In memory of the great biblical eschatologian
Geerhardus Vos (1862–1949)

Biblical Eschatology

Biblical Eschatology

Covenant Eschatology for the Global Mission Age

Jeong Koo Jeon

Foreword by D. Clair Davis

WIPF & STOCK · Eugene, Oregon

BIBLICAL ESCHATOLOGY
Covenant Eschatology for the Global Mission Age

Wipf & Stock
An Imprint of Wipf and Stock Publishers
199 W. 8th Ave., Suite 3
Eugene, OR 97401

www.wipfandstock.com

PAPERBACK ISBN: 978-1-6667-1625-2
HARDCOVER ISBN: 978-1-6667-1626-9
EBOOK ISBN: 978-1-6667-1627-6

09/15/21

Contents

Foreword

I DELIGHT IN THE task kindly given me, of writing a Foreword for this book by my very illustrious student and friend Jeong Koo Jeon. It is much more than one more good academic book among many, for its message is vitally needed by all of us in Christ's church today. Just what is our godly hope right now? Of course it centers around the love of Jesus for all who trust and follow him, 'Trust and Obey, it's the only way, to be happy in Jesus, trust and obey.' But how do those two fit together? How shall we battle Satan and our own pride to obey our holy God?

There are two alleged solutions that Jeon powerfully rejects. The liberals have no room at all for God's final judgment against sin, with the holy God sending sinners to an everlasting Hell, and the evangelical dispensationalists have held that God's judgment was in the Old Testament only, with right now only his grace in play. But we know that neither can be right, that when our holy God comes graciously into our lives, he comes in his own godly relationship to us, his covenant with its 'do this and live.' His gracious blessing comes with his call to godly holiness: how shall we grasp that in our hearts?

Of course they belong together, but how? Those Methodists had reminded us that 'we must be born again,' that radical life-change is God's calling to us, and with them many seasons of repentance and revival followed. God's people saw how God's call to their holiness had been radically minimized. Then the holiness people added their 'second grace of grace,' a kind of second conversion, for asking and receiving holy hearts and lives. But the crucial question remained, how does this belong with 'Christ our righteousness,' our justification? With our Jesus himself?

John Murray showed us what we had long overlooked: our sanctification is not another step on our way, but is with us right at the beginning of our journey with our Savior and Lord, 'definitively.' We are 'united with

Christ' from the beginning, in every way there is. Then added to Murray came Meredith Kline with his deepening work on God's covenant, who showed us how our place with God always depends on God's command to obey him—but Jesus has done that for his followers! "Obey" has not vanished, but it has been kept, forever! Our God declares to us in his covenant lawsuit, in his holy judgment we are righteous in his sight.

God's people now grasp the depth of their trust in Christ's obedience to his Father and ours. Previously Norman Shepherd's "obedient faith" seemed confusing as the grand Reformation insight of "faith alone in Christ alone" had been obscured. But then we had made "faith" the noun and "obedient" its adjective. With Kline and his faithful disciple Jeon we see beautifully the other way around, still centered on obedience, but Jesus' own, in whom we joyfully trust. "Trusting obedience," building on our Jesus and his own obedience unto death, thank you Kline and Jeon! Begin with Kline's covenant lawsuit, our Father's righteous judgment of the surpassing Glory of his Beloved Son's own obedience. Now we're ready to see Jeon building further on that, first in his earlier *Biblical Theology: Covenants and the Kingdom of God in Redemptive History* and now even more in this successor. Our God is the Holy One who demands holiness from us—gloriously totally fulfilled for us in his beloved son!

What especially blesses us as we meditate through his work is his detailed unpacking of so many covenants in the Word, not just with Adam and Jesus, but a grand look at David's and Moses' covenants too, and then the covenanting in the hard time of waiting for the Savior. He pastorally reminds us that God's covenant love and our missional calling belong intimately together. Jesus has told us clearly that they all hate him and will hate us too. When we forget that, we find it too easy to conclude that since no one likes what we say about Jesus, we must not have that sharing-our-faith gift. What if that's the way we should expect it to be, for all of us, and that out of God's kindness to us we can still boldly move ahead with the good news? This is our calling, it's terribly hard and with our loving Lord always at our side. We are boldly in our holy God's presence, so why not even more boldly as we proclaim to those who deny him, at least at first?

Jeon helps us so much with eschatology. Remember when it was a theological add-on, something about the distant future that no one really understood or thought about, but still a necessary addendum? But what if we finally understand that eschatology is right now? The grand already in our already/not yet? Christ is risen, already; Father gives us the Spirit, already; we bring Jesus to the lost and dying world, already. Yes, we wait eagerly for you, Lord Jesus, come quickly—but you are with us, we have all we need for life and godliness because of your love, but with joy in our hearts we see our calling to tell the world of you, boldly indeed! We see that in our little neighborhood but globally too. We hear those hard stories of rejection and suppression and martyrdom everywhere and we pray in gospel hope for our sisters and brothers in the world of the gospel already.

There is so much more in Jeon. For me the most surprising and blessed were the many references to Jonathan Edwards. Edwards in a discussion of covenant? Of course, he saw the Lord in all his glory, and he labored so long to show him to so many others! As we "go thou and do likewise," all of us, we eagerly return to Jeon again and again, we know our need. "Our Father who art in Heaven, Hallelujah!" We do believe that. "Take up your cross daily and be my disciples." We believe that too. Out of what we believe now we root out our remaining most loved sins; we see the unbelief and foolish idolatry still in our lives, and boldly ask to see it more clearly, Jesus, that we may battle Satan's lies with our God's great truth, so glad that God has decisively won his and our lawsuit, already.

There is a valuable appendix to the book, on *Calvin and the Two Kingdoms*, not directly related but very helpful. What does it mean that we still believe in "the separation of church and state, even when our society is radically unbelieving?" Are we glad that Calvin urged the execution of Servetus because of his heresy? Jeon is convincing that we need to understand how common grace and special grace relate to each other to understand the issues and come to the correct conclusion. When we do, we agree with the American amendment to our creed, that we do not ask the state to fix our theology, while we still passionately call upon our God to care for the confusion and evil in our society, with his common grace.

Dr. D. Clair Davis
Professor of Church History, Emeritus
Westminster Theological Seminary

Preface

IT IS MY SPECIAL honor to write and publish *Biblical Eschatology* as we live in the Global Mission Age before the second coming of Jesus Christ. The book compliments *Biblical Theology* (2017) which was written for readers, scattered as the New Covenant diaspora in the global mission field. In that regard, I strongly recommend readers to read both books together.

Many godly individuals, churches, and different organizations have supported my research, teaching, and writing ministry with prayer along with generous financial assistance. I would like to mention just a few names to express my special thanks: Dr. Chang-Wook Kang; Dr. Sahng Yeon Kim; Reverend Jangseock Hong and his congregation, Hasana Church; Reverend Owen Lee and his church, Christ Central Presbyterian Church; Reverend Taeseon Yoon and his church, Immanuel Church of America.

In the process of writing *Biblical Eschatology*, I thoroughly enjoyed it with great awe and humble mindset to rely on the guidance and illumination of the Holy Spirit. Besides, I have had a profound admiration toward the sincere believers and great thinkers such as Augustine, John Calvin, John Owen, Francis Turretin, Jonathan Edwards, Charles Hodge, Herman Bavinck, Geerhardus Vos, Cornelius Van Til, and Meredith G. Kline. Especially the writings of Vos and Kline have been a breakthrough for the backbone and formulation of *Biblical Eschatology*.

The editors of two journals provided me permission to republish those journal articles in my book: "Calvin and the Two Kingdoms: Calvin's Political Philosophy in Light of Contemporary Discussion." *Westminster Theological Journal* 72/2 (2010): 299–320; "The Noahic Covenants and Redemptive Judgment." *The Confessional Presbyterian* 15 (2019): 148–62, 220. My former professor and role model of a godly believer Dr. D. Clair Davis gave me a very inspirational, comprehensive, and thoughtful foreword. My copyeditor Miss Carolyn Hoehner improved the quality of my book through very careful proofreading and editing.

As I prepared to publish my *Biblical Eschatology* in the early Spring of 2020, the COVID-19 global pandemic began to spread like wildfire, and at the same time, I was diagnosed as a colon cancer patient. After a successful surgery, I have received a series of chemotherapy treatments. In this difficult time, many godly people supported me and my family with fervent prayer and encouragement. In particular, I give my special thanks to my pastor Reverend Daniel Shinjong Paeq, and the congregation at Bethel Korean Presbyterian Church for their prayer, encouragement, and personal care.

May the Lord abundantly bless the readers, scattered in the global mission field, having the dual citizenships of earthly and heavenly ones by the grace of God in Jesus Christ! Sometimes, we shout a loud Maranatha with streams of tears amid enormous sufferings and martyrdom in the lives of earthly wilderness which are glorious in the eyes of the Triune God. *Soli Deo Gloria!*

Introduction

PEOPLE DIE WHETHER ONE is rich or poor, powerful or powerless, famous or unknown, beautiful or ugly, and young or old. Everyone has a day of birth and a day of death on the present earth. It is a brutal fact which cannot be denied or ignored. Furthermore, nations and kingdoms rise and fall. No empire or kingdom, no matter how powerful it is, can last forever. World history proves this. The Bible depicts that there will not only be the end of personal life on the earth but also the end of world history. In that sense, eschatology is a proper theological term to be designated. Likewise, Louis Berkhof succinctly describes that the believer's hope for consummation has never died although *eschatology* has not been "the center of Christian thought" throughout church history:

> Speaking generally, it may be said that Christianity never forgot the glorious predictions respecting its future and the future of the individual Christian. Neither the individual Christian nor the Church could avoid thinking about these and finding comfort in them. Sometimes, however, the Church, borne down with the cares of life, or entangled in its pleasures, thought little of the future. Moreover, it happened repeatedly that at one time it would think more of this, and at another time, more of that particular element of its future hope. In days of defection the Christian hope sometimes grew dim and uncertain, but it never died out altogether. At the same time it must be said that there has never been a period in the history of the Christian Church, in which eschatology was the center of the Christian thought. The other loci of Dogmatics have each had their time of special development, but this cannot be said of eschatology.[1]

---

1. Berkhof, *Systematic Theology*, 662.

1

As we might expect, there are several different forms of eschatology that have been influential to the members of the new covenant community in the Global Mission Age. Thus, it is necessary to briefly explore and introduce a concise identification of the different forms of eschatology.

Liberal Theology and Eschatology

In the nineteenth century, classical liberal theology culminated among the German liberal theologians. Representatively, the romantic philosophy of Immanuel Kant and the dialectical view of world history of Hegel were soaked into the minds and practice of German liberal theologians and pastors. In the heart of the German liberal theology is the rejection of the existence and works of the Triune God and the Bible as the inerrant and infallible words of God. In a word, the twin pillars of theology and practice on behalf of the new covenant church were outrightly abandoned and rejected. Because of this rejection, in the minds of liberal theologians, there is no hope for the second coming of Jesus Christ or the believers' glorious bodily resurrection. In that regard, the existence of heaven and hell along with the final judgment was denied as well. So, the eschatological vision for classical liberalism was radically redefined and explained. At best, the progressive advancement and realization of *the moralistic kingdom of God here and now* on the earth, exemplified by Jesus of Nazareth, is the eschatological vision of classical liberalism. Albrecht Ritschl was a representative of the moralistic kingdom of God here and now in the nineteenth century. Denying the future fulfillment of the eternal kingdom of God, he promoted the moralization of the kingdom of God on the present earth. So, Ritschl defines the kingdom of God as "the universal moral kingdom of God" as the teleological goal:

> In Christianity, the Kingdom of God is represented as the common end of God and the elect community, in such a way that it rises above the natural limits of nationality and becomes the moral society of nations. In this respect Christianity shows itself to be the perfect moral religion. . . . In both these respects we have in Christianity a culmination of the monotheistic, spiritual, and teleological religion of the Bible in the idea of the perfected spiritual and moral religion. There can be no doubt that these two characteristics condition each other mutually. Christ made the universal moral Kingdom of God His end, and thus He came to know and decide for that kind of redemption which he achieved

through the maintenance of fidelity in His calling and of His blessed fellowship with God through suffering unto death.[2]

The existential liberal theology, represented by Rudolf Bultmann along with Karl Barth in the twentieth century, is not fundamentally different from the classical liberalism of the nineteenth century although they postulated their distinctive theological ethos. The existential liberal theologians deeply colored theological concepts and languages over the skeleton of existential philosophy which was a dominant philosophical thought in Western Europe in their own time and historical contexts. In doing so, they personified and made subjective all biblical truth, including eschatology through the lens of existentialism. For example, Bultmann radically reinterprets the concept of "the eschatological event" as he demythologizes the bodily resurrection and ascension of Jesus Christ, recorded in the four Gospels:

> According to the New Testament, *Jesus Christ is the eschatological event*, the action of God by which God has set an end to the old world. In the preaching of the Christian Church the eschatological event will ever again become present and does become present ever and again in faith. The old world has reached its end for the believer, he is 'a new creature in Christ.' For the old world has reached its end with the fact that he himself as 'the old man' has reached his end and is now 'a new man,' a free man.
>
> It is the paradox of the Christian message that the eschatological event, according to Paul and John, is not to be understood as a dramatic cosmic catastrophe but as happening within history, beginning with the appearance of Jesus Christ and in continuity with this occurring again and again in history, but not as the kind of historical development which can be confirmed by any historian. It becomes an event repeatedly in preaching and faith. Jesus Christ is the eschatological event not as an established fact of past time but as repeatedly present, as addressing you and me here and now in preaching.[3]

As a result, Bultmann's eschatological vision in light of existentialism promotes *eschatology here and now* which centers the personal and subjective encounter with the kerygmatic word without any real hope of the future fulfillment of the eschatological kingdom of God. In that sense, Bultmann's existential liberalism also demythologizes the biblical

2. Ritschl, *Christian Doctrine of Justification and Reconciliation*, 10.

3. Bultmann, *History and Eschatology*, 151–52.

prophecies of the second coming of Jesus Christ, bodily resurrection, and the final judgment.

Dispensational Premillennialism and Eschatology

The appearance of the dispensational hermeneutics and theology ever since in the middle of the nineteenth century through Nelson Darby was in many ways a turning point of evangelical theology and eschatology. Dispensational eschatology spread rapidly in the United States of America in the twentieth century. The hallmark of dispensationalism is a sharp distinction between Israel and the church. Certainly, there are different forms of dispensationalism such as classical dispensationalism, modified dispensationalism, and progressive dispensationalism. However, the earthly millennial kingdom, centered in Jerusalem along with a distinction between Israel and the church is a common denominator of different forms of dispensational eschatology. In doing so, the exponents of dispensational eschatology reject that the second coming of Jesus Christ and the final judgement are the same day; a truth warranted by biblical eschatology.[4]

As the contemporary promoters of dispensational eschatology and theology, MacArthur and Mayhue separate their view from historic premillennialism. In doing so, they identify it as "futuristic premillennialism" which emphasizes the future fulfillment of Revelation 6–18 during the Great Tribulation and the role of the nation of Israel during the Great Tribulation and earthly millennial kingdom, prophesied in the Old and New Testaments:

> First, futuristic premillennialism holds that Daniel's seventieth week and the seal, trumpet, and bowl judgments of Revelation 6—18 are future from the present standpoint in history. So not only is the millennial kingdom future, but special tribulation period with its divine judgments is also future. This explains why futuristic premillennialism is 'futuristic.' Futuristic premillennialism also holds that the nation of Israel will have an important identity and role in the coming tribulation period and millennial kingdom. Old Testament and New Testament prophecies concerning Israel and Israel's role in the future must be fulfilled

4. For the wide ranges of dispensational premillennialism, see Blaising, "Premillennialism," 157–227; Ryrie, *Basic Theology*; Ryrie, *Dispensationalism*; Scofield, *Scofield Reference Bible*.

literally with the nation of Israel. Thus, futuristic premillennialism rejects all forms of replacement theology or supersessionism
that see the church as the replacement or fulfillment of Israel in
any way that denies the future theological significance of God's
promises to Israel as a nation. Not only does God have a plan for
individuals and the church, he also has a plan for the nations of
the earth, and Israel has a role of leadership and service to the
nations in Jesus's kingdom (Isa. 2:2–4). The millennium will be
a time when all aspects of the covenants and promises made to
Israel will be fulfilled for Israel.[5]

As such, dispensational hermeneutics and theology, portrayed in
eschatology, is not Christocentric and Christotelic but Israelcentric and
Israeltelic which don't have redemptive historical balance and continuity.
In doing so, it loses the proper vision and balance of biblical eschatology. Unfortunately, dispensational theology and eschatology have widely
permeated American evangelicalism so far. Moreover, it has been very
influential to the global mission field because many American missionaries from the early part of the twentieth century have been armed with
dispensational theology and eschatology and introduced it to the evangelical churches all over the world.

Historic Premillennialism and Eschatology

Dispensational eschatology began to spread like wildfire from the beginning of the twentieth century to American evangelical churches.
However, there were some theologians who rejected dispensational
hermeneutics and theology in North America but accepted *the earthly
millennial kingdom as biblical* after the second coming of Jesus Christ. In
that regard, they modified and sharpened their eschatology as historic
premillennialism, distancing themselves from dispensationalism.[6] Gru-

---

5. MacArthur and Mayhue, *Biblical Doctrine*, 891.

6. For example, Carl McIntire Jr. (1906–2002) formed Faith Theological Seminary
in 1937 as a conservative Presbyterian minister in Wilmington, Delaware. One of the
distinctive characteristics was to hold and maintain historic premillennialism at a
seminary which was designed to train future Presbyterian ministers. In the following
year, under the leadership of Carl McIntire, a denomination of the Bible Presbyterian
Church was formed, and its founders revised the sections of the eschatology of the
Westminster Confession of Faith, the Larger Catechism, and the Shorter Catechism,
inserting as a confessional standard the following: the earthly millennial kingdom, believer's bodily resurrection at the day of the second coming of Christ, and unbeliever's

dem as a contemporary exponent of historic millennialism summarizes the diverse spectrum of historic premillennialism as follows:

> According to this viewpoint, the present church age will continue until, as it nears the end, a time of great tribulation and suffering comes on the earth. . . . After that time of tribulation *at the end of the church age, Christ will return to earth to establish a millennial kingdom.* When he comes back, believers who have died will be raised from the dead, their bodies will be reunited with their spirits, and *these believers will reign with Christ on earth for one thousand years.* . . . During this time, Christ will be physically present on the earth in his resurrected body, and will reign as King over the entire earth. The believers who have been raised from the dead, and those who were on earth when Christ returns, will receive glorified resurrection bodies that will never die, and in these resurrection bodies they will live on the earth and reign with Christ. Of the unbelievers who remain on earth, many (but not all) will return to Christ and be

---

bodily resurrection and final judgment after the earthly millennial kingdom before their adoption.

I had an opportunity to have a personal conversation in 1996 at McIntire's home in New Jersey. He told me that he was heavily exposed to dispensational eschatology when he grew up because itinerary bible teachers and revival speakers often came to his home church and taught dispensational eschatology which was a very popular movement back then among evangelical churches. He told me that his theological education at Princeton Theological Seminary and Westminster Theological Seminary helped him abandon dispensational eschatology but not premillennialism itself. That was the reason why he strongly committed to historic premillennialism when he founded Faith Theological Seminary and Bible Presbyterian Church.

Upon the heavy influence of Vernon Grounds (1914–2010) the graduate of Faith Theological Seminary, who served as the president for many years at Denver Seminary, it has become a theological institution that promotes historic premillennialism. For the contemporary defense of historic premillennialism among the faculty of Denver Seminary and others, see Blomberg and Chung, *Case for Historic Premillennialism*.

By the way, Chung fundamentally misreads and misrepresents as he argues that "amillennialism is the product of a gnostic reading of Revelation 20:1–6." We do not think that he has theological sensitivity that historic premillennialism is not compatible with the confessional standards of the Reformation and Post-reformation era: "But what of the Reformers, especially Calvin? If Reformation and Reformed theology recovered much of genuine biblical teaching on so many doctrines, and given the interrelationship among all of the major doctrines of systematic theology, must not amillennialist eschatology necessarily follow? Chung shows how the traditional Reformed covenant theology has spiritualized the biblical teachings on the material and institutional dimensions of redemption. For Chung, amillennialism is the product of a gnostic reading of Revelation 20:1–6." Blomberg and Chung, *Case for Historic Premillennialism*, xviii–xix.

saved. Jesus will reign in perfect righteousness and there will be peace throughout the earth. Many premillennialists hold that the earth will be renewed and we will in fact see the new heavens and the new earth at this time (but it is not essential to premillinnialism to hold to this, for one could be a premillennialist and hold that the new heavens and new earth will not occur until after the final judgment). At the beginning of this time Satan will be bound and cast into the bottomless pit so that he will have no influence on the earth during the millennium (Rev. 20:1–3). According to the premillennial viewpoint, at the end of the thousand years Satan will be loosed from the bottomless pit and will join forces with many unbelievers who have submitted outwardly to Christ's reign but have inwardly been seething in rebellion against him. Satan will gather these rebellious people for battle against Christ, but they will be decisively defeated. Christ will then raise from the dead all the unbelievers who have died throughout history, and they will stand before him for final judgment. After the final judgment has occurred, believers will enter into the eternal state.[7]

A similar phenomenon has occurred in the global mission field. With the lead of some leading theologians, the historic premillennialism has become a very influential form of eschatology in the global mission field within evangelical churches, transcending denominations.[8]

7. Grudem, *Systematic Theology*, 1112. For the thoughts of historic premillennialism from different perspectives, see Ladd, *Blessed Hope*; Ladd, *Commentary on the Revelation of John*; Ladd, *Crucial Questions about the Kingdom of God*; Ladd, *Gospel of the Kingdom*; Ladd, "Historic Premillennialism," 17–40.

8. For example, Hyung Ryong Park (1897–1978) and Yun Seon Park (1905–88) were very influential conservative Presbyterian theologians in the twentieth century in Korea, transcending denominations. They held and taught historic premillennialism as the most biblical form of eschatology throughout their teaching and writing careers. Nevertheless, they didn't pursue to revise the sections of eschatology from the Westminster Standards unlike the founders of the Bible Presbyterian Church in North America which were adopted as the confessional standard in the Presbyterian denominations in Korea. In that sense, we think that both were not aware that the teachings of eschatology of the Westminster Standards are not harmonious with historic premillennialism. However, it is our view that either dispensational premillennialism or historic premillennialism is not compatible with the teachings of the Westminster Standards. Cf. Park, *Dr. Hyung Ryong Park Systematic Theology*; Park, *Commentary on the Revelation of St. John*.

Postmillennialism and Eschatology

Since the early seventeenth century, many faithful believers began adventuring to North America, crossing the Atlantic Ocean with long and wild sail, to escape harsh persecution against churches and believers in Europe. As they arrived in America, they worked tirelessly and built new communities. Pastors and theologians led people's spiritual lives and formed new churches in the middle of new communities. We call them puritan pastors and theologians; those who devoted their lives to preaching, teaching, and pastoral counseling in the New England area. The most puritan pastors and theologians had a very optimistic vision about the role of churches in the world. They had an optimistic vision of building Christian villages, cities, and nations as the good news of the gospel spread more and more to different communities and nations. In that sense, many puritan pastors adopted postmillennialism as biblical.[9] It seems that before the second coming of Jesus Christ we can witness the visible reality of Christian communities, cities, and nations undergoing *cultural transformation* wherever the gospel permeates deeply.[10] Kenneth Gentry briefly defines postmillennialism as its defender and promoter:

> *Postmillennialism expects the proclaiming of the Spirit-blessed gospel of Jesus Christ to win the vast majority of human beings to salvation in the present age. Increasing gospel success will gradually produce a time in history prior to Christ's return in which faith, righteousness, peace, and prosperity will prevail in the affairs of people and of nations. After an extensive era of such conditions the Lord will return visibly, bodily, and in great glory, ending history with the general resurrection and the great judgment of all humankind.* Hence, our system is *post*millennial in that the Lord's glorious return occurs *after* an era of "millennial" conditions. Thus, the postmillennialist confidently proclaims in a unique way that history is "His story."[11]

This view underestimates the deep-seated problem of sin and its divergent and destructive effects in the present age. Moreover, it loses a proper vision of the New Covenant Age as the eschatological age which

9. Jonathan Edwards was one of the representative Puritan pastors, having a postmillennial vision in New England in the eighteenth century. See Edwards, *History of the Work of Redemption.*

10. For the streams of thoughts of postmillennialism, see Gentry, "Postmillennialism," 13–57; Mathison, *Postmillennialism.*

11. Gentry, "Postmillennialsim," 13–14.

is the last days of suffering and persecution against the new covenant church until the second coming of Jesus Christ.

Full Preterism and Eschatology

One of the turning points in redemptive history was the fall of Jerusalem and the destruction of Jerusalem temple in A.D. 70 through the military campaign of the Roman Empire during the reign of Emperor Vespasian. Some theologians perceived the historical event in A.D. 70 was, in fact, the event of the second coming of Jesus Christ and the final judgment. In doing so, they insist that the date of the book of Revelation was before A.D. 70 because they believe the prophecies of Revelation were already fulfilled in A.D. 70, including the day of the second coming of Jesus Christ and the final judgment. In that sense, they viewed all the prophecies in relation to the final judgment along with the second coming of Jesus Christ which they viewed as having already happened that year. This view has been called full preterism. Charles Meek as a contemporary promoter of full preterism describes the comprehensive picture of full preterism:

> This is the view that we will present for your consideration. The term preterism comes from the Latin word *praeter*, which means *past*. Preterists hold that most if not all prophetic events have already been fulfilled with the events of the first century. . . . His Second Coming in judgment and consummate completion of eschatological promises were fulfilled in AD 70. The apostles thought Jesus would return in their generation, and they were right. While this may seem foreign to you, we believe that numerous passages in both the Old Testament and New Testament prove the preterist view to be worthy of your consideration. . . . The basis for the Christian's hope has been fulfilled, just as the inspired writers expected. It has already been realized! Because we believe that the promises of his Second Coming have been fulfilled, we have even greater confidence that the promise of our own eternal life is a reality. As it says in Revelation 14:13: "Blessed are the dead who die in the Lord from now on." . . . Preterism is an optimistic eschatology. Christians do not need to fear a coming tribulation, it has already occurred. Preterists also believe that we need not wait in hades until the end of time to be reunited with our physical bodies and to be with our Lord

in heaven; we go to heaven immediately upon physical death in our glorified bodies to be with God and the saints of all time.[12]

However, I think that full preterism is *heresy* because they simply reject the future day of the second coming of Jesus Christ and the final judgment. To be sure, however, it is true that its exponents and followers are very conservative in terms of their beliefs over other biblical doctrines.

Amillennialism and Biblical Eschatology

The exponents of amillennialism view the one thousand years' reign in Revelation 20:1–6 symbolically and figuratively. In doing so, they understand the present age between the first and second coming of Jesus Christ is the eschatological age where the souls of the martyred and deceased believers are reigning with the exalted Jesus Christ in *heaven*. Nevertheless, they are not optimistic like the exponents of postmillennialism about world history and the surrounding cultures of the new covenant community in that period on the present earth. To be sure, the amillennialists share with the postmillennialists that the day of the Lord as the day of the second coming of Jesus Christ and the day of the final judgment are the same day. I take amillennialism as the most biblical form of eschatology, warranted by the teachings of the Bible.[13] Geerhardus Vos as one of the most profound advocates of biblical eschatology succinctly summarizes the general picture of amillennialism as follows:

12. Meek, *Christian Hope through Fulfilled Prophecy*, 46–47, 296–97. Meanwhile, partial preterists argue the two different comings of Jesus Christ, to separate themselves from full preterism. As Meek summarizes, they argue that the coming of Jesus Christ in A.D. 70 was "metaphorical coming" while there will be "a literal-physical 'consummate coming' of Christ" at the end of world history: "Unlike full preterists, partial preterists hold that in addition to the 'metaphorical coming' of Christ in judgment in AD 70, there will be a literal-physical 'consummate coming' of Christ at the end of time. Full preterists believe that the New Testament speaks only of one second coming, and that while some texts concerning the second coming have no clear time-reference associated with them, they must be interpreted in light of the texts that do have a time-reference constraint to the first century. Partial preterists argue on the basis of inference that because God came in judgment on multiple occasions in the Old Testament, it would be consistent for Jesus to have two 'second' comings—one in AD 70 and one at the end of time." Meek, *Christian Hope through Fulfilled Prophecy*, 48.

13. For the divergent spectrums of amillennialism, see Hoekema, *The Bible and the Future*; Kline, *God, Heaven and Har Magedon*; Riddlebarger, *A Case for Amillennialism*; Strimple, "Amillennialism," 81–129; Vos, *The Pauline Eschatology*.

That history, in the course of which we are situated, will have a conclusion. It is not an endless process but a genuine history that ends in a definite goal and has a boundary and limits. As it had a beginning, it will have an ending. That ending will come as a crisis, and everything that has to do with this crisis belongs to the 'doctrine of the last things.' . . . The end comes at the close of world history for everything at the same time. What belongs to that end and is connected with it we call general eschatology. But for the individual the end also comes with his departure from this life, from this age. By his death he is lifted above this age in its earthly development, and in a certain sense brought closer to the age to come. Indeed, in Scripture the antithesis between the two world-*times* intersects with the antithesis between two world-*places*. The new Jerusalem, the future city, the heavenly kingdom will be revealed when this age empties into the future age. Therefore, relocation of dwelling place is always an exchange of age.[14]

As we begin to discuss the unfolding mystery of biblical eschatology, revealed in the Bible, we will examine the general pattern of *covenant eschatology*, envisioned in the Bible in light of the progressive character of biblical revelation and doctrines of eschatology. In doing so, we will demonstrate the typological or pictorial implication of the distinction between the covenant of works and the covenant of grace, applied for redemptive judgments, and its future application for the final redemptive judgment. Furthermore, we will analyze God's constant covenant lawsuits, mobilizing prophets, Jesus Christ, apostles, and faithful believers, based upon the covenant of works before he executes redemptive judgments.

We will contour that God revealed the pattern of *covenant eschatology* in redemptive history, moving back to the time of Noah on a universal scale. We will examine that God demonstrated the pattern of the final judgment, separating the covenant community and non-covenant community through the flood judgment which was an act of redemptive judgment at the time of Noah. Later, in the historical context of the Abrahamic covenant, God visibly executed the pattern of covenant eschatology through the redemptive judgment against the cities of Sodom and Gomorrah. In doing so, God saved the covenant community leading them to Zoar while all the inhabitants, including infants, were the subjects of curses and death, based upon the covenantal standard of the covenant of works in the first Adam.

14. Vos, *Reformed Dogmatics*, 5:251–53.

Furthermore, with the inauguration of the Mosaic covenant, God showed the pattern of covenant eschatology as well in the process of the conquest of Canaan while the covenant community of Israel on behalf of Yahweh waged the holy war against its dwellers. The blessings or curses upon the covenant community of Israel, based upon the Mosaic covenant of law, were the visible signs and types of the existence of *the invisible heaven and hell*. With the inauguration of the Davidic covenant, the blessings and curses of the Mosaic covenant of law were continued. So, God administered his covenant lawsuit by constantly sending out his faithful prophets and, in the end, he executed the covenant curse against the northern kingdom of Israel in 722 B.C. by using the military power of the Assyrian Empire and the fall of Jerusalem and Babylonian exile of the southern kingdom of Judah in 586 B.C through the means of the Babylonian Empire.

We will explore that the New Covenant Age was inaugurated with the first coming of Jesus Christ. Nevertheless, the Mosaic covenant of law for the covenant community of Israel was still valid even under the new covenant. In that regard, God used the four Gospels and the book of Acts as the historic process of the covenant lawsuit against disobedient Israel through Jesus Christ, apostles, and other faithful believers. In the end, God finally executed the final judgment against the kingdom of Israel in A.D. 70, based upon the Mosaic covenant of law through the military power of the Roman Empire. Jesus Christ will come back again on the day of the Lord as the final judge and consummator. The day of the second coming of Jesus Christ will be the day of the final redemptive judgment. The means of the final redemptive judgment will be the heavenly fire, already typified through the redemptive judgment against Sodom and Gomorrah. In doing so, God the Father will finally remove the benefits of the covenant of common grace, inaugurated in Genesis 3:16–19, and resumption in Genesis 8:20—9:17 after the Noahic flood judgment.

We will pay close attention to the implication of the distinction between the covenant of works and the covenant of grace in the final redemptive judgment. The covenantal background of the final judgment for believers will be the covenant of grace in the last Adam while the covenant of works in the first Adam will be the covenant standard against unbelievers. Let us begin to enjoy a pilgrimage together, adventuring the divergent patterns of covenant eschatology, visibly demonstrated in the grand drama of redemptive history in the Bible as the covenantal canon.

Chapter One

The Noahic Covenants and
Redemptive Judgment

IN GENERAL, LIBERAL THEOLOGIANS consider the account of Genesis 1–11, including the episode of the flood judgment, as a myth which does not reflect historical accounts. Recently, some evangelical scholars began to perceive Genesis 1–11 as "theological history," taking on a middle ground between history and myth. Representatively, Longman and Walton insist that "the flood story of the Bible," recorded in Genesis 6–9 is neither myth nor history but "theological history" which reflects "the hyperbolic presentation" of "real events of the past through the use of figurative language." Here, they summarize their logic:

> We do not believe the flood story of the Bible is myth, but neither do we believe the author of Genesis 6–9 intends to give us a straight forward depiction of the event that lies behind it. We believe there is an event that inspired the story; after all, Genesis 6–9 is theological *history.* However, we believe the best understanding of Genesis 1–11, which of course includes the flood account, is that it talks about real events of the past through the use of the figurative language. In the case of the flood story, we have identified the use of hyperbole to describe the flood. But there is a real event behind the story just as there was an actual conquest behind the hyperbolic presentation of Joshua's conquest as presented in Joshua 1–12.[1]

However, I believe that the account of the flood judgment in Genesis 6–9 is the reflection of a real historic event at the time of Noah without

1. Longman and Walton, *Lost World of the Flood*, 145.

any exaggeration and distortion, written by the prophet Moses under the inspiration of the Holy Spirit. Moreover, God demonstrated *the pattern of biblical eschatology* through the Noahic flood within the historic context of the Prediluvian Noahic covenant in Genesis 6:5—8:19.[2]

We can learn several elements of *biblical eschatology* from the judgment of the Noahic flood. First, it was a redemptive judgment in which God separated the covenant community from the non-covenant community. In addition, it was not a local but a universal judgment because it alludes to the final universal judgment which will happen on the day of the second coming of Jesus Christ. The Noahic flood judgment was a visible judgment as seen in the covenant lawsuit based on the Edenic covenant of works which was broken by the first Adam. Furthermore, it was a verification of the validity of the imputation of the original sin, which was imputed to all the descendants of the first Adam. Lastly, God showed a typological picture of the glorious union of the new earth with "the holy city, new Jerusalem" (Rev 21:2) when the Ark was united with the present earth as the earth dried up after the flood judgment.[3]

Meanwhile, after the Noahic flood judgment, God restored and resumed the covenant of common grace through the postdiluvian Noahic covenant in Genesis 8:20—9:17. In doing so, God secured world history on the present earth until the final judgment comes through the means of the covenant between God and all humanity including the earth. God's continuation of the covenant of common grace, originally

---

2. For biblical theological discussions of the distinction between the prediluvian and postdiluvian Noahic covenants, see Horton, *Introducing Covenant Theology*, 111–28; Jeon, *Biblical Theology*, 33–57; Kline, *Kingdom Prologue*, 212–62.

3. For the eschatological understanding of the flood judgment, see Vos, *Eschatology of the Old Testament*, 81–83. Interestingly, Vos describes the Noahic covenant as "the general covenant" which can be identified as the covenant of common grace while he views the covenant of grace as "the *foedus speciale*" which God made with the elect. In doing so, he doesn't make a proper distinction between the Prediluvian and Postdiluvian Noahic covenants which is warranted: "Szegedin, Musculus, Polanus, Wollebius, and others make a distinction between the *foedus generale*, the general covenant, which God established with all creatures, animals as well as men, and the *foedus special ac sempiternum*, the special and eternally enduring covenant that is made with the elect. For the first, the covenant with all creatures, one can appeal to God's covenant-making with Noah. With that, God promised that the orderings of heaven and of earth would not again be disrupted by a flood and placed the rainbow as a sign and seal of it. . . . In Genesis 6:13; 9:9; and the following verses, between God and Noah. Here, however, it is said repeatedly that it is a covenant between God and every living soul, not excluding the animals. Thus it is not simply the covenant of grace. It is a covenant of nature." Vos, *Reformed Dogmatics*, 2:122–27.

inaugurated in Genesis 3:16–19, not only provided stability for humanity after the flood judgment, but also the presence of the church as a covenant community, saving the elect until the second coming of Jesus Christ on the present earth.

The Noahic Flood and Redemptive Judgment

God is not only love, but also holiness and righteousness. God visibly demonstrates his infinite holiness and righteousness through the Noahic flood judgment. After the completion of the Ark by the faithful and obedient Noah, the Noahic covenant community entered into the Ark based on God's commandment. Entering into the Ark was a process in which there was a visible separation of the Noahic covenant community and non-covenant community.

Jesus Christ as the mediator of the new covenant was a redemptive historical theologian who exemplified mastery in the interpretation of the Hebrew Bible in light of redemptive history patterned in the creation, Fall, redemption, and consummation. In fact, Jesus Christ was an infallible redemptive historical theologian during his public ministry in his sermons and teachings so that his disciples as the original apostles, as well as the apostle Paul, were able to follow his example of redemptive historical interpretation of the Hebrew Bible after the Pentecost event under the inspiration of the Holy Spirit. In his famous Olivet Discourse, Jesus Christ compared the flood judgment at the time of Noah with the final judgment on the day of his second coming:

> [36]"But concerning that day and hour no one knows, not even the angels of heaven, nor the Son, but the Father only. [37]As were the days of Noah, so will be the coming of the Son of Man. [38]For as in those days before the flood they were eating and drinking, marrying and giving in marriage, until the day when Noah entered the ark, [39]and they were unaware until the flood came and swept them all away, so will be the coming of the Son of Man. [40]Then two men will be in the field; one will be taken and one left. [41]Two women will be grinding at the mill; one will be taken and one left. [42]Therefore, stay awake, for you do not know on what day your Lord is coming. [43]But know this, that if the master of the house had known in what part of the night the thief was coming, he would have stayed awake and would not have let his house be broken into. [44]Therefore you also must

be ready, for the Son of Man is coming at an hour you do not
expect. (Matt 24:36–44)[4]

In Jesus Christ's address to his disciples, we find a remarkable truth.
The day of "the coming of the Son of Man" (vv. 37, 39) as his second coming is the same day of the final judgment, separating the elect from the
reprobate (vv. 41–42). God separated the Noahic covenant community
and non-covenant community. The Noahic covenant community entered
into the ark and God closed the door of the ark, and began to pour out
his infinite wrath against the non-covenant community. Similarly, on the
day of "the coming of the Son of man," God will execute his final judgment, visibly separating the elect and reprobate. Verses 40–41, "[40]Then
two men will be in the field; one will be taken and one left. [41]Two women
will be grinding at the mill; one will be taken and one left," are a parabolic
expression of the separation of the elect and reprobate on the day of the
final judgment when Jesus Christ returns.

God sovereignly set *the day of the Lord* which was the day of the
visible appearance of glorious theophany and judgment. When the day of
the Lord came, Noah's family entered into the ark that Noah as a faithful
servant of God built for 120 years while enduring persecution by idol
worshipers who were hostile against God and the covenant community.
After the Noahic covenant community entered into the ark, God appeared as theophanic glory and closed the door of the ark which was the
ark of salvation on the original earth. By doing this, God did not provide
further opportunity to enter the ark, rather he closed and sealed the door.
The beautiful glory closed the door of the ark, which was an earthly picture of the invisible heaven. Closing the door of the ark meant that God
finished the process of the visible separation of the covenant community
and non-covenant community:

---

4. Vos properly compares between the Noahic flood judgment and the final judgment at the time of the second coming of Christ in light of eschatology: "Finally,
the New Testament places the epoch of Noah in parallel with the second coming of
Christ (cf. Matt 24:37; Luke 17:26). These passages point out a comparison between
the sinfulness immediately preceding the two periods under consideration. But it is
especially the suddenness of the coming of Christ that is stressed in this connection.
First Peter 3:20ff. compares the water of baptism with that of the flood. Both have an
eschatological significance and are directed toward salvation. The water was an instrument of the world-judgment and separated godly and ungodly as it does in baptism."
Vos, *Eschatology of the Old Testament*, 82.

11In the six hundredth year of Noah's life, in the second month, on the seventeenth day of the month, on that day all the fountains of the great deep burst forth, and the windows of the heavens were opened. 12And rain fell upon the earth forty days and forty nights. 13On the very same day Noah and his sons, Shem and Ham and Japheth, and Noah's wife and the three wives of his sons with them entered the ark, 14they and every beast, according to its kind, and all the livestock according to their kinds, and every creeping thing that creeps on the earth, according to its kind, and every bird, according to its kind, every winged creature. 15They went into the ark with Noah, two and two of all flesh in which there was the breath of life. 16And those that entered, male and female of all flesh, went in as God had commanded him. And the LORD shut him in. (Gen 7:11–16)

We need to pay special attention to verse 13: "On the very same day Noah and his sons, Shem and Ham and Japheth, and Noah's wife and the three wives of his sons with them entered the ark." In particular, "on the very same day" (בְּעֶצֶם הַיּוֹם הַזֶּה) is a crucial key which indicates that the flood judgment was *a concomitant event* between the blessings of life and curses of death. Here, we find God's remarkable wisdom. God separated two different groups of people when the flood judgment happened on the day of the Lord. Nevertheless, there is a logical and chronological order when God divided the two different groups. First, God secured the Noahic covenant community, sending them in and closing the ark before he demonstrated his infinite wrath against the sinners who were hostile against the kingdom of God. Afterwards, God as a righteous Judge began to display his incredible, infinite, fearful, and merciless judgment upon the original earth where the sinners against God lived.

It is noteworthy that God did not deploy manmade weapons although they are the fruits of the covenant of common grace inaugurated in Genesis 3:16–19. Rather, God used the flood as the means of his glorious and righteous judgment. This is a visible demonstration of God's infinite wisdom. When God displays his redemptive judgment, he does not need help from arrogant and sinful humans. This pattern continues when God executed his redemptive judgments as we see in the historic episodes of the judgments of Sodom and Gomorrah and the Red Sea, among others.[5]

---

5. However, there was an exception. When the covenant community of Israel conquered the promised land, God commanded the armies of Israel to fight holy war on

Longman and Walton deny the authenticity of the flood judgment which occurred at the time of Noah. In doing so, they insist that the flood was not global but local by reading and evaluating the flood episode in Genesis 6–9 in light of the ancient Near Eastern cultures and religions:

> For reasons described in other parts of this book, we do not believe the flood was worldwide, but we do believe it was particularly devastating. We don't think it is possible to date the event, locate the event, or reconstruct the event in our own terms. That is not a problem because the event itself, with which everyone in the Near East is familiar, is not what is inspired. What *is* inspired and thus the vehicle of God's revelation is the literary-theological explanation that is given by the biblical author. We are interested in how the compiler of Genesis used the flood and how he described what God was doing in and with the flood.[6]

However, we believe that the flood judgment was not a local but global and universal judgment which covered the whole earth. The universal flood judgment was God's sovereign revelation that the Final judgment will be global and universal, as the judgment will be at the second coming of Jesus Christ, the final parousia. Due to the flood judgment all the people outside of the ark perished because holy and righteous God displayed his redemptive judgment against their sins in which they followed not God but gods of that time.

---

behalf of Yahweh. It is a typological demonstration of God's infinite wisdom to reveal that the glorified believers at the day of the final judgment will participate to judge the reprobate alongside Jesus Christ who will be coming as the final consummator and judge.

6. Longman and Walton, *Lost World of the Flood*, 85. We believe the root problem lies in their view of the Bible which is deeply rooted in their adaptation and implications of the historical critical reading of the Bible, which is the presupposition of liberal theologians. Endorsing the historical critical reading of the Pentateuch with adaptation of the redaction criticism, they plainly reject the Mosaic authorship of the Pentateuch as well: "As intriguing as it is, however, we are not saying this particular flood generated the story of the flood. We do not believe we can reconstruct the historical event from the biblical account. However, we are confident, due to the genre (theological history) of Genesis 6–9 and in our affirmation that the Bible is true in all that it affirms, that there was a historical event. Our conclusion is that the Black Sea flood is the *type* of devastating flood that could have ultimately inspired the biblical account, even if it is not itself the biblical event. Whatever the precise historical event, the story was told from generation to generation, eventually forming the basis for the *toledot* . . . coming down to the Israelite narrators and the later redactors of the final form of the Pentateuch who used the story of Noah and the flood for their important theological message." Longman and Walton, *Lost World of the Flood*, 149.

When the final parousia comes, God will separate the elect and reprobate, granting the eternal kingdom of God for the elect in the last Adam while the reprobate in the first Adam will be thrown into the kingdom of Satan which will be the completion of hell. God desired to demonstrate and reveal the pattern of final judgment through the Noahic flood judgment. In doing so, God did not separate the elect and reprobate, rather the covenant community and non-covenant community through the flood judgment in the original earth. For example, Ham was a member of the Noahic covenant community, therefore he was able to enter the ark and escape the flood judgment. In addition, Ham participated in worship as a son of the Noahic covenant family. Nevertheless, the Bible depicts Ham not as one of the members of the elect who was chosen by God before the creation of the world to be saved in Christ in the milieu of the covenant of redemption (the *pactum salutis*), which was made among the Father, the Son, and the Holy Spirit. Calvin rightly shows that Ham was not a member of the invisible church although he was saved in the ark during the flood judgment as a member of the visible church, interpreting "and Ham, the father of Canaan" in Genesis 9:22:

> It is received by common consent, that piety towards parents is the mother of all virtues. This Ham, therefore, must have been of a wicked, perverse, and crooked disposition; since he not only took pleasure in his father's shame, but wished to expose him to his brethren. And this is no slight occasion of offense; first, that Noah, the minister of salvation to men, and the chief restorer of the world, should, in extreme old age, lie intoxicated in his house; and then, that the ungodly and wicked Ham should have proceeded from the sanctuary of God. God had selected eight souls as a sacred seed, thoroughly purged from all corruption, for the renovation of the Church: but the son of Noah shows, how necessary it is for men to be held as with the bridle of God, however they may be exalted by privilege. The impiety of Ham proves to us how deep is the root of wickedness in men; and that it continually put forth its shoots, except where the power of the Spirit prevails over it. But if, in the hollowed sanctuary of God, among so small a number, one fiend was preserved; let us not wonder if, at this day, in the Church, containing a much greater multitude of men, the wicked are mingled with the good.[7]

---

7. Calvin, *Genesis*, 9:22, in *Calvin's Commentaries*.

In that sense, Ham will not inherit the eternal kingdom of God when the final redemptive judgment comes at the second coming of Jesus Christ although he escaped the flood judgment.

It is noteworthy to recognize the method of God's judgment at the time of Noah. God completely destroyed everything outside of the ark, killing all the humans of that time. In doing so, God withdrew his benefits of the covenant of common grace that he bestowed to the elect and reprobate without any discrimination after he inaugurated the covenant of common grace in Genesis 3:16–19. God withdrew the common blessings, kindness, love, and mercy that he graciously and temporarily bestowed upon the reprobate and world in his original earth. When the day of the Lord arrived, God waged holy war against the sinful humans and world that followed the spirit of the kingdom of Satan. It was the war of total destruction (*cherem*) which was later commanded by God to the covenant community of Israel when they entered the promised land. In that sense, God used holy war when he executed his redemptive judgment through the Noahic flood, thus putting an end to the covenant of common grace.

Furthermore, the physical death of the reprobates outside of the ark was not the end of the story. God sent all the souls of the cursed people from the flood judgment to hell. As mentioned, what happened outside of the ark in the flood judgment was the visible picture or type of hell, cursing all the non-covenant community with physical death.[8] Furthermore,

---

8. A classic example of preaching about the existence and reality of heaven and hell can be found in Edwards, *Sinners in the Hands of an Angry God*. Edwards vividly describes and illustrates the reality of "everlasting wrath" of hell as follows: "It is everlasting wrath. It would be dreadful to suffer this fierceness and wrath of Almighty God one moment; but you must suffer it to all eternity. There will be no end to this exquisite horrible misery. When you look forward, you shall see a long forever, a boundless duration before you, which will swallow up your thoughts, and amaze your soul; and you will absolutely despair of ever having any deliverance, any end, any mitigation, any rest at all. You will know certainly that you must wear out long ages, millions of millions of ages, in wrestling and conflicting with this almighty merciless vengeance; and then when you have so done, when so many ages have actually been spent by you in this manner, you will know that all is but a point to what remains. So that your punishment will indeed be infinite." Edwards, *Sinners in the Hands of an Angry God*, 36.

Some scholars and theologians of an evangelical posture deny the existence of heaven and hell. This phenomenon is at best against the principle of the good news of the gospel and dual aspects of God's redemptive judgment, revealed in the Bible. For example, an influential evangelical theologian, John Stott denied the existence of eternal hellish punishment. Edwards and Stott, *Evangelical Essentials*, 313–20. Supporting the annihilation of the wicked, Stott denies that there will be eternal punishment in

he sent the souls of all the dead to hell which is now the invisible realm as well. To be sure, all the souls sent to hell through the flood judgment will experience bodily resurrection when the final parousia comes. However, their bodily resurrection will not be the glorious bodily resurrection of "the resurrection of life" (v. 29) as it will be for the elect in the last Adam. It will be the bodily resurrection of the wicked as "the resurrection of judgment" (v. 29), so that they will be thrown into the kingdom of Satan which will be the completion of hell (John 5:25–29).[9]

The Covenant Lawsuit and the Verification of the Original Sin

God is a covenantal God who makes, remembers, and faithfully keeps his covenants. God never forgets his covenants because he is omnipotent and omniscient. Surprisingly, the backdrop of the judgment of the Noahic flood goes back to the holy garden of Eden where God made the covenant of works with the first Adam. When God made the covenant of works with the first Adam in Genesis 2:15–17, he represented all

---

hell against the reprobate: "The third argument in favor of the concept of annihilation concerns the biblical vision of *justice*. Fundamental to it is the belief that God will judge people 'according to what they [have] done' (e.g. Revelation 20:12), which implies that the penalty inflicted will be commensurate with the evil one. . . . I am hesitant to have written these things, partly because I have a great respect for longstanding tradition which claims to be a true interpretation of Scripture, and do not lightly set it aside, and partly because the unity of the world-wide Evangelical constituency has always meant much to me. But the issue is too important to suppress, and I am grateful to you for challenging me to declare my present mind. I do not dogmatise about the position to which I have come. I hold it tentatively. But I do plead for frank dialogue among Evangelicals on the basis of Scripture. I also believe that the ultimate annihilation of the wicked should at least be accepted as a legitimate, biblically founded alternative to their eternal conscious torment." Edwards and Stott, *Evangelical Essentials*, 318–20.

9. Interpreting John 5:29, Vos affirms the bodily resurrection of the elect and reprobate at the final Parousia in light of "the completeness of the theodicy" which will be visibly manifested in the completion of the eschatological kingdom of God: "In John 5:29, Jesus draws a formal distinction between 'the resurrection of life' and 'the resurrection of judgment.' At this point we once more verify that our Lord's doctrine of the resurrection rests on a broader basis than that of individual soteriology. The raising of the dead forms part of a process of cosmic proportions which draws within its range the entire physical universe and therefore extends to the wicked as well as the righteous. Even in the case of the wicked the resurrection of the body and the recompense in the body are necessary to the completeness of the theodicy which forms the essence of the final coming of the kingdom." Vos, *Redemptive History and Biblical Interpretation*, 322.

his descendants because he was the representative covenantal head. So, God remembered this covenant when he executed the flood judgment against the non-covenant community. However, God saved the Noahic covenant family in the ark in light of the covenant of grace, inaugurated in Genesis 3:14–15 while he executed the judgment of death to all the people outside of the ark in the milieu of the covenant of works broken by the first Adam.[10]

In that sense, the Noahic flood was God's redemptive judgment, executing the judgment of death through his covenant lawsuit based upon the Edenic covenant of works. Certainly, the first Adam was not under the covenant of grace but the covenant of works as the representative covenant head of his descendants after him (Gen 2:15–17).[11] As the first

10. Vos properly categorizes two different groups of people after the fall. The elect are receiving spiritual benefits "under the covenant of grace" while the reprobate are condemned "under the covenant of works." In light of that, it is proper to view that God occasionally executed his redemptive judgment against non-covenant community through the covenant lawsuit based upon the Edenic covenant of works as the type of the Final judgment: "Insofar as the covenant of works went beyond the natural relationship between God and man, it has passed away for those who are under the covenant of grace. Still here, too, one should distinguish carefully. . . . The non-elect natural man is also still under the covenant of works, if one takes the covenant of works only in its broadest sense. He is not under it in the sense that his life here on earth would still be a probation, for he is put to the test and succumbed in Adam. He is one fallen, not one who is tested. He is under it insofar as his punishable culpability is at its root connected with Adam's breaking of the covenant, whether he would acknowledge it or not. By the breaking of the covenant of works, he did not revert to his natural relationship." Vos, *Reformed Dogmatics*, 2:44–46.

11. Growing numbers of scholars and theologians deny the historical and logical orders of the covenant of works and the covenant of grace as well as law and gospel or grace which are the essential hermeneutical and theological tools for the good news of the Gospel and God's sovereign grace, granting salvation and eschatological kingdom to hopeless sinners after the fall. For example, Niehaus denies the validity of the distinction between the covenant of works and grace, mixing works and grace together, which is at best a monocovenantalism: "But what can explain God's gracious act? His grace does not avert justice, because the man and the woman would still die. God must remain true to all of his covenantal commitments because doing so actually means that he remains true to his own nature, out of which covenantal relationships and commitments arise. But he also does the one thing that his covenant does not require: He reinstates his fallen vassals so that the covenant might continue. And so it did, with humans ruling and multiplying, although in a sinful and fallen world. On such grounds (as well as those noted earlier), it becomes clear that the Adamic or Creation covenant cannot simply be called a covenant of works. The continuation of the covenant clearly does not depend on the obedience, or the successful work, of the vassals, for the covenant has continued in spite of their disobedience—because God himself has graciously continued it. The Noahic covenant, which (as we discuss later)

Adam ate the forbidden fruit from the tree of the knowledge of good and evil in the holy garden of Eden with his wife Eve due to Satan's temptation, he broke the covenant of works. The breaking of the covenant of works by the first Adam was not an isolated event which resulted with minor consequences. The impact and implication of the broken covenant of works in the holy garden of Eden are more significant and serious than we can ever imagine. Adam and Eve were expelled from the holy garden of Eden although they were saved by God's grace through faith in the coming Messiah. Nevertheless, they lost the right to live in the holy garden of Eden because it was the earthly projection of the glorious heaven and sinners lost their special privilege to live.

God remembered the broken covenant of works when he executed his redemptive judgment, separating the Noahic covenant community and non-covenant community. God poured out his righteous wrath against sinners outside of the ark through the covenant lawsuit, based upon the broken covenant of works in the holy garden of Eden. Simultaneously, God destroyed the holy garden of Eden through his flood judgment although it was the earthly picture of the invisible heaven. The Noahic covenant community was saved in the ark because they were the recipients of the benefits of the covenant of grace, which was inaugurated in Genesis 3:14–15 when gracious God introduced the primitive gospel to Adam and Eve in the name of woman's offspring, the coming Messiah.

Growing numbers of scholars within the so-called evangelical community have begun to reject original sin and its imputation.[12] Representatively, Longman, sharing his opinion with Walton, rejects the idea of original sin, claiming that it does not have any biblical support. Rather, it was an invention of Augustine in the early church without any biblical warrant:

---

is a renewal of the Adamic covenant, only fortifies this position, since it guarantees further the continuance of the key provisions of the Adamic or Creation covenant. We therefore submit again that, on such grounds, the concept of a *covenant of works* is not adequate to explain all the aspects of the Adamic covenant. It cannot account even for the most fundamentally important fact about the covenant—namely, that it continues after the Fall and continues to this day. Therefore, this foundational covenant is no covenant of works but, rather, a covenant of grace *and* works. We will see that the same is true, *mutatis mutandis*, of all the divine—human covenants." Niehaus, *Biblical Theology*, 1:79–80.

12. For a biblical and theological affirmation and discussion of the original sin and its immediate imputation, see Murray, *Imputation of Adam's Sin*.

In short, the idea that we inherit a sin nature, guilt, and death from Adam (and Eve) does not derive from the Old Testament or Paul, but from the thinking of Augustine. Now Augustine was one of the greatest theological thinkers of all time, but he was not infallible. Augustine got off to a bad start by mistranslating the Greek of Romans 5:12 which properly rendered says "just as sin entered the world through one man, and death through sin, and in this way death came to all people, *because* (*eph hō*) all sinned." Augustine translated "because" as "in whom" (*in quo*), thus changing Paul's point that we all are guilty because of our own sin to the idea that we are all guilty because of Adam's sin.[13]

However, God revealed the reality of original sin and its immediate imputation throughout the history of the Old Testament. I claim that God demonstrated the visible reality of the original sin and its imputation from the historic episode of the flood judgment. God's judgment against the non-covenant community outside of the Ark even included innocent babies and embryos. It was one of the characteristics of God's redemptive judgment through the Noahic flood. In doing so, God vividly revealed and verified the original sin as the result of the first Adam's sin and imputed to his descendants, including innocent babies, as he broke the covenant of works:

> [17]The flood continued forty days on the earth. The waters increased and bore up the ark, and it rose high above the earth.

---

13. Longman, *Story of God Bible Commentary*, 72. Similarly, Walton rejects the biblical doctrine of the original sin, arguing that Augustine falsely formulated it without the biblical support and warrant: "Augustine pushes beyond what Paul says, and Paul has moved beyond what Genesis says. In Old Testament theology there is no apparent necessity for asserting the fall, though they understand the reality of sin. Even in Paul, it is not original sin that pervades his writing but the need for the savior. . . . If Augustine's model has been undermined on both counts (starting point and mechanism), one might think that it would have collapsed under its own unwieldiness. The theory, however, has become so deeply entrenched in the history of theological thought and development that it has taken on a life of its own almost independent from its essential roots. Perhaps the time has come for the church to reconsider how original sin is formulated and understood. . . . Another critique of Augustine's model comes from the recognition that he was working from a Latin translation of Romans 5:12. This is what led him to believe that Paul was saying that all sinned 'in Adam' whereas the Greek text has been purported to actually say 'in this way death came to all people, because all sinned' (NIV), indicating that we all sin *because* Adam sinned. This is a good illustration of what a big difference a little word can make, and in this case the result is a huge and longstanding debate among theologians as well as exegetes." Walton, *Lost World of Adam and Eve*, 155–57.

18The waters prevailed and increased greatly on the earth, and the ark floated on the face of the waters. 19And the waters prevailed so mightily on the earth that all the high mountains under the whole heaven were covered. 20The waters prevailed above the mountains, covering them fifteen cubits deep. 21And all flesh died that moved on the earth, birds, livestock, beasts, all swarming creatures that swarm on the earth, and all mankind. 22Everything on the dry land in whose nostrils was the breath of life died. 23He blotted out every living thing that was on the face of the ground, man and animals and creeping things and birds of the heavens. They were blotted out from the earth. Only Noah was left, and those who were with him in the ark. 24And the waters prevailed on the earth 150 days. (Gen 7:17–24)

I will highlight verses 21–23 again because those verses emphasize that no one survived outside of the Ark:

21And all flesh died that moved on the earth, birds, livestock, beasts, all swarming creatures that swarm on the earth, and all mankind. 22Everything on the dry land in whose nostrils was the breath of life died. 23He blotted out every living thing that was on the face of the ground, man and animals and creeping things and birds of the heavens. They were blotted out from the earth. Only Noah was left, and those who were with him in the ark. (Gen 7:21–23)

Likewise, verses 21–23 provide us a vivid picture of the nature of God's redemptive judgment upon the non-covenant community during the flood judgment. No humans, including babies and embryos, except the Noahic covenant community survived. They all died through God's merciless judgement. It gives us a comprehensive outlook that God will execute his final judgment through the covenant lawsuit based upon the covenant of works which was made with the first Adam in the holy garden of Eden.[14] All humans in the first Adam considered as reprobates

---

14. As he rejects original sin and its imputation to his descendents, Walton denies that the first Adam was the first human on the earth, falsely arguing that Adam and Eve were "the first *significant* humans." However, to be sure, the Bible clearly reveals and teaches that Adam and Eve were the first humans on the original earth: "In conclusion, rather than understanding Scripture as necessitating the view that Adam and Eve are the first humans, in light of their specific role concerned with access to God in sacred space and relationship with him, we might alternatively consider the possibility that they are the first *significant* humans. As with Abram, who was given a significant role as the ancestor of Israel (though not the first ancestor of Israel), Adam and Eve would be viewed as established as significant by their election. This would be true

will face the final judgment of God's fire and be thrown into the eternal kingdom of Satan.[15] On the other hand, all humans in the last Adam as the elect will be separated from the final judgment of fire, and inherit the eternal kingdom of God. This is a glorious consummation of heaven because Jesus Christ fulfilled all the requirements of the broken covenant of works and paid full penalty of sins on behalf of the elect through his sinless life and redemptive death on the cross as the last Adam.

The Pictorial Pattern of the Eternal Kingdom of God

After the completion of the flood judgment upon the wicked world, God began to dry up the flooded earth through his mighty wind. The flood

whether or not other people were around. Their election is to a priestly role, the first to be placed as sacred space. The forming accounts give them insight into the nature of humanity, but they also become the first significant humans because of their role in bringing sin into the world. . . . Adam was the 'first' man, given the opportunity to bring life, but he failed to achieve that goal. Christ, as the 'last' man, succeeded as he provided life and access to the presence of God for all as our great high priest (see 1 Cor 15:45)." Walton, *Lost World of Adam and Eve*, 114–15.

15. Supporting theistic evolution in light of the harmony of the Bible and science, Walton falsely argues that there was "death before the fall" and human beings were "created mortal." Perhaps, that is a logical conclusion because he denies the original sin, its imputation to his descendents, and God's judgment with physical death against the first Adam and his descendents. In doing so, he removes the possibility of the existence of eternal blessings of heaven and eternal curses of hell: "We have now laid the groundwork for considering the possibility that there was death before the death. In chapter eight we examined information to support the idea that humankind was created mortal. There we concluded that Paul's statement about why we humans are all subject to death was that in sinning we had lost access to the antidote found in the tree of life. . . . If we consider the model in which there were humans either preceding Adam and Eve or contemporary with Adam and Eve, we need to contemplate their vulnerability to suffering and death. If death and suffering can be feasibly inherent in a non-ordered world and be retained in a partially ordered world, then any pre-fall human population would have been in a state of innocence (not sinlessness) since they were not yet being held accountable, even though they *were* in the image of God. In this scenario we would expect to find predation, animal death, human death and violent behavior. Endowment with the image of God and the initiation of sacred place would provide the foundation for accountability through law and revelation. When Adam and Eve sinned, as representative priests for humanity, their sin brought disorder and accountability and made the antidote to death inaccessible. That disorder infects each one of us when we come into existence as human beings. Non-order is not being resolved according to the original plan (God teamed up with human vice-regents), and disorder brought the need for resolution through the work of Christ." Walton, *Lost World of Adam and Eve*, 159.

judgment was not only God's redemptive judgment upon the wicked original world, but also the process of recreation of the present earth. In that sense, the flood judgment was a means to purify the original earth. The holy and righteous God removed and cursed the non-covenant community who worshiped idols and went against God in their hearts. Simultaneously, God recreated the present earth so that history may continue on the present earth with a habitable and stable environment until the final judgment.

Vos captures the dual aspects of the flood judgment as the complete destruction of the original world and the new creation of the present earth:

> The cosmical extent of the deluge-event is both negative and positive. First, negatively, the flood destroyed the world (cf. Gen. 6). This is a catastrophic world-judgment. This fact is confirmed by pagan mythology, where it is associated with the chaos-flood out of which the world arose. The creation and the deluge both have cosmic significance. It was not confined to man; but the purpose was that God repented that he had created the world. Second, positively, it is the commencement of a new world-order. The waters receded on the first day of the month and the first month of the year (cf. Gen. 8:13); therefore, a new year. . . . Now the deluge and the post-diluvian order of things prefigure eschatological crisis and the eschatological state. In other words, the deluge and "new creation" are typical of the absolute end of the world and the final renewal of the world.[16]

Vos summarizes the flood judgment on the original earth and the new creation of the present earth as a remarkable contrast of God's redemptive drama which was demonstrated by the righteous and creative God. As God dried up the flooded earth through his supernatural wind, the newly created earth began to emerge. This was beautiful because God created the present earth with his mighty water and wind, restoring a habitable environment for humans, as well as all earthly creatures. Nevertheless, the present earth is not the *new earth* which will be perfected and realized when the final redemptive judgment comes with the heavenly fire. Rather, God recreated the present earth as a habitable and blessed environment so that both the covenant community and non-covenant community can live together under the benefits of God's covenant of common grace.

16. Vos, *Eschatology of the Old Testament*, 81.

The Noahic covenant community was surprised by the beauty of the present earth when they came out of the ark because God as the almighty architect and creator beautifully recreated the present earth through the flood judgment. In addition, the ark safely arrived on the Mount Ararat and the Noahic covenant community walked out of the ark along with the animals:

> ¹³In the six hundred and first year, in the first month, the first day of the month, the waters were dried from off the earth. And Noah removed the covering of the ark and looked, and behold, the face of the ground was dry. ¹⁴In the second month, on the twenty-seventh day of the month, the earth had dried out. ¹⁵Then God said to Noah, ¹⁶"Go out from the ark, you and your wife, and your sons and your sons' wives with you. ¹⁷Bring out with you every living thing that is with you of all flesh- birds and animals and every creeping thing that creeps on the earth- that they may swarm on the earth, and be fruitful and multiply on the earth." ¹⁸So Noah went out, and his sons and his wife and his sons' wives with him. ¹⁹Every beast, every creeping thing, and every bird, everything that moves on the earth, went out by families from the ark. (Gen 8:13–19)

The Noahic ark was an earthly and visible picture of the invisible heaven. When Noah saw the completed ark, he gazed and yearned for the invisible heaven through his faith which was typified by the ark. So, God presented the reality of *heaven* in the earthly and visible ark. God will consummate the new heaven and new earth and unite the new earth with "the holy city, new Jerusalem, coming down out of heaven from God" (Rev 21:2) when the final redemptive judgment happens on the day of the second coming of Jesus Christ. The apostle John saw a glorious pictorial vision through a revelation of the consummation of the eternal kingdom of God on the day of the final judgment:

> Then I saw a new heaven and a new earth, for the first heaven and the first earth had passed away, and the sea was no more. ²And I saw the holy city, new Jerusalem, coming down out of heaven from God, prepared as a bride adorned for her husband. ³And I heard a loud voice from the throne saying, "Behold, the dwelling place of God is with man. He will dwell with them, and they will be his people, and God himself will be with them as their God. ⁴He will wipe away every tear from their eyes, and death shall be no more, neither shall there be mourning

nor crying nor pain anymore, for the former things have passed away. (Rev 21:1–4)

The apostle John saw the pictorial vision that God will unite the invisible heaven with the new earth. Hoekema rightly observes that John's pictorial vision is the vision of the glorious union between "holy city, new Jerusalem" and the new earth:

> Verse 2 shows us the "holy city, new Jerusalem," standing for the entire glorified church of God, coming down out of heaven on earth. This church, now totally without spot or blemish, completely purified from sin, is now "prepared as a bride adorned for her husband," ready for the marriage of the Lamb (see Rev 19:7). From this verse we learn that the glorified church will not remain in a heaven far off in space, but will spend eternity on the new earth. From verse 3 we learn that the dwelling place of God will no longer be away from the earth but on the earth. Since where God dwells, there heaven is, we conclude that in the life to come heaven and earth will no longer be separated, as they are now, but will be merged. Believers will therefore continue to be in heaven as they continue to live on the new earth. "He will dwell with them, and they shall be his people" are the familiar words of the central promise of the covenant of grace (cf. Gen 17:7; Exod 19:5–6; Jer 31:33; Ezek 34:30; II Cor 6:16; Heb 8:10; 1 Pet 2:9–10). The fact that this promise is repeated in John's vision of the new earth implies that only on that new earth will God finally grant his people the full riches which the covenant of grace includes. Here we receive the firstfruits; there we shall receive the full harvest.[17]

The ark, as the visible type of invisible heaven, was united with the new earth because God removed evil from the original earth through the flood judgment. What Noah as a prophet saw through his own eyes from the opened door of the ark after the flood judgment was the typological picture of "a new heaven and a new earth" and "the holy city, new Jerusalem, coming down out of heaven from God, prepared as a bride adorned for her husband," united with "a new earth" that the apostle John saw through a revelation (vv. 1–2).

---

17. Hoekema, *Bible and the Future*, 284–85.

The Recovery of the Covenant of Common
Grace and World History

The Noahic flood was God's redemptive judgment against sinners and the sinful world at the time of Noah on the original earth. God displayed his infinite and righteous wrath. In doing so, he honored and glorified himself. Simultaneously, God displayed his infinite holiness and righteousness. In doing so, God provided the typological pattern and picture of the final judgment and biblical eschatology. Nevertheless, the Noahic flood judgment was not the final judgment so that world history can continue until the second coming of Jesus Christ under God's grace on the present earth.

Providing the continuity and stability of world history after the flood judgment on the present earth, God secured this through a means of the covenant of common grace as we observe in Genesis 8:20—9:17. Displaying a rainbow in the sky after the flood judgment was a sign of the covenant of common grace which promises that world history will be secured on the present earth until the final judgment.

God commanded the original cultural mandate to Adam and Eve in the garden of Eden after he created the original heavens and the earth:

> 26Then God said, "Let us make man in our image, after our like-ness. And let them have dominion over the fish of the sea and over the birds of the heavens and over the livestock and over all the earth and over every creeping thing that creeps on the earth." 27So God created man in his own image, in the image of God he created him; male and female he created them. 28And God blessed them. And God said to them, "Be fruitful and mul-tiply and fill the earth and subdue it and have dominion over the fish of the sea and over the birds of the heavens and over every living thing that moves on the earth." 29And God said, "Behold, I have given you every plant yielding seed that is on the face of all the earth, and every tree with seed in its fruit. You shall have them for food. 30And to every beast of the earth and to every bird of the heavens and to everything that creeps on the earth, everything that has the breath of life, I have given every green plant for food." And it was so. 31And God saw everything that he had made, and behold, it was very good. And there was evening and there was morning, the sixth day. (Gen 1:26–31)

When God created Adam and Eve, he created them in his own im-age, he engraved the moral law in their hearts, and he clothed them with his holiness, righteousness, and wisdom. So, they were able to govern the holy garden of Eden for the glory of God as vicegerents. God did not consider sin when he gave his original cultural mandate to Adam and Eve in the holy garden of Eden because it was given in the historical context before the fall. Adam and Eve as the Edenic covenant community had a duty to carry out the original cultural mandate, being fruitful and increasing in number, filling the earth and subduing it as the vicegerents for the glory of God. However, they failed to carry out their original cultural mandate when they broke the covenant of works, eating the forbidden fruit from the tree of the knowledge of good and evil through the temptation of Satan (Gen 3:1–7). Afterwards, gracious God introduced the good news of the gospel in the name of the woman's offspring, the coming Messiah (Gen 3:14–15). Remarkably, God introduced the covenant of common grace before he expelled Adam and Eve from the holy garden of Eden (Gen 3:16–19). In doing so, God provided a stable environment outside of the garden of Eden, so that world history after the Fall continued until the original sinful world faced the flood judgment at the time of Noah. Therefore, it was necessary for God to command a new cultural mandate in the world where the covenant community and non-covenant community can dwell together on the present earth:

> And God blessed Noah and his sons and said to them, "Be fruitful and multiply and fill the earth. [2]The fear of you and the dread of you shall be upon every beast of the earth and upon every bird of the heavens, upon everything that creeps on the ground and all the fish of the sea. Into your hand they are delivered. [3]Every moving thing that lives shall be food for you. And as I gave you the green plants, I give you everything. [4]But you shall not eat flesh with its life, that is, its blood. [5]And for your lifeblood I will require a reckoning: from every beast I will require it and from man. From his fellow man I will require a reckoning for the life of man. [6]"Whoever sheds the blood of man, by man shall his blood be shed, for God made man in his own image. [7]And you, be fruitful and multiply, teem on the earth and multiply in it." (Gen 9:1–7)

Likewise, the new cultural mandate after the flood judgment was not identical but similar to the original cultural mandate given to Adam and Eve because the new cultural mandate was given to the Noahic covenant community in the historical context of the resumption of the covenant of common grace. Moreover, the new cultural mandate was suitable in the fallen and sinful world where the covenant community and non-covenant community may live together until the day of the second coming of Christ.

The Noahic covenant community in the ark was the covenant community in the theocratic kingdom which typified the heavenly kingdom of God. However, the theocratic kingdom in the ark was over as soon as the covenant community walked out of the ark after the flood judgment ended and the present earth was created. As the theocratic kingdom in the ark faded away, God gave a new cultural mandate to the Noahic covenant community in the historical context of the resumption of the covenant of common grace. In that sense, as God recovered the covenant of common grace in Genesis 8:20—9:17, the Noahic covenant community began to live their lives as *the diaspora and pilgrims* on the present earth. Moses noted that "the sons of Noah" going out from the ark began to disperse: "**18**The sons of Noah who went forth from the ark were Shem, Ham, and Japheth. (Ham was the father of Canaan.) **19**These three were the sons of Noah, and from these the people of the whole earth were dispersed" (Gen 9:18–19). We need to focus on verse 19: "These three were the sons of Noah, and from these the people of the whole earth were dispersed." Here, Moses emphasized that the people from "the sons of Noah" began to scatter after the flood judgment. This is significant because the Noahic covenant community after the flood judgment lived their lives as *the diaspora and pilgrims*. It is noteworthy that they lived their lives as the diaspora after the resumption of the covenant of common grace in Genesis 8:20—9:17.

Nevertheless, Noah's descendants as the Babel community rejected living their lives as the diaspora, and began to build the Tower of Babel. The Tower of Babel was a symbol of the wicked sinners' arrogance against God, idolizing their knowledge, intelligence, power, skill, strength, and wisdom. As we have indicated, God gave the new cultural mandate to the Noahic covenant community after the flood judgment (Gen 9:1–7). An aspect of the new cultural mandate is to "be fruitful and multiply and fill the earth" (v.1). In order for this to happen, they had to disperse and spread continuously, building new communities in new areas on the present earth.

However, the Babel community decided to stop dispersing and filling the earth, rather gathered together against God, becoming the servants of the kingdom of Satan. Genesis 11:4 summarizes the comprehensive picture of the Babel community, building "a city and a tower," heading "its tops in the heavens," and rejecting to disperse over "the face of the whole earth;" actions that were against God's new cultural mandate:

> Now the whole earth had one language and the same words. ²And as people migrated from the east, they found a plain in the land of Shinar and settled there. ³And they said to one another, "Come, let us make bricks, and burn them thoroughly." And they had brick for stone, and bitumen for mortar. ⁴Then they said, "Come, let us build ourselves a city and a tower with its top in the heavens, and let us make a name for ourselves, lest we be dispersed over the face of the whole earth." ⁵And the LORD came down to see the city and the tower, which the children of man had built. ⁶And the LORD said, "Behold, they are one people, and they have all one language, and this is only the beginning of what they will do. And nothing that they propose to do will now be impossible for them. ⁷Come, let us go down and there confuse their language, so that they may not understand one another's speech." ⁸So the LORD dispersed them from there over the face of all the earth, and they left off building the city. ⁹Therefore its name was called Babel, because there the LORD confused the language of all the earth. And from there the LORD dispersed them over the face of all the earth. (Gen 11:1–9)

Once again, dispersing and scattering over the present earth was God's will under the principle of the new cultural mandate. However, the Babel community became the servants of the kingdom of Satan who were in their hearts against the kingdom of God. Verse 4 reads, "Then they said, 'Come, let us build ourselves a city and a tower with its top in the heavens, and let us make a name for ourselves, lest we be dispersed over the face of the whole earth.'" This demonstrates the culmination of the wicked thoughts and actions of the Babel community against God. Moreover, the statement "lest we be dispersed over the face of the whole earth" (v. 4) is the reflection of the spirit of *anti-diaspora* of the Babel community as well. Afterwards, the triune God came down to the Babel community and cursed them by confusing their one language so that they were not able to communicate amongst each other. We need to pay special attention to verse 9: "Therefore its name was called Babel, because there the LORD confused the language of all the earth. And from there the LORD dispersed them over the face of all the earth." This verse signifies that the Lord cursed the Babel community, confusing their one language and forcefully dispersing them, filling "the face of all the earth" to live their lives as *diaspora or pilgrims* which was an important aspect of the new cultural mandate.

When God resumed the covenant of common grace in Genesis 8:20—9:17, he revealed several regulations for the covenant community to follow and obey. They are the regulations of food law, the prohibition of eating animal blood, and the institution of capital punishment.[18] The regulation of the food law is related to the formation and maintenance of the theocratic kingdom after the fall outside of the garden of Eden. The garden of Eden was the original theocratic kingdom before the fall on the earth. After the fall, God formed a theocratic kingdom in the ark. After the inauguration of the Sinaitic covenant, God instituted a theocratic kingdom in the promised land. The earthly theocratic kingdoms before and after the fall are the types of the theocratic kingdom in heaven. The distinction between clean and unclean animals is closely related to the formation of theocratic kingdoms after the fall. In redemptive history, God reveals the distinction between clean and unclean animals in the process of the formation of the theocratic kingdom in the ark:

> Then the LORD said to Noah, "Go into the ark, you and all your household, for I have seen that you are righteous before me in this generation. **2**Take with you seven pairs of all clean animals, the male and his mate, and a pair of the animals that are not clean, the male and his mate, **3**and seven pairs of the birds of the heavens also, male and female, to keep their offspring alive on the face of all the earth. (Gen 7:1–3)

As God made the distinction between clean and unclean animals before the Noahic covenant community entered the ark, God demonstrates that the theocratic kingdom in the ark would be inaugurated with the visible execution of the flood judgment. As the theocratic kingdom in the ark was over after the flood judgment, God removed the distinction between clean and unclean animals. In that sense, it is significant to recognize that the distinction between clean and unclean animals is closely tied to the formation and continuation of the theocratic kingdom on the earth after the fall. Furthermore, it is important to recognize that God allowed the covenant community to consume all the animals without any distinction between clean and unclean animals in the historical

18. For a biblical theological discussion of the distinction between clean and unclean animals, the prohibition of eating animal blood, and the institution of capital punishment in light of the resumption of the covenant of common grace in Genesis 8:20—9:17, see Jeon, *Biblical Theology*, 46–57; Kline, *Kingdom Prologue*, 250–60.

context of the resumption of the covenant of common grace after the flood judgment.

After the Sinaitic covenant was inaugurated, God formed a theocratic kingdom of Israel in the promised land. Once again, God made a distinction between clean and unclean animals, as well as clean and unclean people. This distinction was removed in the historical context of the resumption of the covenant of common grace in Genesis 8:20—9:17. Therefore, the covenant community of Israel had to follow the regulations of food law, given by God through the Mosaic law (Lev 11:1–47; Deut 14:1–21). God commanded them not to eat the unclean living creatures under the Mosaic covenant. The violation of the regulations of food law was capital punishment: stoning to death in the covenant community of Israel.

However, as the New Covenant Age was inaugurated through the life, death, resurrection, ascension, and session at the right hand of God Jesus Christ, the mediator of the new covenant, the distinction between clean and unclean animals along with clean and unclean people are permanently removed by God in Jesus Christ for the new covenant community. The Pentecost event was the audible and visible sign of the beginning of the New Covenant Age, as well as the inauguration of the theocratic kingdom in heaven. In this manner, the eschatological kingdom of God was inaugurated with the beginning of Jesus Christ's reign at the right hand of God in heaven. Therefore, God permanently removed the distinction between clean and unclean animals on behalf of the new covenant community so that the members of the new covenant community are able to consume all the living creatures for the glory of God in Jesus Christ (Acts 10: 9–23; 1 Cor 8:1–13; 10:23–33).

Although God removed the distinction between clean and unclean animals under the new cultural mandate, he prohibited consuming animal blood: "But you shall not eat flesh with its life, that is, its blood" (Gen 9:4). It was God's sovereign wisdom for the covenant community that he commanded them not to eat animal blood. It is God's pedagogical lesson that animal blood, shed and offered in altar worship after the inauguration of the covenant of grace in Genesis 3:14–15, is the type of the final sacrifice and redemptive blood, shed and offered on the Golgotha by Jesus Christ. After the inauguration of the new covenant, animal sacrifice was continued in the temple of Jerusalem. That is the reason why the Jerusalem Council, under the inspiration of the Holy Spirit, prohibited the consumption of animal blood even after the inauguration of the New Covenant Age (Acts 15:19–29). God executed his judgment through the covenant lawsuit against the covenant community of Israel who disobeyed the Mosaic covenant of law. He used the pagan soldiers of the Roman Empire to remove the covenant community of Israel from the promised land which was a holy land and poured his infinite wrath against them in A.D. 70. In doing so, God permanently removed earthly altar worship and terminated the old covenant order. In that sense, the new covenant community as *the diaspora or pilgrims* is no longer obligated to abstain from animal blood after A.D. 70.

As God recovered the covenant of common grace in Genesis 8:20—9:17, he manifested his wisdom to keep communities, societies, and various nations out of anarchy with the institution of capital punishment.[19] In light of the mission of God, it is necessary to have stable communities and nations so that believers as *the covenant diaspora or pilgrims* may proclaim the good news of the gospel as they are constantly dispersed and scattered unto the ends of the earth. In God's command of the new cultural mandate, he prohibited the killing of an innocent human:

19. God revealed the covenant of common grace in Genesis 3:16–19 after he proclaimed the *protevangelium* in Genesis 3:15 in light of the covenant of grace. After God expelled Adam and Eve from the garden of Eden, God revealed the institution of the contemporary state as the visible realm under the covenant of common grace to Cain. Kline views Genesis 4:15 as the origin of the state in light of the covenant of common grace, inaugurated in Genesis 3:16–19: "There is then no reference in Gen 4:15 to an unspecified wonder-sign that God performed for Cain's assurance, with the reader left to speculate about what it might have been. And certainly the language does not suggest a 'mark of Cain' imprinted on his body. Such interpretations assume that Cain was being given a special individual guarantee, but that, as we have seen, is not the point of the passage. It is rather concerned with a general world-order that would condition the life of all men. The meaning of the passage will therefore be brought out if we translate, not 'And Yahweh gave a sign to Cain,' but 'Thus Yahweh signified to Cain that . . . '

The author's concern with the subject of God's judicial relation to men is attested once again in Gen 4 when he turns from the Cainite succession to the line of Seth (vv. 25, 26). For he capsulates the nature of this community in their act of confessing (naming) Yahweh as covenant Lord to whom their judicial appeal was directed. There is, of course, a radical difference between the exercise of God's *imperium* that is in view in Gen 4:15, and his vindication of the blood of Abel and the martyr-seed of the woman restored in the line of Seth and continuing to the last judgment (cf. Rev 6:10, 11). To Cain, God signified that for mankind in general he would provide in his common grace an institutional agent to bear the sword of his wrath in the temporal course of world history (cf. Rom 13:4). For the people of his covenant, God's judicial vindication is an act of his saving grace, a coming in personal immediacy as their eschatological, redemptive Avenger." Kline, "Oracular Origin of State," 60–61.

> [5]And for your lifeblood I will require a reckoning: from every beast I will require it and from man. From his fellow man I will require a reckoning for the life of man. [6]"Whoever sheds the blood of man, by man shall his blood be shed, for God made man in his own image." (Gen 9:5–6)

God honors the unique sanctity of human life and institutes capital punishment as he says, "Whoever sheds the blood of man, by man shall his blood be shed, for God made man in his own image" (v. 6).[20] The institution of capital punishment demonstrates that God created man as the *imago Dei* which indicates that God clothed man with God's righteousness, holiness, and wisdom, engraving the ten commandments as moral law in man's heart. The violation of the sixth commandment "You shall not murder" (Exod 20:13) is a serious crime not only against the sanctity of human life but also God's commandment. God's institution of capital punishment in the historical context of the command of the new cultural mandate suggests that God made a proper distinction between church and state. Therefore, the prosecution and execution against criminals who commit the crime of killing innocent people do not belong to the ministry of church but to the legal responsibility of the state.

Reading and interpreting Jesus Christ's famous "Sermon on the Mount," many people assume that he was a pacifist during his earthly ministry (Matt 5:1—7:29). Picturing Jesus Christ as the founder of pacifism, based upon the teachings of "The Sermon on the Mount" is a fundamental misreading and misapplication of his teachings.[21] In short, Jesus

20. Interpreting Genesis 9:6, Calvin affirms capital punishment that God bestowed the authority to the magistrates of state "for the avenging of slaughter" so that the murderer may be punished with death penalty: "Therefore, however magistrates may connive at the crime, God sends executioners from other quarters, who shall render unto sanguinary men their reward. God so threatens and denounces vengeance against the murderer, that he even arms the magistrate with the sword for the avenging of slaughter, in order that the blood of men may not be shed with impunity." Calvin, *Genesis*, 9:6, in *Calvin's Commentaries*.

21. Richard Hays is a representative scholar who colors Jesus Christ's teaching on the Sermon on the Mount as the founder of pacifism or nonviolence. The fundamental problem lies in the fact that he doesn't read it in light of the proper distinction between church and state: "Our exegetical investigation of Matthew 5:38–48 has led to the conclusion that the passage teaches a norm of nonviolent love of enemies. Within the context of Matthew's Gospel, the directive to 'turn the other cheek' functions as more than a bare rule; instead, as a 'focal instance' of discipleship, it functions metonymically, illuminating the life of a covenant community that is called to live in radical faithfulness to the vision of the kingdom of God disclosed in Jesus' teaching and example.

Christ's message through "The Sermon on the Mount" is not a call to pacifism but to eschatological mission, given to the new covenant community so that believers under the New Covenant Age may exercise the heart attitude and spirit of "Love your enemies and pray for those who persecute you" (v. 44). Likewise, the message of the heart attitude for eschatological mission is summed up well here:

> 43"You have heard that it was said, 'You shall love your neighbor and hate your enemy.' 44But I say to you, Love your enemies and pray for those who persecute you, 45so that you may be sons of your Father who is in heaven. For he makes his sun rise on the evil and on the good, and sends rain on the just and on the unjust. 46For if you love those who love you, what reward do you have? Do not even the tax collectors do the same? 47And if you greet only your brothers, what more are you doing than others? Do not even the Gentiles do the same? 48You therefore must be perfect, as your heavenly Father is perfect. (Matt 5:43–48)

The message "Love your enemies and pray for those who persecute you" is the message of eschatological mission which should be followed and practiced by believers under the New Covenant Age. God bestows the benefits of the covenant of common grace, recovered in Genesis 8:20—9:17 without any discrimination between the elect and reprobate so that he sovereignly takes care of the elect and reprobate with temporary and earthly blessings as long as the world history continues on the present earth. Jesus Christ as the mediator of the new covenant in fact revealed that God temporarily blesses and loves even the reprobate, bestowing the blessings of the covenant of common grace when he proclaimed, "For he makes his sun rise on the evil and on the good, and sends rain on the just and on the unjust." (v. 45). Likewise, Jesus Christ made a proper distinction between the covenant of common grace and

---

Taken alone, this text would certainly preclude any justification for Jesus' disciples to resort to violence. The question that we must now consider is how Matthew's vision of the peaceful community fits into the larger witness of the canonical New Testament. Do the other texts in the canon reinforce the Sermon on the Mount's teaching on nonviolence, or do they provide other options that might allow or require Christians to take up the sword? . . . Clearly it is *possible* for a Christian to be a soldier, possible for a Christian to fight. But if we ask the larger question about the vocation of the community, the New Testament witness comes clearly into focus: the community is called to the work of reconciliation and—as a part of that vocation—suffering even in the face of great injustice. When the identity of the community is understood in these terms, the place of the soldier within the church can only be seen as anomalous." Hays, *Moral Vision of the New Testament*, 329, 337.

the covenant of grace, as well as a proper distinction between church and state as the theocratic kingdom of Israel in the promised land began to fade away with the inauguration of the New Covenant Age.

The New Covenant Age was inaugurated with Jesus Christ's life, death, bodily resurrection, ascension, session at the right hand of God in heaven, and the Pentecost event. The exalted and glorified Jesus Christ already began to rule the visible and invisible realms as "King of kings and Lord of lords" (Rev 17:14; 19:16). The exalted Jesus Christ rules the church as the head of the church through the indwelling works of the Holy Spirit and the word of God. However, he rules the state *indirectly*, appointing government authorities. In that sense, a proper distinction between church and state should be maintained until the second coming of Jesus Christ. In light of that, even under the new covenant, the continuity of capital punishment is valid. For example, the apostle Paul affirmed that God endowed to the government authorities to execute penalties, including capital punishment against criminals:

> Let every person be subject to the governing authorities. For there is no authority except from God, and those that exist have been instituted by God. 2Therefore whoever resists the authorities resists what God has appointed, and those who resist will incur judgment. 3For rulers are not a terror to good conduct, but to bad. Would you have no fear of the one who is in authority? Then do what is good, and you will receive his approval, 4for he is God's servant for your good. But if you do wrong, be afraid, for he does not bear the sword in vain. For he is the servant of God, an avenger who carries out God's wrath on the wrongdoer. 5Therefore one must be in subjection, not only to avoid God's wrath but also for the sake of conscience. 6For the same reason you also pay taxes, for the authorities are ministers of God, attending to this very thing. 7Pay to all what is owed to them: taxes to whom taxes are owed, revenue to whom revenue is owed, respect to whom respect is owed, honor to whom honor is owed. (Rom 13:1–7)

When the apostle Paul wrote the epistle to the Romans, the New Covenant Age was already inaugurated approximately for about two decades. The good news of the gospel began to spread powerfully "in all Judea and Samaria, and to the end of the earth" under the guidance of the Holy Spirit through the missionary endeavors of the original apostles, apostle Paul, and other believers as Jesus Christ prophesied to the original apostles right before his ascension to heaven (Acts 1:8). As Jesus

Christ maintained a proper distinction between church and state during his earthly ministry, the apostle Paul maintained a proper distinction between church and state under the inspiration of the Holy Spirit so that he was able to affirm that the execution of penalties, including capital punishment belong to the governing authority of state, which was ordained by God. Paul insists that the state is "the servant of God" who rules and executes penalties against criminals on behalf of God. In particular, Paul warrants capital punishment and its careful and proper execution by government authorities in verse 4: "For he is God's servant for your good. But if you do wrong, be afraid, for he does not bear the sword in vain. For he is the servant of God, an avenger who carries out God's wrath on the wrongdoer."[22] Paul's remarks, "But if you do wrong, be afraid, for he does not bear the sword in vain" highlight that God ordained the execution of capital punishment against killers of innocent humans and that the proper execution of capital punishment does not belong to the ministry of church but to the governing authority of state until the second coming of Jesus Christ.

Summary

Through the Noahic flood judgment God demonstrated a type of the final judgment, separating the Noahic covenant community in the ark and the non-covenant community outside of the ark. Jesus Christ as the consummate redemptive historical theologian compared the Noahic flood judgment with the final judgment which will occur on the day of his second coming (Matt 24:36–44). It is noteworthy that "on the very same day" (Gen 7:13) signifies that the flood judgment was *a concomitant event* between the blessings of life in the ark and curses of death outside of the ark. Nevertheless, there was *a logical and chronological order* that

---

22. Reflecting Rom 13:4, Calvin properly argues that God bestowed the authority for the magistrate of state to execute capital punishment against "the guilty with death." In doing so, Calvin adds that the magistrate executes "God's vengeance," obeying his commands: "This is the same as if it had been said, that he is an executioner of God's wrath; and this he shows himself to be by having the sword, which the Lord has delivered into his hand. This is a remarkable passage for the purpose of proving the right of the sword; for if the Lord, by arming the magistrate, has also committed to him the use of the sword, whenever he visits the guilty with death, by executing God's vengeance, he obeys his commands. Contend then do they with God who think it unlawful to shed the blood of wicked men." Calvin, *Romans*, 13:4, in *Calvin's Commentaries*.

God saved the Noahic covenant community in the ark before he poured out his infinite wrath of death against the non-covenant community.

The flood judgment was not a local but global judgment which covered the entire original earth. The universal flood judgment was God's pictorial and typological demonstration that the final judgment will also be global and universal on the day of the second coming of Jesus Christ. God did not separate the elect and reprobate, rather the covenant community and non-covenant community through the flood judgment. For example, Ham was saved during the flood judgment; he entered into the ark as a member of the Noahic covenant community. Nevertheless, the Bible does not describe Ham as a member of the elect who receives the benefits of salvation and redemptive blessings (Gen 9:22–25).

God waged holy war against the original wicked world and non-covenant community who followed the spirit of the kingdom of Satan. In doing so, God temporarily withheld the benefits of the covenant of common grace, inaugurated in Genesis 3:16–19. The physical death of the non-covenant community was only the beginning of God's infinite wrath, based upon his infinite holiness and righteousness. He sent the souls of all the dead to hell which is an invisible realm. Certainly, the souls in hell will experience the bodily resurrection of the wicked as "the resurrection of judgment" on the day of the second coming of Jesus Christ. They will be thrown into the kingdom of Satan which will be the consummation of hell (John 5:25–29).

God's covenantal background to execute his flood judgment against the non-covenant community was the Adamic covenant of works, made in Genesis 2:15–17. God remembered the covenant of works which was broken by the first Adam when he poured out his wrath during the flood judgment. He poured out his wrath against the sinners outside of the ark, including innocent babies through the covenant lawsuit, based upon the broken covenant of works by the first Adam (Gen 7:17–24). In doing so, he revealed the reality of original sin and its immediate imputation to all the descendants of the first Adam.

The flood judgment was not only God's redemptive judgment upon the original sinful world, but also the recreation process of the present earth. The present earth emerged as God dried up the flooded earth through his creative and mighty wind (Gen 8:13–19). God demonstrated the pictorial and typological pattern of the eternal kingdom of God as the ark arrived on Mount Ararat after the flood judgment. In fact, Noah saw the typological picture of "a new heaven and a new earth" and "the holy city, new Jerusalem, coming down out of heaven from God, prepared as a bride adorned for her husband," united with "a new earth" when the apostle John saw the prophetic vision through a revelation (Rev 22:1–2).

The Noahic flood judgment was not the final judgment so that world history could continue until the second coming of Jesus Christ. God provided the continuity and stability of world history on the present earth through the recovery of the covenant of common grace in Genesis 8:20—9:17.

God gave the original cultural mandate to Adam and Eve in the garden of Eden before the fall (Gen 1:26–31). However, God adjusted the original cultural mandate into the new cultural mandate so that the covenant community and non-covenant community could dwell together in the midst of the present earth, created by the flood judgment (Gen 9:1–7). In addition, God gave the new cultural mandate in the fallen and sinful world until the day of the second coming of Jesus Christ.

The Noahic covenant community began to live their lives as *the diaspora and pilgrims* in the present earth after the flood judgment (Gen 9:18–19). An important aspect of the new cultural mandate is to "be fruitful and multiply and fill the earth" (Gen 9:1). In order to do so, people had to be scattered and constantly building new communities in new areas on the present earth. Nevertheless, the Babel community as the servants of the kingdom of Satan rejected this command. Therefore, the Lord cursed the Babel community by confusing their one language and forcefully dispersing them to live their lives as *the diaspora and pilgrims*.

When God resumed the covenant of common grace in Genesis 8:20—9:17, he revealed several regulations for the covenant community such as food law, the prohibition of eating animal blood, and the institution of capital punishment. God revealed the distinction between clean and unclean animals in the process of the formation of the theocratic kingdom in the ark (Gen 7:1–3). As the theocratic kingdom in the ark was over after the flood judgment, God removed the distinction between clean and unclean animals. In doing so, God allowed the covenant community to consume all the animals in the historical context of the resumption of the covenant of common grace (Gen 9:3).

Although God removed the distinction between clean and unclean animals, allowing the covenant community to consume all the animals through the new cultural mandate, he prohibited consuming animal blood (Gen 9:4). It is God's pedagogical lesson that animal blood offered in altar worship after the inauguration of the covenant of grace in Genesis

3:14–15 is the type of the final sacrifice offered on the Golgotha by Jesus Christ as the mediator of the new covenant. The new covenant community as *the diaspora or pilgrims* is no longer obligated to abstain from animal blood after A.D. 70 because God permanently terminated altar worship and the old covenant order with the fall of Jerusalem.

God prohibited the killing of innocent humans in the context of his command of the new cultural mandate (Gen 9:5–6). God's institution of capital punishment in the historical context of the resumption of the covenant of common grace suggests that God made a proper distinction between church and state. In that sense, the prosecution and execution against the criminals of the crime of killing innocent people do not belong to the ministry of church but to the legal responsibility of the state under the New Covenant Age until the day of the second coming of Jesus Christ.

Chapter Two

The Abrahamic Covenant and Redemptive Judgment

GOD REVEALED BIBLICAL ESCHATOLOGY in the historical context of the Prediluvian Noahic covenant by redemptive judgment (Gen 6:5—8:19). After the flood judgment, God demonstrated several patterns of biblical eschatology in the historical context of the formation of the Abrahamic covenant and in the Exodus of the Israelites as the covenant descendants of Abraham.[1]

In another instance, we will explore that God carries out the glorious pattern of final judgment by means of a mighty fire upon Sodom and Gomorrah in the historical context of the Abrahamic covenant (Gen 18:16—19:29).

At the end of the Israelites' Egyptian bondage for 430 years, God demonstrated a type of final judgment, making a life and death distinction between the covenant children of Israel and the non-covenant children of Egypt. God used the blood of the original Passover lamb to signify the final lamb of God to execute his redemptive judgment. This separated the firstborn sons of Israel from Egypt, including the first-born of the cattle of Israel from Egypt (Exod 11:1—12:51).

Lastly, we will explore that God used the Red Sea during the Exodus as a glorious scene and theatre of redemptive judgment that separated the covenant community of Israel and the non-covenant community of Egyptian soldiers. God visibly demonstrated the pattern of biblical

---

1. For a biblical theological analysis of the Abrahamic covenant and the kingdom of God, see Jeon, *Biblical Theology*, 58–84.

eschatology and final judgment before the covenant community of Israel reached Mount Sinai where God made the Sinaitic covenant.

Sodom and Gomorrah and Redemptive Judgment

God ratified the Abrahamic covenant and made a sworn oath to the covenant as the theophanic Glory, the visible presence of God, by passing through the cursed and torn animal pieces (Gen 15:1–21). Afterwards, God revealed circumcision as the sign of the Abrahamic covenant when Abraham was ninety-nine years old (Gen 17:1–26). According to God's command, Abraham circumcised his son Ishmael and "all the men of his house, those born in the house and they bought with money from a foreigner," including himself (v. 27). The circumcision was the seal and sign of the covenant of grace in the context of the Abrahamic covenant. It was given and applied to the body of the covenant people because it was related to the benefits of redemptive blessings, including salvation by God's grace. Immediately before God revealed circumcision as the sign of the Abrahamic covenant, God changed Abram's name to Abraham; a promise that God will grant "all the land of Canaan" as "an everlasting possession" which is the sign of inheritance of the eternal kingdom of God:

> [4]"Behold, my covenant is with you, and you shall be the father of a multitude of nations. [5]No longer shall your name be called Abram, but your name shall be Abraham, for I have made you the father of a multitude of nations. [6]I will make you exceedingly fruitful, and I will make you into nations, and kings shall come from you. [7]And I will establish my covenant between me and you and your offspring after you throughout their generations for an everlasting covenant, to be God to you and to your offspring after you. [8]And I will give to you and to your offspring after you the land of your sojournings, all the land of Canaan, for an everlasting possession, and I will be their God." (Gen 17:4–8)

Circumcision was applied to the males in the Abrahamic covenant community because the Abrahamic covenant as the covenant of grace was directly related to the redemptive blessings, including personal salvation. It was also the sign and seal of the covenant community as the visible church, set apart from the world. Under the Mosaic covenant, God commanded the covenant community to continue circumcision. In a sense, the circumcision of the covenant community under the Mosaic covenant was related to the preparation of God's holy war against the

inhabitants of the promised land. For example, God prepared the covenant community of Israel with circumcision before God waged holy war
against the non-covenant community in the promised land under the
Sinaitic covenant (Josh 5:1–9). The whole Exodus generation were circumcised, but they perished except for Joshua and Caleb "because they
did not obey the voice of the Lord; the Lord swore to them that he would
not let them see the land that the Lord had sworn to their fathers to give
to us, a land flowing with milk and honey" (v. 6). All the Israelites who
were born during the forty-year wilderness were circumcised by Joshua
according to the Lord's command before the Lord commanded holy war
against the inhabitants of the promised land. In that sense, "the circum-
cising of the whole nation" before the conquest of the promised land with
holy war was closely related to the execution of redemptive judgment in
the promised land (vv. 8–9).[2]

Interestingly, God chose the cities of Sodom and Gomorrah to execute his redemptive judgment.[3] These cities were corrupt and followed
the spirit of the kingdom of Satan (Gen 19:1–11). Before God executed
his redemptive judgment, God sent two angels to rescue Abraham's
nephew Lot's covenant family who resided in Sodom. The two angels
revealed the imminent destruction of Sodom to Lot and Lot, as the head
of the covenant family, informed his sons-in-law to flee because the Lord
was about to destroy the city. Nevertheless, Lot's two sons-in-law did not
heed Lot's warning:

> [12]Then the men said to Lot, "Have you anyone else here? Sons-
> in-law, sons, daughters, or anyone you have in the city, bring
> them out of the place. [13]For we are about to destroy this place,
> because the outcry against its people has become great before
> the LORD, and the LORD has sent us to destroy it." [14]So Lot
> went out and said to his sons-in-law, who were to marry his

---

2. For a biblical theological discussion of the close relationship between circumcision and holy war, see Jeon, *Biblical Theology*, 121–25.

3. Reading the story of the judgment of Sodom and Gomorrah in light of a historical critical perspective, Rad rejects to see it as a historic event but a "saga" which was a
mythological tradition: "It has long been known that the story of Sodom was an independent saga. Now, however, as its beginning and end show, it has been incorporated
into the large Abraham story as a very striking occurrence. . . . The older form of the
saga reported only one judgment on Sodom, which came upon the city because of the
unchastity which did not stop even with divine messengers. Now, however, the visit
of the heavenly being is an act of judgment and at the same time a last chance to test
Sodom." Rad, *Genesis*, 216.

daughters, "Up! Get out of this place, for the LORD is about to destroy the city." But he seemed to his sons-in-law to be jesting. (Gen 19:12–14)

When the day of the Lord's judgment came upon the two cities, the angels as God's agents guided Lot's covenant family out from the city of Sodom. The covenant community safely escaped to the city of Zoar before the Lord sent his fiery judgment on Sodom and Gomorrah:

> 15As morning dawned, the angels urged Lot, saying, "Up! Take your wife and your two daughters who are here, lest you be swept away in the punishment of the city." 16But he lingered. So the men seized him and his wife and his two daughters by the hand, the LORD being merciful to him, and they brought him out and set him outside the city. 17And as they brought them out, one said, "Escape for your life. Do not look back or stop anywhere in the valley. Escape to the hills, lest you be swept away." 18And Lot said to them, "Oh, no, my lords. 19Behold, your servant has found favor in your sight, and you have shown me great kindness in saving my life. But I cannot escape to the hills, lest the disaster overtake me and I die. 20Behold, this city is near enough to flee to, and it is a little one. Let me escape there- is it not a little one?- and my life will be saved!" 21He said to him, "Behold, I grant you this favor also, that I will not overthrow the city of which you have spoken. 22Escape there quickly, for I can do nothing till you arrive there." Therefore the name of the city was called Zoar. (Gen 19:15–22)

Here, we find the pattern of biblical eschatology. There was a logical and chronological order when God executed redemptive judgment upon Sodom and Gomorrah. First, God removed Lot's family as the covenant community from the territory of redemptive judgment. God sovereignly chose the city of Zoar for Lot's covenant family as a holy city. Second, God began to execute his fiery judgment against Sodom and Gomorrah:

> 23The sun had risen on the earth when Lot came to Zoar. 24Then the LORD rained on Sodom and Gomorrah sulfur and fire from the LORD out of heaven. 25And he overthrew those cities, and all the valley, and all the inhabitants of the cities, and what grew on the ground. 26But Lot's wife, behind him, looked back, and she became a pillar of salt. 27And Abraham went early in the morning to the place where he had stood before the LORD. 28And he looked down toward Sodom and Gomorrah and toward all the land of the valley, and he looked and, behold,

the smoke of the land went up like the smoke of a furnace. [29]So
it was that, when God destroyed the cities of the valley, God
remembered Abraham and sent Lot out of the midst of the over-
throw when he overthrew the cities in which Lot had lived. (Gen
19:23–29)[4]

After Yahweh took away Lot's covenant family, "the sun had risen on
the earth" (v. 23). Yahweh executed his redemptive judgment on Sodom
and Gomorrah. The Lord did not use manmade weapons in his execution of judgment although human inventions are one of the benefits of
the covenant of common grace. Instead, the Lord used supernatural
and heavenly power: "Then the LORD rained on Sodom and Gomorrah sulfur and fire from the LORD out of heaven" (v. 24). On the other
hand, verse 28: "And he looked down toward Sodom and Gomorrah and
toward all the land of the valley, and he looked and, behold, the smoke of
the land went up like the smoke of a furnace" highlights that Abraham,
as the head of the Abrahamic covenant community, witnessed Yahweh's
judgment upon Sodom and Gomorrah although he did not escape from
Sodom like Lot's covenant family. In fact, Yahweh revealed to Abraham
the judgment upon Sodom and Gomorrah. Listening to the prophecy,
Abraham interceded for the pagan cities of Sodom and Gomorrah where
his nephew Lot's covenant family lived. However, Yahweh told Abraham
that because Sodom had not even ten righteous people, it will face judgment (Gen 18:16–33). Abraham witnessed the realization of Yahweh's
direct prophecy about the imminent judgment upon Sodom and Gomorrah. Once again, God revealed the pattern of biblical eschatology:
he will not use manmade weapons, including nuclear or atomic bombs,
which are the culmination of scientific and technological endeavors in
the modern era, when the day of the Lord comes with the second coming
of Jesus Christ.[5]

4. Vos reads and interprets the judgment upon Sodom and Gomorrah as "the
eschatology of judgment" as well as the flood judgment at the time of Noah: "Redemptive eschatology is more than revelation. The typical signification of the deluge lies on
the judgment side and not primarily on the side of redemption. The eschatology of
nature is typical of the eschatology of redemption. Revelation in the patriarchal history foreshadows eschatology along the line of redemption. The expression 'fire and
brimstone' (Gen. 19:24) in connection with the destruction of the cities of the plain is
expressive of the eschatology of judgment. This, however, is probably the chief, if not
the only exception. But the main emphasis is on the redemptive side." Vos, *Eschatology
of the Old Testament*, 85.

5. Interpreting the historic episode of Genesis 19, Poythress notes that the

Moreover, we need to highlight and revisit verses 24–25: "**24**Then the LORD rained on Sodom and Gomorrah sulfur and fire from the LORD out of heaven. **25**And he overthrew those cities, and all the valley, and all the inhabitants of the cities, and what grew on the ground." After Lot's covenant family safely arrived in the city of Zoar, "Then the Lord rained on Sodom and Gomorrah sulfur and fire from the Lord out of heaven" (v. 24). This suggests that Yahweh's holy war against the cities of Sodom and Gomorrah began after Lot's covenant family safely escaped to the city of Zoar, a sanctuary city prepared by Yahweh. In particular, "sulfur and fire from the Lord out of heaven" is God's first visible revelation of the divine means of final judgment when the Parousia comes. As we know, God used the mighty water when he demonstrated his redemptive judgment against the original world in the historical context of the Prediluvian Noahic covenant (Gen 6:5—8:19). However, he will use fire from heaven when the final parousia comes as God confirmed this through the apostle Peter (2 Pet 3:1–13). When the day of judgment came upon Sodom and Gomorrah, Yahweh demonstrated his infinite righteousness and holiness against sinful people who worshiped idols and practiced homosexuality. The inhabitants of Sodom and Gomorrah abused the land of Yahweh and made it a land of idol worship. Therefore, he temporarily withheld the benefits of the covenant of common grace although he resumed it in Genesis 8:20—9:17 through the Post-diluvian Noahic covenant.

Verse 25 vividly summarizes the total destruction within the territories of Sodom and Gomorrah: "And he overthrew those cities, and all the valley, and all the inhabitants of the cities, and what grew on the ground." God destroyed not only "all the inhabitants of the cities" who resided there but also all the living beings, including animals and

---

judgment upon Sodom and Gomorrah becomes "a permanent example of God's just judgment and a permanent picture foreshadowing the last judgment." In addition, he adds that God's presence on the judgment of Sodom and Gomorrah is "a foretaste of the theophany of God's presence at the last judgment": "We may move on to Genesis 19. We earlier decided that the two angels that come to Sodom are created angels rather than a direct appearance of God. But it is still true that they are participants in the 'court' of God, and that they come to Sodom reflecting the glory of God. Here we see the presence of God in a broad sense, through the presence of angelic representatives who bear his word and his authority. The rescue of Lot and the destruction of Sodom and Gomorrah both reflect the glory of God and his power. The destruction of Sodom and Gomorrah becomes a permanent example of God's just judgment and a permanent picture foreshadowing the last judgment. . . . The presence of God in the destruction of Sodom and Gomorrah is a foretaste of the theophany of God's presence at the last judgment." Poythress, *Theophany*, 259.

trees. Furthermore, all the standing houses, monuments, and beautiful sites were burned and destroyed. In short, God did not show any mercy against Sodom and Gomorrah but total destruction, including innocent babies.[6] Certainly, it is a very difficult historic event to understand when we read about this event in the Bible. However, God revealed the pattern of not only biblical eschatology but also final judgment. God executed his merciless judgment against all the non-covenant people in Sodom and Gomorrah based upon the result of the covenant lawsuit in light of the broken covenant of works in the garden of Eden by the first Adam. All the inhabitants of Sodom and Gomorrah belonged to the first Adam who broke the covenant of works and ate the forbidden fruit of the knowledge of good and evil (Gen 2:15–17; 3:1–7).[7] The fact that even innocent ba-

6. Jonathan Edwards demonstrates that the Noahic flood judgment and judgment upon Sodom and Gomorrah were the visible manifestations of "God's wrath against sin" which was the consequence of the first Adam's breaking of the covenant of works. Furthermore, he argues that the judgment upon Sodom and Gomorrah was God's infinite wrath against sin which was "the liveliest image of hell." Likewise, Edwards interprets the judgment through the Noahic flood and the fiery judgment upon Sodom and Gomorrah in light of the Final judgment of hell: "But some external awful manifestations of God's wrath against sin were on some accounts especially necessary before the giving of the law; and therefore, before the flood, the terrors of the law handed down by tradition from Adam served. Adam lived nine hundred and thirty years himself, to tell the church of God's awful threatenings denounced in the covenant made with him, and how dreadful the consequences of the fall were, as he was an eye witness and subject; and others, that conversed with Adam, lived until the flood. And the destruction of the world by the flood served to exhibit the terrors of the law, and manifest the wrath of God against sin; and so to make men sensible of the absolute necessity of redeeming mercy. And some that saw the flood were alive in Abraham's time.

But this was now in a great measure forgotten; now therefore God was pleased again, in a most amazing manner, to show his wrath against sin, in the destruction of these cities; which was after such a manner as to be the liveliest image of hell of any thing that ever had been; and therefore the apostle Jude says, 'They suffer the vengeance of eternal fire,' Jude 7. God rained storms of fire and brimstone upon them. The way that they were destroyed probably was by thick flashes of lightning. The streams of brimstone were so thick as to burn up all these cities; so that they perished in the flames of divine wrath. By this might be seen the dreadful wrath of God against the ungodliness and unrighteousness of men; which tended to show men the necessity of redemption, and so to promote that great work." Edwards, *A History of the Work of Redemption*, 64.

7. The antithesis between the covenant of works and covenant of grace along with the proper distinction between law and gospel is vitally important not only for the proper vision of redemptive history as creation, fall, redemption, and consummation but also proper understanding of soteriology. Nowadays, it is a general tendency to ignore or reject it. For example, Thomas Schreiner as a conservative New Testament scholar argues that the first Adam was under "the covenant of creation," avoiding the

bies were killed by God's merciless judgment in Sodom and Gomorrah once again verifies the immediate imputation of the original sin as soon as the first Adam broke the covenant of works in the garden of Eden.

In fact, God's fiery judgment upon Sodom and Gomorrah is a typological picture of the judgment in hell while Lot's covenant family's escape to Zoar is a typological demonstration of the eternal blessings in heaven. In other words, God reveals the existence of heaven and hell not only to Lot's covenant community but also to all the covenant communities thereafter through the decisive redemptive judgment.[8]

---

term the covenant of works: "It is understandable why doubts arise about a creation covenant since the term *covenant* is lacking. When we add to this the unique circumstances of Adam and Eve in the garden, further ammunition is added to the argument that *covenant* is not quite the right term. A word should be said about terminology before going further. Those who believe that there was a covenant with Adam use different terms to label it, such as 'covenant of life,' 'covenant of nature,' or 'covenant of works.' The same general idea is involved, whatever the terminology. I prefer 'covenant of creation' because it fits with an overarching view of redemptive history, enabling us to see how this covenant integrates with other covenants. In other words, God inaugurated history with creation and will consummate it with the new creation, and thus the old creation anticipates and points forward to the new creation. Still, there is no need to linger on the matter of terminology since the vital issue is the nature of the covenant." Schreiner, *Covenant and God's Purpose for the World*, 19–20.

Schreiner's monocovenantalism, rejecting the evangelical distinction between law and gospel, becomes visibly evident in his analysis of justification by faith alone (*sola fide*). He insists that present justification is by faith alone (*sola fide*) while final justification is by works. At the same time, he argues present salvation is by grace alone (*sola gratia*) while final salvation is by works: "When some hear the Reformation cry of *sola fide*—"Faith alone!"—they assume that it means that good works are an optional part of the Christian life or that they play no role at all in our final justification or salvation. Such a perspective radically misunderstands the New Testament witness, while also distorting the historical and biblical meaning of *sola fide*. The New Testament clearly teaches that bare faith cannot save, and that works are necessary for final justification or final salvation. As we will see, this latter notion does not compromise or deny *sola fide* when it is properly understood." Schreiner, *Faith Alone*, 191.

8. Adopting a historical critical reading of the Bible, Peter Enns denies the existence of heaven and hell, insisting that the concept of hell doesn't come from the Bible but "by way of medieval Christian theology," even suggesting that Jesus never used the word hell: "For one thing, our idea of 'hell,' with demons, pitchforks, and eternal flaming agony, comes to us by way of medieval Christian theology. That idea of hell isn't found in the Bible. Actually, we'd be best off stopping the word 'hell' together, since even Jesus never uses it. In the Gospels the word is *Gehenna*, which is a Greek translation of the Old Testament Hebrew *ge'hinnom* meaning 'Valley of Hinnom'—an actual valley located just outside the walls of Jerusalem. The Old Testament prophet Jeremiah has issues with the Valley of Hinnom: the residents of Jerusalem sacrificed their children there to foreign gods." Enns, *The Bible Tells Me So*, 42.

Verse 26 provides us a very significant pedagogical lesson: "But Lot's wife, behind him, looked back, and she became a pillar of salt." On the way to Zoar, Yahweh's place prepared as a safe haven, Lot's wife looked back with compassion and mercy toward the cities of Sodom and Gomorrah that were facing God's catastrophic judgment. As a note, the covenant community were called to live holy lives, set themselves apart from the corrupt world, and love and preach the good news of the gospel to unbelievers and idol worshipers. However, when the day of judgment comes, the days of love, mercy, and compassion are finished because it is time for God's infinite wrath to pour out on the corrupt people and world based upon the principle of the covenant of works in the first Adam. This is the reason why God made Lot's wife "a pillar of salt" to give a symbolic lesson to not only Lot's covenant community, but also to the future covenant community.[9]

Jesus Christ as the founder of redemptive historical hermeneutics and the mediator of the new covenant interpreted the judgments of Noahic flood and Sodom and Gomorrah in light of *eschatology*. In doing so, he related the judgments of Noahic flood and Sodom and Gomorrah to the final judgment which will come at the day of the second coming of "the Son of Man." Through the first coming of Jesus Christ in his incarnation, public ministry, sacrificial death, resurrection, ascension and session at the right hand of God the Father, the eschatological kingdom of God was inaugurated. Moreover, the eschatological kingdom of God will be consummated on the day of the second coming of Jesus Christ. In that sense, Jesus Christ interpreted and saw the judgments of the Noahic flood and Sodom and Gomorrah as the prefigurement of the final judgment:

> **20**Being asked by the Pharisees when the kingdom of God would come, he answered them, "The kingdom of God is not

9. Calvin interprets that although Lot's wife became "a statue of salt," her soul was saved and will be blessed with the glorious bodily resurrection like other believers: "When, however, it is said, that Lot's wife was changed into a statue of salt, let us not imagine that her soul passed into the nature of salt; for it is not to be doubted, that she lives to be a partaker of the same resurrection with us, though she was subjected to an unusual kind of death, that she might be made an example to all. However, I do not suppose Moses to mean, that the statue had the taste of salt; but that it had something remarkable, to admonish those who passed by. . . . And although it is not lawful to affirm anything respecting her eternal salvation; it is nevertheless probable, that God, having inflicted temporal punishment, spared her soul; insamuch as he often chastises his own people in the flesh, that their soul may be saved from eternal destruction." Calvin, *Genesis*, 19:26, in *Calvin's Commentaries*.

coming with signs to be observed, ^{21}nor will they say, 'Look, here it is!' or 'There!' for behold, the kingdom of God is in the midst of you." ^{22}And he said to the disciples, "The days are coming when you will desire to see one of the days of the Son of Man, and you will not see it. ^{23}And they will say to you, 'Look, there!' or 'Look, here!' Do not go out or follow them. ^{24}For as the lightning flashes and lights up the sky from one side to the other, so will the Son of Man be in his day. ^{25}But first he must suffer many things and be rejected by this generation. ^{26}Just as it was in the days of Noah, so will it be in the days of the Son of Man. ^{27} They were eating and drinking and marrying and being given in marriage, until the day when Noah entered the ark, and the flood came and destroyed them all. ^{28}Likewise, just as it was in the days of Lot- they were eating and drinking, buying and selling, planting and building, ^{29}but on the day when Lot went out from Sodom, fire and sulfur rained from heaven and destroyed them all—^{30}so will it be on the day when the Son of Man is revealed. ^{31}On that day, let the one who is on the housetop, with his goods in the house, not come down to take them away, and likewise let the one who is in the field not turn back. ^{32}Remember Lot's wife. ^{33}Whoever seeks to preserve his life will lose it, but whoever loses his life will keep it. ^{34}I tell you, in that night there will be two in one bed. One will be taken and the other left. ^{35}There will be two women grinding together. One will be taken and the other left." ^{36} ^{37}And they said to him, "Where, Lord?" He said to them, "Where the corpse is, there the vultures will gather." (Luke 17:20–37)

Jesus Christ described the last days of the original world as "in the days of Noah" in which the non-covenant community outside of Noah's covenant family lived as idol worshipers, defiling the original earth. However, after Noah's covenant family entered the ark of salvation, Yahweh executed his redemptive judgment against the non-covenant community through the flood (vv. 26–27). Here, Jesus Christ as the founder of the redemptive historical hermeneutics defines the pattern of eschatology, briefly explaining the judgment of the Noahic flood. In fact, "in the days of Noah" was *the last days* in the original world. The last days at the time of Noah began as God commanded Noah to build the Ark and continued until the completion of the Ark. God sovereignly set the last days of the original world as 120 years: "Then the LORD said, 'My Spirit shall not abide in man forever, for he is flesh: his days shall be 120 years'" (Gen 6:3).[10] It is remarkable to know that God revealed to Noah 120 years as *the last days* of the original world at the time of Noah as he made the Prediluvian Noahic covenant. Noah faithfully began to build the Ark while he proclaimed repentance through his words and action as the head of the covenant community. In light of God's redemptive judgment, the period of 120 years was the period of God's covenant lawsuit, based upon the covenant of works against the original corrupt and sinful world. God also used Noah and his covenant family as a vessel for missions against the corrupt world for 120 years while they built the Ark. And *the day of the Lord* as the day of judgment was the day that God commanded Noah and his covenant family to enter into the ark. God's redemptive judgment was begun with the mighty water. Similarly, Jesus Christ interpreted *the last days* of Sodom and Gomorrah as "in the days of Lot" (v. 28). Indeed, "in the days of Lot" was *the last days* of Sodom and Gomorrah. The last days were the period between the beginning of Lot's covenant families' dwelling in Sodom and Gomorrah and before the day of the fiery judgment. From the perspective of the mission of God, the last days of Sodom and Gomorrah were the days of missionary endeavors through the life and worship of Lot's covenant family. Jesus Christ viewed the day of judgment upon Sodom and Gomorrah as the prefigurement of the day of the final judgment through verses 29–30, "**29**but on the day when Lot went out from Sodom, fire and sulfur rained from heaven and destroyed them all: **30**"so will it be on the day when the Son of Man is

---

10. Calvin rightly interprets 120 years of Genesis 6:3 as "a time of repentance to be granted to the whole world" where Noah built the Ark during the period, proclaiming the message of repentance: "Certain writers of antiquity, such as Lactantius, and others, have too grossly blundered, in thinking that the term of human life was limited within this space of time; whereas, it is evident, that the language used in this place refers not to the private life of any one; but to a time of repentance to be granted to the whole world. Moreover, here also the admirable benignity of God is apparent, in that he, though wearied with the wickedness of men, yet postpones the execution of extreme vengeance for more than a century." Calvin, *Genesis*, 6:3, in *Calvin's Commentaries*.

Similarly, Kline interprets 120 years as the period of God's covenant lawsuit against the original corrupt world at the time of Noah after God commanded to build the ark in the historical context of the Prediluvian Noahic covenant: "God's lawsuit against the world conducted through his Spirit-inspired prophets (cf. 1 Pet 3:19, 20) was reaching its climax. In only 120 years, God would blot out man and his world (cf. v. 7). This division (5:1—6:8) thus reviews the history of the world that then was (2 Pet 3:5, 6) from creation (5:1, 2) to its final judgment, a prophetic paradigm of overall eschatology. God's verdict (6:3) arose from his judgment that the increase of mankind (v. 1) was matched by an increase in human depravity, deep and totally pervasive (v. 5; cf. vv. 11, 12)." Kline, *Genesis*, 32.

revealed." Likewise, Jesus Christ's description of "the days of the Son of Man" (v. 26) is actually *the last days* in the present age which depicts the period between the first and second comings of Jesus Christ. In fact, *the last days* in the present age have begun through Jesus Christ's incarnation, public ministry, sacrificial death, resurrection, ascension, session at the right hand of God the Father, and the Pentecost event. Simultaneously, the eschatological kingdom of God was inaugurated as the exalted Jesus Christ began to rule at the right hand of God the Father in heaven. The day of the final judgment will be "on the day when the Son of Man is revealed" (v. 30) as Jesus Christ anticipated and prophesied as the great prophet. We need to pay special attention to Jesus Christ's expression "on the day" which is a singular day. It signifies the day of the final judgment which will be the day of the second coming of Jesus Christ.

The apostles after the Pentecost event followed Jesus Christ's redemptive historical hermeneutics through the inspiration of the Holy Spirit as he exemplified in his teachings and proclamations during his public ministry. Peter as the apostle also demonstrated redemptive historical hermeneutics in his interpretation of the judgments of the Noahic flood and upon Sodom and Gomorrah under the inspiration of the Holy Spirit:

> **4**For if God did not spare angels when they sinned, but cast them into hell and committed them to chains of gloomy darkness to be kept until the judgment; **5**if he did not spare the ancient world, but preserved Noah, a herald of righteousness, with seven others, when he brought a flood upon the world of the ungodly; **6**if by turning the cities of Sodom and Gomorrah to ashes he condemned them to extinction, making them an example of what is going to happen to the ungodly; **7**and if he rescued righteous Lot, greatly distressed by the sensual conduct of the wicked **8**(for as that righteous man lived among them day after day, he was tormenting his righteous soul over their lawless deeds that he saw and heard); **9**then the Lord knows how to rescue the godly from trials, and to keep the unrighteous under punishment until the day of judgment, **10**and especially those who indulge in the lust of defiling passion and despise authority. (2 Pet 2:4–10a)

Peter emphasizes that God executed his redemptive judgment with the flood against "the ancient world" which was the original world while he granted the blessings of life to "Noah, a herald of righteousness" and Noah's covenant family (v. 5). Similarly, God completely destroyed "the cities of Sodom and Gomorrah" while he saved "righteous Lot." In addition, Peter notes that the judgment of Sodom and Gomorrah was an example of what will happen to the reprobate on the day of the final judgment (vv. 6–7). Similarly, Jude interprets the event of the Exodus and judgment of Sodom and Gomorrah from the Christocentric perspective and eschatology:

> [5]Now I want to remind you, although you once fully knew it, that Jesus, who saved a people out of the land of Egypt, afterward destroyed those who did not believe. [6]And the angels who did not stay within their own position of authority, but left their proper dwelling, he has kept in eternal chains under gloomy darkness until the judgment of the great day— [7]just as Sodom and Gomorrah and the surrounding cities, which likewise indulged in sexual immorality and pursued unnatural desire, serve as an example by undergoing a punishment of eternal fire. (Jude 5–7)

Jude warns that God's judgment upon Sodom and Gomorrah was the visible type of "a punishment of eternal fire" in hell.[11]

The Original Passover and Redemptive Judgment

After 430 years of bondage in Egypt, God delivered the people of Israel as the Abrahamic covenant community from Egypt. God performed supernatural miracles during the deliverance as the Lord and king of the kingdom of God. When Moses became eighty years old after forty years in the wilderness in Median, God called and appointed Moses as the leader of the covenant people of Israel.[12] Before he delivered the covenant

11. Interpreting Jude 7, Calvin explains that the fiery judgment upon Sodom and Gomorrah was "a type of the eternal fire" which will be fully realized in hell: "And Jude also mentions in what follows, that the fire through which the five cities perished was a type of the eternal fire. Then God at that time exhibited a remarkable example, in order to keep men in fear till the end of the world. Hence it is that it is so often mentioned in Scripture; nay, whenever the prophets wished to designate some memorable and dreadful judgment of God, they painted it under the figure of sulphurous fire, and alluded to the destruction of Sodom and Gomorrah. It is not, therefore, without reason that Jude strikes all ages with terror, by exhibiting the same view. . . . We ought to observe that he devotes them to eternal fire; for we hence learn, that the dreadful spectacle which Moses describes, was only an image of a much heavier punishment." Calvin, *Jude*, 7, in *Calvin's Commentaries*.

12. Edwards interprets the process of Yahweh's calling of Moses and the Exodus from the Christocentric and Christotelic perspectives. In doing so, he identifies "the

community of Israel from the slavery of Egypt, Yahweh reminded Moses about the Abrahamic covenant that he made with Abraham, and Yahweh confirmed with Isaac and Jacob:

> But the LORD said to Moses, "Now you shall see what I will do to Pharaoh; for with a strong hand he will send them out, and with a strong hand he will drive them out of his land." [2]God spoke to Moses and said to him, "I am the LORD. [3]I appeared to Abraham, to Isaac, and to Jacob, as God Almighty, but by my name the LORD I did not make myself known to them. [4]*I also established my covenant with them to give them the land of Canaan, the land in which they lived as sojourners.* [5]Moreover, I have heard the groaning of the people of Israel whom the Egyptians hold as slaves, and I have remembered my covenant. [6]Say therefore to the people of Israel, 'I am the LORD, and I will bring you out from under the burdens of the Egyptians, and I will deliver you from slavery to them, and I will redeem you with an outstretched arm and with great acts of judgment. [7]I will take you to be my people, and I will be your God, and you shall know that I am the LORD your God, who has brought you out from under the burdens of the Egyptians. [8]*I will bring you into the land that I swore to give to Abraham, to Isaac, and to Jacob. I will give it to you for a possession. I am the LORD.'"* [9]Moses spoke thus to the people of Israel, but they did not listen to Moses, because of their broken spirit and harsh slavery. (Exod 6:1–9)

---

angel of the Lord" in Exodus 3:2–3 as Christ and the covenant community of Israel in Egypt as "the church of God": "The first thing that offers itself to be considered, is the redemption of the church of God out of Egypt; the most remarkable of all the Old Testament redemptions of the church of God, and which was the greatest pledge and forerunner of the future redemption of Christ, of any; and is much more insisted on in scripture than any other of those redemptions. And indeed it was the greatest type of Christ's redemption of any providential event whatsoever. This redemption was by Jesus Christ, as is evident from this, that it was wrought by him that appeared to Moses in the bush; for that was the person that sent Moses to redeem that people. But that was Christ, as is evident, because he is called the angel of the Lord, Ex. iii. 2, 3. The bush represented the human nature of Christ, that is called the branch. The bush grew on Mount Sinai or Horeb, which is a word that signifies a dry place, as the human nature of Christ was a root out of a dry ground. The bush burning with fire, represented the sufferings of Christ, in the fire of God's wrath. It burned and was not consumed; so Christ, though he suffered extremely, yet perished not; but overcame at last, and rose from his sufferings. Because this great mystery of the incarnation and sufferings of Christ was here represented, therefore Moses says, 'I will turn aside, and behold this great sight.' A great sight he might well call it, when there was represented, God manifest in the flesh, and suffering a dreadful death, and rising from the dead." Edwards, *History of the Work of Redemption*, 68–69.

Yahweh reminded Moses that Abraham, Isaac, and Jacob lived in the promised land as *pilgrims and diaspora* while the covenant community of Israel lived their pilgrimage in Egypt. Verse 4 reads, "I also established my covenant with them to give them the land of Canaan, the land in which they lived as sojourners." This confirms that Yahweh will grant the promised land not only as the land of *pilgrims and diaspora* as Abraham and his covenant family made a covenant pilgrim journey, but also a permanent dwelling place for the covenant community of Israel. Nevertheless, the Abrahamic covenant community lived in the promised land as *pilgrims and diaspora*, highlighted by the expression of "they lived as sojourners" before they migrated to the land of Egypt. However, the promised land the covenant community of Israel will enter will be not a place of diaspora or sojourners but a permanent dwelling place because the promised land was the earthly picture of the everlasting kingdom of God which will be consummated in the second coming of Jesus Christ. Likewise, the heart of the promises of the Abrahamic covenant was to *grant* "the land of Canaan" to the covenant descendants of Abraham and in the lines of Isaac, Jacob, and Jacob's twelve tribes. God revealed to Moses that the Exodus would not come naturally but with God's supernatural power. In particular, God's prophetic words to Moses, "I am the LORD, and I will bring you out from under the burdens of the Egyptians, and I will deliver you from slavery to them, and I will redeem you with an outstretched arm and with great acts of judgment" (v. 6), indicate that the Exodus will be visibly realized through God's supernatural acts of judgment against Egypt which represented the kingdom of Satan while the covenant community of Israel in Egypt represented the kingdom of God under the leadership of Moses.

Afterwards, Yahweh made the land of Egypt the historic battleground between the kingdom of God and kingdom of Satan. In light of that, Yahweh sovereignly executed the ten plagues against the land and people of Egypt while he was protecting "the land of Goshen" where the covenant community of Israel was dwelling. Yet, Yahweh hardened Pharaoh's heart and he did not let the covenant community of Israel go until the tenth plague was visibly executed (Exod 7:14—12:32).[13] It is quite

13. Kline views and interprets the ten plagues in the process of the Exodus as God's redemptive judgments that separated between the covenant community of Israel and the non-covenant community of Egypt: "In this event we see the principle of redemptive judgment intruded into common grace history. Redemptive judgments, whether typological anticipations of the ultimate judgment or the antitypical eschatological

remarkable to note that God separated the covenant community of Israel and the non-covenant community of Egypt when he executed the series of ten plagues. In doing so, God temporarily lifted the benefits of the covenant of common grace toward the land and people of Egypt. For example, when Yahweh executed the judgment of the fourth plague of flies, he set apart "the land of Goshen" where the covenant community of Israel was dwelling:

> 20Then the LORD said to Moses, "Rise up early in the morning and present yourself to Pharaoh, as he goes out to the water, and say to him, 'Thus says the LORD, "Let my people go, that they may serve me. 21Or else, if you will not let my people go, behold, I will send swarms of flies on you and your servants and your people, and into your houses. And the houses of the Egyptians shall be filled with swarms of flies, and also the ground on which they stand. 22But on that day I will set apart the land of Goshen, where my people dwell, so that no swarms of flies shall be there, that you may know that I am the LORD in the midst of the earth. 23Thus I will put a division between my people and your people. Tomorrow this sign shall happen."'" 24And the LORD did so. There came great swarms of flies into the house of Pharaoh and into his servants' houses. Throughout all the land of Egypt the land was ruined by the swarms of flies. (Exod 8:20–24)

The covenant community of Israel along with "the land of Goshen" represented the kingdom of God while the people of Egypt in "all the land of Egypt" represented the kingdom of Satan. In that sense, Yahweh visibly separated the two different communities in the process of the execution of the fourth plague of flies. Verses 22 and 23 clearly reveals Yahweh's intention to visibly separate the covenant community of Israel and non-covenant community of Egypt: "22But on that day I will set apart the land of Goshen, where my people dwell, so that no swarms of flies shall be there, that you may know that I am the LORD in the midst of the earth. 23Thus I will put a division between my people and your people. Tomorrow this sign shall happen" Likewise, "all the land of Egypt" was

---

judgment itself, discriminate strictly along covenantal lines in the execution of the curse and blessing. The exodus narrative repeatedly mentions the Lord's distinguishing of his people from the Egyptians. He is said to put a difference between the Israelites, their land and cattle on the one side and the Egyptians and their property on the other (Exod 8:22, 23 [18:19]; 9:4, 6, 26; 10:23; 11:7). Climactic in this play of Yahweh's sovereignty were the tenth plague and the crisis at the sea." Kline, *God, Heaven and Har Magedon*, 115.

ruined "by the swarms of flies" while "no swarms of flies" were in the land of Goshen (v. 24) "on that day" as the day of judgment.

Moreover, through the judgment of the fifth plague of the Egyptian livestock, Yahweh once again visibly made "a distinction between the livestock of Israel and the livestock of Egypt (Exod 9:4). In doing so, the judgment of the fifth plague only fell upon "all the livestock of the Egyptians" while he spared "the livestock of the people of Israel" (Exod 9:6).

In addition, Yahweh visibly separated "all the land of Egypt" and "the land of Goshen" in his execution of judgment in the seventh plague of hail (Exod 9:13–35). Remarkably, "the land of Goshen" as the temporary dwelling place of the covenant community of Israel was free from the judgment of hail. In this process, Yahweh manifested his infinite holiness and righteousness by using the prophet Moses' staff as the means to display and execute Yahweh's miraculous judgment:

> 22Then the LORD said to Moses, "Stretch out your hand toward heaven, so that there may be hail in all the land of Egypt, on man and beast and every plant of the field, in the land of Egypt." 23Then Moses stretched out his staff toward heaven, and the LORD sent thunder and hail, and fire ran down to the earth. And the LORD rained hail upon the land of Egypt. 24There was hail and fire flashing continually in the midst of the hail, very heavy hail, such as had never been in all the land of Egypt since it became a nation. 25The hail struck down everything that was in the field in all the land of Egypt, both man and beast. And the hail struck down every plant of the field and broke every tree of the field. 26Only in the land of Goshen, where the people of Israel were, was there no hail. (Exod 9:22–26)

As we read, Yahweh granted Moses as the prophet to participate and conduct Yahweh's judgment. Moses' staff is used against the land of Egypt: "Then Moses stretched out his staff toward heaven, and the LORD sent thunder and hail, and fire ran down to the earth. And the LORD rained hail upon the land of Egypt."

Likewise, Yahweh made a distinction between the covenant community of Israel in the land of Goshen and the non-covenant community of Egypt throughout the various plagues against the people and land of Egypt. In doing so, Yahweh demonstrated that only he is the true almighty God and Lord to the covenant community of Israel and the divine judge against the idol worshipers of Egypt.

As Pharaoh, the king of Egypt, did not let the covenant community of Israel go, Yahweh executed the tenth and final plague against the nation of Egypt (Exod 11:1—12:32). Moses' prophetic warning about the plague of the firstborn on Pharaoh and Egypt was, in fact, the covenant lawsuit, based upon the covenant of works in the first Adam because the first-born sons include innocent babies (Exod 11:1–10). Revealing the tenth and final plague, Moses gave a prophetic message to Pharaoh that "the Lord makes a distinction between Egypt and Israel" (Exod 11:7). We find that Yahweh made a distinction between the covenant community and the non-covenant community when he executed redemptive judgment. Before Yahweh executed the tenth and final plague, he instructed Moses and Aaron in the proper preparation of the original Passover, including its meaning and implications (Exod 12:1–20).[14] Calling "all the elders of Israel," Moses told them the instructions about the original Passover:

> [21]Then Moses called all the elders of Israel and said to them, "Go and select lambs for yourselves according to your clans, and kill the Passover lamb. [22]Take a bunch of hyssop and dip it in the blood that is in the basin, and touch the lintel and the two door-posts with the blood that is in the basin. None of you shall go out of the door of his house until the morning. [23]For the LORD will pass through to strike the Egyptians, and when he sees the blood on the lintel and on the two doorposts, the LORD will pass over the door and will not allow the destroyer to enter your houses to strike you. [24]You shall observe this rite as a statute for you and for your sons forever. [25]And when you come to the land that the LORD will give you, as he has promised, you shall keep this ser-vice. [26]And when your children say to you, 'What do you mean by this service?' [27]you shall say, 'It is the sacrifice of the LORD's Passover, for he passed over the houses of the people of Israel in Egypt, when he struck the Egyptians but spared our houses.'"

14. A biblical theological analysis on the original Passover in light of the modern criticism, expounded by the historical critical school, see Vos, *Biblical Theology*, 119–21.

John J. Collins, following the historical critical tradition, denies the historical ac-count of the original Passover in the process of the Exodus. He sees that the Passover was "a rite of spring, practiced by shepherds," and it was inserted in the Exodus later: "Before the Israelites depart from Egypt, they celebrate the Passover. This celebration is found only in the Priestly source. Just as P grounded the Sabbath in the story of creation, so it grounds the Passover in the story of the exodus. . . . The Passover was probably originally a rite of spring, practiced by shepherds, but it was associated with the exodus before the Priestly account was composed. P provides the most detailed and explicit account in the Bible of the supposed origin of the Passover in the context of the exodus." Collins, *Introduction to the Hebrew Bible*, 114.

And the people bowed their heads and worshiped. [28]Then the
people of Israel went and did so; as the LORD had commanded
Moses and Aaron, so they did. (Exod 12:21–28)

Moses' instruction to "all the elders of Israel" to kill "the Passover
lamb" is significant in light of redemptive history because Yahweh reveals
for the first time through Moses that the Messiah will come as the Passover lamb (v. 21). In fact, the statement of "kill the Passover lamb" is the
redemptive historical reverberation of the Messiah's sacrificial death on
the cross at Golgotha. According to the guidelines of Moses, the covenant
community of Israel killed the Passover lamb and touched "the lintel and
the two doorposts with the blood" (v. 21). Dipping "a bunch of hyssop"
in the blood of the Passover lamb, each household of Israel touched "the
lintel and the two doorposts with the blood" that is in the basin. The
covenant community of Israel did not go out of the door of their houses
until the morning (v. 22).

The apostle Paul did not know that Jesus of Nazareth was crucified
and slaughtered as the final Passover lamb. However, he reflected Jesus
Christ's sacrificial death on the cross as the mediator of the new cov-
enant after the road to Damascus conversion experience. He realized the
Passover lambs, slaughtered at the Passover feast were pointing to Jesus
Christ who was slaughtered and sacrificed at Golgotha. Paul was boldly
able to state that "Christ, our Passover lamb, has been sacrificed" (v. 7).
Paul as a redemptive historical theologian read and interpreted Jesus
Christ's death on the cross as the sacrificial death of the Passover lamb:

> [6]Your boasting is not good. Do you not know that a little leaven
> leavens the whole lump? [7]Cleanse out the old leaven that you
> may be a new lump, as you really are unleavened. For Christ, our
> Passover lamb, has been sacrificed. [8]Let us therefore celebrate
> the festival, not with the old leaven, the leaven of malice and
> evil, but with the unleavened bread of sincerity and truth. (1
> Cor 5:6–8)

In fact, Jesus Christ is not only "our Passover lamb" but also the final
Passover Lamb so that God's people under the new covenant do not need
Passover lambs to be slaughtered and sacrificed on the earthly altar.

As the covenant community of Israel completed their preparation of
the original Passover, Yahweh executed his redemptive judgment against
the nation of Egypt. At midnight Yahweh cursed the nation of Egypt with
the death of "all the firstborn," including "all the firstborn of the livestock"

(v. 29). All of the Egyptians rose up in the night, including King Pharaoh, in utter shock. A great cry shook the entire nation of Egypt because all of the firstborn Egyptians, including "the first born of Pharaoh", and livestock were dead due to Yahweh's curse at midnight of the original Passover (v. 30). Nevertheless, Yahweh did not execute the full scope of redemptive judgment against the nation of Egypt because the land of Egypt was not the promised land to grant to the covenant community of Israel. It was the land of *diaspora and a pilgrimage* for the covenant descendants of Abraham, Isaac, and Jacob. This is why Yahweh executed his redemptive judgment in a limited scope against the nation of Egypt at midnight during the original Passover in the process of the Exodus:

> **29**At midnight the LORD struck down all the firstborn in the land of Egypt, from the firstborn of Pharaoh who sat on his throne to the firstborn of the captive who was in the dungeon, and all the firstborn of the livestock. **30**And Pharaoh rose up in the night, he and all his servants and all the Egyptians. And there was a great cry in Egypt, for there was not a house where someone was not dead. **31**Then he summoned Moses and Aaron by night and said, "Up, go out from among my people, both you and the people of Israel; and go, serve the LORD, as you have said. **32**Take your flocks and your herds, as you have said, and be gone, and bless me also!" **33**The Egyptians were urgent with the people to send them out of the land in haste. For they said, "We shall all be dead." **34**So the people took their dough before it was leavened, their kneading bowls being bound up in their cloaks on their shoulders. **35**The people of Israel had also done as Moses told them, for they had asked the Egyptians for silver and gold jewelry and for clothing. **36**And the LORD had given the people favor in the sight of the Egyptians, so that they let them have what they asked. Thus they plundered the Egyptians. **37**And the people of Israel journeyed from Rameses to Succoth, about six hundred thousand men on foot, besides women and children. **38**A mixed multitude also went up with them, and very much livestock, both flocks and herds. **39**And they baked unleavened cakes of the dough that they had brought out of Egypt, for it was not leavened, because they were thrust out of Egypt and could not wait, nor had they prepared any provisions for themselves. **40**The time that the people of Israel lived in Egypt was 430 years. **41**At the end of 430 years, on that very day, all the hosts of the LORD went out from the land of Egypt. **42**It was a night of watching by the LORD, to bring them out of the land of Egypt; so this same night is a night of watching kept

to the LORD by all the people of Israel throughout their generations. (Exod 12:29–42)

Once again, we need to visit verse 29: "At midnight the LORD
struck down all the firstborn in the land of Egypt, from the firstborn of
Pharaoh who sat on his throne to the firstborn of the captive who was in
the dungeon, and all the firstborn of the livestock." It signifies that Yahweh fought the holy war of the total destruction against "all the firstborn
in the land of Egypt." In this process, Yahweh displayed his wrath in light
of his infinite holiness and righteousness against "all the firstborn" in
the non-covenant community which represented the kingdom of Satan.
Through the visible separation between "all the firstborn in the land of
Egypt" and the covenant community of Israel in the land of Goshen, Yahweh indirectly reveals that he executed the judgment of death upon little
children in Egypt through the covenant lawsuit, based upon the broken
covenant of works in the first Adam. Yahweh's judgment of death upon
the little and innocent children of Egypt is also the historical verification
of the imputation of the original sin.[15] Moreover, he saved the covenant
community of Israel in the land of Goshen, including the firstborn in
light of the covenant of grace in the last Adam.[16]

15. John Walton interprets the Old Testament in light of the ancient Near Eastern
culture and religions. In doing so, he denies the historical Adam, the fall, and the
original sin. Furthermore, he rejects the biblical doctrine of the existence and works
of Satan and demons: "As demonstrated in this chapter, the Old Testament contains
very little of our Christian theology about evil, sin, Satan, and demons. In the Old
Testament, evil includes moral failure, but it is not itself defined in moral terms. The
ancient Israelites had no concept of original sin (though they did recognize a universal
sinful inclination) or of the fall (as articulated with all its ramifications in contemporary Christian theology). Sin was recognized as imposing a burden, but it was more
commonly considered in terms of its disruption to God's order. It was a source of
disorder primarily related to the covenant. The satan character in the Old Testament
is not the devil, not the chief of the demons, and was not considered a fallen angel. . . .
Neither satan nor demons tempted, possessed, or took any active role in human events
(except on rare occasions when God directed the event). Only the vaguest hints would
indicate that the Israelites would have adopted the ancient Near Eastern view that
many illnesses were caused by demons. At the same time, no polemic or disagreement
of that perspective can be found in the Old Testament either." Walton, *Old Testament
Theology for Christians*, 214–15.

16. Poythress properly recognizes *the historical order* of the covenant of works and
the covenant of grace which is foundational for the proper understanding of redemptive history and soteriology: "The whole of biblical history can be viewed as the out-
working of two covenants: the covenant of works that God made with Adam before the
fall, and the covenant of grace after the fall. . . . The use of the concept of the covenant

Certainly, as he executed his redemptive judgment upon "all the firstborn in the land of Egypt," Yahweh remembered that the king of Egypt ordered Hebrew midwives to kill the newly born male infants of Israelites. Nevertheless, the Hebrew midwives disobeyed the order, fearing God as the covenant members of the Abrahamic covenant:

> 15Then the king of Egypt said to the Hebrew midwives, one of whom was named Shiphrah and the other Puah, 16 "When you serve as midwife to the Hebrew women and see them on the birthstool, if it is a son, you shall kill him, but if it is a daughter, she shall live." 17But the midwives feared God and did not do as the king of Egypt commanded them, but let the male children live. 18So the king of Egypt called the midwives and said to them, "Why have you done this, and let the male children live?" 19The midwives said to Pharaoh, "Because the Hebrew women are not like the Egyptian women, for they are vigorous and give birth before the midwife comes to them." 20So God dealt well with the midwives. And the people multiplied and grew very strong. 21And because the midwives feared God, he gave them families. 22Then Pharaoh commanded all his people, "Every son that is born to the Hebrews you shall cast into the Nile, but you shall let every daughter live." (Exod 1:15–22)

Remembering the order of the king of Egypt to kill the all the newly born male infants, Yahweh decisively executed the death penalty to "all the firstborn in the land of Egypt." As Yahweh displayed his judgment of death upon "all the firstborn in the land of Egypt," including "all the firstborn of the livestock," Pharaoh summoned Moses and Aaron for the Exodus. As a result, the covenant community of Israel as the Abrahamic covenant diaspora and pilgrims left the land of Egypt after 430 years of slavery.

After the Exodus, Yahweh instituted the Passover to commemorate the original Passover, giving some instructions to Moses and Aaron (Exod 12:43–50). Moreover, Yahweh commanded Moses to consecrate him "all the firstborn" who will be born "among the people of Israel, both of man and of beast" (Exod 13:1–2). In addition, Yahweh, through the

---

of grace does not imply that we would ignore the differences between different historical covenants, with Noah, Abraham, Moses, and David, or Jeremiah's promise of the new covenant (Jer 31:31 34). Rather, the covenant of grace is a theological category expressing the unity of *one* way of salvation throughout the course of biblical history. Salvation is by grace through faith, on the basis of Christ's work. The concept of the covenant of grace encourages us to focus on this one salvation expressed in the various historical covenants." Poythress, *Theophany*, 25.

prophet Moses, commanded to keep the Feast of Unleavened Bread for seven days every year when the covenant community of Israel entered the promised land in which Yahweh made a sworn oath to Abraham, Isaac, and Jacob through the Abrahamic covenant (Exod 13:1–16).

Crossing the Red Sea and Redemptive Judgment

As the covenant community of Israel after 430 years of slavery departed the land of Goshen in the process of the Exodus, a beautiful phenomena appeared in front of them. It was the visible glory of Yahweh which appeared and went before them. The beautiful glory of Yahweh, filled in heaven, descended and led them "the way of the wilderness toward the Red Sea" (v. 18). Remarkably, Yahweh led the covenant community of Israel by day and night in the pillars of cloud and fire (vv. 21–22). Likewise, Yahweh not only guided the covenant community of Israel on the way of the Exodus, but also protected and shielded them from any attack and danger:

> [17]When Pharaoh let the people go, God did not lead them by way of the land of the Philistines, although that was near. For God said, "Lest the people change their minds when they see war and return to Egypt." [18]But God led the people around by the way of the wilderness toward the Red Sea. And the people of Israel went up out of the land of Egypt equipped for battle. [19]Moses took the bones of Joseph with him, for Joseph had made the sons of Israel solemnly swear, saying, "God will surely visit you, and you shall carry up my bones with you from here." [20]And they moved on from Succoth and encamped at Etham, on the edge of the wilderness. [21]And the LORD went before them by day in a pillar of cloud to lead them along the way, and by night in a pillar of fire to give them light, that they might travel by day and by night. [22]The pillar of cloud by day and the pillar of fire by night did not depart from before the people. (Exod 13:17–22)

We need to pay special attention to verse 21: "And the LORD went before them by day in a pillar of cloud to lead them along the way, and by night in a pillar of fire to give them light, that they might travel by day and by night." Certainly, "a pillar of cloud" by day and "a pillar of fire" by night looked beautiful and holy in the eyes of the covenant community of Israel because the pillars of cloud and fire were the visible signs of the presence of the invisible Yahweh. In addition, a pillar of cloud by day protected the covenant community of Israel from scorching heat while a pillar of fire by night provided light and heat during cold nights.

However, the mind of Pharaoh king of Egypt was hardened and changed and he began to pursue the covenant community of Israel with "six hundred chosen chariots and all the other chariots of Egypt with officers over all of them" (Exod 14: 7–8). As Pharaoh and his mighty army chased and drew near, the people of Israel feared greatly and they complained against Yahweh and Moses. In the midst of this crisis, Moses, as the leader and prophet, comforted them by reminding them of Yahweh's victorious holy war against the Egyptians (Exod 14:10–14).

Yahweh revealed to Moses that he will fight a holy war against Pharaoh and his mighty army. In doing so, he revealed to Moses that the people of Israel will be able to go through the Red Sea as "dry ground" when Moses lifts up his staff and stretches out his hand over the Red Sea. Then Yahweh will fight a holy war against the Egyptians who will chase after them through the divided Red Sea:

> [15]The LORD said to Moses, "Why do you cry to me? Tell the people of Israel to go forward. [16]Lift up your staff, and stretch out your hand over the sea and divide it, that the people of Israel may go through the sea on dry ground. [17]And I will harden the hearts of the Egyptians so that they shall go in after them, and I will get glory over Pharaoh and all his host, his chariots, and his horsemen. [18]And the Egyptians shall know that I am the LORD, when I have gotten glory over Pharaoh, his chariots, and his horsemen." (Exod 14:15–18)

After Yahweh revealed the method of holy war to Moses, he began to separate "the host of Egypt and the host of Israel" (v. 20). In doing so, "the angel of God" moved and went behind "the host of Israel." "The pillar of cloud" moved from the front of the people of Israel and stood behind them (v. 19).[17] Likewise, the separation between the Egyptian warriors and the covenant community of Israel was the beginning of Yahweh's holy war:

17. Calvin interprets "the angel of God" as "God's only-begotten Son" after he reflects Paul's description in 1 Corinthians 10:4 where Paul explains that Christ guided and spiritually fed the covenant community of Israel in the process of the Exodus and wilderness: "He, who has been called 'Jehovah' hitherto, is now designated by Moses 'the Angel;' not only because the angels who represent God often borrow His name, but because this Leader of the people was God's only-begotten Son, who afterwards was manifested in the flesh, as I have shewn the authority of Paul. (1 Cor 4) It may be remarked, also, that He is said to have moved here and there, as He shewed some token

> [19]Then the angel of God who was going before the host of Israel moved and went behind them, and the pillar of cloud moved from before them and stood behind them, [20]coming between the host of Egypt and the host of Israel. And there was the cloud and the darkness. And it lit up the night without one coming near the other all night. (Exod 14:19–20)

As Yahweh prepared for holy war at the Red Sea against the Egyptians, he separated the non-covenant community of Egypt and the covenant community of Israel. The glory cloud stood between the two groups. The thick darkness covered and overshadowed the people of Egypt while the beautiful light of glory lighted and shined upon the people of Israel during the dark night. In fact, the visible separation of the two groups between thick darkness and bright light signifies that Yahweh separated the kingdom of God and the kingdom of Satan. In that sense, the glory cloud and fire separated the covenant community of Israel and the non-covenant community of the Egyptian warriors. As Yahweh separated two different communities between the thick darkness and bright light, he began to execute his redemptive judgment against the Egyptian warriors who chased the covenant community of Israel.

Yahweh used Moses as the prophet to execute his redemptive judgment against Pharaoh's warriors at the Red Sea. Moses lifted up his staff and stretched out his hands over the Red Sea as Yahweh had instructed him. Moses as the prophet and leader of the covenant community of Israel had a privilege to conduct and execute the redemptive judgment although Yahweh fought the holy war against the king of Egypt and his mighty warriors. Remarkably, the waters of the Red Sea were divided. The covenant community of Israel went into the Red Sea "on dry ground" (vv. 21–22). They safely crossed the Red Sea under the guidance of the glory fire and cloud. At the same time, Pharaoh and his warriors pursued and went into the midst of the Red Sea with the intention to kill the people of Israel. However, Yahweh threw Pharaoh and his warriors into panic "in the pillar of fire and of cloud" (vv. 23–25):

> [21]Then Moses stretched out his hand over the sea, and the LORD drove the sea back by a strong east wind all night and

---

of His power and assistance. Most clearly, too, does it appear, that the glory of God, whilst it enlightens the faithful, overshadows the unbelievers, on the other hand, with darkness. No wonder, then, if now-a-days the brightness of the Gospel should blind the reprobate. But we should ask of God to make us able to behold His glory." Calvin, *Exodus*, 14:19, in *Calvin's Commentaries*.

made the sea dry land, and the waters were divided. [22]And the people of Israel went into the midst of the sea on dry ground, the waters being a wall to them on their right hand and on their left. [23]The Egyptians pursued and went in after them into the midst of the sea, all Pharaoh's horses, his chariots, and his horsemen. [24]And in the morning watch the LORD in the pillar of fire and of cloud looked down on the Egyptian forces and threw the Egyptian forces into a panic, [25]clogging their chariot wheels so that they drove heavily. And the Egyptians said, "Let us flee from before Israel, for the LORD fights for them against the Egyptians." (Exod 14:21–25)

As the covenant community of Israel safely crossed the Red Sea, Yahweh commanded Moses to stretch out his hand over the Red Sea. When Moses stretched out his hand over the Red Sea, the waters returned to their normal state. All of sudden, the waters of the Red Sea became the means of holy war against Pharaoh and his Egyptian warriors and they all died at the hands of Yahweh's redemptive judgment:

[26]Then the LORD said to Moses, "Stretch out your hand over the sea, that the water may come back upon the Egyptians, upon their chariots, and upon their horsemen." [27]So Moses stretched out his hand over the sea, and the sea returned to its normal course when the morning appeared. And as the Egyptians fled into it, the LORD threw the Egyptians into the midst of the sea. [28]The waters returned and covered the chariots and the horsemen; of all the host of Pharaoh that had followed them into the sea, not one of them remained. [29]But the people of Israel walked on dry ground through the sea, the waters being a wall to them on their right hand and on their left. [30]Thus the LORD saved Israel that day from the hand of the Egyptians, and Israel saw the Egyptians dead on the seashore. [31]Israel saw the great power that the LORD used against the Egyptians, so the people feared the LORD, and they believed in the LORD and in his servant Moses. (Exod 14:26–31)[18]

18. John J. Collins as a historical critical scholar rejects the historical accounts of the story of the Exodus. And he argues that they are "full of legendary details." In this manner, he considers the story of the Red Sea crossing as a legendary account: "In the end, very little can be said about the exodus as history. It is likely that some historical memory underlies the story, but the narrative as we have it is full of legendary details and lacks supporting evidence from archaeology or from nonbiblical sources. The story of the crossing of the sea seems to have arisen from attempts to fill out the allusions in the hymn preserved in Exodus 15. That hymn celebrates some defeat of a pharaoh, but the references to drowning are poetic, and cannot be pressed for

Verse 28 indicates the result of Yahweh's holy war, using the water of the Red Sea: "The waters returned and covered the chariots and the horsemen; of all the host of Pharaoh that had followed them into the sea, not one of them remained." In fact, the prophet Moses summarizes the visible reality of Yahweh's holy war against Pharaoh and his mighty soldiers. Moreover, it is a comprehensive and visible picture of the total destruction of the holy war, killing Pharaoh the king of Egypt, his warriors, horses, and even destroying colorfully decorated chariots. In contrast, the waters became the means of protection and shield for the covenant community of Israel and they walked "on dry ground" through the Red Sea. Moses highlights Yahweh's blessings of life upon the covenant community of Israel: "But the people of Israel walked on dry ground through the sea, the waters being a wall to them on their right hand and on their left" (v. 29).

Yahweh's drowning of Pharaoh and his warriors at the Red Sea was a redemptive historical reversal. Yahweh remembered the king of Egypt's order to throw all the male babies of Israel into the Nile River: "Every son that is born to the Hebrews you shall cast into the Nile, but you shall let every daughter live" (Exod 1:22). Moreover, as we know, Moses was thrown into the Nile River in a basket after his mother hid him for three months for survival and then she was not able to hide Moses anymore. Paradoxically, he was, however, rescued by the daughter of Pharaoh at the river (Exod 2:1–10). Moses' survival highlighted the failure of Pharaoh's plot to kill all the newborn male children of Israel. Remembering the historic episode of Pharaoh's plot to kill the newborn male babies of Israel in the Nile River, Yahweh decisively drowned the king of Egypt and his warriors under the water of the Red Sea. Moses, who survived in the water of the Nile River when he was a Hebrew baby, became the masterful and dramatic conductor of Yahweh's redemptive judgment at the Red Sea by using his staff in his hand. In short, it was a glorious reversal of the drama of redemptive history through Yahweh's redemptive judgment at the Red Sea.

Yahweh rejoiced to set the day of judgment against the Egyptian warriors at the Red Sea. In fact, the day of judgment was *the day of the Lord* in which Yahweh separated the covenant community of Israel and the non-covenant community of the Egyptian warriors. As the covenant community of Israel witnessed "the Egyptians dead on the seashore" (v. 30), they sang the glorious Song of Moses to Yahweh together (Exod

historical information." Collins, *Introduction to the Hebrew Bible*, 119.

15:1–21).[19] It was the song of Yahweh's glorious victory against Pharaoh king of Egypt and his warriors in the Red Sea. The glorious victory song of the kingdom of God spread out over the dead corpses of the Egyptians on the seashore. Once again, the victory song highlights the visible reality of Yahweh's holy war and redemptive judgment, separating the non-covenant community of Egypt and covenant community of Israel: "For when the horses of Pharaoh with his chariots and his horsemen went into the sea, the LORD brought back the waters of the sea upon them, but the people of Israel walked on dry ground in the midst of the sea" (v. 19).[20] Looking back at the Red Sea event, the author of Hebrews identifies that the covenant community of Israel passed through "the Red Sea as on dry land" while the Egyptians were drowned at the time of Yahweh's execution of redemptive judgment through his holy war (Heb 11:29).

Crossing the Red Sea by the covenant community of Israel, the covenant descendants of Abraham were, in fact, God's grand redemptive display where he powerfully demonstrated the pattern of *biblical eschatology*. At the Red Sea, God separated the covenant community of Israel and the non-covenant community of the Egyptian soldiers. He gloriously executed his redemptive judgment between the blessings of life and the

19. Vos identifies Exodus 15:1–18 as "the victory hymn," and indicates that it is "eschatological and messianic" as the Psalter: "The content of Psalter is eschatological and messianic. We consider here the eschatological material in its dynamic aspect. Notice first the emphasis upon the kingship of Jehovah. As King he judges and rules. The following are a few of the Psalms in which this is pronounced: 22:29 (28); 47; 93; 96; 97; 99; 146. The victory hymn in Exodus 15:1–18 conveys the identical thought. These may be explained from the thought that they are processional hymns or perhaps derived from the ancient custom of carrying the ark. At any rate, they seem to celebrate a military event. The eschatological throne is not on the earth, but in heaven, and this thought reveals what is really meant by judging and subjugating nations, i.e., the kingship is to be absolutely universal (c.f. Pss. 47:2; 48; 96–99; 146; also 2 Kgs 11:12)." Vos, *Eschatology of the Old Testament*, 141.

20. Denying the historic account of the crossing of the Red Sea in Exodus 14:1–31, Cross argues that "lyric poems" "in the Song of the Sea" in Exodus 15 and "the Song of Deborah" in Judges 5 are earlier than "prose narrative accounts" in Exodus 14 and Judges 4: "Further, if, as I shall argue, the epic was a creation of the league and had a special function in the cultus of its pilgrim shrines, we expect its form to have been poetic. There can be no question of early Israel eschewing poetry as somehow inappropriate as a vehicle for recounting the mighty acts of Yahweh or Israel's early times. We possess lyric poems with strong narrative content in the Song of the Sea (Exodus 15) and the Song of Deborah (Judges 5). In both instances we possess side-by-side prose narrative accounts (Exodus 14 and Judges 4), and in both instances the poetry is earlier, the prose secondary and derivative. We see the process of prosaizing poetic composition before our eyes." Cross, *From Epic to Canon*, 32.

curses of death in the midst of the redemptive theater of the Red Sea.[21]
In fact, the covenant community of Israel tasted the blessings of heaven
while the non-covenant community of Egypt foretasted the curses of hell
through God's execution of redemptive judgment at the Red Sea.[22]

21. Peter Enns reinterprets "the stories of creation, Noah, and the exodus" in light
of "mythically robed" stories which deny their genuine historical character: "THE
BIBLE has one more mythically robed story involving God and water: the story of
Noah and the flood. Israel's storytellers drew a clear linking the stories of creation,
Noah, and the exodus. . . . I understand how this might take some getting used to for
readers with certain expectations of the Bible—like it should avoid myth and just give
us more or less history as we understand the term. But especially here in reading the
stories of Israel's deep past we need to be extra careful not to allow *our* point of view to
dictate how the Bible behaves. A story like the exodus story is what happens when, as I
said previously, God lets his children tell the story—in ways *they* understand and that
is packed with meaning for *them*." Enns, *Bible Tells Me So*, 124–26.

22. Denying original sin, John Walton also rejects the biblical doctrine of heaven
and hell as well: "Now, as little more than an afterthought, we can offer a few comments on what we know of these benefits (to be accurate, eternal life is the benefit,
paired with the benefit of avoiding hell). We have learned that the Old Testament has
no concept of hell, no words for hell, no place for hell in the ideology, and it therefore
has no teaching to offer about it. One's perceptions about hell are typically shaped by
one's beliefs about other doctrines—primarily sin and salvation. We should also note
that even the New Testament is indeterminate about hell. A survey of New Testament
passages reveals a mix between those that seem to suggest eternal torment and those
that are used to support annihilation. This is not the place to engage this discussion,
but our interaction with the Old Testament may suggest that in our theological formu-
lations we should be willing to reconsider the illocutions of these passages. Options
would include: threat, warning, deterrent, or instruction concerning metaphysical
eschatology. . . . However, most descriptors of hell involve sensory attack or depriva-
tion, and these are descriptions that are deeply embedded in the ancient Near Eastern
cultural river." Walton, *Old Testament Theology for Christians*, 264–65.

Similarly, N. T. Wright rejects the biblical doctrine of heaven and hell as he has
denied the biblical doctrines of justification by faith alone (*sola fide*), and salvation by
grace alone (*sola gratia*) in the light of the soteriology of the Second Temple Judaism,
rejecting the antithesis between law and gospel as a hermeneutical and theological
tools: "Part of the difficulty of the topic, as with the others we have been studying,
is that the word *hell* conjures up an image gained more from medieval imagery than
from the earliest Christian writings. . . . But, as with his language about heaven, so
with his talk of Gehenna: once Christian readers had been sufficiently distanced from
the original meaning of the words, alternative images would come to mind, generated not by Jesus or the New Testament but by the stock of images, some of them
extremely lurid, supplied by ancient and medieval folklore and imagination. . . . Hell,
and final judgment, is not a major topic in the letters (though when it comes it is very
important, as for instance in Romans 2:1–16); it is not mentioned at all in Acts; and
the vivid pictures toward the end of the book of Revelation, while being extremely
important, have always proved among the hardest parts of scripture to interpret with
any certainty. All this should warn us against the cheerful double dogmatism that has

Summary

After the flood judgment, God visibly revealed the several patterns of *biblical eschatology* in the historical context of the Abrahamic covenant and in the process of the Exodus of the Abrahamic covenant community.

In the Prediluvian Noahic covenant, God displayed the pattern of biblical eschatology through the flood judgment. Later, God demonstrated the visible pattern of final judgment by the fiery judgment upon Sodom and Gomorrah through the means of heavenly fire in the historical context of the Abrahamic covenant (Gen 18:16—19:29). Jesus Christ as the founder of the redemptive historical hermeneutics interpreted the judgment upon Sodom and Gomorrah in light of *the last days* in the present age and *the day of the Son of Man* which will be the second coming of Jesus Christ.

In the process of the Exodus, God revealed the pattern of biblical eschatology, separating the covenant children of Israel and the non-covenant children of Egypt. God used the blood of the Passover lamb to execute his redemptive judgment, granting the blessings of life to the firstborn sons of Israel while he cursed the firstborn sons of Egypt along with the firstborn of the cattle with death. In doing so, God revealed that the Messiah will come as the final Passover lamb and be slaughtered as the final sacrificial lamb at Golgotha.

The visible showdown and war between the kingdom of God and the kingdom of Satan culminated at the Red Sea. Yahweh showcased the Red Sea as a glorious theater of redemptive judgment, separating the covenant community of Israel and the non-covenant community of Pharaoh and his Egyptian warriors. Yahweh fought the holy war, demonstrating the pattern of biblical eschatology and final judgment. In doing so, he granted the blessings of life to the covenant community of Israel while he executed the curses of death to the Egyptian warriors, even destroying their horses and chariots. In doing so, Yahweh visibly demonstrated the classical paradigm of holy war with total destruction. Moreover, Moses as the prophet conducted Yahweh's redemptive judgment against Pharaoh and his warriors by using the staff in his hands. This suggests that Jesus

---

bedeviled discussion of these topics—the dogmatism, that is, both of the person who knows exactly who is and who isn't 'going to hell' and of the universalist who is absolutely certain that there is no such place or that if there is it will, at the last, be empty." Wright, *Surprised by Hope*, 175–77.

Christ will conduct the final redemptive judgment when he comes back again as the judge and consummator.

Chapter Three

The Mosaic Covenant and Redemptive Judgment

THE COVENANT COMMUNITY OF Israel as the descendants of the Abrahamic covenant experienced a series of God's miracles in the Exodus after 430 years of bondage in Egypt. In the Exodus, God demonstrated redemptive judgments, separating the covenant community of Israel and the non-covenant community of Egypt as seen in the curse of the first-born male of Egyptians in the original Passover and judgment at the Red Sea against Pharaoh and his warriors.

As Israel arrived at Mount Sinai, Yahweh made his covenant with them through the mediator Moses (Exod 19–24). In doing so, Israel became a holy nation which typified the eternal kingdom of God. The believers under the Mosaic covenant were saved under the principle of the covenant of grace, inaugurated in Genesis 3:15. Nevertheless, Israel as a holy nation was under the Mosaic covenant of law so that both blessings and curses as dual sanctions were visibly applied to the nation of Israel. In that sense, we will explore Yahweh's blessings and curses upon Israel after the inauguration of the Mosaic covenant on Mount Sinai typified the blessings of heaven and curses of hell. We may identify this as *the old covenant eschatology*.[1]

We will explore three historical accounts of Israel's apostasy: breaking the Mosaic covenant of law, namely the golden calf (Exod 32:1–35); the exploration of the promised land by the twelve spies (Num 13:1–14:38); and the rebellion of Korah, Dathan, and Abiram (Num 16:1–50).

---

1. For a biblical theological discussion on the Mosaic covenant and the kingdom of God, see Jeon, *Biblical Theology*, 85–130.

We will also discuss the subsequent God's covenant lawsuit against the breakers of the covenant and the announcement and execution of the covenant curses of death.

One of the promises of the Abrahamic covenant was the covenant community of Israel's inheritance of the promised land of Canaan. In the context of the Mosaic covenant, God commanded Israel to fight a holy war with total destruction (*cherem*) against the inhabitants of the promised land. We will identify how the conquest of Canaan was the process of God's redemptive judgment, separating the covenant community of Israel and the non-covenant community of the Canaanites. In that respect, we will argue that the holy war during the conquest of Canaan, especially represented in the conquest of Jericho, was the type of final holy war which will occur at the second coming of Christ which will separate the elect and reprobate.

John and Harvey Walton insist that the Canaanites in the promised land should not be considered "as having violated the moral principles of the Law." Furthermore, they argue that Canaanites are not able to break "the covenant because they are not in a covenant relationship with Yahweh" while Israel broke the Mosaic covenant:

> It is not uncommon for people to read about the Canaanites and the conquest and conclude that the Canaanites are being punished because they were not holy. We have been contending in several of the previous propositions that the Canaanites cannot be considered as having violated the moral principles of the law. . . . When Israelites are unfaithful to the Torah, they are not breaking God's universal moral law; they are breaking the covenant. As discussed in proposition eight, Canaanites cannot break the covenant because they are not in a covenant relationship with Yahweh.[2]

However, it is our assessment that their analysis is a fundamental misreading of the background of Yahweh's command of total destruction (*cherem*). Spiritually speaking, the Canaanites were under the first Adam who broke the covenant of works (Gen 2:15–17) although they were not under the Mosaic covenant. In light of that, we will explore that Yahweh executed the redemptive judgment with the curses of death against the Canaanites in the milieu of the covenant of works in the first Adam which

---

2. Walton and Walton, *Lost World of the Israelite Conquest*, 103.

the principles were republished and written in the Ten Commandments on the two stone tablets.

The Mosaic Covenant of Law and Old Covenant Eschatology[3]

God made a covenant with the Abrahamic covenant community when they arrived on Mount Sinai after the Exodus (Exod 19–24). The covenant community of Israel made a sworn oath to the Mosaic covenant in the presence of Yahweh as they shouted together, "All that the Lord has spoken we will do" (Exod 19:8; 24:3, 7).[4] The dual sanctions of blessings and curses were specifically applied throughout the nation of Israel. Therefore, after the inauguration of the Mosaic covenant, Yahweh blessed the nation of Israel when they obeyed the Mosaic laws. However, he cursed them when they disobeyed the Mosaic laws.

After the inauguration of the Mosaic covenant, Moses and Joshua stayed at Mount Sinai for forty days and forty nights to receive the tablets of stone (Exod 24:12–18). On Mount Sinai, Yahweh provided Moses the comprehensive instructions and designs of the tabernacle and its furnishings, enveloped in the glory of the Lord while the covenant community of Israel waited in the wilderness at the foothills of Mount Sinai (Exod 25:1—31:18).

However, when Moses took a while to come down from Mount Sinai, the covenant community of Israel went to Aaron and suggested

---

3. For a brief exploration on the concept of the old covenant eschatology, see Jeon, *Biblical Theology*, 100–107.

4. Vos identifies God's visible presence in the process of making the Sinaitic covenant as "the Sinai Theophany." In doing so, he views "the Sinai Theophany" has "the eschatological significance" which is "typical of what will happen at the end of the world" when Jesus Christ comes back again: "Like the deluge, God's appearance on Sinai contains an eschatological element. However, in the deluge, the negative destruction-idea of the world's crisis is brought out. Here at Sinai, the constructive, positive element of redemption is presented. This is further brought out by viewing it in its historical setting. In its context the eschatological significance is clear because it is the climax of the events of the exodus. These events were the redemption of Israel and are typical of the messianic redemption in the New Testament. The terms of our salvation are derived from this. Now the New Testament redemption has the inherent character of gravitating toward an end and this same feature must be sought in its typical forecast; i.e., the climax at Sinai is typical of what will happen at the end of the world." Vos, *Eschatology of the Old Testament*, 105.

the making of gods. Aaron gathered gold from the Israelites and made a golden calf as an object of worship:

> When the people saw that Moses delayed to come down from the mountain, the people gathered themselves together to Aaron and said to him, "Up, make us gods who shall go before us. As for this Moses, the man who brought us up out of the land of Egypt, we do not know what has become of him." [2]So Aaron said to them, "Take off the rings of gold that are in the ears of your wives, your sons, and your daughters, and bring them to me." [3]So all the people took off the rings of gold that were in their ears and brought them to Aaron. [4]And he received the gold from their hand and fashioned it with a graving tool and made a golden calf. And they said, "These are your gods, O Israel, who brought you up out of the land of Egypt!" [5]When Aaron saw this, he built an altar before it. And Aaron made proclamation and said, "Tomorrow shall be a feast to the LORD." [6]And they rose up early the next day and offered burnt offerings and brought peace offerings. And the people sat down to eat and drink and rose up to play. (Exod 32:1–6)

Aaron's and the Israelites' patience did not last for forty days and forty nights which was the duration of Moses' time with God on Mount Sinai. The people of Israel not only made a golden calf but also built an altar. They offered burnt offerings and peace offerings as manifestations of the highest form of apostasy, violating the first and second commandments of the Ten Commandments. In doing so, both Aaron and the Israelites broke the Sinaitic covenant of law.[5]

---

5. As we have already noted, the people of Israel after the inauguration of the Mosaic covenant (Exod 19–24) were saved by God's grace alone (*sola gratia*), by faith alone (*sola fide*) and in Christ alone (*solo Christo*), based upon the principle of the covenant of grace, inaugurated in Gen 3:15. Nevertheless, the principle of the Mosaic covenant of law was applied for the national life of Israel with the dual sanctions such as the blessings of life and curses of death after the prophetic announcement of covenant lawsuits. However, Schreiner as a monocovenantalist who denies the covenant of works before the Fall also rejects the implications of the Mosaic covenant of law. In doing so, he identifies the Mosaic covenant purely as "gracious," still applying and using the concept of "covenant lawsuit" which is self-contradictory and confusing. Instead, we argue that God's covenant lawsuits and the subsequent curses of death are not applied based upon the principle of the covenant of grace but limited to the violation or breaking of the Adamic covenant of works and the Mosaic covenant of law: "The covenant with Israel was gracious, for the Lord freed his people from Egyptian slavery. In some ways, it was an extension of the covenant with Abraham and Adam, for Israel was called as God's son and as a kingdom of priests to display the righteousness of

As the apostasy was prevalent among the covenant people of Israel, Yahweh told Moses on Mount Sinai about the imminent covenantal curse. God delivered the covenant lawsuit based upon the Sinaitic covenant:

> **7**And the LORD said to Moses, "Go down, for your people, whom you brought up out of the land of Egypt, have corrupted themselves. **8**They have turned aside quickly out of the way that I commanded them. They have made for themselves a golden calf and have worshiped it and sacrificed to it and said, 'These are your gods, O Israel, who brought you up out of the land of Egypt!'" **9**And the LORD said to Moses, "I have seen this people, and behold, it is a stiff-necked people. **10**Now therefore let me alone, that my wrath may burn hot against them and I may consume them, in order that I may make a great nation of you." (Exod 32:7–10)

Yahweh's words to Moses, "These are your gods, O Israel, who brought you up out of the land of Egypt!" (v. 8) were the Israelites' shouts at the foot of Mount Sinai which was the climax of their apostasy. At this critical moment, Moses as the mediator of the Sinaitic covenant interceded for the people of Israel to forgive their sins and appealed to the promise of the Abrahamic covenant which was confirmed to Abraham, Isaac, and Israel (Exod 32:11–13). In the end, God answered Moses' intercessory prayer as we read, "And the LORD relented from the disaster that he had spoken of bringing on his people" (Exod 32:14).

After God's answer and response to the intercessory prayer, Moses came down along with Joshua on Mount Sinai with "the two tablets of the testimony," where God engraved the Ten Commandments. Near the camp of Israel at the foot of Mount Sinai, Moses saw the golden calf and the Israelites' dancing around this idol. Moses threw the stone tablets and broke them. Then Moses took the golden calf, burned it with fire, turned

---

the Lord to the world as they kept the covenant stipulations. The covenant with Israel was patterned after suzerain-vassal treaties in the ancient Near East. Blessings were promised for obedience and curses for disobedience. Israel was called as a theocracy to live under Yahweh's lordship, and that demanded the submission of every member of the nation, for he had entered into covenant with the entire nation.

We see in the history of Israel that they failed to abide by the covenant stipulations, summarized in the Ten Commandments, and thus they were sent into exile. The prophets declared in covenant lawsuits, which detailed Israel's violation of the covenant, that judgment was coming. Jeremiah and others, however, also prophesied a new covenant (Jer. 31:31–34), one in which the law would be inscribed on the heart." Schreiner, *Covenant and God's Purpose for the World*, 72.

it into powder, threw it on the water, and commanded the covenant community of Israel to drink it (Exod 32:15–20).

As Israel was unrepentant to their sins, God commanded Moses to execute the covenant curses of death, based upon the Sinaitic covenant of law through the hands of the sons of Levi:

> 25And when Moses saw that the people had broken loose (for Aaron had let them break loose, to the derision of their enemies), 26then Moses stood in the gate of the camp and said, "Who is on the LORD's side? Come to me." And all the sons of Levi gathered around him. 27And he said to them, "Thus says the LORD God of Israel, 'Put your sword on your side each of you, and go to and fro from gate to gate throughout the camp, and each of you kill his brother and his companion and his neighbor.'" 28And the sons of Levi did according to the word of Moses. And that day about three thousand men of the people fell. 29And Moses said, "Today you have been ordained for the service of the LORD, each one at the cost of his son and of his brother, so that he might bestow a blessing upon you this day." (Exod 32:25–29)

Verse 28 signifies that God executed his covenant curses of death against the unrepentant people of Israel, breaking the Sinaitic covenant of law: "And the sons of Levi did according to the word of Moses. And that day about three thousand men of the people fell." The historic episode of the golden calf indicates that the dual sanctions of the blessings and curses were applied after the inauguration of the Sinaitic covenant in the national life of Israel. When Israel was faithful to the covenant, God blessed the nation of Israel. However, when they were disobedient to the covenant, God cursed them with death. In doing so, God demonstrated the real existence of the blessings of heaven and the curses of hell in a typological manner although heaven and hell are invisible realms in the present world.

After the historic episode of the golden calf and God's covenant curses of death against the disobedient Israel, Moses went up alone on Mount Sinai and cut "two tablets of stone like the first" according to Yahweh's guideline. He stayed there with Yahweh for forty days and forty nights while fasting. Yahweh wrote "on the tablets the words of the covenant, the Ten Commandments" (v. 28). Afterwards, Moses returned to the covenant community of Israel from Mount Sinai "with the two tablets of the testimony," and the skin of Moses' face shone "because he had been talking with God" (v. 29). When Aaron and the people of Israel saw Moses, they were afraid to come near him because "the skin of his face" was shining. Afterwards, the covenant community of Israel went to Moses, and he spoke all the things that Yahweh had spoken with him on Mount Sinai. After Moses spoke to Israel, he put a veil over his shining face. However, Moses removed the veil when he spoke with Yahweh (Exod 34:1–34).

Israel built the tabernacle and constructed it along with all its furnishings under the guidelines and leadership of Moses as Yahweh had already provided the masterful designs (Exod 35:1—39:43). As Israel dedicated the completed tabernacle and all its furnishings according to the guidelines of God through the leadership of the prophet Moses, the glory of the Lord appeared and filled the tabernacle:

> [34]Then the cloud covered the tent of meeting, and the glory of the LORD filled the tabernacle. [35]And Moses was not able to enter the tent of meeting because the cloud settled on it, and the glory of the LORD filled the tabernacle. [36]Throughout all their journeys, whenever the cloud was taken up from over the tabernacle, the people of Israel would set out. [37]But if the cloud was not taken up, then they did not set out till the day that it was taken up. [38]For the cloud of the LORD was on the tabernacle by day, and fire was in it by night, in the sight of all the house of Israel throughout all their journeys. (Exod 40:34–38)

In fact, *the glory of the Lord* (כְּבוֹד יְהוָה) was the visible sign of the presence of the invisible God, which dwelt in the midst of the covenant community of Israel. Moses identified the tabernacle as "the tent of meeting" which was a movable temple. The glory of the Lord as the visible form of cloud and fire was present throughout the historic process of the Exodus. However, it appeared over the tabernacle and guided the Israelites throughout the journey in the wilderness. Therefore, Israel moved according to the direction of the glory cloud during the day. They stopped walking whenever the cloud as the visible sign of God's presence stopped moving. During the night, fire as the shining glory of the Lord was over the tabernacle, providing light and protecting the covenant community of Israel from any harm or attacks.[6]

6. Vos interprets the Mosaic tabernacle in light of redemptive historical continuity and eschatology. He views Jesus Christ as "the antitypical tabernacle" who is the embodiment of the eschatological or final tabernacle: "The typical significance of the tabernacle should be sought in close dependence upon its symbolic significance. We must ask: where do these religious principles and realities, which the tabernacle

Meanwhile, Yahweh commanded Israel to prepare the military campaign through Moses before they left the Desert of Sinai toward the promised land (Num 1:1—10:10). The campaign included a census of the warriors among the covenant people of Israel "from twenty years old and upward" besides Levites (Num 1:1–46) and an arrangement of the camp according to Yahweh's design (Num 2:1–34).

As Israel finished preparing their military campaign according to the guidelines of God, the glory cloud lifted "from over the tabernacle of the testimony" (v. 11). They began to march, leaving "the wilderness of Sinai" where the Sinaitic covenant was inaugurated. As the *shekinah* Glory cloud stopped moving "in the wilderness of Paran," they settled there:

> [11]In the second year, in the second month, on the twentieth day of the month, the cloud lifted from over the tabernacle of the testimony, [12]and the people of Israel set out by stages from the wilderness of Sinai. And the cloud settled down in the wilderness of Paran. [13]They set out for the first time at the command of the LORD by Moses. (Num 10:11–13)

As the beautiful glory cloud lifted over the tabernacle, the entire nation of Israel began to move for the first time after the inauguration of the Mosaic covenant on Mount Sinai. It signified that God was present in the midst of Israel from the beginning of the Exodus and throughout the wilderness journey toward the promised land. In particular, verse 13 highlights that Israel at last began to move toward the promised land: "They set out for the first time at the command of the LORD by Moses." They

---

served to teach and communicate, reappear in the subsequent history of redemption, lifted to their consummate history? First we discover them in the glorified Christ. Of this speaks the Evangelist [John 1.14]. The Word became flesh is the One in whom God came to the tabernacle among men, in order to reveal to them His grace and glory. In John 2.19–22 Jesus Himself predicts that the Old Testament temple, which His enemies by their attitude towards Him are virtually destroying, He will build up again in three days, i.e., through the resurrection. This affirms the continuity of the Old Testament sanctuary and His glorified Person. In Him will be forever perpetuated all that tabernacle and temple stood for. The structure of stone may disappear; the essence proves itself eternal. In Col 2.9, Paul teaches that in Him the fullness of the Godhead dwells bodily. With these passages should be compared the saying of Jesus to Nathanael [John 1.51] where He finds in Himself the fulfillment of what Jacob had called the house of God, the gate of heaven. In all these cases the indwelling of God in Christ serves the same ends which the Mosaic tabernacle provisionally served. He as the antitypical tabernacle is revelatory and sacramental in the highest degree." Vos, *Biblical Theology*, 154–55.

left the memorable sight of Mount Sinai where they made the Sinaitic covenant with God through the prophet Moses and built the tabernacle.

Yahweh commanded Moses to send out twelve warrior spies who represented the twelve tribes to spy out the promised land as the final stage of preparation of holy war against the land of Canaan. He gave an opportunity for the twelve warrior representatives to explore the land of Canaan which was promised and granted to the descendants of Abraham, Isaac, and Jacob through the Abrahamic covenant. Moses sent them from the wilderness of Paran to the promised land according to the command of Yahweh (Num 13:1–25). As the twelve spies spied out the promised land for forty days, they witnessed the rich blessings at the Valley of Eshcol:

> [21]So they went up and spied out the land from the wilderness of Zin to Rehob, near Lebo-hamath. [22]They went up into the Negeb and came to Hebron. Ahiman, Sheshai, and Talmai, the descendants of Anak, were there. (Hebron was built seven years before Zoan in Egypt.) [23]And they came to the Valley of Eshcol and cut down from there a branch with a single cluster of grapes, and they carried it on a pole between two of them; they also brought some pomegranates and figs. [24]That place was called the Valley of Eshcol, because of the cluster that the people of Israel cut down from there. (Num 13:21–24)

As the twelve spies witnessed the abundant fruits of grapes, pomegranates, and figs at the Valley of Eshcol, they brought some fruits back to the covenant community of Israel who were waiting in the wilderness of Paran.

After forty days, they came back to "all the congregation of the people of Israel in the wilderness of Paran, at Kadesh" (v. 26). They showed the fruits of the promised land. However, the ten spies' report, with the exception of Caleb and Joshua, was very negative which reflected that they did not see the promised land through the lens of faith and obedience. The promised land was deeply rooted in the promise of the Abrahamic covenant, a sworn oath by God (Num 13:25–29). In the midst of an audible and visible crisis due to the bad report given by the ten spies, Caleb tried to soothe the covenant community of Israel. But the ten spies discouraged Israel again not to enter the land of Canaan (Num 13:30–33).

Tragically, the congregation of Israel did not listen to the faithful report of Caleb and Joshua as the eyewitnesses who reported based upon the promise of the Abrahamic covenant. Paying attention to the faithless and disobedient ten spies' report, they complained against Moses and Aaron, inevitably complaining against Yahweh. Once again, Caleb and Joshua tried to calm them down by explaining and summarizing the blessed nature of the promised land. In the end, the angry Israelites tried to stone Moses and Aaron (Num 14:1–10).

At the moment of absolute chaos and crisis, the glory of the Lord appeared at the tent of the meeting to Israel, and Yahweh pronounced the brief words of the covenant lawsuit against them to the prophet Moses:

> [11]And the LORD said to Moses, "How long will this people despise me? And how long will they not believe in me, in spite of all the signs that I have done among them? [12]I will strike them with the pestilence and disinherit them, and I will make of you a nation greater and mightier than they." (Num 14:11–12)

Verse 12 states "I will strike them with the pestilence and disinherit them, and I will make of you a nation greater and mightier than they." This verse summarizes the comprehensive picture of the covenant curses of death to the disobedient Israel while he promises Israel as a nation will inherit the promised land. As Moses listened to Yahweh's covenant lawsuit with the curses of death against the covenant community of Israel, he interceded for the forgiveness of sins of Israel (Num 14:13–19). Yahweh responded to Moses' intercessory prayer as the mediator of the Mosaic covenant on behalf of the disobedient Israel that indeed he forgave their sins. Nevertheless, he confirmed that he will curse the disobedient Israelites with the curses of death, based upon the covenant lawsuit in light of the Mosaic covenant of law, except for Caleb and the little ones:

> [20]Then the LORD said, "I have pardoned, according to your word. [21]But truly, as I live, and as all the earth shall be filled with the glory of the LORD, [22]none of the men who have seen my glory and my signs that I did in Egypt and in the wilderness, and yet have put me to the test these ten times and have not obeyed my voice, [23]shall see the land that I swore to give to their fathers. And none of those who despised me shall see it. [24]But my servant Caleb, because he has a different spirit and has followed me fully, I will bring into the land into which he went, and his descendants shall possess it. [25]Now, since the Amalekites and the Canaanites dwell in the valleys, turn tomorrow and set out for the wilderness by the way to the Red Sea." (Num 14:20–26)

Afterwards, Yahweh commanded Moses and Aaron to tell the disobedient Israelites from twenty years old and older, except for Caleb and

Joshua, they will receive the curses of death and bear forty years in the wilderness. The curses of death against the disobedient Israelites from twenty years and older, except for Caleb and Joshua, and forty years in the wilderness are in fact the covenantal curses through the covenant lawsuit, based upon the Mosaic covenant of law:

> [26]And the LORD spoke to Moses and to Aaron, saying, [27]"How long shall this wicked congregation grumble against me? I have heard the grumblings of the people of Israel, which they grumble against me. [28]Say to them, 'As I live, declares the LORD, what you have said in my hearing I will do to you: [29]your dead bodies shall fall in this wilderness, and of all your number, listed in the census from twenty years old and upward, who have grumbled against me, [30]not one shall come into the land where I swore that I would make you dwell, except Caleb the son of Jephunneh and Joshua the son of Nun. [31]But your little ones, who you said would become a prey, I will bring in, and they shall know the land that you have rejected. [32]But as for you, your dead bodies shall fall in this wilderness. [33]And your children shall be shepherds in the wilderness forty years and shall suffer for your faithlessness, until the last of your dead bodies lies in the wilderness. [34]According to the number of the days in which you spied out the land, forty days, a year for each day, you shall bear your iniquity forty years, and you shall know my displeasure.' [35]I, the LORD, have spoken. Surely this will I do to all this wicked congregation who are gathered together against me: in this wilderness they shall come to a full end, and there they shall die." (Num 14:26–35)

Yahweh used pictorial language to describe the covenantal curses of death and forty years of the wilderness vividly to Moses (vv. 29–35). Meanwhile, Yahweh promised the blessings of life to faithful Caleb and Joshua and the children and youth who were younger than twenty years old. "But your little ones, who you said would become a prey, I will bring in, and they shall know the land that you have rejected" (v. 31) promises the little ones with Caleb and Joshua will enjoy the special privilege to inherit the promised land after the suffering of forty years in the wilderness.

Yahweh respected Moses, who played the role of prosecutor, as the prophet. After Yahweh's covenant lawsuit was spoken to the disobedient Israelites through the prophet Moses, Yahweh *immediately* executed the curses of death as the infinitely righteous judge against the ten spies who gave such a bad report about the land of Canaan:

> ³⁶And the men whom Moses sent to spy out the land, who
> returned and made all the congregation grumble against him
> by bringing up a bad report about the land— ³⁷the men who
> brought up a bad report of the land- died by plague before the
> LORD. ³⁸Of those men who went to spy out the land, only Josh-
> ua the son of Nun and Caleb the son of Jephunneh remained
> alive. (Num 14:36–38)

We clearly see that the dual sanctions of blessings of life and curses
of death were applied in the national life of Israel after the inauguration
of the Sinaitic covenant. "The men who brought up a bad report of the
land died by plague before the LORD. Among the men who went to spy
out the land, only Joshua the son of Nun and Caleb the son of Jephunneh
lived" (vv. 37–38) vividly shows us that Yahweh radically made a separation between the curses of death and blessings of life with respect to the
ten disobedient spies and faithful Caleb and Joshua.

Yet again, we find a significant pattern of Yahweh's covenant lawsuit,
based upon the Mosaic covenant of law. Yahweh first spoke to the prophet Moses about the covenantal curses of death, based upon the Mosaic
covenant of law when Israel broke the covenant. Moses as the prophet
spoke Yahweh's living words of the covenant lawsuit against the disobedient Israel. In that sense, the prophet played a role of prosecutor against
the disobedient Israel. Then Yahweh as the righteous Judge executed the
judgment of death against Israel who broke the Mosaic covenant of law.

We need to explore another historic episode of the rebellion of Korah, Dathan, and Abiram against Moses and Aaron and God's judgment
with the curses of death (Num 16:1–50). It demonstrates the general pattern of the disobedience of the covenant people, the covenant lawsuit,
and God's execution of the covenant curses of death against the disobedient people.

Korah, Dathan, Abiram, and On along with "a number of the people
of Israel" gathered together and argued against Moses and Aaron, challenging the distinctiveness of the office of the priests:

> Now Korah the son of Izhar, son of Kohath, son of Levi, and
> Dathan and Abiram the sons of Eliab, and On the son of Peleth,
> sons of Reuben, took men. ²And they rose up before Moses, with
> a number of the people of Israel, 250 chiefs of the congregation,
> chosen from the assembly, well-known men. ³They assembled
> themselves together against Moses and against Aaron and said
> to them, "You have gone too far! For all in the congregation are

holy, every one of them, and the LORD is among them. Why then do you exalt yourselves above the assembly of the LORD?" (Num 16:1–3)

Yahweh communicated to Moses and Aaron his covenant lawsuit against Korah, Dathan, Abiram, and their supporters (Num 16:20–24). Moses as the prophet delivered God's covenant lawsuit against Korah, Dathan, Abiram, and their supporters with the covenantal curses of death:

> 25Then Moses rose and went to Dathan and Abiram, and the elders of Israel followed him. 26And he spoke to the congregation, saying, "Depart, please, from the tents of these wicked men, and touch nothing of theirs, lest you be swept away with all their sins." 27So they got away from the dwelling of Korah, Dathan, and Abiram. And Dathan and Abiram came out and stood at the door of their tents, together with their wives, their sons, and their little ones. 28And Moses said, "Hereby you shall know that the LORD has sent me to do all these works, and that it has not been of my own accord. 29If these men die as all men die, or if they are visited by the fate of all mankind, then the LORD has not sent me. 30But if the LORD creates something new, and the ground opens its mouth and swallows them up with all that belongs to them, and they go down alive into Sheol, then you shall know that these men have despised the LORD." (Num 16:25–30)

After Moses as the prophet finished speaking the words of God's covenant lawsuit against the disobedient Korah and his followers' family members, the judgment of the curses of death fell upon them. The judgment of death was exactly what Moses prophesied:

> 31And as soon as he had finished speaking all these words, the ground under them split apart. 32And the earth opened its mouth and swallowed them up, with their households and all the people who belonged to Korah and all their goods. 33So they and all that belonged to them went down alive into Sheol, and the earth closed over them, and they perished from the midst of the assembly. 34And all Israel who were around them fled at their cry, for they said, "Lest the earth swallow us up!" 35And fire came out from the LORD and consumed the 250 men offering the incense. (Num 16:31 35)

"So they and all that belonged to them went down alive into Sheol, and the earth closed over them, and they perished from the midst of the assembly" (v. 33) highlights that Moses' prophetic words during the covenant lawsuit was exactly fulfilled in the execution of the curses of death. We need to pay attention to verse 35: "And fire came out from the LORD and consumed the 250 men offering the incense." In addition to Korah and his followers and their family members, this verse suggests that Yahweh administered the curses of death against 250 non-priests who were offering the incense that was designated to be conducted only by the priests, the descendants of Aaron.

Again, we find the pattern of God's execution of the dual sanctions such as blessings and curses under the Mosaic covenant. When Korah and his followers were disobedient to the Mosaic covenant, God spoke his covenant lawsuit against the disobedient people and their family members. Moses as the prophet delivered the words of the covenant lawsuit against them. Afterwards, God carried the curses of death against Korah, his followers, and their family members.

As we explored, Yahweh delivered the message of curse against the disobedient Israel through the prophet Moses in the context of the report of twelve spies after they came back from spying the land of Canaan for forty days (Num 14:20–38). Yahweh executed the covenantal curses of death during the forty years of wilderness against the disobedient ten spies and those who were twenty years old and older because of their disobedience.

At last, Israel arrived at the plain of Moab and God renewed the Sinaitic covenant with Israel through the prophet Moses, the mediator of the covenant. The prologue of Deuteronomy verifies that the Israelites lived their lives for forty years in the wilderness which was one of the covenantal curses upon them due to their disobedience (Deut 1:1–4).

In the context of the renewal of the Sinaitic covenant in the plain of Moab, Moses as the prophet confirmed that Yahweh executed the curses of death against those warriors who were twenty years old and older among the Israelites during the forty years in the wilderness:

> [13]"Now rise up and go over the brook Zered." So we went over the brook Zered. [14]And the time from our leaving Kadesh-barnea until we crossed the brook Zered was thirty-eight years, until the entire generation, that is, the men of war, had perished from the camp, as the LORD had sworn to them. [15]For indeed the hand of the LORD was against them, to destroy them from the camp, until they had perished. [16]So as soon as all the men of war had perished and were dead from among the people,

> **17**the LORD said to me, **18**"Today you are to cross the border
> of Moab at Ar. **19**And when you approach the territory of the
> people of Ammon, do not harass them or contend with them,
> for I will not give you any of the land of the people of Ammon
> as a possession, because I have given it to the sons of Lot for a
> possession." (Deut 2:13–19)

Moses as the prophet reminded the covenant community of Israel
that Yahweh executed the curses of death during the forty years in the
wilderness against the disobedient Israelites who listened to the unfaithful report of the ten spies. Here, we need to be sure that believers under
the Mosaic covenant were saved by the principle of the covenant of grace,
inaugurated in Genesis 3:15. The elect among the covenant community
of Israel were saved by grace alone (*sola gratia*) and justified by faith
alone (*sola fide*) and in Christ alone (*solo Christo*). Nevertheless, the dual
sanctions of the blessings of life and curses of death under the Mosaic
covenant were applied within the national life of Israel. In doing so, God
provided a pedagogical lesson to Israel that the blessings of heaven and
curses of hell indeed exist. In fact, the faithful believers under the Mosaic
covenant meditated the blessings of heaven when they enjoyed God's
abundant material and spiritual blessings while they realized the curses
of hell when the curses of death befell on the disobedient Israelites. We
can properly identify this as *the old covenant eschatology*.

The Conquest of Canaan and Redemptive Judgment

Many bible readers, not to mention bible scholars and theologians, have
a difficult time understanding the stories of the conquest of Canaan in
the book of Joshua. How could a loving and compassionate God command Israel to kill all the inhabitants of Canaan, including innocent
babies, when they entered the promised land? It is a puzzling command.
However, we can comprehend God's cruel command if we read and understand it in light of *eschatology*. In fact, God visibly demonstrates *the
pattern of biblical eschatology* in the process of the conquest of Canaan,
written in the book of Joshua.[7] We would like to explore Israel's holy war

7. Modern historical critical scholars, following the lead of Martin Noth's hypothesis of the Deuteronomistic history, reject the historic account of the conquest
of Canaan, recorded in the book of Joshua. James Kugel as one of the followers of the
Deuteronomistic history summarizes it as follows: "Meanwhile, in 1943, a German
biblical scholar, Martin Noth, worked out on his own a new hypothesis concerning

against the city of Jericho because it describes the most detailed account

the relationship between Deuteronomy and the subsequent historical books (Joshua, Judges, 1 and 2 Samuel, and 1 and 2 Kings), and his accounting of things won immediate acceptance among Western scholars.

Noth believed that the group of laws and exhortations that form the center of Deuteronomy (4:44—30:20) constituted, with a few adjustments, the 'original' book of Deuteronomy, the one that had been found in the Jerusalem temple in Josiah's time. That book was thus essentially a law code, many of whose provisions embod ied D's characteristic ideology—radical devotion to Israel's God, fervent opposition to anything smacking of 'Canaanite' worship, along with an evident concern for the downtrodden ('the stranger, the widow, and the orphan'), a rather abstract conception of God, and a broad perspective on the surrounding world.

Noth thought that someone—the 'Deuteronomistic historian'—had taken this law code and used it as the starting point for composing a long history of Israel, from the time of Moses to the Babylonian exile. This writer was someone who was steeped in the ideology of Deuteronomy, but he must have lived long afterward; since this history ended with the Babylonian exile, Noth, concluded, he must have composed his work sometime in the sixth century BCE.

How did this historian proceed? First, Noth believed, he composed the opening four chapters of Deuteronomy, in which Moses reviews the people's desert wanderings. This would serve as an introduction to the old law code, the 'original' Deuteronomy. The same historian then ended the book with an account of Moses' death. To this he then added the bulk of his work—a thoroughgoing history of Israel, starting with Joshua and the conquest of the land, then on to the period of the Judges, David's rise to power, the United Monarchy, and so forth down to the fall of Jerusalem and the Babylonian exile. This whole history thus stretched from the beginning of Deuteronomy to the end of 2 Kings." Kugel, *How to Read the Bible*, 371.

Childs as the architect of canonical criticism also adopts Noth's hypothesis of the Deuteronomistic history, noting that the theology of the book of Joshua was "an extension of the theology of Deuteronomy" through the editing process by a Deuteronomistic historian: "The next major level within the witness was correctly seen by Noth when he ascribed to a Deuteronomistic historian the shaping of the present structure of the book of Joshua. This editor brought the conquest traditions into a unified whole and provided a theological framework to the book (chs 1 and 23) which was an extension of the theology of Deuteronomy. Accordingly, God led Israel as the unified, chosen people to possession of the land, and as long as Israel was obedient to the divine will, no one could stand for." Childs, *Biblical Theology*, 145–46.

Growing numbers of evangelical scholars adopt Noth's historical critical hypothesis of Deuteronomistic history. For example, Longman and Dillard adopt it with more evangelical posture: "The result of these debates has been a wide range of assessments about the historicity and date of the book of Joshua. . . . Dates assigned to the book have been as late as the post exilic period, when the issue of possessing the land was again before Israel. Conservative scholars have commonly assigned a time not long after the events (Woudstra 1981) or early in the monarchy (Harrison 1969, 673). Making such determinations is very difficult. While one may reject the negative skepticism of the more critical approaches, a distinction is still necessary between the date of sources and the later editor(s) who produced the book in its present form. The book does share the viewpoint of the Deuteronomistic History (Joshua—Kings) and could

in the process of the conquest of Canaan in the book of Joshua, providing the pattern of biblical eschatology.[8]

After forty years in the wilderness, God renewed the Mosaic covenant in the plain of Moab. We may identify the entire book of Deuteronomy as the renewal of the Sinaitic covenant. In doing so, the covenant community of Israel prepared to cross the Jordan River and conquer the promised land of Canaan which was promised to Abraham, Isaac, and Jacob with God's sworn oath. Once again, God emphasized the method of war in the process of the conquest of Canaan through the prophet Moses in the historical context of the renewal of the Sinaitic covenant:

> When the LORD your God brings you into the land that you are entering to take possession of it, and clears away many nations before you, the Hittites, the Girgashites, the Amorites, the Canaanites, the Perizzites, the Hivites, and the Jebusites, seven nations more numerous and mightier than yourselves, [2]and when the LORD your God gives them over to you, and you defeat them, then you must devote them to complete destruction. You shall make no covenant with them and show no mercy to them. [3]You shall not intermarry with them, giving your daughters to their sons or taking their daughters for your sons, [4]for they would turn away your sons from following me, to serve other gods. Then the anger of the LORD would be kindled against you, and he would destroy you quickly. [5]But thus shall you deal with them: you shall break down their altars and dash in pieces their pillars and chop down their Asherim and burn their carved images with fire. [6]For you are a people holy to the LORD your God. The LORD your God has chosen you to be a people for his treasured possession, out of all the peoples who are on the face of the earth. [7]It was not because you were more in number than

---

reflect some compositional or editorial work as late as the exilic editor of Kings (2 Kings 25:27–30)." Longman and Dillard, *Introduction to the Old Testament*, 127.

8. John and Harvey Walton define the conquest of Canaan as "rhetorical hyperbole" which denies the historic account, recorded in the book of Joshua. It is because they read the conquest of Canaan through the lens of the historical critical methodology, especially Martin Noth's hypothesis of the Deuteronomistic history: "The same is true of Israelite literature, including the conquest in Joshua. We should assume that a military campaign of some kind occurred, and since the record is inspired we should assume that the writer's interpretation of the event is accurate, at least insofar as it claims to represent the purposes of God. But the actual details of the totality of the destruction or the quantity of victims is likely couched in rhetorical hyperbole, in accordance with the expectations of the genre." Walton and Walton, *Lost World of the Israelite Conquest*, 178.

any other people that the LORD set his love on you and chose
you, for you were the fewest of all peoples, [8]but it is because the
LORD loves you and is keeping the oath that he swore to your
fathers, that the LORD has brought you out with a mighty hand
and redeemed you from the house of slavery, from the hand of
Pharao-h king of Egypt. [9]Know therefore that the LORD your
God is God, the faithful God who keeps covenant and steadfast
love with those who love him and keep his commandments, to a
thousand generations, [10]and repays to their face those who hate
him, by destroying them. He will not be slack with one who hates
him. He will repay him to his face. [11]You shall therefore be careful to do the commandment and the statutes and the rules that I
command you today. (Deut 7:1–11)

Moses as the prophet comprehensively summarized the method of
war when the covenant community of Israel entered the promised land
in verse 2: "And when the LORD your God gives them over to you, and
you defeat them, then you must devote them to complete destruction.
You shall make no covenant with them and show no mercy to them."
Afterwards, God revealed to Israel two different kinds of war which are
common grace war and holy war (Deut 20:9–20). The common grace war
respects international law and regulations in the process of waging war
(Deut 20:9–15). However, holy war is the war of total destruction, temporarily lifting the benefits of the covenant of common grace, inaugurated
in Genesis 3:16–19 and recovered and renewed in Genesis 8:20—9:17
through the postdiluvian Noahic covenant (Deut 20:16–20).[9] Certainly,
God's command for total destruction (*cherem*) against the inhabitants
of the promised land was the holy war which should be viewed in light
of the consideration of the final judgment which will take place at the
second coming of Christ.[10]

---

9. For a biblical theological discussion on a proper distinction between common
grace war and holy war, see Jeon, *Biblical Theology*, 78–79; Kline, *Structure of Biblical
Authority*, 162–64.

10. As John and Harvey Walton denies the genuine historic account of the conquest of Canaan, written in the book of Joshua, they radically redefine the concept of
"total destruction" (*cherem*) which removes the biblical and eschatological concept
of holy war from it: "The idea that the conquest is an act of genocide is based on
the assumption that the *herem* of the Canaanite nations is a command to kill people
of a particular ethnicity (derived from Deut. 7:2). The idea that the *herem* is divine
punishment for offense against God is based on the assumption that the *herem* of
Israelite idolaters in Deuteronomy 13:15 (also Ex 22:20) is a command to carry out a
death sentence in consequence for a particular crime. Both of these assumptions are

After the renewal of the Sinaitic covenant at the plain of Moab, Moses climbed Mount Nebo and Yahweh showed Moses the promised land. However, he died on Mount Nebo in the land of Moab. Although he desired to enter the promised land, Yahweh did not allow him (Deut 34:1–7). Certainly, the Bible clearly reveals that Moses, as the mediator of the Sinaitic covenant, was saved by God's grace under the principle of the covenant of grace and his soul went to the glorious and holy heaven immediately after his death. Nevertheless, he was not able to enter the promised land. Yahweh directly revealed to Moses before his death the reason why he was not able to enter the promised land:

> **48**That very day the LORD spoke to Moses, **49**"Go up this mountain of the Abarim, Mount Nebo, which is in the land of Moab, opposite Jericho, and view the land of Canaan, which I am giving to the people of Israel for a possession. **50**And die on the mountain which you go up, and be gathered to your people, as Aaron your brother died in Mount Hor and was gathered to his people, **51**because you broke faith with me in the midst of the people of Israel at the waters of Meribah-kadesh, in the wilderness of Zin, and because you did not treat me as holy in the midst of the people of Israel. **52**For you shall see the land before you, but you shall not go there, into the land that I am giving to the people of Israel." (Deut 32:48–52).

Yahweh revealed the reason why Moses received the curse of death at the end of the forty years in the wilderness instead of entering the promised land. Verse 51 is a comprehensive statement from Yahweh: "Because you broke faith with me in the midst of the people of Israel at the waters of Meribah-kadesh, in the wilderness of Zin, and because you did not treat me as holy in the midst of the people of Israel." Moses as the mediator of the Sinaitic covenant and prophet failed to manifest Yahweh's holiness in the midst of the covenant community of Israel "at the waters of Meribah, in the wilderness of Zin." Through Moses' death on Mount Nebo in the land of Moab, we have a clear picture that some

---

false. *Herem* does not mean 'destroy'; it means 'remove from use.' . . . The (infamous) command to '*herem* them . . . show no mercy' in Deuteronomy refers, as we have demonstrated, to destroying identities, not people, as is indicated by the destruction of identity markers (that is cult objects) in Deuteronomy 7:5. The list of things Israelites are to do to them consists of breaking down their altars, smashing their sacred stones, cutting down their Ashera poles, and burning their idols in the fire; it does not include killing every last one of them." Walton and Walton, *Lost World of the Israelite Conquest*, 179, 193.

faithful believers as the members of God's eternal election in Christ under the Sinaitic covenant received the curses of death when they violated or broke the Mosaic covenant of law.

With the death of Moses, Joshua took over the leadership role under the blessings and endorsement of Yahweh that Moses used to have in the process of the Exodus, the inauguration of the Sinaitic covenant, and leading the covenant community of Israel during the forty years in the wilderness (Deut 34:1–12). After the death of Moses, Yahweh commanded Joshua to conquer the promised land and lead Israel (Josh 1:1–9).

At last, Israel crossed the Jordan River under the leadership of Joshua just as they had crossed the Red Sea under the leadership of Moses (Josh 3:1–17). Crossing the Jordan River meant not only officially ending the forty years in the wilderness for Israel but also finally entering into the promised land. Certainly, the pictorial languages of crossing the Jordan River were reminiscent of crossing the Red Sea which was the visible culmination of the historic process of the Exodus:

> [14]So when the people set out from their tents to pass over the Jordan with the priests bearing the ark of the covenant before the people, [15]and as soon as those bearing the ark had come as far as the Jordan, and the feet of the priests bearing the ark were dipped in the brink of the water (now the Jordan overflows all its banks throughout the time of harvest), [16]the waters coming down from above stood and rose up in a heap very far away, at Adam, the city that is beside Zarethan, and those flowing down toward the Sea of the Arabah, the Salt Sea, were completely cut off. And the people passed over opposite Jericho. [17]Now the priests bearing the ark of the covenant of the LORD stood firmly on dry ground in the midst of the Jordan, and all Israel was passing over on dry ground until all the nation finished passing over the Jordan. (Josh 3:14–17)

Crossing the Jordan River was a marvelous and miraculous scene. As "the priests bearing the ark of the covenant of the LORD" stood in the midst of the Jordan River, it became "dry ground." Remarkably, "the ark of the covenant of the LORD" became a visible means of blessings for Israel. Verse 17 states, "And all Israel was passing over on dry ground until all the nation finished passing over the Jordan," emphasizing that the entire covenant community of Israel entered the promised land by crossing the Jordan River through the miraculous works of Yahweh. Verse 17 indicates that the inheritance of the promised land was in fact

Yahweh's gift to Israel which was one of the fulfillments of the promises of the Abrahamic covenant.

The stories of Israel's crossing the Jordan River spread to the various kings in the land of Canaan. The kings were terrified: "As soon as all the kings of the Amorites who were beyond the Jordan to the west, and all the kings of the Canaanites who were by the sea, heard that the LORD had dried up the waters of the Jordan for the people of Israel until they had crossed over, their hearts melted and there was no longer any spirit in them because of the people of Israel" (Josh 5:1). In that sense, we can say that the widespread news of Israel's miraculous crossing of the Jordan River was in fact the covenant lawsuit against the kings and dwellers in the land of Canaan which signified the imminent redemptive judgment of Yahweh.

Under the old covenant, God commanded the covenant community of Israel to keep two sacraments: circumcision and the Passover. God commanded to circumcise every male after eight days of their birth as the visible sign of the member of the covenant community in the historic context of the Abrahamic covenant. The Passover was to commemorate the original Passover, which separated between the blessings of life for Israel and the curses of death against the first born sons of Egypt. Jesus Christ as the mediator of the new covenant instituted and commanded the practice of two sacraments within the new covenant church: baptism and the Lord's Supper. In doing so, water baptism replaced circumcision as the Lord's Supper replaced the Passover.

Remarkably, as the final stage of the preparation of holy war against Jericho, Yahweh commanded the circumcision of "the sons of Israel" because all the males who were born during the forty years in the wilderness did not receive the sacrament of circumcision (Josh 5:2–9). Israel kept the Passover, eating the produce of the promised land for the first time: the unleavened bread and parched grain at Gilgal. As they enjoyed eating the produce of the promised land, Yahweh ceased sending the manna from heaven which was daily bread for them during the forty years in the wilderness (Josh 5:10–12). Moreover, receiving circumcision and celebrating the Passover at Gilgal for the elect within the covenant community of Israel, signifies that they were recipients of the redemptive blessings of the covenant of grace, including justification by faith alone (*sola fide*) and salvation by grace alone (*sola gratia*) and in Christ alone (*solo Christo*) although the nation of Israel was under the dual sanctions of the curses of death and blessings of life in light of the Mosaic covenant of law.

Here, we need to highlight the historic scene of the circumcision of Israel more closely because the circumcision of all the males, born during the forty years in the wilderness, was related to Yahweh's holy war against the dwellers in the land of Canaan:

> [2]At that time the LORD said to Joshua, "Make flint knives and circumcise the sons of Israel a second time." [3]So Joshua made flint knives and circumcised the sons of Israel at Gibeath-haaraloth. [4]And this is the reason why Joshua circumcised them: all the males of the people who came out of Egypt, all the men of war, had died in the wilderness on the way after they had come out of Egypt. [5]Though all the people who came out had been circumcised, yet all the people who were born on the way in the wilderness after they had come out of Egypt had not been circumcised. [6]For the people of Israel walked forty years in the wilderness, until all the nation, the men of war who came out of Egypt, perished, because they did not obey the voice of the LORD; the LORD swore to them that he would not let them see the land that the LORD had sworn to their fathers to give to us, a land flowing with milk and honey. [7]So it was their children, whom he raised up in their place, that Joshua circumcised. For they were uncircumcised, because they had not been circumcised on the way. [8]When the circumcising of the whole nation was finished, they remained in their places in the camp until they were healed. [9]And the LORD said to Joshua, "Today I have rolled away the reproach of Egypt from you." And so the name of that place is called Gilgal to this day. (Josh 5:2–9)

Verse 6 once again confirms that Yahweh executed the covenantal curses of death and the forty years in the wilderness against the people of Israel who were disobedient after the historic event of spying on the promised land for forty days (Num 13:1—14:38). When all the males were circumcised, Israel's warriors were ready to fight the holy war on behalf of Yahweh because the circumcision was the visible, embodied sign of the covenant people of God against the idol worshipers who dwelt in the land of Canaan.[11]

---

11. For a biblical theological discussion about the close relationship between circumcision and God's holy war in the Old Testament, see Jeon, *Biblical Theology*, 122–23.

After the sacraments of circumcision and the Passover were over, Israel's military campaign against Jericho was launched. Firstly, Yahweh instructed Joshua the military commander in chief the process of holy war against Jericho (Josh 6:1–5). Then the Israelites executed holy war against Jericho according to the guidelines of Joshua (Josh 6:6–21).

The armies of Israel walked around the city of Jericho for six days once a day with "the ark of the covenant of the Lord" which included the two stone tablets with the Ten Commandments as the principle of the covenant of works, broken by the first Adam. In light of Yahweh's redemptive judgment against Jericho, the six days of walking around the city was the period of Yahweh's covenant lawsuit before he executed the curses of death to all the residents of Jericho:

> 8And just as Joshua had commanded the people, the seven priests bearing the seven trumpets of rams' horns before the LORD went forward, blowing the trumpets, with the ark of the covenant of the LORD following them. 9The armed men were walking before the priests who were blowing the trumpets, and the rear guard was walking after the ark, while the trumpets blew continually. 10But Joshua commanded the people, "You shall not shout or make your voice heard, neither shall any word go out of your mouth, until the day I tell you to shout. Then you shall shout." 11So he caused the ark of the LORD to circle the city, going about it once. And they came into the camp and spent the night in the camp. 12Then Joshua rose early in the morning, and the priests took up the ark of the LORD. 13And the seven priests bearing the seven trumpets of rams' horns before the ark of the LORD walked on, and they blew the trumpets continually. And the armed men were walking before them, and the rear guard was walking after the ark of the LORD, while the trumpets blew continually. 14And the second day they marched around the city once, and returned into the camp. So they did for six days. (Josh 6:8–14)

As we explored, God demonstrates his covenant lawsuit against the disobedient Israel in light of the Mosaic covenant of law. However, God did not make the Mosaic covenant with the residents in the land of Canaan, including Jericho. What kind of covenant did God have in mind when he appealed the covenant lawsuit against them? In short, it was the Adamic covenant of works (Gen 2:15–17). Spiritually speaking, there are only two kinds of people after the fall on the earth: those who are in the first Adam who broke the covenant of works along with him and those who are in the last Adam, Christ, as the mediator of the covenant of grace who fulfilled the requirement of the Adamic covenant of works and paid the full penalty of the sins of the elect. In that sense, the inhabitants of Jericho were the former. The period of six days, walking and circling around the city of Jericho by the army of Israel with "the ark of the covenant of the Lord" was *the judicial period of the covenant lawsuit*, based upon the covenant of works against the dwellers of Jericho who broke the covenant. In other words, the period of six days was the judicial process of the covenant lawsuit against those who broke the Adamic covenant of works.[12]

In light of *eschatology*, the six days walking around the city of Jericho by the armies of Israel were *the last days*: the period of the covenant lawsuit, based upon the Adamic covenant of works. However, the seventh day was *the day of the Lord* where Yahweh executed the judgment of the curses of death against all the people of Jericho, including innocent babies, while he secured the blessings of life for the covenant community of Israel:

> [15]On the seventh day they rose early, at the dawn of day, and marched around the city in the same manner seven times. It was only on that day that they marched around the city seven times. [16]And at the seventh time, when the priests had blown the trumpets, Joshua said to the people, "Shout, for the LORD has given you the city. [17]And the city and all that is within it shall be devoted to the LORD for destruction. Only Rahab the prostitute and all who are with her in her house shall live, because she hid the messengers whom we sent. [18]But you, keep yourselves from the things devoted to destruction, lest when you have devoted them you take any of the devoted things and make the camp of

---

12. In "the ark of the covenant of the Lord" the Ten Commandments written in the two stone tablets were included. Amazingly, the Ten Commandments were the principle of the covenant of works as the basis of the covenant lawsuit against the dwellers of Canaan, including the city of Jericho.

The Westminster divines understood that God engraved the moral law to the hearts of Adam and Eve as the *imago Dei*, and the moral law was the principle of "a covenant of works" for the first Adam. After the fall, the moral law continued to be "a perfect rule of righteousness" and was carried "by God upon Mount Sinai, in ten commandments, and written in two tables": "1. God gave to Adam a law, as a covenant of works, by which He bound him and all his posterity, to personal, entire, exact, and perpetual obedience, promised life upon the fulfilling, and threatened death upon the breach of it, and endued him with power and ability to keep it. 2. This law, after his fall, continued to be a perfect rule of righteousness; and, as such, was delivered by God upon Mount Sinai, in ten commandments, and written in two tables: the first four commandments containing our duty towards God; and the other six, our duty to man." *Westminster Confession of Faith*, 19.1–2.

Israel a thing for destruction and bring trouble upon it. [19]But all silver and gold, and every vessel of bronze and iron, are holy to the LORD; they shall go into the treasury of the LORD." [20]So the people shouted, and the trumpets were blown. As soon as the people heard the sound of the trumpet, the people shouted a great shout, and the wall fell down flat, so that the people went up into the city, every man straight before him, and they captured the city. [21]Then they devoted all in the city to destruction, both men and women, young and old, oxen, sheep, and donkeys, with the edge of the sword. (Josh 6:15–21)

The seventh day was *the day of the Lord* which was the day of the execution of redemptive judgment against the city of Jericho. The armies of Israel circled and walked around Jericho six times without blowing the trumpets. It was God's wisdom to reveal the suddenness of the curses of death in redemptive judgment. Then, at the seventh time, the priests blew the trumpets and the people of Israel gave a loud shout and the wall of Jericho collapsed as Yahweh had already revealed. Verse 21, "Then they devoted all in the city to destruction, both men and women, young and old, oxen, sheep, and donkeys, with the edge of the sword," vividly draws the nature of the curses of death against Jericho which include not only all the people but also all the animals. In short, it provides us the comprehensive picture of total destruction (*cherem*). We need to highlight the phrase "both men and women, young and old" which includes innocent babies. The fact that innocent babies along with unborn babies were included in the curses of death in judgment against Jericho verifies the imputation of the original sin which is the result of the breaking of the covenant of works by the first Adam.[13]

---

13. God created man as the image of God, and engraved the Ten Commandments as the moral law. After the fall, everyone outside of the last Adam is under the curse of the covenant of works to be fulfilled. In light of that, the Canaanites were under the curse of the law as the covenant of works. However, John and Harvey Walton as they deny the historicity of Adam, also reject that the Canaanites were under the covenant of works and that God engraved the moral law onto their hearts: "Neither the covenant nor the law was revealed to the *Canaanites*; the covenant never applied to them, either in its blessings or its curses. Therefore they cannot be indicted on the basis of not obeying it. They can, however, be held up as a negative example and a foil of the ideal of the covenant order. The language used to describe the Canaanites in Leviticus and Deuteronomy is not an accusation and is not a rationale for war. It is a brilliant appropriation of literary tropes and typology designed to simultaneously emphasize Israel's dependence on Yahweh, extol the covenant order as the ideal state of being, and warn the Israelites of the consequences of covenant infidelity." Walton and Walton,

There is a glorious, visible connection between the trumpet sounds at Jericho and the trumpet sounds when the final day of the Lord comes, as Jesus Christ reveals in his famous Olivet discourse:

> **29**"Immediately after the tribulation of those days the sun will be darkened, and the moon will not give its light, and the stars will fall from heaven, and the powers of the heavens will be shaken. **30**Then will appear in heaven the sign of the Son of Man, and then all the tribes of the earth will mourn, and they will see the Son of Man coming on the clouds of heaven with power and great glory. **31**And he will send out his angels with a loud trumpet call, and they will gather his elect from the four winds, from one end of heaven to the other. (Matt 24:29–31)

Echoing the priests' trumpet sounds *at the day of the Lord* in the city of Jericho, Jesus Christ prophesied that there will be "a loud trumpet call" when he returns as the final Judge after the present age which is the New Covenant Age. Verse 31, "And he will send out his angels with a loud trumpet call, and they will gather his elect from the four winds, from one end of heaven to the other," indicates that the trumpet sounds at the final day of the Lord will not be by the earthly trumpets but by heavenly trumpets which will be the defining moment of not only the second coming of Jesus Christ but also the visible execution of the final judgment.[14]

Lost World of the Israelite Conquest, 156.

14. Interpreting the conquest of Canaan from the Christocentric and Christotelic perspectives, Edwards highlights that "the sound of the trumpets of the priests" typified "the sound of the gospel by the preaching of the gospel ministers" while the walls of Jericho signified "the walls of satan's kingdom." In addition, he emphasizes that the promised land was "a great type of heaven" which was possessed by Israel: "The next thing I would observe, was God's bringing the people of Israel under the hand of Joshua, and settling them in that land where Christ was to be born, and which was the great type of the heavenly Canaan, which Christ has purchased. This was done by Joshua, who was of Joseph's posterity, and was an eminent type of Christ, and is therefore called the shepherd, the stone of Israel, in Jacob's blessing of Joseph, Gen. xlix. 24. Being such a type of Christ, he bore the name of Christ. . . . God wonderfully possessed his people of this land, conquering the former inhabitants of it, and the mighty giants, as Christ conquered the devil; first conquering the great kings of that part of the land that was on the eastern side of Jordan, Sihon king of the Amorites, and Og king of Bashan; and then dividing the river Jordan, as before he had done the Red Sea; causing the walls of Jericho to fall down at the sound of the trumpets of the priests; that sound typifying the sound of the gospel by the preaching of the gospel ministers, the walls of the accursed city Jericho signifying the walls of Satan's kingdom. . . . Thus God gave the people whence Christ was to proceed, the land where he was to be born, and live, and preach, and work miracles, and die, and rise again, and whence he was to ascend into heaven, as the land which was

The apostle Paul encapsulates the comprehensive pattern of eschatology in 1 Corinthians 15:1–58. In doing so, Paul under the inspiration of the Holy Spirit notes that there will be the bodily resurrection of believers "at the last trumpet" (ἐν τῇ ἐσχάτῃ σάλπιγγι) which will be blown at the final day of the Lord:

> **50**I tell you this, brothers: flesh and blood cannot inherit the kingdom of God, nor does the perishable inherit the imperishable. **51**Behold! I tell you a mystery. We shall not all sleep, but we shall all be changed, **52***in a moment, in the twinkling of an eye, at the last trumpet. For the trumpet will sound, and the dead will be raised imperishable, and we shall be changed* [ἐν ἀτόμῳ, ἐν ῥιπῇ ὀφθαλμοῦ, ἐν τῇ ἐσχάτῃ σάλπιγγι· σαλπίσει γὰρ καὶ οἱ νεκροὶ ἐγερθήσονται ἄφθαρτοι καὶ ἡμεῖς ἀλλαγησόμεθα.]. **53**For this perishable body must put on the imperishable, and this mortal body must put on immortality. (1 Cor 15:50–53)

Paul describes believers' bodily resurrection as "a mystery" (μυστήριον) which will be visibly realized when Jesus Christ comes back again with the heavenly cantata which will be the song of the arrival of the final judgment. Nevertheless, God will not use a manmade trumpet at the second coming of Jesus Christ although it is a beautiful musical instrument. Rather, he will create the most glorious sound of trumpet without manmade instruments.

As we explored, Yahweh used the armies of Israel to execute the redemptive judgment against the inhabitants of the city of Jericho at the priests' last trumpet. In doing so, he separated the covenant community of Israel with the blessings of life and the pagan dwellers with the curses of death in the city of Jericho. God typologically demonstrated the blessings of heaven and curses of hell. However, "the last trumpet" at the final day of the Lord will be the heavenly trumpet, the audible sign of the execution of the final redemptive judgment, which will separate the glorious bodily resurrection of the believers and the bodily resurrection of the wicked.

Paul also notes "the last trumpet" as "the sound of the trumpet of God" which will be the sound of the heavenly trumpet. Certainly, it will be the decisive and glorious sound of the second coming of Jesus Christ, the bodily resurrection, and the final judgment:

a great type of heaven, which is another thing whereby a great advance was made in the affair of redemption." Edwards, *History of the Work of Redemption*, 84–85.

13But we do not want you to be uninformed, brothers, about
those who are asleep, that you may not grieve as others do who
have no hope. 14For since we believe that Jesus died and rose
again, even so, through Jesus, God will bring with him those
who have fallen asleep. 15For this we declare to you by a word
from the Lord, that we who are alive, who are left until the coming of the Lord, will not precede those who have fallen asleep.
16For the Lord himself will descend from heaven with a cry of
command, with the voice of an archangel, and with the sound
of the trumpet of God. And the dead in Christ will rise first.
17Then we who are alive, who are left, will be caught up together
with them in the clouds to meet the Lord in the air, and so we
will always be with the Lord. 18Therefore encourage one another with these words. (1 Thess 4:13–18)

Verse 16 vividly reveals the audible and visible picture of the moment of the second coming of Jesus Christ: "For the Lord himself will descend from heaven with a cry of command, with the voice of an archangel,
and with the sound of the trumpet of God. And the dead in Christ will
rise first." In particular, Paul emphasizes that there will be three harmonious sounds as he describes, "With a cry of command, with the voice of
an archangel, and with the sound of the trumpet of God." Certainly, the
phrase "with the sound of the trumpet of God" (ἐν σάλπιγγι θεου) indicates
that there will be the sound of the heavenly glory for the elect as they meet
Jesus Christ "in the air" with the glorious bodily resurrection, but it will be
the sound of the curses of hell for the reprobate. Likewise, God used the
sound of the trumpets, blown by the priests, on the day of the Lord when
he executed the redemptive judgment against the city of Jericho under the
old covenant. However, God will use the sound of the heavenly trumpet
at the final day of the Lord when he will visibly demonstrate the final redemptive judgment at the end of the New Covenant Age.[15]

15. MacArthur and Mayhue as the major exponents of dispensational premille-
nialism fundamentally misread and misinterpret Paul's passages of 1 Corinthians
15:50–58 and 1 Thessalonians 4:13–18. They interpret the passage in light of "a pretribulational rapture," separating between "the rapture and Christ's second coming
to earth." At best, this is a culmination of unbiblical concept of rapture, promoted
by dispensational hermeneutics and eschatology: "Fifth, 1 Thessalonians demands a
pretribulational rapture. Suppose that some other rapture view is here. What then we
expect to find in 1 Thessalonians 4? The reverse of the concerns reflected there. To
begin, we would expect the Thessalonians to be rejoicing that their loved ones are
home with the Lord and will not endure the horrors of the tribulation. But instead,
we discover that the Thessalonians are actually grieving because they fear their loved

Meanwhile, Israel's holy war on behalf of Yahweh culminated by setting fire against Jericho. However, Joshua as a commander in chief was commanded by God to rescue Rahab the prostitute and her father's family. Therefore, the two warriors who spied Jericho went to Rahab's home, following the scarlet cord in the window and saved them:

> [22]But to the two men who had spied out the land, Joshua said, "Go into the prostitute's house and bring out from there the woman and all who belong to her, as you swore to her." [23]So the young men who had been spies went in and brought out Rahab and her father and mother and brothers and all who belonged to her. And they brought all her relatives and put them outside the camp of Israel. [24]And they burned the city with fire, and everything in it. Only the silver and gold, and the vessels of bronze and of iron, they put into the treasury of the house of the LORD. [25]But Rahab the prostitute and her father's household and all who belonged to her, Joshua saved alive. And she has lived in Israel to this day, because she hid the messengers whom Joshua sent to spy out Jericho. (Josh 6:22–25)

Rahab the prostitute and her father's family were rescued and survived the culmination of holy war. As we know, Rahab hid Israel's two spies on the roof of her house when the pursuers of Jericho tried to find them. Therefore, the two spies were saved by Rahab. They told Rahab when Israel came and attacked Jericho to tie the scarlet cord in the window of her house while Rahab and her father's family should stay inside the house (Josh 2:1–24). Here, it is noteworthy to explore Rahab's incredible confessional statement before the two spies went to sleep on the roof.

---

ones will miss the rapture. Only a pretribulational rapture accounts for this grief. . . . Seventh, events at Christ's return to earth after the tribulation differ from the rapture. If one compares what happens at the rapture in 1 Thessalonians 4:13–18 and 1 Corinthians 15:50–58 with what happens in the final events of Christ's second coming in Matthew 24–25, at least eight significant contrasts or differences can be observed, which demand that the rapture and Christ's second coming occur at different times. . . . Additionally, several of Christ's parables in Mathew 13 confirms differences between the rapture and Christ's second coming to earth. In the parable of the wheat and the tares, the tares (unbelievers) are taken out from among the wheat (believers) at the climax of the second coming (Matt 13:30, 40), while believers are removed among unbelievers at the rapture (1 Thess 4:15–17). In the parable of the dragnet, the bad fish (unbelievers) are taken out from among the good fish (believers) at the culmination of Christ's second coming (Matt. 13:48–50), while believers are removed from among unbelievers at the rapture (1 Thess 4:15–17). Finally, there is no mention of the rapture in the detailed second-coming texts Matthew 24 and Revelation19." MacArthur and Mayhue, *Biblical Doctrine*, 901–2.

Rahab heard the miraculous stories about the Exodus, culminated in the Red Sea and Israel's victorious wars against Sihon and Og:

> [8]Before the men lay down, she came up to them on the roof [9]and said to the men, "I know that the LORD has given you the land, and that the fear of you has fallen upon us, and that all the inhabitants of the land melt away before you. [10]For we have heard how the LORD dried up the water of the Red Sea before you when you came out of Egypt, and what you did to the two kings of the Amorites who were beyond the Jordan, to Sihon and Og, whom you devoted to destruction. [11]And as soon as we heard it, our hearts melted, and there was no spirit left in any man because of you, for the LORD your God, he is God in the heavens above and on the earth beneath. [12]Now then, please swear to me by the LORD that, as I have dealt kindly with you, you also will deal kindly with my father's house, and give me a sure sign [13]that you will save alive my father and mother, my brothers and sisters, and all who belong to them, and deliver our lives from death." (Josh 2:8–13)

Rahab's confessional statement suggests that the inhabitants of the city of Jericho heard the miraculous stories about the Exodus and God's miraculous works for Israel's forty years in the wilderness. But only Rahab the prostitute responded with faith and obedience among the people of Jericho. What is remarkable is that Rahab believed Israel's God as her God and Lord. Verse 11 points out that Rahab abandoned the gods of the Canaanites who were at best manmade false gods: "And as soon as we heard it, our hearts melted, and there was no spirit left in any man because of you, for the LORD your God, he is God in the heavens above and on the earth beneath." She realized that the God of Israel is the true God and Lord who created the heavens and the earth. Moreover, Rahab carefully listened to the two spies' words and followed their suggestions with obedience under the guidance and illumination of the Holy Spirit:

> [17]The men said to her, "We will be guiltless with respect to this oath of yours that you have made us swear. [18]Behold, when we come into the land, you shall tie this scarlet cord in the window through which you let us down, and you shall gather into your house your father and mother, your brothers, and all your father's household. [19]Then if anyone goes out of the doors of your house into the street, his blood shall be on his own head, and we shall be guiltless. But if a hand is laid on anyone who is with you in the house, his blood shall be on our head. [20]But if you tell this

business of ours, then we shall be guiltless with respect to your oath that you have made us swear." [21]And she said, "According to your words, so be it." Then she sent them away, and they departed. And she tied the scarlet cord in the window. [22]They departed and went into the hills and remained there three days until the pursuers returned, and the pursuers searched all along the way and found nothing. (Josh 2:17–22)

We need to pay special attention to verse 21: "And she tied the scarlet cord in the window." As Rahab tied "the scarlet cord in the window," she meditated on the coming Messiah's infinite meritorious obedience on the cross as the mediator of the new covenant. Later, on the day of the Lord, the two spies identified Rahab the prostitute's house when they saw "the scarlet cord in the window" which symbolizes the blood of the new covenant, shed by Jesus Christ. In that sense, Rahab was not only saved during the seventh-day redemptive judgment against Jericho but also saved by God's grace and received eternal life as a gift through faith. In short, Rahab was the recipient of redemptive blessings of the covenant of grace. Moreover, the survival of Rahab the prostitute and her father's family manifest God's heart for the gentiles under the Mosaic covenant. They became the members of the covenant community of Israel by God's grace.[16]

Incidentally, Achan violated Yahweh's command of the holy war against the city of Jericho. After the victorious holy war against Jericho, the armies of Israel tried to conquer Ai, but they were miserably defeated (Josh 7:1–9).[17] Eventually, Yahweh explained to Joshua that Israel violated

16. Interpreting Josh 2:1, Calvin emphasizes that Rahab the prostitute was saved by God's grace and admitted into "the body of the chosen people," becoming "a member of the Church." In doing so, he exemplified redemptive historical hermeneutics: "My conclusion therefore is, that they obtained admission privily, and immediately betook themselves to a hiding place. Moreover, in the fact that a woman who had gained a shameful livelihood by prostitution was shortly after admitted into the body of the chosen people, and became a member of the Church, we are furnished with a striking display of divine grace which could thus penetrate into a place of shame, and draw forth from it not only Rahab, but her father and the other members of her family." Calvin, *Joshua*, 2:1, in *Calvin's Commentaries*.

17. John Collins as a liberal historical critical scholar argues that the story of Ai, recorded in Josh 7:1—8:29 is "a fiction" as he radically reinterprets the conquest of Canaan in light of the Deuteronomistic history: "The story of the attack on Ai is most probably also a fiction designed to give a clear illustration of the Deuteronomist's theology. When the initial attack fails, it is assumed that the reason is not inadequate manpower or strategy, but the displeasure of the Lord. Sure enough, the Lord informs Joshua that Israel has broken the covenant by disobeying a commandment. The specific commandment in question is the ban, which Achan had broken by taking things for

the Mosaic covenant which included the method of the holy war. In doing so, he delivered the words of the covenant lawsuit against the violator of the method of the holy war, based upon the Mosaic covenant of law:

> [10]The LORD said to Joshua, "Get up! Why have you fallen on your face? [11]Israel has sinned; they have transgressed my covenant that I commanded them; they have taken some of the devoted things; they have stolen and lied and put them among their own belongings. [12]Therefore the people of Israel cannot stand before their enemies. They turn their backs before their enemies, because they have become devoted for destruction. I will be with you no more, unless you destroy the devoted things from among you. [13]Get up! Consecrate the people and say, 'Consecrate yourselves for tomorrow; for thus says the LORD, God of Israel, "There are devoted things in your midst, O Israel. You cannot stand before your enemies until you take away the devoted things from among you." [14]In the morning therefore you shall be brought near by your tribes. And the tribe that the LORD takes by lot shall come near by clans. And the clan that the LORD takes shall come near by households. And the household that the LORD takes shall come near man by man. [15]And he who is taken with the devoted things shall be burned with fire, he and all that he has, because he has transgressed the covenant of the LORD, and because he has done an outrageous thing in Israel.'" (Josh 7:10–15)

In like manner, Yahweh commanded Joshua as the commander of Israel to execute the covenantal curses of death against the persons among Israel who violated the given method of the holy war against Jericho. In the process of Yahweh's covenant lawsuit against the violator of the method of the holy war, we can find out that the curses of death against Israel were based upon the Mosaic covenant of law which was already renewed in the book of Deuteronomy. Receiving Yahweh's words about the covenant lawsuit, Joshua found out Achan among Israel as the violator of the principle of the holy war and executed the curses of death against Achan and his family members according to the command of Yahweh:

> [19]Then Joshua said to Achan, "My son, give glory to the LORD God of Israel and give praise to him. And tell me now what you

---

himself. The specificity of the commandment is not crucial, however. The point is that a commandment has been broken. After the perpetrator has been executed, the Israelites are able to capture Ai and destroy it. Perhaps the most remarkable aspect of the story is the sense of corporate responsibility." Collins, *Introduction to the Hebrew Bible*, 196.

have done; do not hide it from me." **20**And Achan answered Joshua, "Truly I have sinned against the LORD God of Israel, and this is what I did: **21**when I saw among the spoil a beautiful cloak from Shinar, and 200 shekels of silver, and a bar of gold weighing 50 shekels, then I coveted them and took them. And see, they are hidden in the earth inside my tent, with the silver underneath." **22**So Joshua sent messengers, and they ran to the tent; and behold, it was hidden in his tent with the silver underneath. **23**And they took them out of the tent and brought them to Joshua and to all the people of Israel. And they laid them down before the LORD. **24**And Joshua and all Israel with him took Achan the son of Zerah, and the silver and the cloak and the bar of gold, and his sons and daughters and his oxen and donkeys and sheep and his tent and all that he had. And they brought them up to the Valley of Achor. **25**And Joshua said, "Why did you bring trouble on us? The LORD brings trouble on you today." And all Israel stoned him with stones. They burned them with fire and stoned them with stones. **26**And they raised over him a great heap of stones that remains to this day. Then the LORD turned from his burning anger. Therefore, to this day the name of that place is called the Valley of Achor. (Josh 7:19–26)

Verse 24 demonstrates that all Israel along with Joshua participated in the performing death penalty against Achan and his family members, including animals: "And Joshua and all Israel with him took Achan the son of Zerah, and the silver and the cloak and the bar of gold, and his sons and daughters and his oxen and donkeys and sheep and his tent and all that he had. And they brought them up to the Valley of Achor." The death penalty against Achan and his family members suggests that Yahweh was serious in his execution of the holy war against Jericho which was the visible type of the final holy war which will occur when Jesus Christ returns at *the final day of the Lord*. The historic episode of the curses of death against Achan and his family is another confirmation that God administered the curses of death and blessings of life after the process of the covenant lawsuit based upon the Mosaic covenant of law. In doing so, God typologically reveals the curses of hell and blessings of heaven which we define as *the old covenant eschatology*.

Summary

After the inauguration of the Mosaic covenant on Mount Sinai (Exod 19–24), Israel was born as the holy nation identifiable as the theocratic kingdom of Israel. Under the Mosaic covenant, individual believers were saved by the principle of the covenant of grace, inaugurated in Gen 3:15. Nevertheless, Israel as a nation was under the dual sanctions of the covenant curses of death and blessings of life according to the principles of the Mosaic covenant of law because Israel as the covenant community made a sworn oath to the covenant before Yahweh.

After the inauguration of the Mosaic covenant of law, God administered the covenant curses of death and blessings of life according to Israel's attitude to the covenant because Israel was the Theocratic Kingdom which typified the eternal kingdom of God. The historic episode of making a golden calf as the visible object of worship was a representation of Israel's apostasy. Informing Israel's apostasy to Moses, God delivered his covenant lawsuit against Israel, based upon the Mosaic covenant of law. God executed the covenant curses of death where three thousand men among Israel died (Exod 32:25–29). In doing so, God visibly showed Israel the reality of the blessings of heaven and curses of hell.

In the process of the preparation of the holy war against the promised land, God commanded to send out twelve spies to explore the land of Canaan. Moses sent out twelve spies according to God's command (Num 13:1–24). After they returned from the promised land, they reported before Israel what they witnessed. Nevertheless, ten spies except for Caleb and Joshua reported negatively about the land and suggested not to enter the land of Canaan (Num 13:25–33). Unfortunately, the congregation of Israel did not listen to Caleb's and Joshua's faithful report but the unfaithful report by the ten spies (Num 14:1–10). Afterwards, God announced his covenant lawsuit against the unfaithful and disobedient ten spies and the disobedient Israel who followed the unfaithful ten spies' report, informing that all who are twenty years old and older among the unfaithful Israel, except for Joshua and Caleb and innocent children, will die in the wilderness. Israel will also have to suffer for forty years in the wilderness. The unfaithful ten spies immediately faced the curses of death by the plague while Joshua and Caleb enjoyed the blessings of life (Num 14:11–38). Likewise, God demonstrated the curses of death against the unfaithful ten spies and Israel who followed the unfaithful report made by the ten spies. But Joshua and Caleb with their faithful report, based upon *the promise of the Abrahamic covenant*, along with innocent children among Israel received the blessings of life although they suffered for forty years in the wilderness. Moreover, they entered the promised land which was one of the central promises in the Abrahamic covenant.

We found another corporate apostasy and disobedience within Israel after the inauguration of the Mosaic covenant of law in the historic episode of Korah, Dathan, and Abiram against Moses and Aaron. This historic episode reflects the general pattern of the disobedience of the covenant people, God's covenant lawsuit, and God's deliverance of the curses of death against the disobedient Israelites (Num 16:1–50). Korah and his followers and their family members received the curses of death as the earth opened and swallowed them up. In addition, God executed the curses of death against 250 non-priests as they offered the incense, designated to be offered only by the priests, the descendants of Aaron (Num 16:31–35).

As such, the dual sanctions of the blessings of life and curses of death were visibly demonstrated in the national life of Israel after the inauguration of the Mosaic covenant. The faithful believers foretasted the blessings of heaven when they received God's gracious material and spiritual blessings while they witnessed the curses of hell when the covenantal curses of death befell upon the disobedient Israelites. We identified this as *the old covenant eschatology.*

Modern readers of the Bible are deeply puzzled when they read the cruel stories of the conquest of Canaan, vividly highlighted in the book of Joshua. However, we can properly understand God's cruel command of the total destruction (*cherem*) if we interpret and understand it from the perspective of *eschatology.* As a matter of fact, God showed the covenant community of Israel *the pattern of biblical eschatology* through the process of the conquest of Canaan.

Representatively, Israel's holy war against the city of Jericho was a classical paradigm of redemptive judgment, comprehensively described and explained in the book of Joshua (Josh 5:13—6:27). In the process of waging the holy war, the armies of Israel walked around the city of Jericho for six days once a day "with the ark of the covenant of the Lord" which carried inside the Ten Commandments written on the two stone tablets (Josh 6:8–14). We considered the six days of walking around the city was *the period of God's covenant lawsuit* before he demonstrated the curses of death against all the residents of Jericho. From the perspective of eschatology, the six days circling and walking around the city of Jericho by the armies of Israel were *the last days*, defining the period of God's covenant lawsuit, based upon the Adamic covenant of works (Gen 2:15–17). However, the seventh day was *the day of the Lord* as God poured his infinite wrath and executed the judgment of the curses of death against all the residents of Jericho, including innocent children and unborn babies.

Case in point, the seventh day was *the day of the Lord* which was the day of God's execution of redemptive judgment which separated the covenant community of Israel and the dwellers of the city of Jericho. In short, it was a separation between the covenant blessings of life for Israel and the covenant curses of death for the inhabitants of Jericho. It provided a comprehensive and typological picture of the final judgment which will occur at the final day of the Lord in the second coming of Jesus Christ (Josh 6:21–25).

The priests' trumpet sound on the seventh day when the armies of Israel marched around the city of Jericho for the seventh time was the typological picture of the glorious sound of "a loud trumpet call" at the final day of the Lord as Jesus Christ revealed in his Olivet discourse. And there will be a visible separation between the elect and reprobate (Matt 24:29–31). Paul connects the sound "at the last trumpet" with the arrival of the final day of the Lord. Indeed, it will be the eschatological song of the day of the final judgment, immediately following the glorious bodily resurrection of believers both dead and alive (1 Cor 15:50–53). In fact, "the last trumpet" at the final day of the Lord will be the heavenly last trumpet because it will be the audible sign of the day of the final redemptive judgment, visibly separating the glorious bodily resurrection of the believers and the bodily resurrection of the wicked. Furthermore, Paul relates "the last trumpet" as "the sound of the trumpet of God" to emphasize the fact that it will be the sound of the heavenly trumpet. It will be the glorious sound heard universally at the second coming of Jesus Christ as the consummator and judge, bodily resurrection, and the final judgment (1 Thess 4:13–18). Similarly, God used the sound of the trumpets, blown by the priests at the day of the Lord, when he displayed the redemptive judgment against the city of Jericho under the old covenant. But he will use the sound of the heavenly trumpet at the final day of the Lord and then execute the final redemptive judgment after the end of the New Covenant Age.

Israel's holy war on behalf of Yahweh was highlighted by setting fire against Jericho. Before that, Joshua as a commander in chief was commanded by God to rescue Rahab the prostitute and her father's family.

The two spies who spied out Jericho beforehand entered Rahab's home and saved her and her family by following "the scarlet cord in the window" (Josh 6:22–25). Rahab was not only saved during the seventh day redemptive judgment against Jericho but also saved by God's grace and received eternal life as the gift through faith (Josh 2:8–22). Rahab the prostitute was the recipient of redemptive blessings of the covenant of grace. Furthermore, the survival of Rahab and her father's family in the milieu of "the scarlet cord in the window" demonstrates God's heart for the Gentile mission even under the old covenant. Indeed, "the scarlet code in the window" was the cross in the window of Rahab the prostitute's house. As they survived the redemptive judgment against Jericho, they became the members of the covenant community of Israel by God's grace alone.

Israel fought the victorious holy war against the city of Jericho, executing the redemptive judgment with the covenant curses of death against the dwellers of Jericho, based upon the covenant of works in the first Adam. Immediately following that event, the armies of Israel were miserably defeated as they tried to conquer Ai (Josh 7:1–9). God revealed the reason why Israel was defeated because one man violated the method of the holy war when he took "some of the devoted things." God emphasized to Joshua that it was the transgression of the Mosaic covenant of law. In doing so, God commanded Joshua to execute the curses of death with fire against the person, along with all his belongings, within Israel who violated the given method of the holy war against Jericho (Josh 7:10–15). In the process of God's covenant lawsuit against the violator of the method of the holy war, we found out that the curses of death against Israel were based upon the Mosaic covenant of law. Joshua found out Achan within Israel as the violator of the method of the holy war and all of Israel participated in the execution against Achan and his family members, including animals at the valley of Achor (Josh 7:19–26). The historical episode of death against Achan and his family within Israel is another confirmation that God exercised the curses of death and blessings of life after the process of the covenant lawsuit based on the Mosaic covenant of law. In doing so, God typologically demonstrated the existence of the curses of hell and blessings of heaven which we defined as *the old covenant eschatology*.

Chapter Four

The Davidic Covenant and Redemptive Judgment

WITH THE RATIFICATION OF the Davidic covenant, Israel officially became the Davidic Kingdom which was the earthly type of the eternal kingdom of God (2 Sam 7:1–17; 1 Chr 17:1–15).[1] The official establishment of the kingdom of Israel in the promised land was in fact the earthly fulfillment of one of the promises of the Abrahamic covenant. In that sense, God continued to exercise the promissory blessings of the Abrahamic covenant after the inauguration of the Davidic covenant. God also administered the Mosaic covenant of law even after the ratification of the Davidic covenant for *the continuation of the earthly kingdom of Israel* which applied the dual sanctions of blessings and curses.

The kingdom of Israel after David and Solomon was divided into the northern kingdom of Israel and the southern kingdom of Judah. Afterwards, God consistently sent out prophets to the covenant community for their repentance as they often fell into idol worship. This act broke the Mosaic covenant of law.

Growing numbers of so-called evangelical scholars who are negatively influenced by the historical critical reading of the Bible reject the existence of heaven and hell. For example, John Walton as an Old Testament scholar abandons the biblical doctrine of the existence of heaven and hell:

> Now, as little more than an afterthought, we can offer a few comments on what we know of these benefits (to be accurate, eternal

1. For a biblical theological discussion on the Davidic covenant and the kingdom of God, see Jeon, *Biblical Theology*, 131–71.

life is the benefit, paired with the benefit of avoiding hell). We have learned that the Old Testament has no concept of hell, no words for hell, no place for hell in the ideology, and it therefore has no teaching to offer about it. One's perceptions about hell are typically shaped by one's beliefs about other doctrines—primarily sin and salvation. We should also note that even the New Testament is indeterminate about hell. A survey of New Testament passages reveals mix between those that seem to suggest eternal torment and those that are used to support annihilation.[2]

However, we will explore how God provided a picture of the existence of heaven and hell through the rise and fall of Israel. Specifically, the northern kingdom of Israel fell through the military campaign of the Asyrian Empire in 722 B.C., and the southern kingdom of Judah fell subsequently, and God drove survivors into the Babylonian exile in 586 B.C. In the process, God sent his faithful prophets, warning them of God's pending judgment. In light of God's judgment against the covenant community, the prophetic messages reflected God's covenant lawsuit which was based upon the Mosaic covenant of law. It is our assessment that *the pattern of the judgment of the old covenant eschatology* culminated in the fall of the northern kingdom of Israel and the southern kingdom of Judah. Through *the pattern of the old covenant eschatology*, God provided the typological picture of the existence of the blessing of heaven and curse of hell.

Meanwhile, God made a judgment against the Assyrian Kingdom through the military campaign of the Babylonian Empire although God used it before to punish the covenant community of the northern kingdom of Israel. Similarly, God used the Persian Empire to make a judgment against the Babylonian Empire which was already used by God as a means to make a judgment against the covenant community of the southern kingdom of Judah. In doing so, God demonstrated his absolute sovereignty over the rise and fall of the pagan earthly kingdoms and nations and showed that he is the ultimate Great King and Lord of the heavens and earth as the God of Israel.

2. Walton, *Old Testament Theology for Christians*, 264.

The Covenant Lawsuit and the Fall of
the Northern Kingdom of Israel

The history of the Divided Kingdoms, recorded from 1 Kings 12:1 to 2 Kings 25:30, is actually the history of God's covenant lawsuit against the covenant community who broke the Mosaic covenant of law with their apostasy and disobedience. The Chronicler wrote the same history from a different perspective with wondrous symphonic harmony, written under the inspiration of the Holy Spirit (2 Chr 10:1—36:23).[3]

The author of Kings briefly summarizes the fall of the northern kingdom of Israel through the military attack of the armies of "Shalmaneser of king of Assyria" when Hoshea was reigning as the last king "in Samaria over Israel." The capital city, Samaria, was surrounded by the armies of the Assyrian Empire for three years. At last, Samaria was captured and fell:

> In the twelfth year of Ahaz king of Judah, Hoshea the son of Elah began to reign in Samaria over Israel, and he reigned nine years. [2]And he did what was evil in the sight of the LORD, yet not as the kings of Israel who were before him. [3]Against him came up Shalmaneser king of Assyria. And Hoshea became his vassal and paid him tribute. [4]But the king of Assyria found treachery in Hoshea, for he had sent messengers to So, king of Egypt, and offered no tribute to the king of Assyria, as he had done year by year. Therefore the king of Assyria shut him up and bound him in prison. [5]Then the king of Assyria invaded all the land and came to Samaria, and for three years he besieged it. [6]In the ninth year of Hoshea, the king of Assyria captured Samaria, and he carried the Israelites away to Assyria and placed them in

---

3. Following the lead of Martin Noth's radical concept of Deuteronomistic history, Collins discredits all miraculous events, labeling them as hyperbolic or mythological expressions, recorded in the books of Joshua, Judges, 1 and 2 Samuel, and 1 and 2 Kings. In light of the radical Deuteronomistic history, he also denies the historical harmony between Samuels and Kings, and Chronicles: "Much of the Chronicler's History can be seen to derive from biblical materials, especially from 2 Samuel and 1—2 Kings. . . . While the Chronicler may have had occasional access to independent historical information, the great bulk of the cases where he departs from Deuteronomistic history can be explained by his theological and ideological preferences. In many cases, such as the reign of Manasseh, he displays astonishing freedom in manipulating the historical record. Chronicles describes history as the author thought it should have been. It is not a reliable source for historical information about preexilic Israel or Judah." Collins, *Introduction to the Hebrew Bible*, 459.

Halah, and on the Habor, the river of Gozan, and in the cities of the Medes (2 Kgs 17:1–6).

Verse 6 summarizes the seizure of Samaria and dispersion of the covenant community of Israel into the Assyrian exile in the regions of Halah and other areas. In light of this diaspora, the covenant community became *the old covenant diaspora* outside of the promised land with God's curse, based upon breaking of the Mosaic covenant of law.

Furthermore, the author of Kings attributes the fall of the northern kingdom of Israel by the military attack of the Assyrian Empire to the covenant community's disobedience to God through idol worship:

> [7]And this occurred because the people of Israel had sinned against the LORD their God, who had brought them up out of the land of Egypt from under the hand of Pharaoh king of Egypt, and had feared other gods [8]and walked in the customs of the nations whom the LORD drove out before the people of Israel, and in the customs that the kings of Israel had practiced. [9]And the people of Israel did secretly against the LORD their God things that were not right. They built for themselves high places in all their towns, from watchtower to fortified city. [10]They set up for themselves pillars and Asherim on every high hill and under every green tree, [11]and there they made offerings on all the high places, as the nations did whom the LORD carried away before them. And they did wicked things, provoking the LORD to anger, [12]and they served idols, of which the LORD had said to them, "You shall not do this." (2 Kgs 17:7–12)

Likewise, the author of Kings comprehensively summarizes the sins of "the people of Israel" which became the ultimate reason for God's curse against them and the Assyrian exile. In addition, the author of Kings indicates that God pronounced his covenant lawsuit by sending forth his faithful prophets and warning against "Israel and Judah:"

> [13]Yet the LORD warned Israel and Judah by every prophet and every seer, saying, "Turn from your evil ways and keep my commandments and my statutes, in accordance with all the Law that I commanded your fathers, and that I sent to you by my servants the prophets." [14]But they would not listen, but were stubborn, as their fathers had been, who did not believe in the LORD their God. [15]*They despised his statutes and his covenant that he made with their fathers and the warnings that he gave them. They went after false idols and became false, and they followed the nations that were around them, concerning whom the LORD*

had commanded them that they should not do like them. [16]And
they abandoned all the commandments of the LORD their God,
and made for themselves metal images of two calves; and they
made an Asherah and worshiped all the host of heaven and
served Baal. [17]And they burned their sons and their daughters
as offerings and used divination and omens and sold themselves
to do evil in the sight of the LORD, provoking him to anger.
[18]Therefore the LORD was very angry with Israel and removed
them out of his sight. None was left but the tribe of Judah only.
(2 Kgs 17:13–18)

Verse 13 indicates that God constantly sent prophets to the covenant
community of Israel and Judah to get them to repent of their sins and idol
worship.[4] In light of God's judgment, sending forth prophets to the covenant community for repentance is the process of God's covenant lawsuit
against them who broke the covenant.[5] It is very important to identify the
fundamental basis of God's covenant lawsuit against the covenant community of Israel. To be clear, it was not the Abrahamic covenant but the
Mosaic covenant of law. God never appealed his covenant lawsuit based
upon the promissory covenant which was represented in the Abrahamic
covenant in the Old Testament. In that sense, we need to pay special attention to verse 15 which states that "they despised his statutes and his
covenant that he made with their fathers and the warnings that he gave
them." This verse describes how Israel broke God's covenant which was
made with their ancestors. Once again, we need to identify how the
covenant made with Israel on Mount Sinai was *breakable* because Israel
made a sworn oath before God. In that sense, God had a sovereign right
to his covenant lawsuit through the mouths of the prophets and seers,
based upon the Sinaitic covenant of law before he executed his judgment

---

4. Responding to the agnostic view of the origin of the prophets in the Old Testament, promoted by historical critical scholars, Robertson properly designates Moses
as the origin of the prophets who led Israel as the mediator between God and his
covenant people: "So according to the biblical testimony, prophetism in Israel had its
historical origin with the establishment of the theocratic nation in the Mosaic period.
As the foundational law of the covenant was being revealed, the prophetic office came
into being. As a consequence, in starkest contrast with a long history of negatively
critical reconstruction, law and prophecy do not stand over against one another. Instead prophetism originates with the mediation of God's law." Robertson, *Christ of the
Prophets*, 14.

5. For the comprehensive definition and roles of the prophets in the history of
Israel in the Old Testament in light of modern historical critical scholarship, see Vos,
Biblical Theology, 183–296.

against Israel. Verse 18, "Therefore the LORD was very angry with Israel and removed them out of his sight. None was left but the tribe of Judah only," summarizes the historic event of the fall of the northern kingdom of Israel. Moreover, God removed the survivors outside of the promised land. This removal is reminiscent of God's expulsion of Adam and Eve from the garden of Eden after Adam broke the covenant of works in the garden of Eden, the earthly projection of the heavenly kingdom of God. In fact, the promised land was a pictorial type of the eternal kingdom of God. With sin, no one can inherit the eternal kingdom of God. This is why God expelled many from the northern kingdom of Israel outside of the promised land when it fell in 722 B.C.[6]

The author of Kings describes how the divided kingdoms of Israel and Judah did not obey God's commandments. Rather, they fell into sin. The author specifically highlights Jeroboam who made Israel fall into "great sin." Furthermore, verse 22 states, "The people of Israel walked in all the sins that Jeroboam did. They did not depart from them," explaining the historical background of the fall of the northern kingdom of Israel and the Assyrian exile:

> [19]Judah also did not keep the commandments of the LORD their God, but walked in the customs that Israel had introduced. [20]And the LORD rejected all the descendants of Israel and afflicted them and gave them into the hand of plunderers, until he had cast them out of his sight. [21]When he had torn Israel from the house of David, they made Jeroboam the son of Nebat king. And Jeroboam drove Israel from following the LORD and made them commit great sin. [22]The people of Israel walked in all the sins that Jeroboam did. They did not depart from them, [23]until the LORD removed Israel out of his sight, as he had spoken by all his servants the prophets. So Israel was exiled from their own land to Assyria until this day. (2 Kgs 17:19–23)

6. For comprehensive and historical descriptions of the fall of the northern kingdom of Israel through the military campaign of the Assyrian Empire, see Bright, *History of Israel*, 275: "In 724, Shalmaneser attacked. Hoshea, who apparently appeared before his master hoping to make, was taken prisoner. The Assyrians then occupied the land, save for the city of Samaria, which continued to hold out for over two years. Although Shalmaneser's successor, Sargon II, who seized the Assyrian throne on Shalmaneser's death late in 722, repeatedly boasts of having taken Samaria, the Bible is probably correct in attributing its capture to Shalmaneser. The city apparently fell in the late summer or autumn of the year 722/721. Thousands of its citizens—27,290 according to Sargon—were subsequently deported to Upper Mesopotamia and Media, there ultimately to vanish from the stage of history."

Once again, the author of Kings briefly recounts and reiterates the historic event of the fall of the northern kingdom of Israel through the military campaign of the Assyrian Empire:

> ⁹In the fourth year of King Hezekiah, which was the seventh year of Hoshea son of Elah, king of Israel, Shalmaneser king of Assyria came up against Samaria and besieged it, ¹⁰and at the end of three years he took it. In the sixth year of Hezekiah, which was the ninth year of Hoshea king of Israel, Samaria was taken. ¹¹The king of Assyria carried the Israelites away to Assyria and put them in Halah, and on the Habor, the river of Gozan, and in the cities of the Medes, ¹²*because they did not obey the voice of the LORD their God but transgressed his covenant, even all that Moses the servant of the LORD commanded. They neither listened nor obeyed.* (2 Kgs 18:9–12)

In fact, the people of Israel transgressed God's covenant which was the Mosaic covenant of law. Because of this transgression, God used the pagan Empire to curse his covenant people and the promised land. Verse 12 explains and summarizes the backbone of God's covenant lawsuit and the subsequent judgment of curses against the northern kingdom of Israel: "Because they did not obey the voice of the LORD their God but transgressed his covenant, even all that Moses the servant of the LORD commanded. They neither listened nor obeyed." In doing so, the author of Kings emphasizes the importance of the Mosaic covenant of law as the background of God's covenant lawsuit through the prophets and God's execution of curses against the covenant community and the promised land. Through this process, he provided a pictorial visualization of the existence of the curses in hell which will be consummated at the second coming of Jesus Christ.

The historical analysis of the author of Kings makes a beautiful harmony with the prophetic message given through Hosea. Hosea proclaims how Israel broke the covenant as the first Adam broke the covenant of works in the garden of Eden:

> "Come, let us return to the LORD; for he has torn us, that he may heal us; he has struck us down, and he will bind us up. ²After two days he will revive us; on the third day he will raise us up, that we may live before him. ³Let us know; let us press on to know the LORD; his going out is sure as the dawn; he will come to us as the showers, as the spring rains that water the earth." ⁴What shall I do with you, O Ephraim? What shall I do

with you, O Judah? Your love is like a morning cloud, like the dew that goes early away. ⁵Therefore I have hewn them by the prophets; I have slain them by the words of my mouth, and my judgment goes forth as the light. ⁶For I desire steadfast love and not sacrifice, the knowledge of God rather than burnt offerings. ⁷*But like Adam they transgressed the covenant; there they dealt faithlessly with me.* ⁸Gilead is a city of evildoers, tracked with blood. ⁹As robbers lie in wait for a man, so the priests band together; they murder on the way to Shechem; they commit villainy. ¹⁰In the house of Israel I have seen a horrible thing; Ephraim's whoredom is there; Israel is defiled. ¹¹For you also, O Judah, a harvest is appointed, when I restore the fortunes of my people. (Hos 6:1–11)

Hosea succinctly compares the sins of Adam and Israel. As such, "But like Adam they transgressed the covenant; there they dealt faithlessly with me" (v. 7) is a covenantal and redemptive historical comparison that was culminated in the breaking of the covenant of works in the garden of Eden by the first Adam and the Mosaic covenant of law by Israel. Both episodes ended with the expulsion of God's covenant people from the garden of Eden and the promised land.

Once again, Hosea provides an explanation for the covenantal foundation of God's judgment against the northern kingdom of Israel:

Set the trumpet to your lips! One like a vulture is over the house of the LORD, because they have transgressed my covenant and rebelled against my law. ²To me they cry, My God, we—Israel—know you. ³Israel has spurned the good; the enemy shall pursue him. ⁴They made kings, but not through me. They set up princes, but I knew it not. With their silver and gold they made idols for their own destruction. ⁵I have spurned your calf, O Samaria. My anger burns against them. How long will they be incapable of innocence? ⁶For it is from Israel; a craftsman made it; it is not God. The calf of Samaria shall be broken to pieces. ⁷ For they sow the wind, and they shall reap the whirlwind. The standing grain has no heads; it shall yield no flour; if it were to yield, strangers would devour it. ⁸Israel is swallowed up; already they are among the nations as a useless vessel. ⁹For they have gone up to Assyria, a wild donkey wandering alone; Ephraim has hired lovers. (Hos 8:1–9)

Through the prophet Hosea, God revealed how Israel broke the covenant that he made with them. Verse 2, "Because they have transgressed my covenant and rebelled against my law," clearly identifies how Israel transgressed the Mosaic covenant of law, and this transgression became the foundation of God's judgment against the northern kingdom of Israel. Verses 8 and 9 demonstrate how God executed the curses of the covenant and drove survivors of the Assyrian military campaign into Assyrian captivity. As the covenant community of Israel were scattered across the Assyrian Empire, they became *the old covenant diaspora* out of the curse of the God of Israel.

Here, we need to explore the prophetic formula of *the day of judgment* against the Israelites who broke the Mosaic covenant of law. God raised Amos to prophesy when Jeroboam son of Jehoash ruled as the king of Israel. Amos predicted the day of judgment against Israel.[7] In doing so, he designated the prophetic formula of "the day of the Lord" (יוֹם יְהוָה) which signified the day of God's judgment:

> [18]*Woe to you who desire the day of the LORD! Why would you have the day of the LORD? It is darkness, and not light,* [19]*as if a* man fled from a lion, and a bear met him, or went into the house and leaned his hand against the wall, and a serpent bit him. [20]*Is not the day of the LORD darkness, and not light, and gloom with no brightness in it?* [21]"I hate, I despise your feasts, and I take no delight in your solemn assemblies. [22]Even though you offer me your burnt offerings and grain offerings, I will not accept them; and the peace offerings of your fattened animals, I will not look upon them. [23]Take away from me the noise of your songs; to the melody of your harps I will not listen. [24]But let justice roll down like waters, and righteousness like an ever-flowing stream. [25]"Did you bring to me sacrifices and offerings during the forty years in the wilderness, O house of Israel? [26]You shall take up Sikkuth your king, and Kiyyun your star-god—your

---

7. Against the modern critical scholarship which rejects the predictive element of the prophets' prophecy, Vos rightly recognizes that one of the prophetic roles is to predict future events under the inspiration of the Holy Spirit: "Prophecy is a factor of continuity in the history of revelation, both through its retrospective and through its prospective attitude. Its preaching of repentance, and of the sin of apostasy from the norms of the past, links it to the preceding work of Jehovah for Israel in the patriarchal and Mosaic periods. Through its predictive elements it anticipates the continuity with the future. Although the name 'prophet' may not mean 'foreteller,' none the less foretelling is an essential part in the prophet's task. The prophets themselves emphasize this so much that one cannot consider it to be incidental [Amos 3.7] . . . Eschatological interest is sometimes a species of comfort to the pious soul. For all these reasons it is a cheap modernizing tendency to belittle the predictive element in prophecy." Vos, *Biblical Theology*, 188.

images that you made for yourselves, ²⁷*and I will send you into
exile beyond Damascus," says the LORD, whose name is the God
of hosts.* (Amos 5:18–27)

Certainly, "the day of the Lord" (יוֹם יְהוָה) in verses 18 and 20 was
the prophecy of the day of the fall of the northern kingdom of Israel.
Verse 27 of "*and I will send you into exile beyond Damascus*" confirms
the close relationship between "the day of the Lord" and the fall of Israel.
Furthermore, in light of the progressive character of God's special revelation, "the day of the Lord" was the divine revelation of the coming of the
day of God's judgment against Israel, a people who failed to repent from
apostasy and idol worship.

As we observed, God used the Assyrian Empire to curse the northern kingdom of Israel. The northern kingdom of Israel fell causing survivors to disperse throughout the Assyrian Empire to form *the old covenant
diaspora.* However, God used another pagan empire, the Babylonian
Empire, to punish the Assyrian Empire which was used as a means to
pour out God's wrath against the covenant community. For example, the
prophet Isaiah prophesied that God would punish the Assyrian Empire:

> ⁵Ah, Assyria, the rod of my anger; the staff in their hands is
> my fury! ⁶Against a godless nation I send him, and against the
> people of my wrath I command him, to take spoil and seize
> plunder, and to tread them down like the mire of the streets.
> ⁷But he does not so intend, and his heart does not so think;
> but it is in his heart to destroy, and to cut off nations not a few;
> ⁸for he says: "Are not my commanders all kings? ⁹Is not Calno
> like Carchemish? Is not Hamath like Arpad? Is not Samaria like
> Damascus? ¹⁰As my hand has reached to the kingdoms of the
> idols, whose carved images were greater than those of Jerusalem
> and Samaria, ¹¹shall I not do to Jerusalem and her idols as I
> have done to Samaria and her images?" ¹²When the Lord has
> finished all his work on Mount Zion and on Jerusalem, he will
> punish the speech of the arrogant heart of the king of Assyria
> and the boastful look in his eyes. (Isa 10:5–12)[8]

8. Adopting the historical critical reading of the book of Isaiah, growing numbers of evangelical scholars adopt between "Isaiah of Jerusalem" and "Second Isaiah
(or Deutero-Isaiah)," separating between Isaiah 1–39 and Isaiah 40–66. For example,
Longman and Dillard, representing the Longman and Dillard School, argue that Isaiah
wrote chapters 1–39 while another prophet during the exile wrote chapters 40–66.
In doing so, they mar the singular authorship of Isaiah and the unity of the book:
"Recognizing that the setting of Deuteronomy 34 requires an author living later than

Once again, God's oracle came to Isaiah, noting that "I will break the Assyrian in my land, and on my mountains trample him underfoot" (v. 25). This prophecy suggests that God would wage his holy war against the Assyrian armies when they invade the land of Judah:

> 24The LORD of hosts has sworn: "As I have planned, so shall it be, and as I have purposed, so shall it stand, 25that I will break the Assyrian in my land, and on my mountains trample him underfoot; and his yoke shall depart from them, and his burden from their shoulder." 26This is the purpose that is purposed concerning the whole earth, and this is the hand that is stretched out over all the nations. 27For the LORD of hosts has purposed, and who will annul it? His hand is stretched out, and who will turn it back? (Isa 14:24–27)

Yahweh's oracle of judgment against the Assyrian Empire is much more clear and definite when he pronounces that "I will break the Assyrian in my land, and on my mountains trample him underfoot; and his yoke shall depart from them, and his burden from their shoulder" (v. 25). This verse predicts that Yahweh will curse the Assyrian armies in the promised land when they wage the war against the southern kingdom of Judah. The oracle was fulfilled later as Isaiah recorded the historic event when Sennacherib king of Assyria waged a military campaign "against all the fortified cities of Judah" during "the fourth year of King Hezekiah" (Isa 36:1—37:38). The city of Jerusalem was surrounded by the Assyrian armies, a hopeless situation for the city. However, at this critical moment, *the angel of the Lord* intruded and waged a holy war against the Assyrian armies:

> 30"And this shall be the sign for you: this year you shall eat what grows of itself, and in the second year what springs from that. Then in the third year sow and reap, and plant vineyards, and eat their fruit. 31And the surviving remnant of the house of

---

Moses, the author traditionally assigned the book, is not materially different from recognizing that the background of Isaiah 40—66 presumes an author living during the exile. Isaiah is not mentioned in the second half of the book. However, the reality of prophetic inspiration is not thereby eliminated: an author living later in the exile foresaw through divine inspiration what God was about to do through Cyrus, just as Isaiah foresaw what God would soon do with Tiglath-Pileser III. . . . This later author saw in Isaiah's prophecies of exile and a remnant events that were transpiring in his own day, and he wrote to develop and apply Isaiah's preaching to his fellow exiles. Although the anonymity of this great prophet is a problem, it is no more unusual than the anonymity of the historical books of the book of Hebrews." Longman and Dillard, *Introduction to the Old Testament*, 303, 311.

Judah shall again take root downward and bear fruit upward. [32]For out of Jerusalem shall go a remnant, and out of Mount Zion a band of survivors. The zeal of the LORD of hosts will do this. [33]"Therefore thus says the LORD concerning the king of Assyria: He shall not come into this city or shoot an arrow there or come before it with a shield or cast up a siege mound against it. [34]By the way that he came, by the same he shall return, and he shall not come into this city, declares the LORD. [35]For I will defend this city to save it, for my own sake and for the sake of my servant David." [36]*And the angel of the LORD went out and struck down a hundred and eighty-five thousand in the camp of the Assyrians. And when people arose early in the morning, behold, these were all dead bodies.* [37]Then Sennacherib king of Assyria departed and returned home and lived at Nineveh. [38]And as he was worshiping in the house of Nisroch his god, Adrammelech and Sharezer, his sons, struck him down with the sword. And after they escaped into the land of Ararat, Esarhaddon his son reigned in his place. (Isa 37:30–38)

As *the angel of the Lord* (מַלְאַךְ יְהוָה) waged a holy war against the Assyrian armies, "a hundred and eighty-five thousand in the camp of the Assyrians" were struck down.[9] In fact, it was God's defense of the holy city, the earthly visible city of the kingdom of God, against the Assyrian armies who represented the power of the kingdom of Satan. Moreover, God remembered the promise of the Davidic covenant, which he promised with his sworn oath that the kingdom of David, succeeded and consummated in Jesus Christ, would be forever.

Later, God announced his oracle against Nineveh, the capital of the Assyrian Kingdom, through the prophet Nahum (Nah 1:1—3:19). The highlight of the fall of Nineveh was vividly prophesied:

[5]He remembers his officers; they stumble as they go, they hasten to the wall; the siege tower is set up. [6]The river gates are opened; the palace melts away; [7]its mistress is stripped; she is carried off, her slave girls lamenting, moaning like doves and beating

---

9. Calvin interprets "the angel of the Lord" as "a single angel" whom God used to execute his judgment, protecting Jerusalem "for the safety of the Church" from Assyrians: "Yet it is more probable, and agrees better with the words of the Prophet, that a single angel was commissioned to execute this judgment, as in the ancient redemption an angel passed through the hole of Egypt to slay the first-born. (Exod. xii. 29.) Although God sometimes executes his vengeance by means of evil angels, yet he chose one of his willing servants, that by means of him he might provide for the safety of the Church." Calvin, *Isaiah*, 37:36, in *Calvin's Commentaries*.

their breasts. [8]Nineveh is like a pool whose waters run away. "Halt! Halt!" they cry, but none turns back. [9]Plunder the silver, plunder the gold! There is no end of the treasure or of the wealth of all precious things. [10]Desolate! Desolation and ruin! Hearts melt and knees tremble; anguish is in all loins; all faces grow pale! [11]Where is the lions' den, the feeding place of the young lions, where the lion and lioness went, where his cubs were, with none to disturb? [12]The lion tore enough for his cubs and strangled prey for his lionesses; he filled his caves with prey and his dens with torn flesh. [13]Behold, I am against you, declares the LORD of hosts, and I will burn your chariots in smoke, and the sword shall devour your young lions. I will cut off your prey from the earth, and the voice of your messengers shall no longer be heard. (Nah 2:5–13)

As Nahum prophesied the fall of Nineveh, the Assyrian Empire already conquered and destroyed the Egyptian city of Thebes. In light of the historic event, he prophesied that Nineveh will follow a similar fate as Thebes (Nah 3:8–11). After drawing a comparative analogy between Thebes and Nineveh, Nahum again ends with his prophecy about the fall of Nineveh with graphic images and description of its final days:

[12]All your fortresses are like fig trees with first-ripe figs- if shaken they fall into the mouth of the eater. [13]Behold, your troops are women in your midst. The gates of your land are wide open to your enemies; fire has devoured your bars. [14]Draw water for the siege; strengthen your forts; go into the clay; tread the mortar; take hold of the brick mold! [15]There will the fire devour you; the sword will cut you off. It will devour you like the locust. Multiply yourselves like the locust; multiply like the grasshopper! [16]You increased your merchants more than the stars of the heavens. The locust spreads its wings and flies away. [17]Your princes are like grasshoppers, your scribes like clouds of locusts settling on the fences in a day of cold- when the sun rises, they fly away; no one knows where they are. [18]Your shepherds are asleep, O king of Assyria; your nobles slumber. Your people are scattered on the mountains with none to gather them. [19]There is no easing your hurt; your wound is grievous. All who hear the news about you clap their hands over you. For upon whom has not come your unceasing evil? (Nah 3:12–19)

From the perspective of the progressive character of God's special revelation, it is remarkable to observe how God revealed the fall of the capital city of Nineveh along with the Assyrian Empire through the prophet Zephaniah:

> **13***And he will stretch out his hand against the north and destroy Assyria, and he will make Nineveh a desolation, a dry waste like the desert.* **14**Herds shall lie down in her midst, all kinds of beasts; even the owl and the hedgehog shall lodge in her capitals; a voice shall hoot in the window; devastation will be on the threshold; for her cedar work will be laid bare. **15**This is the exultant city that lived securely, that said in her heart, "I am, and there is no one else." What a desolation she has become, a lair for wild beasts! Everyone who passes by her hisses and shakes his fist. (Zeph 2:13–15)

Verse 13 highlights how the God of Israel planned to destroy the entire Assyrian Empire and not just the capital city of Nineveh. In fact, the prophetic messages about the fall of Nineveh were fulfilled in 612 B.C when the Babylonian Empire defeated the Assyrian Empire. Later, the entire Assyrian Empire fell due to the military power of the Babylonian Empire in 609 B.C.[10] Since then, the Babylonian Empire became a dominant military and political power in the ancient Near East. From the rise and fall of the Assyrian Empire, God demonstrated how the God of Israel is the only living God who is the Great King who rules the heavens and earth; he is the only Lord who has absolute sovereignty over the destiny of all earthly kingdoms and nations.

---

10. John Bright vividly describes the final days of the Assyrian Empire through the military campaign of "the Babylonians and Medes" as follows: "Within a few years Assyria was fighting for her life against the Babylonians and Medes. . . . Egyptian forces arrived in Mesopotamia in 616 in time to assist in checking Nabopolassar, who had advanced far up the Euphrates and administered to the Assyrians a serious defeat. But the Medes now began to take a decisive part. After various maneuvers, in 614 Cyaxares took Asshur, the ancient Assyrian capital, by storm. Nabopolassar, arriving on the scene too late to participate, concluded a formal treaty with him. Two years later (612) the allies assaulted Nineveh itself and, after a three months' siege, took it and destroyed it utterly; Sin-shar-ishkun perished in the debacle. Remnants of the Assyrian army under Asshur-uballit II retired westward to Haran where, with their back to the Egyptians, they endeavored to keep resistance alive. But in 610 the Babylonians and their allies took Haran, and Asshur-uballit with the wreckage of his forces fell back across the Euphrates into the arms of the Egyptians. An attempt (in 609) to retake Haran failed miserably. Assyria was finished." Bright, *History of Israel*, 315–16.

The Covenant Lawsuit and the Fall of
the Southern Kingdom of Judah

The inspired author of Kings ended the writings of the ancient history of Israel with the fall of the southern kingdom of Judah and the Babylonian exile (2 Kgs 25:1–30). Similarly, the writer of Chronicles ended the narrative of the ancient history of Israel with the fall of Jerusalem and the Babylonian captivity (2 Chr 36:11–23).[11] The prophet Jeremiah also recorded the historic event of the fall of Judah and the Babylonian captivity (Jer 52:1–34). The diverse perspectives of the fall of Jerusalem and the Babylonian captivity highlight the destructive and sad historic event.

The Chronicler sums up the poor spiritual condition of the king Zedekiah along with "all the officers of the priests and the people" in the southern kingdom of Judah as they faced God's imminent judgment:

> [11]Zedekiah was twenty-one years old when he began to reign, and he reigned eleven years in Jerusalem. [12]He did what was evil in the sight of the LORD his God. He did not humble himself

11. Reading Kings and Chronicles in light of a historical critical perspective, Rad denies a harmony of historical accounts and theology between the Kings of "the Deuteronomistic history" and "the Chronicler's historical work." In doing so, he abandons the redemptive historical nature and pattern as revealed in the ancient history of Israel: "A comparison of the Chronicler's historical work with the Deuteronomist's is difficult to carry into effect for the reason that the two works are so very different in purpose. The Deuteronomistic history was a great confession of guilt, for the construction of which the whole history of the monarchy was mustered. The Chronicler wrote in order to legitimate cultic offices founded by David, and in so doing he showed himself to be a representative of the messianic tradition as such. Nevertheless, the great difference in the understanding of the law in the two works calls for comparison. For the Deuteronomist, the law by which he assessed Israel along with her kings was the torah, that is, the summation of Jahweh's turning to Israel in salvation. On this revealed will of Jahweh as it had been formulated in Deuteronomy, Israel had made shipwreck. In the Chronicler too we find this spiritual understanding which still comprehends the law as a unity. But a very much more formal and external mode of reference is commoner, namely in the many cases where he speaks of the correspondence of a certain cultic usage with a canonical ritual regulation. Here a dubious understanding of the law is proclaimed. Is this still a law understood spiritually? Or is it not rather a very much more disjointed law, one which in fact has already become a matter of its letter, and which is composed of many ritual prescriptions taken absolutely? Here, understanding of the unity of the revelation of Jahweh is manifestly waning away. The case of the concept of election is still more dubious. . . . However to the Chronicler these specific acts of election were more important than the one act of the election of Israel. Is not this too a disjointed election, especially when we bear in mind that the Chronicler says nothing at all about the election of Israel—he does not even know of a Covenant Theology." Rad, *Old Testament Theology*, 1:352.

before Jeremiah the prophet, who spoke from the mouth of the LORD. **13**He also rebelled against King Nebuchadnezzar, who had made him swear by God. He stiffened his neck and hardened his heart against turning to the LORD, the God of Israel. **14**All the officers of the priests and the people likewise were exceedingly unfaithful, following all the abominations of the nations. And they polluted the house of the LORD that he had made holy in Jerusalem. (2 Chr 36:11–14)

God sent "his messengers" continuously to the kings and people of Judah to repent of their sins, but they mocked the various prophets who were "the messengers of God." In the end, "the wrath of the Lord" was poured out against the covenant community of Judah:

15The LORD, the God of their fathers, sent persistently to them by his messengers, because he had compassion on his people and on his dwelling place. **16**But they kept mocking the messengers of God, despising his words and scoffing at his prophets, until the wrath of the LORD rose against his people, until there was no remedy. (2 Chr 36:15–16)

Verse 15 highlights how God sent "his messengers" to his covenant people to repent of their sins and idol worship: "The LORD, the God of their fathers, sent persistently to them by his messengers, because he had compassion on his people and on his dwelling place." However, they did not listen to "the messengers of God." Here, we see the pattern of God's judgment against the covenant community under the Davidic covenant. When the covenant community fell into apostasy with idol worship and disobedience, God sent his messengers and spoke against them, pronouncing the covenant lawsuit based upon *the Mosaic covenant of law*. He then executed the judgment against the southern kingdom of Judah through the pagan empire of the Babylonian Kingdom. In doing so, he manifested his title the Great Heavenly Judge.

The Chronicler's indication of God's covenant lawsuit against the covenant community of Judah before his judgment is wondrously harmonious with the writings of Jeremiah the prophet. In a sense, it was the divine redemptive drama orchestrated by the sovereign God, inspiring the prophets and the author of Chronicles through the Holy Spirit:

The word that came to Jeremiah concerning all the people of Judah, in the fourth year of Jehoiakim the son of Josiah, king of Judah (that was the first year of Nebuchadnezzar king of Babylon), **2**which Jeremiah the prophet spoke to all the people of

Judah and all the inhabitants of Jerusalem: ³"For twenty-three years, from the thirteenth year of Josiah the son of Amon, king of Judah, to this day, the word of the LORD has come to me, and I have spoken persistently to you, but you have not listened. ⁴You have neither listened nor inclined your ears to hear, although the LORD persistently sent to you all his servants the prophets, ⁵saying, 'Turn now, every one of you, from his evil way and evil deeds, and dwell upon the land that the LORD has given to you and your fathers from of old and forever. ⁶Do not go after other gods to serve and worship them, or provoke me to anger with the work of your hands. Then I will do you no harm.' ⁷Yet you have not listened to me, declares the LORD, that you might provoke me to anger with the work of your hands to your own harm. (Jer 25:1–7)

Knowing that the covenant community of Judah would not repent of their apostasy, Jeremiah predicted that God would execute his judgment against the southern kingdom of Judah. Some of the survivors would experience the Babylonian captivity for seventy years as detailed in verses 8–14:

⁸"Therefore thus says the LORD of hosts: Because you have not obeyed my words, ⁹behold, I will send for all the tribes of the north, declares the LORD, and for Nebuchadnezzar the king of Babylon, my servant, and I will bring them against this land and its inhabitants, and against all these surrounding nations. I will devote them to destruction, and make them a horror, a hissing, and an everlasting desolation. ¹⁰Moreover, I will banish from them the voice of mirth and the voice of gladness, the voice of the bridegroom and the voice of the bride, the grinding of the millstones and the light of the lamp. ¹¹*This whole land shall become a ruin and a waste, and these nations shall serve the king of Babylon seventy years.* ¹²Then after seventy years are completed, I will punish the king of Babylon and that nation, the land of the Chaldeans, for their iniquity, declares the LORD, making the land an everlasting waste. ¹³I will bring upon that land all the words that I have uttered against it, everything written in this book, which Jeremiah prophesied against all the nations. ¹⁴For many nations and great kings shall make slaves even of them, and I will recompense them according to their deeds and the work of their hands." (Jer 25:8–14)

The apex of Yahweh's oracle of judgment against the southern kingdom of Judah comes with the bold and chilling prediction as described in verse 11. Jeremiah's prophecy was precisely fulfilled as Jerusalem fell in 586 B.C. The fulfilled prophecy led some survivors into the Babylonian exile for seventy years.[12]

We may ask whether there is written evidence of a covenantal background to execute God's judgment against the southern kingdom of Judah. It is very important to find and verify the background of God's covenant lawsuit. In fact, God revealed through the prophet Jeremiah that *the people of Judah broke their covenant with God.* It was the covenantal background of God's covenant lawsuit and subsequent judgment that stood against them. In fact, the entire book of Jeremiah is God's covenant lawsuit against the covenant community of Judah, including Israel who broke the covenant and fell into judgment according to the principles of dual sanctions such as blessings and curses:

> The word that came to Jeremiah from the LORD: [2]"Hear the words of this covenant, and speak to the men of Judah and the inhabitants of Jerusalem. [3]You shall say to them, Thus says the

---

12. Sohn interprets and understands the covenantal relationship between Yahweh and Israel in light of a marriage metaphor which covers "engagement, wedding, married life, divorce, and remarriage." He interprets Yahweh's judgment with death and the Babylonian exile against Israel as "the metaphor of YHWH's divorce of Israel" which is a very insightful observation: "As we have seen, YHWH wrote a certificate of divorce and gave it to Israel, and he stripped her of her garments and exposed her nakedness; he forsook and forgot her. Obviously these images are borrowed from the practice of human divorce. The series of historical events such as Israel's breaking his covenant and being cast out of Canaan and her Babylonian captivities, etc. are delineated in terms of the metaphor of YHWH's divorce of Israel. As covenant making was portrayed in terms of the imagery of marriage, covenant breaking was portrayed in terms of the imagery of divorce. Particularly, it is very significant that YHWH's rejection of Israel as his chosen nation and the subsequent fall of Israel are described through the metaphor of divorce." Sohn, *YHWH, the Husband of Israel*, 61–62.

In addition, Sohn explores the idea of election in the covenantal relationship between Yahweh and Israel. He argues that it is closely related and tied to the metaphor of marriage in the life of ancient Israel: "Since certain election terms are borrowed from marriage terminology, we can safely say, for example, that the people of Israel tried to explain the idea of election from the perspective of human marriage. They understood Yahweh's choosing Israel to be Yahweh's taking Israel as his bride. Since there is no more intimate social metaphor than that of a husband's choosing his bride, it is evident that Yahweh's choosing Israel was considered to be indicative of a close, familial relationship of great import. In addition to this, both a syntactical comparison of the marriage/election formulae and a philological analysis of their Semitic cognates confirm this thesis in detail. With this as a foundation, we can expand our understanding of the related themes of covenant, rejection, remnant, and restoration." Sohn, *Divine Election of Israel*, 5–6.

LORD, the God of Israel: Cursed be the man who does not hear the words of this covenant [4]that I commanded your fathers when I brought them out of the land of Egypt, from the iron furnace, saying, Listen to my voice, and do all that I command you. So shall you be my people, and I will be your God, [5]that I may confirm the oath that I swore to your fathers, to give them a land flowing with milk and honey, as at this day." Then I answered, "So be it, LORD." [6]And the LORD said to me, "Proclaim all these words in the cities of Judah and in the streets of Jerusalem: Hear the words of this covenant and do them. [7]For I solemnly warned your fathers when I brought them up out of the land of Egypt, warning them persistently, even to this day, saying, Obey my voice. [8]Yet they did not obey or incline their ear, but everyone walked in the stubbornness of his evil heart. Therefore I brought upon them all the words of this covenant, which I commanded them to do, but they did not." [9]Again the LORD said to me, "A conspiracy exists among the men of Judah and the inhabitants of Jerusalem. [10]*They have turned back to the iniquities of their forefathers, who refused to hear my words. They have gone after other gods to serve them. The house of Israel and the house of Judah have broken my covenant that I made with their fathers.* [11]Therefore, thus says the LORD, behold, I am bringing disaster upon them that they cannot escape. Though they cry to me, I will not listen to them. (Jer 11:1–11)

Yahweh confirmed that he granted the promised land to the covenant descendents of Abraham, Isaac, and Jacob as he made a sworn oath to the Abrahamic covenant. Verse 5 verifies Yahweh's word of confirmation to the prophet Jeremiah that the inheritance of the promised land was God's grant to the covenant community, based on the promise of the Abrahamic covenant. To be sure, the ongoing echo of "*The house of Israel and the house of Judah have broken my covenant that I made with their fathers*" (v. 10) goes back to Mount Sinai where God made a covenant with Israel through the prophet Moses after the miraculous event of the Exodus (Exod 19–24). In that regard, Yahweh's word to Jeremiah was about *breaking the covenant* by the covenant community of Judah including Israel. At that time, God already executed his judgment against the northern kingdom of Israel through the Assyrian military in 722 B.C.

[17]Therefore, thus says the LORD: You have not obeyed me by proclaiming liberty, every one to his brother and to his neighbor; behold, I proclaim to you liberty to the sword, to pestilence, and to famine, declares the LORD. I will make you a horror to all

the kingdoms of the earth. [18]And the men who transgressed my covenant and did not keep the terms of the covenant that they made before me, I will make them like the calf that they cut in two and passed between its parts— [19]the officials of Judah, the officials of Jerusalem, the eunuchs, the priests, and all the people of the land who passed between the parts of the calf. [20]And I will give them into the hand of their enemies and into the hand of those who seek their lives. Their dead bodies shall be food for the birds of the air and the beasts of the earth. [21]And Zedekiah king of Judah and his officials I will give into the hand of their enemies and into the hand of those who seek their lives, into the hand of the army of the king of Babylon which has withdrawn from you. [22]Behold, I will command, declares the LORD, and will bring them back to this city. And they will fight against it and take it and burn it with fire. I will make the cities of Judah a desolation without inhabitant. (Jer 34:17–22)

Yahweh explains the background of his covenant lawsuit against the people of Judah and the prophecy of the subsequent judgment. We remember the covenant ratification ceremony of the Abrahamic covenant in Genesis 15:1–20. Verse 17 provides a wondrous pictorial language of the highlights of the ceremony: "when the sun had gone down and it was dark, behold, a smoking fire pot and a flaming torch passed between these pieces." The reference to "a smoking fire pot and a flaming torch passed between these pieces" shows us the visible reality of the fiery phenomena of God's shining glory. It was the awesome scenery of God's sworn oath before a mere, undeserving sinner Abraham. Yet, God made a sworn oath by passing in the midst of the cursed and torn animal; an oath which suggests that all the promises of God to Abraham will progressively and surely be fulfilled in the foregoing redemptive history.

Having that in mind, we need to observe a contrasting element of the covenant oath which was made by the people of Judah in Jeremiah 34:17–22. Verses 18 and 19 provide a very good idea of God's covenant lawsuit and the subsequent display of covenantal curses. Moreover, verse 19 states, "The officials of Judah, the officials of Jerusalem, the eunuchs, the priests, and all the people of the land who passed between the parts of the calf." This verse highlights that the covenant community of Judah made a sworn oath to the covenant in the presence of God. Of course, it was not a visible reflection of the covenant ratification ceremony of the Abrahamic covenant but the Mosaic covenant (Exod 19–24). In that sense, as we have seen through Jeremiah's prophecy, God claimed his covenant lawsuit based on the Mosaic covenant of law (Exod 19–24) which was renewed at the plain of Moab (Deut 1:1—34:12) and Shechem (Josh 24:1–33), and later with the covenant people of Judah.

Here, we need to go back to the original context of the Mosaic covenant on Mount Sinai, made between God and Israel through the prophet Moses. God spoke to Israel through Moses about the dual sanctions of blessings and curses. The blessings of the covenant are briefly summarized in Leviticus 26:1–13 while the curses of the covenant are graphically and extensively described in Leviticus 26:14–45. Surprisingly, God anticipated Israel's disobedience and apostasy. Accordingly, God predicted that he would display his covenantal curses against Israel and that eventually some of the survivors would be expelled from the promised land:

> 27"But if in spite of this you will not listen to me, but walk contrary to me, 28then I will walk contrary to you in fury, and I myself will discipline you sevenfold for your sins. 29You shall eat the flesh of your sons, and you shall eat the flesh of your daughters. 30And I will destroy your high places and cut down your incense altars and cast your dead bodies upon the dead bodies of your idols, and my soul will abhor you. 31And I will lay your cities waste and will make your sanctuaries desolate, and I will not smell your pleasing aromas. 32And I myself will devastate the land, so that your enemies who settle in it shall be appalled at it. 33And I will scatter you among the nations, and I will unsheathe the sword after you, and your land shall be a desolation, and your cities shall be a waste. (Lev 26:27–33)

Yet, God told Israel that he would restore the exiled covenant community back to the promised land *if* they sincerely repent of their sins. In doing so, he would remember *the promise of the Abrahamic covenant* when he forgives their sins and restores them back to the promised land:

> 40"But if they confess their iniquity and the iniquity of their fathers in their treachery that they committed against me, and also in walking contrary to me, 41so that I walked contrary to them and brought them into the land of their enemies- if then their uncircumcised heart is humbled and they make amends for their iniquity, 42*then I will remember my covenant with Jacob, and I will remember my covenant with Isaac and my covenant with Abraham, and I will remember the land.* 43But the land shall be abandoned by them and enjoy its Sabbaths while it lies desolate without them, and they shall make amends for their

iniquity, because they spurned my rules and their soul abhorred my statutes. **44**Yet for all that, when they are in the land of their enemies, I will not spurn them, neither will I abhor them so as to destroy them utterly and break my covenant with them, for I am the LORD their God. **45***But I will for their sake remember the covenant with their forefathers, whom I brought out of the land of Egypt in the sight of the nations, that I might be their God: I am the LORD."* (Lev 26:40–45)

God is emphatic when he spoke, "Then I will remember my covenant with Jacob, and I will remember my covenant with Isaac and my covenant with Abraham, and I will remember the land" (v. 42). It is a clear confirmation that God would forgive the sins of Israel and restore them back to the promised land *if* they would sincerely repent, as promised by the Abrahamic covenant. Furthermore, we need to pay attention to the end of God's speech about the curses of the covenant which we see in verse 45: "But I will for their sake remember the covenant with their forefathers, whom I brought out of the land of Egypt in the sight of the nations, that I might be their God: I am the LORD." Once again, God's speech affirms and verifies that the restoration of the exiled covenant community to the promised land will not be based upon the Mosaic covenant of law *but the promise of the Abrahamic covenant.*[13]

After forty years in the wilderness, God renewed the Mosaic covenant at the plain of Moab, as written in the book of Deuteronomy (Deut 1:1—34:12). Through Moses' speech, God laid out the dual sanctions of blessings and curses once again. For instance, Moses spoke the blessings of the covenant in Deuteronomy 28:1–14. Afterwards, he laid out the contents of the curses of the covenant in Deuteronomy 28:15–68. In doing so, anticipating the disobedience and apostasy of Israel, Moses prophesied that God would curse Israel and they would experience the

13. Robertson demonstrates his insightful analysis that the prophets' prophecy about Israel's fall and restoration was based upon the prophecy of the Mosaic law, although more specific data was added in light of the progressive character of God's special revelation: "So when the prophets explain to Israel its moral duties, they introduce nothing new. They also expound the portions of the law that had been misunderstood. In terms of threats of judgment, the prophets describe in detail what the law had spoken in general terms. So Leviticus 26 speaks of the coming day when the life of the disobedient nation will hang on a thread, while the prophets go beyond the law and specify Assyria and Babylon as the divine agents of judgment. In terms of promised blessings, the law declares that God will bring back to their land even though he has scattered them (Deut. 30:4). But the prophets are more specific in announcing that the return will occur within seventy years." Robertson, *Christ of the Prophets*, 79.

fall and exile from the promised land (Deut 28:20–68). In the end, Moses, inspired by the Holy Spirit, emphasized that Israel would be exiled *if* they disobey the Mosaic covenant of law:

> And the LORD will scatter you among all peoples, from one end of the earth to the other, and there you shall serve other gods of wood and stone, which neither you nor your fathers have known. [65]And among these nations you shall find no respite, and there shall be no resting place for the sole of your foot, but the LORD will give you there a trembling heart and failing eyes and a languishing soul. [66]Your life shall hang in doubt before you. Night and day you shall be in dread and have no assurance of your life. [67]In the morning you shall say, 'If only it were evening!' and at evening you shall say, 'If only it were morning!' because of the dread that your heart shall feel, and the sights that your eyes shall see. (Deut 28:64–67)

Moses' prophecy is that Israel would become *the old covenant diaspora* outside of the promised land through God's curse when he proclaims, "And the LORD will scatter you among all peoples, from one end of the earth to the other, and there you shall serve other gods of wood and stone, which neither you nor your fathers have known" (v. 64). Further, Moses predicted that God would restore the covenant community back to the promised land when they repent of their sins sincerely in the midst of their exile:

> And when all these things come upon you, the blessing and the curse, which I have set before you, and you call them to mind among all the nations where the LORD your God has driven you, [2]and return to the LORD your God, you and your children, and obey his voice in all that I command you today, with all your heart and with all your soul, [3]then the LORD your God will restore your fortunes and have compassion on you, and he will gather you again from all the peoples where the LORD your God has scattered you. [4]If your outcasts are in the uttermost parts of heaven, from there the LORD your God will gather you, and from there he will take you. [5]And the LORD your God will bring you into the land that your fathers possessed, that you may possess it. And he will make you more prosperous and numerous than your fathers. [6]And the LORD your God will circumcise your heart and the heart of your offspring, so that you will love the LORD your God with all your heart and with all your soul, that you may live. [7]And the LORD your God will put all these curses on your foes and enemies who persecuted

you. [8]And you shall again obey the voice of the LORD and keep all his commandments that I command you today. [9]The LORD your God will make you abundantly prosperous in all the work of your hand, in the fruit of your womb and in the fruit of your cattle and in the fruit of your ground. For the LORD will again take delight in prospering you, as he took delight in your fathers, [10]when you obey the voice of the LORD your God, to keep his commandments and his statutes that are written in this Book of the Law, when you turn to the LORD your God with all your heart and with all your soul. (Deut 30:1–10)

Moses prophesied that the exiled covenant community would return from the pagan nations when they repent sincerely of their sins before the God of Israel. He emphatically highlighted the return of the exiled covenant community as he proclaimed, "The LORD your God will restore your fortunes and have compassion on you, and he will gather you again from all the peoples where the LORD your God has scattered you" (v. 3). Moreover, Moses' prophecy includes how God would punish the pagan nations who persecute Israel as summarized in verse 7: "And the LORD your God will put all these curses on your foes and enemies who persecuted you." Moses' prophecy against the pagan nations was fulfilled through the fall of the Assyrian Empire in 609 B.C. and the Babylonian Empire in 539 B.C., and others.

Meanwhile, Daniel became the member of the Babylonian exile "in the third year of the reign of Jehoiakim king of Judah" with the military campaign of "Nebuchadnezzar king of Babylon" around 605 B.C. Daniel was there with his friends, "Hananiah, Mishael, and Azariah of the tribe of Judah" (Dan 1:1–7).[14]

---

14. Reading the book of Daniel in light of a radical historical criticism, Ehrman denies Daniel as "a historic figure." He sees Daniel 1–6 as fictional stories while he understands Daniel 7–12 as "apocalyptic visions." In doing so, he plainly rejects Daniel's authorship: "Daniel is not a historical figure who makes real-time proclamations to the people of Israel in light of their dire situation and almost certain coming destruction. The first six chapters of the book are collection of short stories about a wise young man Daniel, taken to Babylon after the destruction of Jerusalem. The final six chapters contain a number of apocalyptic visions that Daniel allegedly had. There are good reasons for thinking that these two portions of the book originated separately from one another as different traditions associated with this person Daniel, and they were put together only after both had been circulation for a time. One of the most obvious reasons for thinking so is that they are in fact of different genres of literature. . . . Within Daniel 7–12, we find the first full-fledged instances of Jewish 'apocalypses,' a genre I will define at the appropriate time. For now, we will focus on Daniel 1–6, the

While Daniel was reading the book of Jeremiah, he realized that the Babylonian exile could last seventy years which ended in 539 B.C., the year the Babylonian Empire was overthrown by the Persian Empire (Dan 9:1–2). Understanding this, Daniel prayed with "fasting and sackcloth and ashes," and confessed his own sins along with the sins of "all Israel" (Dan 9:3–19). Once again, Daniel's prayer confirms that God sent forth prophets for the repentance of the sins of the covenant community of Israel and Judah. Nevertheless, they did not repent of their sins which included idol worship. After all, God executed his judgment after the period of his covenant lawsuit through the prophets. And some survivors of Judah went to the Babylonian exile for seventy years:

> 6*We have not listened to your servants the prophets, who spoke in your name to our kings, our princes, and our fathers, and to all the people of the land.* 7To you, O Lord, belongs righteousness, but to us open shame, as at this day, to the men of Judah, to the inhabitants of Jerusalem, and to all Israel, those who are near and those who are far away, in all the lands to which you have driven them, because of the treachery that they have committed against you. 8To us, O Lord, belongs open shame, to our kings, to our princes, and to our fathers, because we have sinned against you. 9To the Lord our God belong mercy and forgiveness, for we have rebelled against him 10and have not obeyed the voice of the LORD our God by walking in his laws, which he set before us by his servants the prophets. 11*All Israel has transgressed your law and turned aside, refusing to obey your voice. And the curse and oath that are written in the Law of Moses the servant of God have been poured out upon us, because we have sinned against him.* 12He has confirmed his words, which he spoke against us and against our rulers who ruled us, by bringing upon us a great calamity. For under the whole heaven there has not been done anything like what has been done against Jerusalem. 13As it is written in the Law of Moses, all this calamity has come upon us; yet we have not entreated the favor of the LORD our God, turning from our iniquities and gaining insight by your truth. 14Therefore the LORD has kept ready the calamity and has brought it upon us, for the LORD our God is righteous in all the works that he has done, and we have not obeyed his voice.

---

short stories associated with this famous, though fictional, character and several of his close friends in their lives together in a foreign land. These stories are obviously post-exilic as they are all about life in exile. They are probably to be dated to the fourth or third century B.C.E." Ehrman, *Bible*, 199.

15And now, O Lord our God, who brought your people out of the land of Egypt with a mighty hand, and have made a name for yourself, as at this day, we have sinned, we have done wickedly. (Dan 9:6–15)

Once again, we can verify the pattern of God's covenant lawsuit, sending out the different prophets when the covenant community continuously disobeyed God's laws with idol worship and God's subsequent judgment upon the covenant community and the promised land through Daniel's prayer. Verse 6 briefly summarizes the history of God's covenant lawsuit, as he sent his "servants and the prophets." Reflecting the falls of the northern kingdom of Israel and southern kingdom of Judah and the Babylonian exiles for seventy years, Daniel confessed that in fact it was the result of breaking of the Mosaic covenant of law, inaugurated on Mount Sinai (Exod 19–24). Through verse 11, which states that "all Israel has transgressed your law and turned aside, refusing to obey your voice. And the curse and oath that are written in the Law of Moses the servant of God have been poured out upon us, because we have sinned against him," Daniel highlights that "all Israel" violated God's law, breaking the Mosaic covenant of law and the curses of the covenant were poured out upon the covenant community and the promised land. Moreover, Daniel, experiencing the Babylonian exile for seventy years, emphasizes God's covenantal curses upon Jerusalem with the vivid description of the city in verse 12.

While Daniel was praying, God sent the angel Gabriel to reveal the "seventy weeks" which prophesied the future redemptive and covenant history, beginning from 539 B.C. which was the year of the return for the people of Judah to the promised land after seventy years captivity:

24"Seventy weeks are decreed about your people and your holy city, to finish the transgression, to put an end to sin, and to atone for iniquity, to bring in everlasting righteousness, to seal both vision and prophet, and to anoint a most holy place. 25Know therefore and understand that from the going out of the word to restore and build Jerusalem to the coming of an anointed one, a prince, there shall be seven weeks. Then for sixty-two weeks it shall be built again with squares and moat, but in a troubled time. 26And after the sixty-two weeks, an anointed one shall be cut off and shall have nothing. And the people of the prince who is to come shall destroy the city and the sanctuary. Its end shall come with a flood, and to the end there shall be war. Desolations

are decreed. [27]And he shall make a strong covenant with many
for one week, and for half of the week he shall put an end to
sacrifice and offering. And on the wing of abominations shall
come one who makes desolate, until the decreed end is poured
out on the desolator." (Dan 9:24–27)

As a reminder, "seventy weeks" suggests that God revealed the future
redemptive and covenantal history, beginning from 539 B.C. through the
angel Gabriel.[15] Verse 25 prophecies the decree of King Cyrus of Persia
in 539 B.C, return to Jerusalem from the Babylonian exile, the rebuilding
of the temple and Jerusalem, and "the coming of an anointed one" which
is the first coming of the Messiah. In fact, there is a beautiful harmony
between the announcement of the angel Gabriel in Daniel and the written testimony of the book of Ezra.

The introduction of the book of Ezra provides a historical background for the angel Gabriel's announcement of the beginning of "seventy weeks" in Daniel 9:24–27:

In the first year of Cyrus king of Persia, that the word of the
LORD by the mouth of Jeremiah might be fulfilled, the LORD
stirred up the spirit of Cyrus king of Persia, so that he made
a proclamation throughout all his kingdom and also put it in
writing: [2]"Thus says Cyrus king of Persia: The LORD, the God
of heaven, has given me all the kingdoms of the earth, and he
has charged me to build him a house at Jerusalem, which is in
Judah. [3]Whoever is among you of all his people, may his God be
with him, and let him go up to Jerusalem, which is in Judah, and
rebuild the house of the LORD, the God of Israel- he is the God
who is in Jerusalem. [4]And let each survivor, in whatever place
he sojourns, be assisted by the men of his place with silver and
gold, with goods and with beasts, besides freewill offerings for
the house of God that is in Jerusalem." (Ezra 1:1–4)[16]

15. For a covenantal and redemptive historical reading with symbolical interpretation of "seventy weeks," see Jeon, *Biblical Theology*, 178–80; Kline, *God, Heaven and
Har Magedon*, 146–54.

16. John Bright provides a comprehensive historical background of the fall of
the Babylonian Empire in 539 B.C. through the military campaign of "the Persian
armies" and Cyrus' policy through "The Edict of Restoration" as follows: "The blow
was even then falling. The Persian armies were already massed on the frontier, and
with the coming of summer they fell to the attack. The situation was hopeless. Apparently desiring to concentrate all his forces both military and spiritual for the defense
of Babylon, Nabonidus brought the gods of outlying cities into the capital—a step
that succeeded in demoralizing the citizens whose gods had been taken away. The

Remarkably, Isaiah's prophecy identifies "Cyrus" king of Persia as the one who will be used by Yahweh to restore the exiled covenant community, temple and Jerusalem (Isa 44:24—45:25). The infallible prediction with the inspiration of the Holy Spirit came as follows:

> **24**Thus says the LORD, your Redeemer, who formed you from the womb: "I am the LORD, who made all things, who alone stretched out the heavens, who spread out the earth by myself, **25**who frustrates the signs of liars and makes fools of diviners, who turns wise men back and makes their knowledge foolish, **26**who confirms the word of his servant and fulfills the counsel of his messengers, who says of Jerusalem, 'She shall be inhabited,' and of the cities of Judah, 'They shall be built, and I will raise up their ruins'; **27**who says to the deep, 'Be dry; I will dry up your rivers'; **28**who says of Cyrus, 'He is my shepherd, and he shall fulfill all my purpose'; saying of Jerusalem, 'She shall be built,' and of the temple, 'Your foundation shall be laid.'" 45:1 Thus says the LORD to his anointed, to Cyrus, whose right hand I have grasped, to subdue nations before him and to loose the belts of kings, to open doors before him that gates may not be closed: (Isa 44:24—45:1)

Verse 28 precisely predicts that Yahweh will use "Cyrus" king of Persia to rebuild the temple and Jerusalem. Of course, it would be fulfilled in a distant future from the time of prophecy. Meanwhile, Isaiah 45: 1 predicts the conquering of different kingdoms, including the Babylonian kingdom, through the armies of Cyrus.[17]

---

decisive engagement took place at Opis on the Tigris, and was a crushing defeat for Babylon. Resistance collapsed. In October, 539, Gobryas took Babylon without a fight. Nabonidus, who had fled, was subsequently taken prisoner. A few weeks later Cyrus himself entered the city in triumph. According to his own inscription, he was welcomed as a liberator by the Babylonians, to whom he showed the utmost consideration. . . . In the first year of his reign in Babylon (538), Cyrus issued a decree ordering the restoration of the Jewish community and cult in Palestine. The Bible gives two reports of this in Ezra 1:2–4 and in ch. 6:3–5. The latter is part of a collection of Aramaic documents (Ezra 4:8 to 6:18) presumably preserved in the Temple and incorporated by the Chronicler in his work, the authenticity of which need not be questioned. It provides that the Temple be rebuilt and the expenses defrayed out of the royal treasury, lays down certain general specifications for the building (naturally enough, since the state was bearing the costs,) and directs that the vessels taken by Nebuchadnezzar be restored to their rightful place." Bright, *History of Israel*, 360–61.

17. As an exponent of radical historical critical methodology, Kugel explains that the presupposition of the historical critical methodology does not accept *the prophetic prediction* which will be fulfilled in the future. It is one of the reasons why liberal

Moreover, the announcement of the decree of Cyrus king of Persia in the book of Ezra also affirms the inerrancy and infallibility of the prophet Jeremiah's prophecy about the seventy-year Babylonian exile and return of the covenant community to the promised land:

> [11]This whole land shall become a ruin and a waste, and these nations shall serve the king of Babylon seventy years. [12]Then after seventy years are completed, I will punish the king of Babylon and that nation, the land of the Chaldeans, for their iniquity, declares the LORD, making the land an everlasting waste. [13]I will bring upon that land all the words that I have uttered against it, everything written in this book, which Jeremiah prophesied against all the nations. [14]For many nations and great kings shall make slaves even of them, and I will recompense them according to their deeds and the work of their hands. (Jer 25:11–14)

To be sure, God used Nebuchadnezzar the king of Babylon, and the military power of the Babylonian Empire, to pour out his covenantal wrath against the southern kingdom of Judah. It was also the fulfillment of Jeremiah's prophecy. Further, God punished the Babylonian Empire, through the Persian Empire as prophesied. As the Babylonian Empire ceded with God's judgment, the Babylonian exile also came to an end as Jeremiah predicted. As the end of the Babylonian exile was prophesied,

---

scholars designates Isaiah 40–66 as "Deutero-Isaiah," or "the second Isaiah" written about the two centuries later after Isaiah 1–39: "Scholars knew perfectly well that there *was* a time when the inhabitants of Judah had been exiled from their land: the time following the Babylonian destruction of Jerusalem in 586 BCE. The exiles had been forced to remain in Babylon until that country fell to the Persian army and Cyrus, the Persian king, issued his famous edict (538 BCE) allowing the Jews to go back to their old homeland. Now, the striking thing about the later chapters of Isaiah is that they actually mention Cyrus by name—twice, in fact. . . . Of course, a prophet might theoretically foresee events centuries before they happen. Still, what sense did it make for Isaiah in the eighth century to be telling his contemporaries about a king who would not come along until two hundred years later—and to be telling them about him without ever explaining who this 'Cyrus' might be, apparently assuming that people would just recognize the name? . . . Considering all such differences, many scholars began to consider the possibility that chapters 40—66 had actually been written some two hundred years *after* the eighth-century Isaiah—they must have been written by an anonymous Jew who lived precisely in the time of Cyrus, when the Babylonian exile was just coming to a close and when Israel's religion was fast becoming one of unequivocal monotheism. Of course, this idea was found to be disturbing to traditional Christian belief, since, as we have seen, passages from those chapters had played a crucial role in the New Testament and other early Christian writings; they seemed to offer no less than a way of interpreting Jesus' life and crucifixion as the fulfillment of a divine plan." Kugel, *How to Read the Bible*, 560–61.

the return of the covenant community to Jerusalem was also prophesied through Jeremiah:

> 36Now therefore thus says the LORD, the God of Israel, concerning this city of which you say, "It is given into the hand of the king of Babylon by sword, by famine, and by pestilence": 37Behold, I will gather them from all the countries to which I drove them in my anger and my wrath and in great indignation. I will bring them back to this place, and I will make them dwell in safety. 38And they shall be my people, and I will be their God. 39I will give them one heart and one way, that they may fear me forever, for their own good and the good of their children after them. 40I will make with them an everlasting covenant, that I will not turn away from doing good to them. And I will put the fear of me in their hearts, that they may not turn from me. 41I will rejoice in doing them good, and I will plant them in this land in faithfulness, with all my heart and all my soul. (Jer 32:36–41)

To be sure, Jeremiah was a member of the Babylonian exile which was the result of God's curse against the covenant community that disobeyed and broke the Mosaic covenant of law. In the midst of the darkest moments in the history of Israel, God promised Jeremiah that the exiled community would return to the promised land. He reminded Jeremiah that he would bless his people with the core promise of the covenant of grace as summarized by "and they shall be my people, and I will be their God" (v. 39). Moreover, God promised that he would make the new covenant which is "an everlasting covenant," as summed up in verse 40. As we confirm the wondrous harmony between the prophecy of the prophetic books and testimony of the historical books in the Old Testament, we stand in awe of the beautiful harmony of the grand and wondrous divine drama of redemptive and covenantal history orchestrated by God the Father, and sealed by the Holy Spirit. The prophecy anticipates the coming of the Son of God as the mediator of the new covenant.[18]

18. Edwards rightly highlights "admirable harmony" among the different books of the Old Testament in light of "the divine authority" which is an epistemological foundation for the proper interpretation and application of the Bible: "What has been said, affords a strong argument for the divine authority of the Old Testament, from that admirable harmony there is in them, whereby they all point to the same thing. For we may see by what has been said, how all the parts of the Old Testament, though written by so many different penmen, and in ages distant one from another, do all harmonize one with another; all agree in one, and all centre in the same thing, and that a future thing; an event which it was impossible any one of them should know but by divine revelation, even the future coming of Christ." Edwards, *History of the Work of Redemption*, 158.

Let us return to the proper interpretation and outlook of the prophecy of "seventy weeks" in Daniel 9:24–27.[19] "Seven weeks" and "sixty-two weeks" in verse 25 may be interpreted as *symbolic years*. In that sense, "seven weeks" was the period of building the Second Temple under Zerubbabel which spanned from 539 B.C to the rebuilding of Jerusalem. Afterwards, "sixty-two weeks" depicted the period which covered the completion of rebuilding the temple and Jerusalem up until the Messiah's sacrificial death as the mediator of the new covenant.[20]

"And he shall make a strong covenant with many for one week:" (v. 27a) is a prophecy of the New Covenant Age which covers the crucifixion of the Messiah as the covenant ratification ceremony of the new covenant to the second coming of Jesus Christ which will be the final day of the

---

19. Ryrie as a classical dispensationalist interprets "seventy weeks" in light of literal interpretation. In doing so, he sees "an interval" between "the first sixty-nine weeks of seven years" and "seventieth week of seven years." He locates the church age as the period of interval, identifying it as a parenthesis. And seventieth week is literal seven years which will mark "the Great Tribulation" for the seven year period: "The Tribulation actually begins with the signing of a covenant between the leader of the 'Federated States of Europe' and the Jewish people. This treaty will set in motion the events of the seventieth week (or seven years) of Daniel's prophecy. There is an interval of undetermined length between the first sixty-nine weeks of seven years each and the last or seventieth week of seven years.

We are living in that interval. It is the time in which God is forming the church, the body of Christ, by saving Jews and Gentiles alike. Since God has not yet finished this present program, the last week of the seventy has not yet begun. When it does, God will once again turn His attention in a special way to His people the Jews and to His holy city Jerusalem, as outlined in Daniel 9:24.

When this last period of seven years begins, 'He will make a firm covenant with the many for one week' (v.27). Who does the 'he' refer to? Grammatically it could refer either to Messiah (v.26) or to 'the prince who is to come,' who will probably be related to the people who destroyed Jerusalem in A.D. 70. The latter view is better, because usually the antecedent nearer to a pronoun is preferred and in this case it is the prince, not Messiah. Then too nothing in the record of Christ's life in any way connects Him with the making (and later breaking) of a seven-year covenant with the Jewish people." Ryrie, *Basic Theology*, 541.

20. Kline summarizes the symbolic interpretation of "the sixty-nine weeks" in verse 25 as follows: "The sixty-nine weeks leading up to Messiah-Ruler are divided into seven weeks and sixty-two weeks (v. 25a). The time of restoration (the Jubilee period of seven weeks) is thus distinguished from the subsequent time of declension (the sixty-two weeks). Dan 9:25b focuses on this seven week period of the restoration of Jerusalem, Daniel's immediate concern, promising the successful rebuilding of the temple-city in spite of adversaries (as later recorded in the historical accounts of 2 Chronicles, Ezra, and Nehemiah)." Kline, *God, Heaven and Har Magedon*, 149.

Lord.[21] "And for half of the week he shall put an end to sacrifice and offering" (v. 27b) emphasizes the period from the sacrificial death of the mediator of the new covenant to the final fall of Israel through which God executed his final judgment against the covenant community of Israel in the promised land through the military campaign of the Roman Empire. In doing so, God terminated the old covenant order in the promised land as well that which was inaugurated in the Mosaic covenant on Mount Sinai (Exod 19–24). Nevertheless, *the eschatological kingdom of God* was inaugurated with Jesus Christ's incarnation, public life, death, resurrection, ascension, session at the right hand of God the Father in heaven, and the Pentecost. Verse 27c, "And on the wing of abominations shall come one who makes desolate, until the decreed end is poured out on the desolator," depicts the period from the final fall of Israel at A.D. 70 until the day of the second coming of Jesus Christ which will be the day of the final judgment and Consummation, visibly separating the eternal kingdom of God from the kingdom of Satan.[22] In short, the seventieth

21. Kline provides a comprehensive covenantal outlook of verses 26 and 27 which is the prophetic vision of the new covenant: "It is important for the proper interpretation of vv. 26 and 27 to recognize they have a parallel structure with correspondence between the successive three parts contained in each of the two verses. The A-sections deal with the covenant of the seventieth week, the New Covenant; both the B and C sections, with the terminating judgment on the Old Covenant order. The fact that the vision thus concludes with a heavy emphasis on the disaster of 70 AD reminds us that this vision belongs to the canon of the Old Covenant, where the divine lawsuit against the apostatizing nation is a major rubric of the prophets' message. Yet, while prosecuting the lawsuit of the Mosaic Covenant, the prophets also proclaimed the promises of the Abrahamic Covenant and thereby were heralds of the Messiah and the New Covenant. So too the prophecy of the seventy weeks makes known that before the collapse of the typal kingdom, the foundation of the enduring messianic kingdom would be laid." Kline, *God, Heaven and Har Magedon*, 149.

22. Robertson represents "the chronological/symbolical understanding" of "seventy sevens" which he interprets "seven weeks" and "sixty-two weeks" as *literal years* while he understands the final seventieth week *symbolically*. Interestingly, he sees the beginning of the seventy weeks as 445 B.C. which was the year of the subsequent return from the exile under Nehemiah: "But a closer adherence to the text itself indicates that the starting point of the seventy weeks of years is not the initial return of the Jews in response to the 536 B.C. decree of Cyrus, but the subsequent return under Nehemiah in approximately 445 B.C. . . . With this starting point for the seventy sevens or 490 years, the subdivision of the seventy weeks of years is as remarkable as the prophecy of Jeremiah concerning the seventy-year length of Israel's captivity. The first unit of seven weeks would total forty-nine years, which would extend from the decree of Artaxerxes to approximately 400 B.C., which corresponds essentially to the time at which old covenant revelation came to its conclusion. The next unit of sixty-two weeks would last for 434 years, coming down to approximately A.D. 30, the time of the life, ministry,

week depicts *the symbolical period of the New Covenant Age* which began with the sacrificial death and bodily resurrection of the Messiah and will end with the second coming of Jesus Christ along with the final redemptive judgment.[23]

As we briefly observed, God used the Babylonian Empire to make a decisive judgment against the Assyrian Empire in 609 B.C., although it was used as a means to curse the northern kingdom of Israel in 722 B.C. Similarly, God used the Persian Empire to pour out his wrath against the Babylonian Empire in 539 B.C., although God used it to make his decisive judgment against the southern kingdom of Judah in 586 B.C. Remarkably, God spoke his coming judgment against the Babylonian Empire through the ministries of prophets (Isa 13:1—14:23; 21:1–10; 46:1—47:15; Jer 50:1—51:64).[24]

God's oracle indicates that the day of judgment against the Babylonian Empire will come and it will be *the day of the Lord*. It suggests

---

death, and resurrection of Jesus the anointed one. The final single week of years has its own distinctive significance, which also must be determined in the framework of a full biblical-theological context." Robertson, *Christ of the Prophets*, 262–63.

23. MacArthur and Mayhue as dispensationalists interpret Daniel's prophecy of the seventieth week with future tribulation for seven years, committing to "the pretribulational rapture view." In doing so, they do not see covenantal and redemptive historical continuity because of *their literal interpretation of the seventy weeks*: "First, the pretribulational rapture view asserts that the church will be raptured before Daniel's seventieth week. Since the entire period of tribulation is the 'wrath of God,' the church must be rescued prior to the tribulation to fulfill God's promise that the church will escape the wrath of God (1 Thess 1:9–10; Rev 3:10). The pretribulational rapture functions as a rescue mission by which Jesus delivers his church from the divine wrath of the tribulation." MacArthur and Mayhue, *Biblical Doctrine*, 898.

24. Some historical critical scholars divide the book of Isaiah into First, Second, and Third Isaiah, denying the predictive aspects and harmony of the book of Isaiah. Bart Ehrman as a radical historical critical scholar summarizes the logic behind the three divisions of the book of Isaiah as follows: "First Isaiah. Chapters 1–39 (with some exceptions) go back to Isaiah of Jerusalem, prophesying in the eighth century B.C.E. He is predicting a coming judgment on the nation of Judah. Second Isaiah. Chapters 40–55 were written by a prophet who shared many of the perspectives of Isaiah of Jerusalem but who was living about 150 years later in the middle of the sixth century after the Babylonian captivity had begun. He is preaching consolation for those Judeans who had suffered because of this military defeat. Third Isaiah. Chapters 56–66 were written by a yet later prophet who appears to have been writing after the exiles had returned from Babylon. He is exhorting the returnees to live in ways pleasing to Yahweh. At some later time, a redactor took these three sets of prophecies and combined them on a single scroll so that all of them appear to derive from Isaiah of Jerusalem; but in reality, only a portion—though a sizeable portion—of them do." Ehrman, *The Bible*, 133.

that the oracle used the judgment formula of the day of the Lord as the decisive judgment day against the Babylonian Empire:

> **6**Wail, for the day of the LORD is near; as destruction from the Almighty it will come! **7**Therefore all hands will be feeble, and every human heart will melt. **8**They will be dismayed: pangs and agony will seize them; they will be in anguish like a woman in labor. They will look aghast at one another; their faces will be aflame. **9***Behold, the day of the LORD comes, cruel, with wrath and fierce anger, to make the land a desolation and to destroy its sinners from it.* **10**For the stars of the heavens and their constellations will not give their light; the sun will be dark at its rising, and the moon will not shed its light. (Isa 13:6–10)

The comprehensive summary of God's wrath against the Babylonian Empire is expressed in "Behold, the day of the LORD comes, cruel, with wrath and fierce anger, to make the land a desolation and to destroy its sinners from it" (v. 9). In doing so, God expressed how the fall of the pagan empires depended upon his absolute sovereignty. As God revealed the judgment day against the Babylonian Empire as the day of the Lord, he also revealed how he would use the military power of "the Medes," the Medo-Persian Empire, to destroy the capital city Babylon and its empire:

> **17***Behold, I am stirring up the Medes against them, who have no regard for silver and do not delight in gold.* **18**Their bows will slaughter the young men; they will have no mercy on the fruit of the womb; their eyes will not pity children. **19**And Babylon, the glory of kingdoms, the splendor and pomp of the Chaldeans, will be like Sodom and Gomorrah when God overthrew them. **20**It will never be inhabited or lived in for all generations; no Arab will pitch his tent there; no shepherds will make their flocks lie down there. **21**But wild animals will lie down there, and their houses will be full of howling creatures; there ostriches will dwell, and there wild goats will dance. **22**Hyenas will cry in its towers, and jackals in the pleasant palaces; its time is close at hand and its days will not be prolonged. (Isa 13:17–22)

Verse 19 comprehensively sums up God's wrath against Babylon on the day of the Lord. God's oracle to Isaiah was in fact looking back to the historical context of the Abrahamic covenant where God cursed the cities of Sodom and Gomorrah, executing his redemptive judgment through holy war. After God's covenant lawsuit through Lot's covenant family in those cities, God executed his wrath, and waged his holy war by sending forth his holy and righteous fire from heaven. In fact, it was the pictorial pattern of the final holy war and judgment which will happen on the final day of the Lord at the second coming of Jesus Christ. To be sure, when God waged holy war against the cities of Sodom and Gomorrah, the covenantal and legal background was the covenant of works, broken by Adam as the federal and representative head (Gen 2:15–17).

Later, God's oracle against the Babylonian Empire came to the prophet Jeremiah again with much more detailed accounts of God's judgment (Jer 50:1—51:64). As God's oracle came to Jeremiah, he mentioned the falls of the northern kingdom of Israel and the southern kingdom of Judah as the past historical fulfillment of God's past oracles as conveyed through his faithful prophets. Furthermore, God's oracle expanded that God would punish the Babylonian Empire as he decisively punished the Assyrian Empire:

> 17"Israel is a hunted sheep driven away by lions. First the king of Assyria devoured him, and now at last Nebuchadnezzar king of Babylon has gnawed his bones. 18Therefore, thus says the LORD of hosts, the God of Israel: Behold, I am bringing punishment on the king of Babylon and his land, as I punished the king of Assyria. 19I will restore Israel to his pasture, and he shall feed on Carmel and in Bashan, and his desire shall be satisfied on the hills of Ephraim and in Gilead. 20In those days and in that time, declares the LORD, iniquity shall be sought in Israel, and there shall be none. And sin in Judah, and none shall be found, for I will pardon those whom I leave as a remnant. (Jer 50:17–20)

Likewise, verse 17 of "Israel is a hunted sheep driven away by lions. First the king of Assyria devoured him, and now at last Nebuchadnezzar king of Babylon has gnawed his bones" summarizes the past historical events which already happened. In fact, the northern kingdom of Israel fell under the military campaign of the Assyrian Empire in 722 B.C. while the southern kingdom of Judah fell through the military campaign of "Nebuchadnezzar king of Babylon" in 586 B.C.

In particular, God's oracle against the Babylonian Empire suggests that it will surely be fulfilled in the near future as his oracle against the Assyrian Empire was already realized in 609 B.C with its fall. Once again, God's oracle though Jeremiah against the Babylonian Empire compares with his wrath against Sodom and Gomorrah as Isaiah did:

> 39"Therefore wild beasts shall dwell with hyenas in Babylon, and ostriches shall dwell in her. She shall never again have

people, nor be inhabited for all generations. **40***As when God overthrew Sodom and Gomorrah and their neighboring cities, declares the LORD, so no man shall dwell there, and no son of man shall sojourn in her.* **41**"Behold, a people comes from the north; a mighty nation and many kings are stirring from the farthest parts of the earth. **42**They lay hold of bow and spear; they are cruel and have no mercy. The sound of them is like the roaring of the sea; they ride on horses, arrayed as a man for battle against you, O daughter of Babylon! **43**"The king of Babylon heard the report of them, and his hands fell helpless; anguish seized him, pain as of a woman in labor. (Jer 50:39–43)

In doing so, God's oracle about the fall of the Babylonian Empire was expressed poetically through vivid imagery. Furthermore, God revealed to Jeremiah that he will use "the kings of the Medes" to seek revenge against the Babylonian Empire. In this regard, we can identify a progressive character of the divine revelation in God's oracles in the prophetic books:

> **11**"*Sharpen the arrows! Take up the shields! The LORD has stirred up the spirit of the kings of the Medes, because his purpose concerning Babylon is to destroy it, for that is the vengeance of the LORD, the vengeance for his temple. . . .* **28**Prepare the nations for war against her, the kings of the Medes, with their governors and deputies, and every land under their dominion. **29**The land trembles and writhes in pain, for the LORD's purposes against Babylon stand, to make the land of Babylon a desolation, without inhabitant. **30**The warriors of Babylon have ceased fighting; they remain in their strongholds; their strength has failed; they have become women; her dwellings are on fire; her bars are broken. **31**One runner runs to meet another, and one messenger to meet another, to tell the king of Babylon that his city is taken on every side; **32**the fords have been seized, the marshes are burned with fire, and the soldiers are in panic. **33**For thus says the LORD of hosts, the God of Israel: The daughter of Babylon is like a threshing floor at the time when it is trodden; yet a little while and the time of her harvest will come." (Jer 51:11–33)

The Medes and Persians were merged into one kingdom through Cyrus around 550 B.C which was the Medo-Persian Empire. In that regard, "the kings of the Medes" may be properly designated as the Medo-Persian Empire. Later, the Babylonian Empire was conquered through the Medo-Persian Empire in 539 B.C. as the prophets prophesied through God's infallible and inerrant oracles.[25]

Summary

As God ratified the Davidic covenant, the kingdom of Israel was visibly formed in the promised land (2 Sam 7:1–17; 1 Chr 17:1–15). The visible formation of the kingdom of Israel was the realization of the one of the promises of the Abrahamic covenant. In that regard, God *remembered* the Abrahamic covenant to exercise the grace of promises after the inauguration of the Davidic covenant. In fact, under the Davidic covenant, God saved believers by God's grace alone (*sola gratia*), by faith alone (*sola fide*) in Christ alone (*solo Christo*), applying the principle of the covenant of grace as inaugurated in Genesis 3:15. Moreover, God applied the Mosaic covenant of law with the dual sanctions of blessings and curses for the *continuation* of the earthly kingdom of Israel in the promised land which visibly typified the eternal kingdom of God.

God sent forth the prophets against the disobedient covenant community of the northern kingdom of Israel and southern kingdom of Judah. In light of God's judgment, the prophets functioned as prosecutors, constantly claiming God's covenant lawsuits which based upon the Mosaic covenant of law, inaugurated on Mount Sinai (Exod 19–24), renewed at Moab (Deut 1–34) and Shechem (Josh 24). Eventually, God cursed the northern kingdom of Israel through the military power of the Assyrian Empire in 722 B.C. and many survivors were scattered to the different

25. Reflecting the predictive elements of the prophecy of Isaiah and Jeremiah, Robertson comprehensively describes that the rise of the Medo-Persian Empire, the fall of the Babylonian Empire, and Israel's restoration from the exile were the fulfillment of the prophetic predictions: "At the heart of the Lord's prediction is this announcement that Israel shall be restored from its exile. A consideration of the circumstances required for this prophesied event to actually occur uncovers its remarkable character. First, the Babylonian Empire had to be conquered by a yet unknown foreign power. Then this foreign power would have to reverse altogether the policy of deportation of conquered peoples that had been practiced by the Babylonians. Finally the Israelite people must be willing to return despite the comfortable lifestyle they had acquired in Babylon during the days of their exile. Yet precisely at the appointed time as predicted by Jeremiah, the Medo-Persian Empire arose. Immediately after his conquest of Babylon, Cyrus their leader issued his decree that deported peoples should be assisted in returning to their homeland. Though only a small number of Jewish exiles responded, the predicted return did occur, and the people of Israel were reestablished in the land of promise." Robertson, *Christ of the Prophets*, 351.

regions outside of the promised land as *the old covenant diaspora*. Similarly, God executed his judgment after the series of his covenant lawsuits against the southern kingdom of Judah through the Babylonian Empire in 586 B.C. and its survivors went into the Babylonian exile for seventy years as God prophesied and spoke through the prophets. Applying the covenantal blessings and curses in the promised land, the sovereign God wanted to demonstrate that the blessings of heaven and curses of hell indeed exist. We identified the historical implication of blessings and curses toward the covenant community as the *old covenant eschatology*.

Although God used the Assyrian and Babylonian Empires to curse the disobedient Israel, who broke the Mosaic covenant of law, he executed his judgment against the pagan empires according to his prophetic oracles. Eventually, God cursed the Assyrian Empire along with the capital city of Nineveh in 609 B.C. through the military power of the Babylonian Empire. Later, God used the Persian Empire to bring judgment against the Babylonian Empire in B.C. 539. In doing so, God demonstrated that the God of Israel has absolute sovereignty in the rise and fall of the different kingdoms and nations on the earth.

The prophets used the eschatological expression of *the day of the Lord* when they spoke against the disobedient Israel. Indeed, it is the formula of the day of God's judgment against Israel. Moreover, the prophets applied the eschatological designation of the day of the Lord for coming God's judgment against the pagan kingdoms and nations such as the Assyrian and Babylonian Empires. The prophets also used the consummative expression of the day of the Lord as the final day of the Lord which will occur at the second coming of Jesus Christ and the day will be the day of final redemptive judgment, separating the eternal kingdom of God and the kingdom of Satan.

Chapter Five

The New Covenant and Redemptive Judgment

THE NEW COVENANT IS the apex and climax of the divine covenants in redemptive history summed up as creation, fall, redemption, and consummation. Remarkably, the Holy Spirit orchestrated the historical process of making the new covenant in the four Gospels, including Mathew, Mark, Luke, and John, each authored by distinct authors, inspired by the Holy Spirit.[1]

In light of God's judgment against the covenant community of Israel, the four Gospels and book of Acts represent the historic process of covenant lawsuits against a disobedient Israel. We will explore how God sent out his faithful servants such as John the Baptist, the Messiah Jesus, apostles and others for the repentance of the sins of Israel and to believe in Jesus of Nazareth as the Messiah who is the fulfillment of the old covenant law and the Prophets. However, the king of Israel beheaded John

---

1. Viewing the four Gospels in light of the historical critical reading, Ehrman denies the authorship of the four Gospels by Matthew, Mark, Luke, and John: "For many years, this view may sound a bit baffling. Weren't the Gospels written by the disciples of Jesus, and didn't they simply record what they saw happen? Scholars have long realized that this is probably not the case at all. We call the Gospels Matthew, Mark, Luke, and John because those are the traditional names associated with them. Two of these authors were allegedly Jesus' disciples: Matthew the tax collector and John the beloved disciple. Two others were companions of the apostles: Mark, the companion of Peter, and Luke, the companion of Paul. . . . These books, on the other hand, were written by later Christians from outside of Palestine who were highly educated and whose native tongue was Greek, not Aramaic. They are anonymous—we don't know who the actual authors were. We continue to call them Matthew, Mark, Luke, and John simply because those are their traditional titles." Ehrman, *Bible*, 261–62.

the Baptist. And the majority of Israel rejected Jesus as the Messiah and crucified him. Furthermore, they stoned Stephen to death, a deacon who defended and witnessed Jesus of Nazareth as the Messiah after the Pentecost in Jerusalem. We will argue that the history of Israel's disobedience, written in the four Gospels and the book of Acts, is clear evidence of God's covenant lawsuits against Israel, based upon the Mosaic covenant of law. God finally executed his final judgment against the kingdom of Israel in the promised land in A.D. 70 through the Roman Empire. In that historic episode, the exalted Jesus Christ executed his judgment against Israel as the heavenly Judge in heaven as King of kings and Lord of lords.

During his earthly ministry, Jesus Christ as the mediator of the new covenant prophesied his second coming and final judgment. After the Pentecost, the apostles carried the same message under the inspiration of the Holy Spirit. We will argue the day of the Lord and the day of the final redemptive judgment are organically related and tied together under the new covenant. In addition, after the final redemptive judgment, there will be a visible separation between the eternal kingdom of God and the kingdom of Satan. Furthermore, we will explore how the new heavens and new earth will be the glorified cosmos or universe while the new earth will be united together with the New Jerusalem which will come down from *heaven*.

The final judgment of the elect will be based upon the covenant of grace in the last Adam while the final judgment of the reprobate will be founded upon the covenant of works in the first Adam. Yet, there will be *gradations* of the heavenly rewards for the elect in the eternal kingdom of God. Similarly, there will be *gradations* of the hellish curses against the reprobate in the kingdom of Satan.

The Covenant Lawsuit and the Final Fall of the Kingdom of Israel

Not many people recognize that the Mosaic covenant of law (Exod 19–24) was directly related and effective when the kingdom of Israel eventually fell through the Roman Empire in A.D. 70. Before the final judgment against the kingdom of Israel, God sent forth his messengers to repent and believe in Jesus as the Messiah who was prophesied to come by prophets in the Old Testament. But, the majority of the covenant community of Israel rejected Jesus of Nazareth as the Messiah. In fact, the four Gospels

and Acts are historical accounts of covenant lawsuits against the disobedient Israel, based upon the Mosaic covenant of law. The authors of the
four Gospels harmoniously report Jesus' incarnation, public life and ministry, crucifixion, and bodily resurrection. In doing so, God demonstrates
the historic process of making the new covenant with the elect through
the mediator Jesus Christ.[2] Nevertheless, in light of the final fall of the
kingdom of Israel in A.D. 70 by the military intervention of the Roman
Empire, Jesus' earthly ministry as portrayed in the four Gospels, is the
ministry of the covenant lawsuit against the disobedient Israel.[3]

Meanwhile, God sent John the Baptist to prepare the way of Jesus
of Nazareth as the Messiah to come as prophesied in the Old Testament.
At the same time, he played a pivotal role as the final prophet of the old
covenant who became a prophetic bridge between the old and new covenants. As he baptized the people of the covenant community of Israel
with water in the Jordan River, he urged them to repent because of God's
coming wrath:

> [7]But when he saw many of the Pharisees and Sadducees coming
> for baptism, he said to them, "You brood of vipers! Who warned
> you to flee from the wrath to come? [8]Bear fruit in keeping with
> repentance. [9]And do not presume to say to yourselves, 'We have
> Abraham as our father,' for I tell you, God is able from these
> stones to raise up children for Abraham. [10]Even now the axe is
> laid to the root of the trees. Every tree therefore that does not
> bear good fruit is cut down and thrown into the fire. [11]I baptize
> you with water for repentance, but he who is coming after me is
> mightier than I, whose sandals I am not worthy to carry. He will
> baptize you with the Holy Spirit and with fire. [12]His winnow-
> ing fork is in his hand, and he will clear his threshing floor and

2. For a biblical theological discussion on the new covenant and the kingdom of
God, see Jeon, *Biblical Theology*, 172–219.

3. Kline provides a proper vision about Yahweh's final judgment against the kingdom of Israel in A.D. 70. Yahweh warned Israel with the historic process of "lawsuit
against the Israelites" who broke the Mosaic covenant. He executed his final judgment
against Israel at the "day of covenant judgment" based upon the Mosaic covenant:
"Likewise in the administering of the Torah covenant the failure of the covenant
people in their national probation led to a day of Yahweh, a day of reckoning. Pressing
the Lord's lawsuit against the Israelites, his prophet-lawyers repeatedly warned that
for those who did not honor their covenant obligations the coming day of the Lord
would bring not light but darkness. Such a day of judicial darkness befell the nation
in the calamity of the Babylonian exile and a second time in the 70 AD destruction of
Jerusalem." Kline, *God, Heaven and Har Magedon*, 188.

gather his wheat into the barn, but the chaff he will burn with unquenchable fire." (Matt 3:7–12)

John the Baptist's prophetic warning in verse 7, "You brood of vipers! Who warned you to flee from the wrath to come?" is the lingering echo of the coming judgment against the disobedient Israel. The Pharisees and Sadducees who were members of different sects of Judaism thought that they were faithful followers of God due to their obedience to the Mosaic law. Nevertheless, their religion was not the religion which was followed and promoted by the Old Testament believers such as Abraham, Isaac, Jacob, Moses, Joshua, David and others. The followers of Judaism at the time of John the Baptist in the first century did not understand the disparity between their religion and that of the Old Testament Israelites. In that regard, John the Baptist's prophetic ministry was a ministry of covenant lawsuits against Israel who rejected Jesus as the Messiah.

John the Baptist was especially privileged to baptize Jesus in the Jordan river (Matt 3:13–17; Mark 1:8–11; Luke 3:21–22). In fact, the visible scene of Jesus' water baptism was the anointing ceremony as the King of the eschatological kingdom of God as "the son of David, the son of Abraham" (Matt 1:1). Jesus did not come to this world to sit at the throne in Jerusalem as the king of Israel but to succeed the Davidic kingdom in the glorious throne of *heaven*. That is why Jesus was not anointed by olive oil like the other kings of Israel but the Holy Spirit. Moreover, the glorious scene of Jesus' water baptism in the Jordan river was the glorious moment of the wondrous presence of God the Father, the Son, and the Holy Spirit. In fact, his baptism audibly and visibly verified the existence and work of the Triune God.[4]

---

4. Adopting radical principles of the historical critical method, Dale Martin argues that the Bible does not embrace or teach the doctrine of the Trinity. Rather, it was the doctrine, "developed later, especially in the fourth-century church councils." Likewise, he rejects the doctrine of the Trinity, labeling it as "anachronistic." In doing so, he denies one of the most important presuppositions of the biblical religion: "In historical criticism, as in the practice of modern historiography more broadly, a great sin is the commission of 'anachronism': one must not retroject an idea or practice into the ancient text or its context that didn't exist at the time. For example, most historical critics would agree that although New Testament authors do speak of the Father, Jesus as the Son, and a Holy Spirit (although it is seldom clear precisely what they mean by the last term, whether it was a 'thing' or a 'person'), it would be anachronistic to read the New Testament as teaching the full doctrine of the Trinity as it became developed later, especially in the fourth-century church circles. It would be even more objectionable to read Genesis as referring to the Trinity. A premodern interpreter may be perfectly

Before Jesus began his earthly and public ministry, he fasted for forty days and forty nights in the wilderness where he was tempted by the devil (Matt 4:1–11; Mark 1:12–13; Luke 4:1–13). It was a major spiritual battle between Satan and Jesus as the last Adam. Jesus, representing the kingdom of God, defeated Satan's challenge in the wilderness. We know that the first Adam as the representative head of the covenant of works failed to defeat Satan's challenge in the garden of Eden (Gen 3:1–7). However, Jesus as the last Adam defeated Satan's challenge in the wilderness. After winning the spiritual battle against Satan, Jesus launched his earthly ministry, proclaiming *the coming of the kingdom of God or the kingdom of Heaven* against the challenges of Satan and his demons.

Around that time, John the Baptist was imprisoned by Herod Antipas, the son of Herod the Great (Matt. 4:12). During the birthday party of the king of Herod Antipas the tetrarch, answering the request of the daughter of Herodias, had John beheaded in prison. Thus, the last prophet of the old covenant was martyred as the forerunner of Jesus Christ (Matt 14:1–12; Mark 6:14–29; Luke 9:7–9).

As Jesus began his public ministry, he went to the different regions in the promised land and proclaimed the good news of the kingdom of God. He visited synagogues which were the center of gatherings and Sabbath worship for the followers of Judaism:

> [35]And Jesus went throughout all the cities and villages, teaching in their synagogues and proclaiming the gospel of the kingdom and healing every disease and every affliction. [36]When he saw the crowds, he had compassion for them, because they were harassed and helpless, like sheep without a shepherd. [37]Then he said to his disciples, "The harvest is plentiful, but the laborers are few; [38]therefore pray earnestly to the Lord of the harvest to send out laborers into his harvest." (Matt 9:35–38)

We need to pay attention to the summary statement of Jesus' teaching and healing ministry as summarized in verse 35. The central location of Jesus' ministry was the synagogues, scattered in the promised land. Moreover, Jesus' teaching and proclamation of the good news of the Gospel and the kingdom of God represented the covenant lawsuit against

---

happy to say that the 'spirit' (or 'wind' in more recent translations) that 'hovers over the space of the deep' in Genesis 1:2 is the Holy Spirit. But a modern critic would object that such a reading is anachronistic, retrojecting a later Christian doctrine into a text whose author could not possibly have known it." Martin, *New Testament History and Literature*, 326–27.

the disobedient Israelites in the promised land. Of course, in doing so, Jesus anticipated the coming of the final judgment against the kingdom of Israel at A.D. 70.

Choosing the twelve original disciples, Jesus sent them to different cities and regions in the promised land. He specifically ordered for them to go "to the lost sheep of the house of Israel" (v. 6), proclaiming "the kingdom of heaven is at hand" (v. 7). Jesus' demand to his disciples indicates that he anticipated the final judgment against the kingdom of Israel:

> [5]These twelve Jesus sent out, instructing them, "Go nowhere among the Gentiles and enter no town of the Samaritans, [6]but go rather to the lost sheep of the house of Israel. [7]And proclaim as you go, saying, 'The kingdom of heaven is at hand.' [8]Heal the sick, raise the dead, cleanse lepers, cast out demons. You received without paying; give without pay. [9]Acquire no gold nor silver nor copper for your belts, [10]no bag for your journey, nor two tunics nor sandals nor a staff, for the laborer deserves his food. [11]And whatever town or village you enter, find out who is worthy in it and stay there until you depart. [12]As you enter the house, greet it. [13]And if the house is worthy, let your peace come upon it, but if it is not worthy, let your peace return to you. [14]And if anyone will not receive you or listen to your words, shake off the dust from your feet when you leave that house or town. [15]Truly, I say to you, it will be more bearable on the day of judgment for the land of Sodom and Gomorrah than for that town." (Matt 10:5–15)

Jesus' command in verses 6 and 7 indicates that the major focus of the disciples' ministry before his death and resurrection was directed to the people of Israel in the promised land. It is because Jesus as the great prophet used the disciples' ministry as the means of covenant lawsuit against a disobedient Israel. As we explore Jesus' anticipation of the final judgment against the kingdom of Israel in the promised land, we need to see "the day of judgment" from the perspective of the eschatological judgment. We ponder upon the eschatological designation of "the day of judgment" after the inauguration of the New Covenant Age through the Pentecost. This eschatological judgment is twofold as follows: "The day of judgment" against Israel which will be terminated as the kingdom of Israel in the promised land in A.D. 70, and "the day of judgment" against the present world which will face the final judgment when Jesus Christ returns. Anticipating the final judgment against a disobedient Israel, Christ compares it with the redemptive judgment upon Sodom and

Gomorrah. Indeed, verse 15, "Truly, I say to you, it will be more bearable on the day of judgment for the land of Sodom and Gomorrah than for that town" powerfully predicts the catastrophic nature of the final judgment against Israel.

Moreover, Jesus as the great prophet foresaw the persecution against his disciples who would execute the mission for the covenant people of Israel in the promised land:

> 16"Behold, I am sending you out as sheep in the midst of wolves, so be wise as serpents and innocent as doves. 17Beware of men, for they will deliver you over to courts and flog you in their synagogues, 18and you will be dragged before governors and kings for my sake, to bear witness before them and the Gentiles. 19When they deliver you over, do not be anxious how you are to speak or what you are to say, for what you are to say will be given to you in that hour. 20For it is not you who speak, but the Spirit of your Father speaking through you. 21Brother will deliver brother over to death, and the father his child, and children will rise against parents and have them put to death, 22and you will be hated by all for my name's sake. But the one who endures to the end will be saved. 23When they persecute you in one town, flee to the next, for truly, I say to you, you will not have gone through all the towns of Israel before the Son of Man comes. (Matt 10:16–23)

Jesus used a metaphor with sheep and wolves to compare his disciples with a disobedient Israel. He considered his disciples as sheep and identified the disobedient Israel as wolves. In verses 16 and 17 he predicted how his disciples would face enormous resistance and persecution in the synagogues which were the center of gatherings and Sabbath worship for the followers of Judaism. Visiting the various towns of Israel, introducing the good news of the gospel in Jesus of Nazareth by the disciples was in fact the historic process of the covenant lawsuits by God. Afterwards, there would be a final judgment against the disobedient Israel. Indeed, Jesus' prediction in verse 23 is the prophecy of the invisible coming of the Son of Man as the Judge against Israel who broke the Mosaic covenant of law in A.D. 70. Nevertheless, the coming of the Son of Man as judge against the disobedient Israel will not be in physical form. Rather, he will be coming as the judge while he will be exercising and executing his judgment in the heavenly throne as the King and Lord of the eschatological kingdom of God, using the Roman Empire.

Jesus performed an abundance of miraculous signs before the people of Israel, especially in the cities of Chorazin, Bathsaida, and Capernaum. But most Israelites in those cities did not welcome Jesus and rejected the good news of the gospel. Observing the disobedience of the Israelites in those cities, Jesus as the great prophet announced the coming of "the day of judgment" which would be more severe than the judgment upon Sodom in the context of the Abrahamic covenant:

> [20]Then he began to denounce the cities where most of his mighty works had been done, because they did not repent. [21]"Woe to you, Chorazin! Woe to you, Bethsaida! For if the mighty works done in you had been done in Tyre and Sidon, they would have repented long ago in sackcloth and ashes. [22]But I tell you, it will be more bearable on the day of judgment for Tyre and Sidon than for you. [23]And you, Capernaum, will you be exalted to heaven? You will be brought down to Hades. For if the mighty works done in you had been done in Sodom, it would have remained until this day. [24]But I tell you that it will be more tolerable on the day of judgment for the land of Sodom than for you." (Matt 11:20–24; cf. Luke 10:1–24)

In doing so, Jesus evaluated the covenant people of Israel in those cities and concluded that their spiritual condition was much worse than that of the gentile cities of Tyre and Sidon. In fact, Jesus' warning of curses for the people of Israel in the cities of Chorazin, Bethsaida, and Capernaum was the covenant lawsuit, based upon the Mosaic covenant of law.

When Jesus prepared for his final entry to Jerusalem before his crucifixion, he gathered his twelve disciples. Anticipating his crucifixion as the great prophet, he predicted that "the chief priest and scribes" who were the religious leaders of people of Israel would condemn "the Son of Man" to crucifixion (v. 19). Nevertheless, "the Son of Man" would be raised from the tomb after the third day (v. 20). Jesus' prediction to his original disciples is significant because it is the prediction of the highlight of the disobedient Israel, represented by the religious leaders of the covenant community of Israel:

> [17]And as Jesus was going up to Jerusalem, he took the twelve disciples aside, and on the way he said to them, [18]"See, we are going up to Jerusalem. And the Son of Man will be delivered over to the chief priests and scribes, and they will condemn him to death [19]and deliver him over to the Gentiles to be mocked

and flogged and crucified, and he will be raised on the third day." (Matt 20:16–19; cf. Mark 10:32–34; Luke 18:31–34)

In fact, Jesus' crucifixion by the religious leaders of the covenant people of Israel was the culmination of disobedience and sins of Israel. In that sense, as he anticipated his once for all sacrificial death, Jesus clearly pronounced to his disciples *God's covenant lawsuit against the disobedient Israel.*

When Jesus entered Jerusalem after the end of his earthly ministry, he was surrounded by his disciples and crowds. He declared a series of judgments against the "scribes and Pharisees" who were the representative religious figures among the covenant people of Israel (Matt 23: 1–36). In the announcement of the last woe against the "scribes and Pharisees," Jesus predicted that they would persecute and kill the prophets and other faithful believers:

> 29"Woe to you, scribes and Pharisees, hypocrites! For you build the tombs of the prophets and decorate the monuments of the righteous, 30saying, 'If we had lived in the days of our fathers, we would not have taken part with them in shedding the blood of the prophets.' 31Thus you witness against yourselves that you are sons of those who murdered the prophets. 32Fill up, then, the measure of your fathers. 33You serpents, you brood of vipers, how are you to escape being sentenced to hell? 34Therefore I send you prophets and wise men and scribes, some of whom you will kill and crucify, and some you will flog in your synagogues and persecute from town to town, 35so that on you may come all the righteous blood shed on earth, from the blood of innocent Abel to the blood of Zechariah the son of Barachiah, whom you murdered between the sanctuary and the altar. 36Truly, I say to you, all these things will come upon this generation. (Matt 23:29–36)

In fact, Jesus' declaration of the series of woes of judgment against "scribes and Pharisees" was the public announcement of the covenant lawsuit against the covenant people of Israel, based upon the Mosaic covenant of law. Later, after the Pentecost, the apostles and other faithful believers scattered to the different regions of the promised land, witnessing Jesus of Nazareth as the Messiah with the proclamation of the good news of the Gospel. Here, Jesus predicted that the "scribes and Pharisees" would persecute the apostles and other faithful believers and some would even be martyred. As such, verse 34 provides a glimpse into the near future persecution and martyrdom of the apostles and others by the religious leaders of Judaism in the first century.

After the announcement of the series of judgment against "scribes and Pharisees," Jesus poured out his lamentation over Jerusalem which kills God's faithful messengers and prophets:

> 37"O Jerusalem, Jerusalem, the city that kills the prophets and stones those who are sent to it! How often would I have gathered your children together as a hen gathers her brood under her wings, and you would not! 38See, your house is left to you desolate. 39For I tell you, you will not see me again, until you say, 'Blessed is he who comes in the name of the Lord.'" (Matt 23:37–39)

Jesus' lamentation as presented in verse 37 summarizes the covenant lawsuit against Israel in light of Israel's disobedience and apostasy. In that regard, the following statement "See, your house is left to you desolate" (v. 38) poetically predicts the desolation of Jerusalem which would take place in A.D. 70 through the military campaign of the Roman Empire.

Jesus predicted a twofold judgment upon the disobedient Israel and the present world in the Olivet Discourse which was given on the Mount of Olives. Through the historical context and introduction of the Olivet Discourse, we find an important fact: Jesus as the great prophet predicted the final judgment upon Jerusalem and destruction of the temple:

> Jesus left the temple and was going away, when his disciples came to point out to him the buildings of the temple. 2But he answered them, "You see all these, do you not? Truly, I say to you, there will not be left here one stone upon another that will not be thrown down." (Matt 24:1–2)

Jesus' prediction provides us a vivid pictorial language against the final destiny of the kingdom of Israel. In that regard, verse 2 highlights the final judgment against Israel and the temple in Jerusalem.[5]

---

5. Interpreting the Olivet Discourse, recorded in Matthew 24:1—25:36, Chafer as an influential dispensational theologian falsely insists that "the judgment of Israel" will occur with "the second advent of Christ" at the end of the seven years of the tribulation before the establishment of "the glorious Messianic kingdom" which would be built in Jerusalem. The presupposition of this unhealthy hermeneutics and eschatology is a sharp distinction between Church and Israel: "In the order in which the future judgment occurs, the judgment of Israel is next. It occurs in connection with the second advent of Christ. That the judgment of Israel precedes the judgment of the nations is indicated by the fact that these judgments are recorded in that order in the Olivet

Israel's disobedience and apostasy culminated in Jesus' condemnation to crucifixion and death on the cross. In fact, the Sanhedrin, the highest court of Israel in the first century, declared Jesus guilty, charging him with the sin of blasphemy which merits death by stoning according to the tradition of the Mosaic law:

> 57Then those who had seized Jesus led him to Caiaphas the high priest, where the scribes and the elders had gathered. 58And Peter was following him at a distance, as far as the courtyard of the high priest, and going inside he sat with the guards to see the end. 59Now the chief priests and the whole Council were seeking false testimony against Jesus that they might put him to death, 60but they found none, though many false witnesses came forward. At last two came forward 61and said, "This man said, 'I am able to destroy the temple of God, and to rebuild it in three days.'" 62And the high priest stood up and said, "Have you no answer to make? What is it that these men testify against you?" 63But Jesus remained silent. And the high priest said to him, "I adjure you by the living God, tell us if you are the Christ, the Son of God." 64Jesus said to him, "You have said so. But I tell you, from now on you will see the Son of Man seated at the right hand of Power and coming on the clouds of heaven." 65Then the high priest tore his robes and said, "He has uttered blasphemy. What further witnesses do we need? You have now heard his blasphemy. 66What is your judgment?" They answered, "He deserves death." 67Then they spit in his face and struck him. And some slapped him, 68saying, "Prophesy to us, you Christ! Who is it that struck you?" (Matt 26:57–68)

Before the Sanhedrin, Jesus himself defended his identity as "the Christ, the Son of God" and "the Son of Man." Then, Caiaphas the high priest, the leader of the Sanhedrin, tore his robes, declaring, "He has uttered blasphemy. What further witnesses do we need? You have now heard his blasphemy. What is your judgment?" (vv. 65–66a). And then the Sanhedrin members unanimously answered and shouted, "He

---

Discourse (Matt. 24:1—25:46); however, both of these great judgments are related to the second advent and occur at the end of the tribulation. Quite in contrast to the experience accorded the Church (cf. John 5:24), the nation Israel must be judged, and it is reasonable to believe that this judgment will include all of that nation who in past dispensations have lived under the covenants and promises. Therefore a resurrection of those generations of Israel is called for and must precede their judgment. The glorious Messianic kingdom has been the hope of the Old Testament saints and in conformity to this hope they ordered their lives." Chafer, *Systematic Theology*, 4:406.

deserves death" (v. 66b). The Sanhedrin's decision to penalize Jesus by death is significant because it was the legal decision of the highest court of the covenant community of Israel. Moreover, after the decision was made, the Sanhedrin members mocked and persecuted Jesus physically. And it is pictorially reflected in verses 67–68.

As Jesus was crucified at Golgotha, shedding his blood of the new covenant as the great high priest, the religious leaders of Judaism in Jerusalem were present as eyewitnesses. Moreover, they mocked the suffering servant:

> 32As they went out, they found a man of Cyrene, Simon by name. They compelled this man to carry his cross. 33And when they came to a place called Golgotha (which means Place of a Skull), 34they offered him wine to drink, mixed with gall, but when he tasted it, he would not drink it. 35And when they had crucified him, they divided his garments among them by casting lots. 36Then they sat down and kept watch over him there. 37And over his head they put the charge against him, which read, "This is Jesus, the King of the Jews." 38Then two robbers were crucified with him, one on the right and one on the left. 39And those who passed by derided him, wagging their heads 40and saying, "You who would destroy the temple and rebuild it in three days, save yourself! If you are the Son of God, come down from the cross." 41So also the chief priests, with the scribes and elders, mocked him, saying, 42"He saved others; he cannot save himself. He is the King of Israel; let him come down now from the cross, and we will believe in him. 43He trusts in God; let God deliver him now, if he desires him. For he said, 'I am the Son of God.'" 44And the robbers who were crucified with him also reviled him in the same way. (Matt 27:32–44)

The mockery of the religious leaders of Israel against the crucified Jesus rang and spread over the hills of Golgotha. This was the culmination of a disobedient Israel's breaking the Mosaic covenant of law. The chief priests, along with the scribes and elders as the religious leaders of Israel, mocked the suffering Jesus on the cross, shouting "42He saved others; he cannot save himself. He is the King of Israel; let him come down now from the cross, and we will believe in him. 43He trusts in God; let God deliver him now, if he desires him. For he said, 'I am the Son of God.'" (vv. 42–43). However, this mockery against the crucified Jesus by the religious leaders of Israel was also the audible and visible evidence of the apex of a disobedient Israel.

With the Pentecost, the New Covenant Age was officially and visibly inaugurated (Acts 2:1–13).[6] And the gospel of the good news of Jesus Christ of Nazareth was powerfully proclaimed through the ministry of the apostles and other faithful believers, along with the supernatural works of the Holy Spirit. Nevertheless, Stephen's speech before the Sanhedrin in Jerusalem became a pivotal moment of God's redemptive history (Acts 6:8—7:60). In his monumental speech, Stephen delivered an inspirational message, interpreting the ancient history of Israel from the Christocentric and Christotelic perspectives from Abraham to Solomon. In the epilogue of his speech, Stephen announced a covenant lawsuit, declaring that the Sanhedrin, as the representative religious and legal body of Israel, violated the Mosaic covenant of law:

> [51]"You stiff-necked people, uncircumcised in heart and ears, you always resist the Holy Spirit. As your fathers did, so do you. [52]Which of the prophets did not your fathers persecute? And they killed those who announced beforehand the coming of the Righteous One, whom you have now betrayed and murdered, [53]you who received the law as delivered by angels and did not keep it." (Acts 7:51–53)

As Stephen declared the covenant lawsuit against the Sanhedrin, he also reminded them of how the faithful prophets who prophesied "the coming of the Righteous One" in the Old Testament were persecuted and martyred by the disobedient Israel. Moreover, he delivered the powerful statement that the Sanhedrin betrayed and murdered the prophesied Righteous One, Jesus Christ of Nazareth. The conclusive and declarative statement, "You who received the law as delivered by angels and did not keep it" (v. 53) is in fact the official announcement of Israel's guilt before the Sanhedrin by the covenant lawsuit through the mouth of Stephen who represented God and was filled with the Spirit of Christ.

---

6. Making a sharp contrast between Israel and the church, Chafer as a major exponent of dispensational theology and eschatology, looks at *Pentecost as the beginning of the Church*. In doing so, he denies that the Old Testament believers were the members of the visible church on earth: "Pentecost is anticipated typically in the wave loaves of Leviticus 23:15–21. It should be noted that the wave loaves were presented exactly after the wave sheaf, which marks the precise period between the first ascension of Christ (John 20:17) and Pentecost. Thus by type, the Church—represented by the loaves—is seen to originate at Pentecost and not in the Old Testament or at the end of the period covered by the Acts. Direct prediction relative to Pentecost was uttered by Christ (John 14:16–17, 26; 15:26; 16:7–15)." Chafer, *Systematic Theology*, 4:393–94.

After the official announcement of guilt against the Sanhedrin by Stephen, the members of the Sanhedrin raged and gnashed their teeth against him. At that critical moment, Stephen saw *the glorious heaven* opened before him. This glorious scene illuminated the works of the Triune God through revelation of God the Father, the Son, and the Holy Spirit. In that regards, the covenant lawsuit against the Sanhedrin through Stephen was legally conducted *in the heavenly court* where the Triune God was gloriously present:

> [54]Now when they heard these things they were enraged, and they ground their teeth at him. [55]But he, full of the Holy Spirit, gazed into heaven and saw the glory of God, and Jesus standing at the right hand of God. [56]And he said, "Behold, I see the heavens opened, and the Son of Man standing at the right hand of God." [57]But they cried out with a loud voice and stopped their ears and rushed together at him. [58]Then they cast him out of the city and stoned him. And the witnesses laid down their garments at the feet of a young man named Saul. [59]And as they were stoning Stephen, he called out, "Lord Jesus, receive my spirit." [60]And falling to his knees he cried out with a loud voice, "Lord, do not hold this sin against them." And when he had said this, he fell asleep. (Acts 7:54–59)

At the climax of Stephen's speech before the Sanhedrin, God revealed the exalted Jesus Christ of Nazareth as Luke briefly describes it from the trinitarian perspective in verse 55. Before being stoned to death by the Sanhedrin, God revealed the crucified Jesus' victory in heavenly realm. Verse 56 says, "Behold, I see the heavens opened, and the Son of Man standing at the right hand of God." This verse reveals how Jesus Christ had already begun to rule the eschatological kingdom of God as King of kings and Lord of lords after his ascension on Mount Olivet. In fact, Stephen's final words to the Sanhedrin were the glorious victory song of the kingdom of God, sung from *heaven* against the vicious and destructive challenge of the kingdom of Satan. In short, the heavenly cantata of victory song was sung through the mouth of Stephen, conducted and orchestrated by the Spirit of the exalted Jesus Christ. In that sense, Stephen's covenant lawsuit against the Sanhedrin was the exalted Jesus Christ's covenant lawsuit against the guilty as the heavenly judge after the inauguration of the new covenant.

After the martyrdom of Stephen by the Sanhedrin, the great persecution against the believers in Jerusalem broke out. So, the believers under the great persecution scattered throughout "the regions of Judea and Samaria, except the apostles" (v. 2). In light of the history of diaspora after Adam and Eve were expelled from the holy garden of Eden after the fall, they became *the origin of the new covenant diaspora*. In fact, the scattered believers became the new covenant diaspora after the inauguration of the New Covenant Age through Jesus' death, resurrection, ascension, and session at the right hand of God, and the Pentecost:

> And Saul approved of his execution. And there arose on that day a great persecution against the church in Jerusalem, and they were all scattered throughout the regions of Judea and Samaria, except the apostles. 2Devout men buried Stephen and made great lamentation over him. 3But Saul was ravaging the church, and entering house after house, he dragged off men and women and committed them to prison. 4Now those who were scattered went about preaching the word. 5Philip went down to the city of Samaria and proclaimed to them the Christ. 6And the crowds with one accord paid attention to what was being said by Philip when they heard him and saw the signs that he did. 7For unclean spirits came out of many who were possessed, crying with a loud voice, and many who were paralyzed or lame were healed. 8So there was much joy in that city. (Acts 8:1–8)

But the evangelistic endeavors of the new covenant diaspora, scattered throughout "the regions of Judea and Samaria" (v. 1), were the historical process of covenant lawsuit against the disobedient Israel before the final fall of the kingdom of Israel in the promised land in A.D. 70.

After Stephen's martyrdom, the great persecution was revived in the Jerusalem church. During the reign of Herod Agrippa I the king of Israel, he executed the apostle James, son of Zebedee and brother of John. He also imprisoned the apostle Peter:

> About that time Herod the king laid violent hands on some who belonged to the church. 2He killed James the brother of John with the sword, 3and when he saw that it pleased the Jews, he proceeded to arrest Peter also. This was during the days of Unleavened Bread. 4And when he had seized him, he put him in prison, delivering him over to four squads of soldiers to guard him, intending after the Passover to bring him out to the people. 5So Peter was kept in prison, but earnest prayer for him was made to God by the church. (Acts 12:1–5)

Luke, under the inspiration of the Holy Spirit, charges God's covenant lawsuit against Herod the king of Israel who persecuted the church, martyred the apostle James, and imprisoned the apostle Peter. Verse 1 comprehensively describes the great persecution against the Jerusalem church under King Herod. God disclosed his covenant lawsuit against Herod the king and the Jews in Luke's summary of the martyrdom of James and imprisonment of Peter (vv. 2–4).

Meanwhile, before his conversion, Paul was one of the foremost persecutors of the church among the followers of Judaism (Acts 8:1–3; 22:4–5; 26:9–11; 1 Cor 15:9; Gal 1:13–14, 23; Phil 3:6). However, through his Damascus Road conversion experience, Paul received the good news of the gospel through the revelation of the exalted Jesus Christ from *heaven*. Immediately, Paul abandoned the monotheism of Judaism and was transformed into a trinitarian apostle and theologian.[7] He then

---

7. As the exponents of the New Perspective on Paul, Wright and Bird radically reinterpret the biblical doctrine of Trinity. Interpreting the doctrine of Trinity in light of *the Jewish monotheism*, they fall into the trap of modalism which ultimately rejects the biblical doctrine of Trinity. Their biggest failure is to not distinguish between the biblical religion of the Old Testament Israel and the religion of Judaism, fallen to the Jewish monotheism which was by nature against the biblical doctrine of the Trinity: "The cross is the place where Paul sees God's justice fully displayed; his Christology, seen as the revision of the Jewish-style monotheism, is the context within which we can best understand it. . . . The second branch of Paul's redefinition of Jewish-style monotheism is closely allied with the first, and concerns the spirit. When Paul articulates the spirit's properties and actions, we find two passages of great power and concentrated theological energy, in which a classically Jewish monotheism is expressed in relation to Jesus and the spirit together. The first is Galatians 4.1–7. Paul's main aim here is to reinforce his central point in the letter that the Galatian Christians are already complete in Christ and do not need to take upon themselves the yoke of Torah. But as he does this, we can watch him also developing the Jewish monotheistic picture of God in a spectacular new way. This is the full, fresh revelation of the God of Abraham, the God of the exodus: he is now to be known, worshipped, and trusted as the God who sends the son and the God who sends the spirit of the son. . . . In all this, across Galatians 4 and Romans 8, Paul is again working within the framework of Jewish-style monotheism. He sees the spirit alongside the son as the agents of the one God, doing what Wisdom was to do, doing what Torah wanted to do but could not. . . . Paul thus regularly spoke of the spirit in ways which indicate that he regarded the spirit, as he regarded the Messiah, as the glorious manifestation of YHWH himself. This conclusion is not dependent on one or two verbal echoes, but relies on the regular and repeated invocation of the various elements of the foundational exodus-narrative. The spirit is, it seems, the ultimate mode of YHWH's personal and powerful presence with, and even in, his people. The Christology of 'divine identity' is thus matched by the pneumatology of 'divine identity,' in both cases focused in particular on the Jewish eschatology of the return of YHWH." Wright and Bird, *New Testament in Its World*, 374–77.

began to preach the death and resurrection of Jesus Christ to both Jews and gentiles as an apostle. Paul visited many synagogues during his three missionary journeys to various cities and preached and taught the gospel and the kingdom of God. Nevertheless, a majority of the Jews opposed Paul's presentation of the gospel and the kingdom of God and persecuted him. After the third missionary journey, Paul returned to Jerusalem but was arrested by the Jews who tried to kill him and was eventually taken to Rome for trial (Acts 21:17—28:31).

Before he was taken to Rome, Paul had an opportunity to defend himself in front of King Herod Agrippa II (Acts 26:1–32). In the midst of his defense, Paul appealed to King Agrippa that his preaching and teaching to the Jews and gentiles were focused on Christ's death and resurrection which was the prophetic fulfillment of the prophets and Moses:

> 19Therefore, O King Agrippa, I was not disobedient to the heavenly vision, 20but declared first to those in Damascus, then in Jerusalem and throughout all the region of Judea, and also to the Gentiles, that they should repent and turn to God, performing deeds in keeping with their repentance. 21*For this reason the Jews seized me in the temple and tried to kill me.* 22To this day I have had the help that comes from God, and so I stand here testifying both to small and great, saying nothing but what the prophets and Moses said would come to pass: 23that the Christ must suffer and that, by being the first to rise from the dead, he would proclaim light both to our people and to the Gentiles. (Acts 26:19–23)

Paul emphatically states in verse 21, "For this reason the Jews seized me in the temple and tried to kill me" (v. 21). It is not only Paul's self-defense of innocence but also covenant lawsuit against the covenant community of Israel that broke the Mosaic covenant of law in their persecution against the church and the apostle Paul. In other words, God pronounced his covenant lawsuit against the covenant community of Israel through the inspired mouth of Paul before King Agrippa.

In sum, throughout his early ministry, Jesus as the great prophet delivered God's covenant lawsuit against the people of Israel who rejected Jesus as the prophesied Messiah in the Old Testament. His covenant lawsuit was culminated by the prophecy of the final fall of Jerusalem and destruction of the temple which was fulfilled by the military campaign of the Roman Empire in A.D. 70. Moreover, Jesus' covenant lawsuit was carried and succeeded through the ministry of the apostles and other faithful believers after the Pentecost with the inspiration of the Holy Spirit as inscripturated in the book of Acts.

The Covenant Lawsuit and World Mission

As we explored, the New Covenant Age was inaugurated through Jesus Christ's incarnation, public life and ministry, sacrificial death, bodily resurrection, ascension and session at the right hand of God the Father, and the Pentecost. In light of God's final judgment on the present world, the New Covenant Age is the age of cosmic covenant lawsuit. This lawsuit is based on the Adamic covenant of works for those who remain in the first Adam, and reject Jesus Christ as their personal Savior and Lord who fulfilled the requirement of the covenant of works, paying the penalty of sins of the elect. In that sense, the apostles' and faithful believers' preaching the good news of the gospel of Jesus Christ after the Pentecost in Jerusalem, Judea, Samaria, and to the ends of the earth was not only the process of eschatological evangelism and mission but also the process of *cosmic covenant lawsuit*, based upon the broken covenant of works by the first Adam. Likewise, we need to closely look at the captivated scene of Jesus Christ's ascension in front of the disciples on the Mount of Olives:

> **6**So when they had come together, they asked him, "Lord, will you at this time restore the kingdom to Israel?" **7**He said to them, "It is not for you to know times or seasons that the Father has fixed by his own authority. **8**But you will receive power when the Holy Spirit has come upon you, and you will be my witnesses in Jerusalem and in all Judea and Samaria, and to the end of the earth." **9**And when he had said these things, as they were looking on, he was lifted up, and a cloud took him out of their sight. **10**And while they were gazing into heaven as he went, behold, two men stood by them in white robes, **11**and said, "Men of Galilee, why do you stand looking into heaven? This Jesus, who was taken up from you into heaven, will come in the same way as you saw him go into heaven." (Acts 1:6–11)

In light of God's eschatological mission, Jesus Christ's final word to his original disciples before his ascension pointed to the global mission from Jerusalem to the ends of the earth. In fact, it was the inspired word of Jesus Christ for *the eschatological mission*, launched after the Pentecost. Likewise, we need to highlight the continuous echo of Jesus Christ's final word before his ascension as recorded in verses 7–8. As a matter of fact, it is Jesus Christ's prophecy as the great prophet that the original apostles, except Judas Iscariot, will launch and lead the eschatological mission "in Jerusalem and in all Judea and Samaria, and to the ends of the earth" through the inspired and infallible guidance of the Holy Spirit.

Paul's Areopagus Speech in Athens is an example of *God's universal covenant lawsuit* against idol worshipers and unbelievers in the gentile mission field (Acts 17:16–34). In the epilogue of his speech, Paul under the inspiration of the Holy Spirit, declared the covenant lawsuit against idol worshipers. In doing so, he persuasively argued that the day of the final judgment is, in fact, coming:

> [29]Being then God's offspring, we ought not to think that the divine being is like gold or silver or stone, an image formed by the art and imagination of man. [30]The times of ignorance God overlooked, but now he commands all people everywhere to repent, [31]because he has fixed a day on which he will judge the world in righteousness by a man whom he has appointed; and of this he has given assurance to all by raising him from the dead." [32]Now when they heard of the resurrection of the dead, some mocked. But others said, "We will hear you again about this." [33]So Paul went out from their midst. [34]But some men joined him and believed, among them Dionysius the Areopagite and a woman named Damaris and others with them. (Acts 17:29–34)

Paul's main point is clear that God demands idol worshipers' repentance in Jesus Christ because the day of the final judgment is coming. Paul juxtaposes *God's universal covenant lawsuit* against the idol worshipers in verse 30. This verse suggests that the world mission age had already launched with the first coming of Jesus Christ. In fact, the Pentecost was the audible and visible seal and sign of the beginning of the world mission age, as well as the inauguration of the New Covenant Age.[8]

---

8. Paying close attention to verses 30 and 31 in light of the eschatological judgment, Pardigon argues that it is "God's universal lawsuit" against idol worshipers because they are the covenant breakers: "The mention of the preparatory proceedings for God's universal lawsuit is syntactically and causally related to God's *commanding* to men to repent. . . . This double turn of event (imminent lawsuit and divine injunction), however, is a rhetorically effective and pressing inducement to repent. . . . It seems rather obvious that the trial initiated by Yahweh is against mankind's idolatry or, to be more precise, against mankind on account of its idolatry, as discussed above. On the one hand, vv. 22–29 make the case that Paul's God alone possesses the power, legitimacy, and authority to judge the whole world—by virtue of being its sole God-Creator-Lord-Benefactor. On the other hand, they also supply ample evidence and the necessary witness to demonstrate man's inexcusable crime against that very same king

As we live in the Global Mission Age, God is intensifying the covenant lawsuit against disobedient people who reject the good news of the gospel in Jesus Christ. God raises many faithful missionaries, pastors, and believers, and in doing so, he scatters them as *the new covenant diaspora* to proclaim the gospel to all nations, tribes, and languages. In light of the second coming of Jesus Christ, the Global Mission is the final stage of God's preparation for his Son's return, executing his covenant lawsuit to the global community. As the second coming approaches, the great persecution against faithful believers will intensify in the global mission field. As such many godly believers' blood will be shed as martyrs for the kingdom of God in Jesus Christ.

Indeed, with the inauguration of the New Covenant Age, many faithful believers were persecuted and martyred. The apostle John himself was persecuted and sent to the island of Patmos in the Mediterranean Sea. He wrote the book of Revelation around the end of the first century through "the revelation of Jesus Christ" to send to "the seven churches, to Ephesus and to Smyrna and to Pergamum and to Thyatira and to Sardis and to Philadelphia and to Laodicea" (Rev 1:1–20).[9] Moreover, Jerusalem

---

and judge—idolatry is among other things a *lese majeste*, a seditious covenant-breaking—therefore establishing his guilt and making his conviction inevitable." Pardigon, *Paul Against the Idols*, 212.

Indeed, this is a brilliant observation to see "God's universal lawsuit" in the context of Paul's Areopagus Speech against idol worshipers in Athens. Moreover, Pardigon identifies idolatry as "a seditious covenant-breaking." However, we need to clarify the concept of "God's universal lawsuit" and "a seditious covenant-breaking" against idolatry in the context of the Gentile mission. It is clearer to identify these concepts as *God's universal covenant lawsuit against idol worshipers who broke the covenant of works in the first Adam under the New Covenant Age.* Cf. Jeon, Review of *Paul Against the Idols*, 237–40.

9. In light of the historical critical reading of the Bible, Bart Ehrman denies the apostle John's authorship of the Book of Revelation as well as the Gospel of John: "The author himself as 'John,' but he gives no further indication of which 'John' he might be. It was a common name in the ancient world. The book was eventually included in the New Testament—after long and protracted debates by the church fathers—once it was widely believed that this John was none other than John the son of Zebedee, author of the fourth Gospel. As we have seen, this historical John—one of Jesus' disciples—almost certainly did not write the Gospel; and whoever did write it is not the same person as the one who authored the book of Revelation, as is obvious to anyone who compares the two writing styles of the books in Greek. Most likely, then, this author really was someone named John, but he is a John that is otherwise unknown." Ehrman, *Bible*, 379.

Similarly, viewing the book of Revelation from the perspective of the historical critical reading, Wright and Bird reject the apostle John's authorship not only of the

finally fell and the kingdom of Israel as a type of the eternal kingdom of God was terminated in A.D. 70 through the military campaign of the Roman Empire.[10] In that context, John saw the glorious heaven where the martyred souls would reign "for a thousand years" with the exalted Jesus Christ, experiencing "the first resurrection" in heaven:

> Then I saw an angel coming down from heaven, holding in his hand the key to the bottomless pit and a great chain. [2]And he seized the dragon, that ancient serpent, who is the devil and Satan, and bound him for a thousand years, [3]and threw him into the pit, and shut it and sealed it over him, so that he might not deceive the nations any longer, until the thousand years were ended. After that he must be released for a little while. [4]Then I saw thrones and seated on them were those to whom the authority to judge was committed. Also I saw the souls of those who had been beheaded for the testimony of Jesus and for the word of God, and who had not worshiped the beast or its image and had not received its mark on their foreheads or their hands. They came to life and reigned with Christ for a thousand years. [5]The rest of the dead did not come to life until the thousand

---

Gospel of John and the Johannine Epistles but also the book of Revelation: "When all is said and done, however, it may be the contrasts between the gospel and Revelation which stand out more starkly. There are striking differences in language, grammar, and mode of discourse. The Greek of John's gospel is simple yet sublime. The Greek of Revelation falls within 'the range of possible registers of Greek usage of the first century.' . . . In the end, we may allow that John's gospel, epistles, and Revelation all come from the same circle, but that different authors are responsible for them. Neither John the son of Zebedee nor John the elder is the 'John' of Revelation. To distinguish him, we call him 'John the Seer.'" Wright and Bird, *New Testament in Its World*, 813–14.

10. David Chilton as a Christian Reconstructionist, dating the book of Revelation before the year of the destruction of Jerusalem and temple in A.D. 70, falsely argues that the book of Revelation is "a prophecy of Covenant wrath against apostate Israel." In doing so, he mistakenly insists that the book of Revelation is "a Covenant Lawsuit against Israel" which led to the final collapse against the kingdom of Israel in 70 A.D. However, we need to be reminded that the book of Revelation in light of the final redemptive judgment is *the prophecy of the covenant lawsuit against the people of all nations* that broke the covenant of works in the first Adam: "Like many other Biblical prophecies, the Book of Revelation is a prophecy of Covenant wrath against apostate Israel, which irrevocably turned away from the Covenant in her rejection of Christ. And, like many other Biblical prophecies, the Book of Revelation is written in the form of the Covenant Lawsuit, with five parts, conforming to the treaty structure of the Covenant. . . . There are other indications within the structure of Revelation that it is a Covenant Lawsuit against Israel. The four sevenfold judgments are arranged in general conformity to the order of Jesus' prophecy against Jerusalem in Matthew 24." Chilton, *Days of Vengeance*, 15, 20.

years were ended. This is the first resurrection. **6**Blessed and holy is the one who shares in the first resurrection! Over such the second death has no power, but they will be priests of God and of Christ, and they will reign with him for a thousand years. (Rev 20:1–6)

In fact, "a thousand years" is a *symbolical period* of time that covers the entire period of the New Covenant Age. Likewise, the New Covenant Age was audibly and visibly inaugurated in the upper room at the Pentecost in the presence of 120 new covenant community members, including the apostles. "The first resurrection" is not the believers' physical bodily resurrection which will occur when Jesus Christ returns. Rather, it describes *the glorified spirits in heaven* after their physical death in the New Covenant Age.[11]

The Day of the Lord and Second Coming of Jesus Christ

After the end of the New Covenant Age, Jesus Christ will return from *heaven*. Indeed, the inauguration of the New Covenant Age took place in the upper room at Pentecost. Ever since, the good news of the gospel of Jesus Christ spread to the ends of the present earth, slowly and surely accomplishing the Great Commission (Matt 28:16–20). The inauguration of the New Covenant Age did not come silently but came with the audible and visible sign and seal, including tongues and fiery forms in the upper room where 120 faithful believers, including the apostles, fervently prayed for the coming of the promised Holy Spirit (Acts 2:1–13).

11. For a covenantal and redemptive historical understanding of Revelation 20:1–6, see Jeon, *Biblical Theology*, 164–67; Kline, *God, Heaven and Har Magedon*, 171–79. Interpreting Revelation 20:1–6 in light of amillennialism, Kline describes "the first resurrection" a reference to "the bodily death of the righteous" during the New Covenant Age: "Similarly, paradoxical terminology is used in referring to the bodily death of the righteous. The real significance of their passage from earthly life is to be found in the nature of the intermediate state into which it translates them. And John sees the Christian dead, the souls of the martyrs beheaded for the testimony of Jesus, living and reigning with Christ for a thousand years (Rev 20:4b). As the event that introduces the Christian into the blessedness of this state of royal-priestly life in the presence of Christ in the heavenly church triumphant (vv. 4–6), bodily death is paradoxically called 'the first resurrection.' What for others is the first death is for believers a veritable resurrection, It is the first resurrection, to be followed by their second resurrection, a bodily resurrection, at the parousia after the thousand years when all the 'first' things pass away and God makes all things new (Rev 21: 4,5)." Kline, *God, Heaven and Har Magedon*, 176.

As the New Covenant Age ends with the completion of the global mission through the infallible guidance and work of the Holy Spirit, mobilizing the faithful servants of God, Jesus Christ will again intrude the present world from *heaven*. Undoubtedly, the second coming of Christ will not be a silent or humble one but a spectacular and visible return for all on the earth to see. Of course, Jesus' first earthly coming was a humble one as a suffering servant. His second coming, however, will be awesome, glorious, thunderous, and visible because he will return as the final Judge and Consummator.

The day of the Lord depicts the day of the second coming of Jesus Christ in the New Testament. At the same time, it signifies the day of the final redemptive judgment which will visibly separate the elect and reprobate. In that regard, we need to explore the vital relationship between the day of the Lord and final redemptive judgment.[12]

After the end of the New Covenant Age, the reign of "the thousand years" of the glorified souls with the exalted Jesus Christ *in heaven* will end as well. And the day of the Lord will follow as the day of the final redemptive judgment after a brief intrusion from the antichrist on the present earth. Before the outbreak of the final battle between the kingdom of God and the kingdom of Satan, Jesus Christ will separate the elect and

---

12. Based on *the dispensational theology and eschatology*, MacArthur and Mayhue improperly argue that there will be *the two different days of the Lord in the future*. One will occur after "the end of the tribulation period," while the other will take place after the earthly millennial kingdom. Moreover, they falsely describe that the day of the Lord will involve "judgment only, not judgment and blessing." In doing so, they deny the fact that the day of the Lord will be once and for all the final judgment day, visibly separating the eternal blessings and curses from the elect and reprobate: "The New Testament writers picked up on the eschatological usage and applied the phrase both to the judgment that will climax the tribulation period and the judgment that will usher in the new earth. The day of the Lord occurs through providential means (Ezek. 30:3) or directly at the hand of God (2 Pet. 3:10). At times, the near fulfillment (Joel 1:15) prefigures the far fulfillment (Joel 3:14). Two periods of the day of the Lord are yet to be fulfilled on earth: (1) the judgment that climaxes the tribulation period (2 Thess. 2:2; Rev. 16–18) and (2) the consummating judgment of this earth after the millennium that ushers in the new earth (2 Pet. 3:10–13; Rev. 20:7—21:1). In sum, the day of the Lord can be summarized in six assertions: 1. The day of the Lord involves judgment only, not judgment and blessings. 2. The day of the Lord occurs twice in God's prophetic plan, not once. 3. The day of the Lord occurs at the end of the tribulation period, not throughout its duration. 4. The day of the Lord occurs again at the end of the millennium, not throughout its duration. 5. The day of the Lord as defined here does not necessarily prove pretribulationism, but it certainly and easily allows for it. 6. The day of the Lord supports futuristic premillennialism." MacArthur and Mayhue, *Biblical Doctrine*, 907.

reprobate. Jesus Christ, as the great prophet during his public ministry, prophesied that there would *simultaneously* be "the resurrection of life" and "the resurrection of judgment," anticipating his second coming:[13]

> 25"Truly, truly, I say to you, an hour is coming, and is now here, when the dead will hear the voice of the Son of God, and those who hear will live. 26For as the Father has life in himself, so he has granted the Son also to have life in himself. 27And he has given him authority to execute judgment, because he is the Son of Man. 28Do not marvel at this, for an hour is coming when all who are in the tombs will hear his voice 29*and come out, those who have done good to the resurrection of life, and those who have done evil to the resurrection of judgment* [καὶ ἐκπορεύσονται οἱ τὰ ἀγαθὰ ποιήσαντες εἰς ἀνάστασιν ζωῆς, οἱ δὲ τὰ φαῦλα πράξαντες εἰς ἀνάστασιν κρίσεως]. (John 5:25–29)

As Jesus prophesied, God the Father will grant the Son the authority to conduct the final judgment, visibly separating believers from unbelievers. Likewise, God will grant believers the glorious bodily resurrection, defined as "the resurrection of life" (ἀνάστασιν ζωῆς) which is the future blessings of the covenant of grace in the last Adam. On the other hand, God will curse unbelievers with "the resurrection of judgment" (ἀνάστασιν κρίσεως) because they are under the curse of the broken covenant of works in the first Adam.[14]

13. Scofield, as a dispensationalist, was a very influential person, spreading dispensational theology and eschatology not only in the English-speaking world but throughout the Global Mission Field in the twentieth century. He unbiblically argues that there will be believers' resurrection before the millennial kingdom and unbelievers' resurrection after the millennial kingdom will be over: "(4) Two resurrections are yet future, which are inclusive of 'all that are in the graves' (John 5:28). These are distinguished as 'of life' (1 Cor. 15. 22. 23; 1 Thess. 4:14–17; Rev. 20. 4), and 'of judgment' (John 5. 28, 29; Rev. 20:11–13). They are separated by a period of one thousand years (Rev. 20. 5). The 'first resurrection,' that 'unto life,' will occur at the second coming of Christ (1 Cor. 15. 23), the saints of the O.T. and church ages meeting Him in the air (1 Thess. 4. 16, 17); while the martyrs of the tribulation, who also have part in the first resurrection (Rev. 20. 4), are raised at the end of the great tribulation. . . . (7) After the thousand years the 'resurrection unto judgment' (John 5. 29) occurs. The resurrection body of the wicked dead is not described. They are judged according to their works, and cast into the lake of fire (Rev. 20. 7–15)." Scofield, *Scofield Study Bible*, 1228.

14. Anticipating the second coming of Jesus Christ at the day of the Lord, Vos draws an organic relation that "resurrection and Judgment are the two correlated acts of the final consummation of things." In that sense, the bodily resurrection of believers and unbelievers will be "a judging-process" which will take place universally and visibly: "Resurrection and Judgment are the two correlated acts of the final

At the end of Jesus Christ's public ministry before his crucifixion, he delivered his famous Olivet Discourse on the Mount of Olives in the presence of his original disciples (Matt 24:1—25:46). In summation, it was a message about the comprehensive picture and guideline of eschatology:

> 29"Immediately after the tribulation of those days the sun will be darkened, and the moon will not give its light, and the stars will fall from heaven, and the powers of the heavens will be shaken. 30Then will appear in heaven the sign of the Son of Man, and then all the tribes of the earth will mourn, and they will see the Son of Man coming on the clouds of heaven with power and great glory. 31And he will send out his angels with a loud trumpet call, and they will gather his elect from the four winds, from one end of heaven to the other. (Matt 24:29–31)

Jesus Christ predicted that his second coming would take place after the brief period of great tribulation which he defined as "the tribulation of those days" (v. 29). Moreover, his second coming will not be silent or humble, but glorious, spectacular, visible, and universal. He will be *globally* visible as he explained that all the people on the earth "will see the Son of Man coming on the clouds of heaven with power and great glory" (v. 30). In relation to this, we need to pay special attention to verse 31: "And he will send out his angels with a loud trumpet call, and they will gather his elect from the four winds, from one end of heaven to the other." This verse suggests that he will visibly separate the elect from reprobate, mobilizing and using his angels as the final Judge as a part of the final judgment.

Jesus Christ, the infallible founder of redemptive historical interpretation of the Old Testament par excellence, compares the day of judgment to the original world at the time of Noah and the day of the final judgment "with the coming of the Son of Man" to the present world:

> 36"But concerning that day and hour no one knows, not even the angels of heaven, nor the Son, but the Father only. 37As were the days of Noah, so will be the coming of the Son of Man. 38For as in those days before the flood they were eating and drinking, marrying and giving in marriage, until the day when Noah

---

consummation of things. They are like twin-woes in the travail by which the age to come is brought to birth. But they are not cleanly separated even at their eschatological emergence. In the resurrection there is already wrapped up a judging-process, at least for believers: the raising act in their case, together with the attending change, plainly involves a pronouncement of vindication." Vos, *Pauline Eschatology*, 261.

entered the ark, [39]and they were unaware until the flood came and swept them all away, so will be the coming of the Son of Man. [40]Then two men will be in the field; one will be taken and one left. [41]Two women will be grinding at the mill; one will be taken and one left. [42]Therefore, stay awake, for you do not know on what day your Lord is coming. [43]But know this, that if the master of the house had known in what part of the night the thief was coming, he would have stayed awake and would not have let his house be broken into. [44]Therefore you also must be ready, for the Son of Man is coming at an hour you do not expect. (Matt 24:36–44)

Jesus Christ uses *a parabolic expression* to explain the process of separation between believers and unbelievers. In doing so, he employs pictorial images of a farmer's field and home of "grinding at the mill" which were common scenes of that time in the promised land. The pictorial identification in verses 41 and 42 is crucially important because it graphically defines *the visible separation process between the elect and reprobate*. In that sense, people who are *taken* will be believers while people who are *left* behind will be unbelievers.[15]

The apostle Paul admonishes the new covenant community in the Thessalonian church that there will be "the coming of the Lord" at the day of the Lord:

[13]But we do not want you to be uninformed, brothers, about those who are asleep, that you may not grieve as others do who have no hope. [14]For since we believe that Jesus died and rose again, even so, through Jesus, God will bring with him those who have fallen asleep. [15]For this we declare to you by a word

15. Kline insightfully argues that the gathering of the resurrected believers at the second coming of Jesus Christ will be the visible process of *a separation* of the elect from the reprobate in the process of the final judgment: "The resurrection-gathering of the saints effects a separation of the sons of the kingdom from the seed of the evil one. This separation is brought out graphically in our Lord's teaching concerning the day of the Son of Man, the day like the Noahic day of judgment. Coming on the clouds of heaven with power and great glory (cf. Matt. 16:27; 2 Thess 1:7) he will send out his angels with a loud trumpet call to gather his elect from one end of heaven to the other (Matt 24:30, 31), but also to gather all evildoers out of his kingdom (Matt 13:41). One of two men in the field will be taken to safety and one left for desolation. One of two women grinding at the mill will be taken and the other left (Matt 24:39–41). The angel reapers will perform their two fold task: the weeds (the Satan-sown wicked) will be gathered and bound in bundles to be burned in the furnace of fire and the wheat (the righteous) will be gathered into the barn, destined to glow like the sun in the kingdom of their Father (Matt 13:30, 39–43)." Kline, *God, Heaven and Har Magedon*, 202.

> from the Lord, that we who are alive, who are left until the com-
> ing of the Lord, will not precede those who have fallen asleep.
> 16For the Lord himself will descend from heaven with a cry of
> command, with the voice of an archangel, and with the sound
> of the trumpet of God. And the dead in Christ will rise first.
> 17Then we who are alive, who are left, will be caught up together
> with them in the clouds to meet the Lord in the air, and so we
> will always be with the Lord. 18Therefore encourage one an-
> other with these words. (1 Thess 4:13–18)

As Jesus Christ returns from *heaven*, there will be the glorious heavenly cantata of the prelude of the final battle between the kingdom of
God and the kingdom of Satan. Paul describes *pictorially* the scene of Jesus Christ's second coming in the air (v. 16). As Jesus Christ comes back,
he will gather all the elect in the air with *the glorified bodies*, separating
them from the corrupt world and the resurrected bodies of the reprobate
before the final holy war is waged against the kingdom of Satan. In that
sense, the Son as the final Judge will separate the elect and reprobate. So,
Paul's statement, "And the dead in Christ will rise first. 17Then we who
are alive, who are left, will be caught up together with them in the clouds
to meet the Lord in the air" (vv. 16b-17a) vividly describes the separation
of the glorified elect with bodily resurrection and transformation from
the corrupt world and the resurrected bodies of the reprobate before the
final holy war.[16] In fact, the glorified believers' *visible union with Christ*
with the holy angels will be the glorious union in the air between Jesus
Christ the bridegroom and the gloriously resurrected and transformed
believers as the bride.[17]

16. Interpreting 1 Thess 4:17, Vos rightly views that it is a pictorial description of
"the glorification of believers" which precedes the final judgment, separating believers
from the reprobate: "It is difficult to conclude anything in this regard. The judge will
certainly be visible to all. On the basis of 1 Thessalonians 4:17, the Lutherans thought
that the judgment would take place in the air. The Reformed sometimes concluded
from this text that believers would receive their judgment in the air, unbelievers below
on the earth. But 1 Thessalonians 4 is not related specifically to the last judgment but
only to the glorification of believers, which in part precedes the judgment, in part
follows it, for which reason also nothing is said about unbelievers." Vos, *Reformed
Dogmatics*, 5:290.

17. Dispensationalists developed the doctrine of "the rapture of the living saints,"
based upon 1 Thess 4:13–18 and other bible passages. Their theological presupposition
is that the church will be caught up *from earth to heaven* before the earthly millennial
kingdom begins. In that sense, *the dispensational doctrine of rapture* is not biblical so
that we must reject it: "Closely related in view of the time and circumstances with the
resurrection of the bodies of believers is the translation, apart from death, of the living

With the completion of the visible separation between believers and unbelievers with the bodily resurrection, the preparation process for the final holy war will be over. Then there will be *the final holy war* between the kingdom of God and the kingdom of Satan. Many believe that world history on the present earth will end due to global warming or World War III. However, the pictorial description of the last day as presented in the Bible does not guide us in that direction. Rather, world history will end with the final holy war which will take place when Jesus Christ returns as the final Judge.

At this point, we need to explore the symbolic pictures and images as revealed in the book of Revelation. Surprisingly, there are the recapitulations of the final holy war in Revelation 16:12–16, 19:11–21, and 20:7–10. Revelation 16:12–16 provides images of the Armageddon Battle[18] while Revelation 19:11–21 includes symbolic pictures of the Battle of the Rider on a White Horse. Moreover, Revelation 20:7–10 is the symbolic description of the Gog and Magog Battle. In that regard, we

---

saints. Having described at length the resurrection of the bodies of the believers who have died (1 Cor 15:35–50), the Apostle goes on to declare a mystery, or sacred secret hitherto unrevealed (1 Cor 15:51–57), namely, that 'we shall not all sleep,' but with essential changes which are wrought in a moment, the child of God goes on in this body to meet the Lord in the air (cf. John 14:1–3; 1 Cor 15:52–52; 1 Thess 4:13–18; 2 Thess 2:1; Heb 9:28)." Chafer, *Systematic Theology,* 4:395.

Similarly, Ryrie as a *dispensationalist* insists *the dispensational doctrine of rapture*: "The Rapture of the church means the carrying away of the church from earth to heaven. The Greek word from which we take the term 'rapture' appears in 1 Thessalonians 4:17, translated 'caught up.' The Latin translation of this verse used the word *rapturo.* . . . Thus there can be no doubt that the word is used in 1 Thessalonians 4:17 to indicate the actual removal of people from earth to heaven. . . . Strictly speaking, only living believers are raptured (though we use the term to include all that happens at that time). This means they will be caught up into the Lord's presence without having to experience physical death." Ryrie, *Basic Theology,* 537–38.

18. Interpreting the Armageddon Battle in Revelation 16:13–16, Riddlebarger insightfully sees that it will occur at the second coming of Christ, which will be the day of the final judgment. Furthermore, he properly argues that the Armageddon Battle is the recapitulation of the same battle, revealed in Revelation 13 and 19:11–21: "Then in Revelation 16:13–16, we read of how the kings of the whole earth are gathered for battle at Armageddon 'on the great day of God Almighty' (v. 14). This is the day, John said, when Jesus returns like a thief in judgment (v. 15) . . . Clearly, Revelation 13, 16, and 19 depict the same event, yet another strong indication of recapitulation in this epistle. What is depicted in Revelation 16 and 19 is judgment day. This is when Jesus Christ returns in wrath to judge the nations, raise the dead, and make all things new." Riddlebarger, *A Case for Amillennialism,* 231.

need to briefly explore the recapitulations of the final holy war as revealed
in those passages.

The Armageddon Battle provides various images of the final holy
war which will occur when Jesus Christ returns.[19] The battle will take
place "on the great day of God the Almighty" which will be the day of
Parousia.[20] The frontiers of the kingdom of Satan against the kingdom
of God will be the dragon, the beast, and the false prophet at the visible
showdown of the final holy war:

> [12]The sixth angel poured out his bowl on the great river Euphra-
> tes, and its water was dried up, to prepare the way for the kings
> from the east. [13]And I saw, coming out of the mouth of the
> dragon and out of the mouth of the beast and out of the mouth
> of the false prophet, three unclean spirits like frogs. [14]For they

19. Beale interprets the Armageddon Battle in Revelation 16:14, the Battle in Revelation 19:19, and the Gog and Magog Battle in Revelation 20:8 as *the same battle* which
is the recapitulation: "The purpose of the deception is 'to gather them together for the
war of the great day of God Almighty.' The same expression occurs in chs. 19 and 20,
where it refers respectively to the beast and the dragon gathering kings together to
fight against Christ at his final coming. . . . The reference here is probably the same as
in chs. 19 and 20: the confrontation between the forces of the beast and Christ at the
end of the age. These three references to the war are based on OT prophecy, especially
from Zechariah 12–14 and possibly Zephaniah 3, which predict that God will gather
the nations together in Israel for the final war of history. . . . In all three places, 16:14;
19:19; and 20:8, the article is used with 'war' (ton polenon) because they are referring
to "the [well-known] 'War of the End' " prophesied in the OT. 20:7–10 shows that
this 'war' is part of the final attack of Satan's forces against the saints. Therefore, it
is the same 'war' as in 11:7, since that battle also is one in which the 'beast' attempts
to annihilate the whole body of believers on earth (see on 11:7–10). In this light, the
definite article may be an article of previous reference, not only to OT prophecy, but
also back to the initial anarthrous description of the last battle in 11:7." Beale, *Book of
Revelation*, 834–35.

20. Interpreting the Armageddon Battle in Revelation 16:12–16 in light of the
dispensational premillennialism, MacArthur insists that it will begin during the Great
Tribulation and end when Jesus Christ arrives in Jerusalem from heaven: "16:14 . . .
kings of the whole world. No longer just the eastern confederacy, but now all the world
begins to gather in Palestine for the final, climactic battle (Ps. 2:2–3; Joel 3:2–4; Zech.
14:1–3). Battle on the great day of God the Almighty. The battle of the Armageddon (Rev. 16:16). It is the great war with God and Christ. . . . The war will end when
Christ arrives (Rev. 19:17–20). . . . 16:16 Armageddon. The Hebrew name for Mount
Megiddo, 60 miles north of Jerusalem. The battle will rage on the nearby plains, site of
Barak's victory over the Canaanites (Judg. 4) and Gideon's victory over the Midianites
(Judg. 7). Napoleon called this valley the greatest battlefield he had ever seen. But the
battle of Armageddon will not be limited to the Megiddo plains—it will encompass the
length of Palestine." MacArthur, *MacArthur Study Bible*, 1963.

are demonic spirits, performing signs, who go abroad to the kings of the whole world, to assemble them for battle on the great day of God the Almighty. 15("Behold, I am coming like a thief! Blessed is the one who stays awake, keeping his garments on, that he may not go about naked and be seen exposed!") 16And they assembled them at the place that in Hebrew is called Armageddon. (Rev 16:12–16)

Jesus Christ as the final Judge will throw the antichrist and the false prophet as his wicked servant into "the lake of fire." In fact, the apostle Paul identified the antichrist as "the man of lawlessness" (2 Thess 2:1–12).

Meanwhile, John saw Jesus Christ riding on "a white horse" through a vision capturing "the beast," the antichrist, along with "the false prophet" and throwing them into "the lake of fire," as they were still alive:

11Then I saw heaven opened, and behold, a white horse! The one sitting on it is called Faithful and True, and in righteousness he judges and makes war. 12His eyes are like a flame of fire, and on his head are many diadems, and he has a name written that no one knows but himself. 13He is clothed in a robe dipped in blood, and the name by which he is called is The Word of God. 14And the armies of heaven, arrayed in fine linen, white and pure, were following him on white horses. 15From his mouth comes a sharp sword with which to strike down the nations, and he will rule them with a rod of iron. He will tread the winepress of the fury of the wrath of God the Almighty. 16On his robe and on his thigh he has a name written, King of kings and Lord of lords. 17Then I saw an angel standing in the sun, and with a loud voice he called to all the birds that fly directly overhead, "Come, gather for the great supper of God, 18to eat the flesh of kings, the flesh of captains, the flesh of mighty men, the flesh of horses and their riders, and the flesh of all men, both free and slave, both small and great." 19And I saw the beast and the kings of the earth with their armies gathered to make war against him who was sitting on the horse and against his army. 20And the beast was captured, and with it the false prophet who in its presence had done the signs by which he deceived those who had received the mark of the beast and those who worshiped its image. These two were thrown alive into the lake of fire that burns with sulfur. 21And the rest were slain by the sword that came from the mouth of him who was sitting on the horse, and all the birds were gorged with their flesh. (Rev 19:11–21)

The appearance and activity of the antichrist, described as "the beast," will be the final visible sign of the second coming of Jesus Christ. When Jesus Christ returns in the air, he will throw the antichrist along with "the false prophet" into "the lake of fire." Verse 20 provides a vivid image of the antichrist and his servant, the false prophet. In fact, "the beast," the antichrist, and "the false prophet" will be thrown into "the lake of fire" by a rider on a white horse who is Jesus Christ as the Judge who will wage the final holy war against the kingdom of Satan.[21]

In redemptive history after the fall, God took Enoch to heaven who was walking with him, setting apart himself from the original corrupt world. Surprisingly, God took Enoch to *heaven* before his physical death (Gen 5:21–24). Later, God took the prophet Elijah from the present earth "by a whirlwind into heaven" while the prophet Elisha watched (2 Kgs 2:1–14). The ascension of Enoch and Elijah without physical death is God's demonstration of the existence of *heaven* to the covenant community. Contrastingly, the Son, in his second coming, will send the antichrist and the false prophet to *hell* before their physical death.

With Jesus Christ's second coming, the gathering of the glorified believers in the air, and disposal of the antichrist and false prophet into "the lake of fire," the preparation of the final holy war against the kingdom of Satan, including reprobate, will end. The covenantal background of the visible separation between the glorified believers in the air and the wicked left behind on the present earth will be the covenant of works and the covenant of grace. In other words, God the Father will grant to *take* the glorified believers into the air to meet Jesus Christ in the milieu of the blessings of the covenant of grace. However, the wicked, with their bodily resurrection, will be *left* on the present earth, based upon the curse of the covenant of works in the first Adam.[22]

21. Vos connects "the lawless one" of 2 Thess 2:8 with "the beast" of Rev 19:20 which can be identified as the antichrist. In doing so, he observes that the beast and the false prophet will be thrown into "living into hell" in contrast with Enoch and Elijah who ascended into *heaven* without tasting physical death: "We note further that the antichrist will be destroyed by the Spirit of the Lord's mouth and by the manifestation of His coming [2 Thess 2:8]. The hostile power that has arrayed itself against His church will collapse as soon as the Lord shows Himself. From Revelation 19:20 the conclusion has been drawn that the antichrist and the false prophet, who has served him, will without dying first, descend living into hell (as it were in contrast with Enoch and Elijah), while the others are killed in order then again to be resurrected." Vos, *Reformed Dogmatics*, 5:289.

22. The antithetical principle between the covenant of works and the covenant of grace is applied not only in the process of personal salvation in redemptive history

And then there will be the final holy war. God the Father will grant the Son to wage the final holy war against the kingdom of Satan. Jesus Christ, the Divine Warrior of the kingdom of God, will fight the final holy war against the kingdom of Satan. He will lead this war, using God's mighty fire to consume Satan and his demons, along with the wicked reprobate who have followed Satan with their minds, hearts, and souls under the curse of the covenant of works in the first Adam. We briefly examined the Armageddon Battle as the final holy war, revealed in Revelation 16:12–16. The same battle is described as the Gog-Magog Battle in Revelation 20:7–10 from a different perspective.[23] In the end, Satan, as the head of the kingdom of Satan, will finally be defeated and thrown into "the lake of fire and sulfur" which will be *the consummated hell*:

> [7]And when the thousand years are ended, Satan will be released from his prison [8]and will come out to deceive the nations that are at the four corners of the earth, Gog and Magog, to gather them for battle; their number is like the sand of the sea. [9]And they marched up over the broad plain of the earth and surrounded the camp of the saints and the beloved city, but fire came down from heaven and consumed them, [10]and the devil who had deceived them was thrown into the lake of fire and

---

but also in the Consummation as Riddlebarger properly demonstrates: "The history of redemption is the progressive unfolding of a covenant of works and a covenant of grace throughout the whole of Scripture. These two covenants—the very essence of covenant theology—will continue to resurface as we speak of the eschatology of both testaments. In the progressive development of these two covenants, Jesus Christ—the only Mediator between God and Man and the Redeemer promised throughout the whole Old Testament—was revealed. . . . The connection between the new creation and the covenant of grace is important to keep in mind. The one who makes all things new, Jesus Christ, is also the Mediator of the covenant of grace. Therefore, new creation and the covenant of grace are forever joined together in the person and work of Jesus Christ." Riddlebarger, *Case for Amillennialism*, 62–63.

23. Kline properly views the Gog and Magog Battle as the recapitulation of the Har Magedon Battle, revealed in Rev 16:12–16 and 19:11–21, which will occur at the day of the second coming of Christ as the process of the final judgment, including bodily resurrection: "In the Revelation 20 depiction of the resurrection-judgment a courtroom vision is juxtaposed to a battle vision. In vv. 7–10 (a recapitulation of the Har Magedon battle scene of Rev 16:12–16 and 19:11–21) the forces of antichrist Gog besieging the city of the saints are consumed by fire falling from heaven. . . . It is when antichrist Gog and Magog have surrounded the ekklesia-camp that the judgment fire falls on them, ending their siege of the saints (Rev 20:9). Both type and antitype final judgments are thus redemptive acts in that they save God's people from the power of their hellish foes." Kline, *God, Heaven and Har Magedon*, 207–9.

sulfur where the beast and the false prophet were, and they will
be tormented day and night forever and ever. (Rev 20:7–10)

The Gog and Magog Battle will be the final holy war between the
kingdom of God and kingdom of Satan.[24] However, Satan and his wicked
armies will be decisively defeated by the Son and his holy armies, including the holy angels and glorified believers. As Yahweh used his heavenly
fire to consume the cities of Sodom and Gomorrah, the Son will not use
manmade weapons like nuclear bombs, chemical weapons, and other
sophisticated weapons, but the heavenly fire. Verse 9 states, "And they
marched up over the broad plain of the earth and surrounded the camp
of the saints and the beloved city, but fire came down from heaven and
consumed them." This provides us with a comprehensive image of the
final showdown between the Son's glorious armies and Satan's wicked
armies. Once again, we can have a very good idea about the fact that the
Son will use the heavenly fire as a means of the final holy war when we
pay close attention to the description of "but fire came down from heaven
and consumed them."

As Hendriksen insightfully describes the Gog and Magog Battle as
the recapitulation of the same battle, namely the Armageddon Battle as revealed in Revelation 16:12–16 and recapitulated in Revelation 19:11–21:

> In other words, we have here in Revelation 20:7–10 a descrip-
> tion of the same battle—not "war"—that was described in
> Revelation16:12ff. and in Revelation 19:19. In all three cases
> we read in the original, *the* battle. Thus, 16:14: "to gather them
> together for *the* battle of the great day of God, the Almighty."
> Again, Revelation 19:19: "gathered together to make *the* battle
> against him." Similarly, here in 20:8: "to gather them together to
> *the* battle." In other words, these are not three different battles.
> We have here one and the same battle. It is the battle of Har-
> Magedon in all three cases. It is the final attack of anti-Christian

---

24. As a dispensationalist, MacArthur sees the Armageddon Battle in Revelation
16:12–16 taking place right during the great tribulation before the second coming
of Christ while he anticipates the Gog and Magog Battle after the earthly millennial
kingdom is over: "20.8 Gog and Magog. The name given to the army of rebels and its
leader at the end of the Millennium. They were names of ancient enemies of the Lord.
Magog was the grandson of Noah (Gen. 10:2) and founder of a kingdom located north
of the Black and Caspian Seas. Gog is apparently the leader of a rebel army known
collectively as Magog. The battle depicted in Rev. 20:8–9 is like the one in Ezek. 38–39;
it is best to see this one as taking place at the end of the Millennium." MacArthur,
MacArthur Study Bible, 1970.

forces upon the Church. The "new" thing that Revelation 20 reveals is what happens to Satan as a result of this battle.[25]

Meanwhile, God's heavenly fire will not only be used as a means to wage the final holy war against Satan, demons, and unbelievers but to also recreate the new heavens and new earth. Agreeably, Peter describes that God will make his final judgment at "the day of judgment." God will pour out his mighty fire upon the present heavens and earth and also the unbelievers:

> This is now the second letter that I am writing to you, beloved. In both of them I am stirring up your sincere mind by way of reminder, [2]that you should remember the predictions of the holy prophets and the commandment of the Lord and Savior through your apostles, [3]knowing this first of all, that scoffers will come in the last days with scoffing, following their own sinful desires. [4]They will say, "Where is the promise of his coming? For ever since the fathers fell asleep, all things are continuing as they were from the beginning of creation." [5]For they deliberately overlook this fact, that the heavens existed long ago, and the earth was formed out of water and through water by the word of God, [6]and that by means of these the world that then existed was deluged with water and perished. [7]But by the same word the heavens and earth that now exist are stored up for fire, being kept until the day of judgment and destruction of the ungodly. (2 Pet 3:1–7)

Peter identifies the day of the second coming of Jesus Christ not only as "the day of judgment" but also "the day of the Lord" and "the day of God." In that sense, "the day of judgment," "the day of the Lord," and "the day of God" are coterminous and all point to the day of the second coming of Jesus Christ and final judgment.[26] Moreover, Peter emphasizes

---

25. Hendriksen, *More Than Conquerors*, 213.

26. Interpreting "the day of the Lord" in 2 Pet 3:10, Chafer as a dispensationalist strangely and falsely argues that it will be the period of one thousand years of the earthly millennial kingdom "by the reign of Christ over Israel and the world on David's throne in Jerusalem accompanied by His Bride—the Church." It is a good example of how Chafer's dispensational hermeneutics loses the proper ground of eschatology: "This lengthened period of a thousand years begins, generally speaking, with the second advent of Christ and the judgments connected therewith, and ends with the passing of the present heaven and the present earth. The second coming of Christ is, to Israel, as 'a thief in the night' (cf. Matt 24:42–44; 1 Thess 5:4; 2 Pet 3:10). It is therefore worthy of special note that Peter, having referred to the truth that a day with the Lord is as a thousand years and a thousand years as a day. . . . The Day of the Lord is characterized by the reign of Christ over Israel and the world on David's throne

how God's final judgment upon the present world will be at the same time *a final process of the new creation* for "new heavens and a new earth" where the glorified believers will inherit and dwell:

> [8]But do not overlook this one fact, beloved, that with the Lord one day is as a thousand years, and a thousand years as one day. [9]The Lord is not slow to fulfill his promise as some count slowness, but is patient toward you, not wishing that any should perish, but that all should reach repentance. [10]But the day of the Lord will come like a thief, and then the heavens will pass away with a roar, and the heavenly bodies will be burned up and dissolved, and the earth and the works that are done on it will be exposed. [11]Since all these things are thus to be dissolved, what sort of people ought you to be in lives of holiness and godliness, [12]waiting for and hastening the coming of the day of God, because of which the heavens will be set on fire and dissolved, and the heavenly bodies will melt as they burn! [13]But according to his promise we are waiting for new heavens and a new earth in which righteousness dwells. (2 Pet 3:8–13)

Peter highlights how the "new heavens and a new earth" will be the dwelling place of the glorified believers with his succinct statement of "But according to his promise we are waiting for new heavens and a new earth in which righteousness dwells" (v. 13). To be sure, however, God's recreation of "new heavens and a new earth" through his mighty fire will not be after the annihilation of the present heaven and earth, but will be the glorification and transformation of the present universe. Put simply, the present heavens and earth are the triune God's beautiful creation. In that sense, they are not the object of annihilation but the glorification and transformation at the day of the Lord.[27]

---

in Jerusalem accompanied by His Bride—the Church. In that time the believers will not only share in Christ's reign and the judgments of mankind (1 Cor 6:2), but also in His judgments of the angels (1 Cor 6:3). The judgment of angels continues throughout the thousand years (1 Cor 15:25–26)." Chafer, *Systematic Theology*, 4:398.

As we know "the day of the Lord" and "the day of God" are coterminous terms which indicate the day of the second coming of Christ in the New Testament. However, Chafer does not recognize this truth, falsely making a distinction between the day of the Lord and the day of God in his interpretation of 2 Peter 3:10, 12: "In distinction from the Day of the Lord which is terminated by the ending of the thousand years and the passing of the present heaven and the present earth (2 Pet. 3:10), is the eternity to come which is designated *the Day of God* (cf. 2 Pet 3:12 with 1 Cor 15:28)." Chafer, *Systematic Theology*, 4:401.

27. Favoring "the annihilation of the present universe" over the renewal of the

After the final holy war is over, all the resurrected people, including both the elect and reprobate, will stand before "a great white throne" for the final judgment.[28] "Books" will be opened for the elect and reprobate for their final judgment.[29] The covenantal standard for the final judgment of reprobate will be the covenant of works, broken in the first Adam with a *gradation of hellish curses* based upon their thoughts and deeds,

---

present universe, MacArthur and Mayhue miss the mark, misinterpreting 2 Pet 3:7–12, Rev 21:1, and other Bible passages: "With this new heaven and new earth be entirely new, another out-of-nothing creation of God, after the first heaven and earth are annihilated? Or are the new heaven and new earth a restoration and renewal of the present planet? The biblical language describing the destruction of the old order argues in favor of a completely new planet, because the old has been put out of existence. John writes that the first heaven and earth 'passed away' (Rev 21:1). Then there is the strong wording of fiery destruction in 2 Peter 3. . . . In further support of the annihilation of the present universe is Jesus's statement, 'Heaven and earth will pass away, but my words will not pass away' (Matt. 24:35). Psalm 102 declares that the earth and the heavens 'will perish' and 'wear out like a garment' (Ps 102:25–26). Isaiah 24:20 states, 'The earth staggers like a drunken man; it sways like a hut . . . and it falls, and will not rise again.' In his first epistle, John writes, 'The world is passing away' (1 John 2:17)." MacArthur and Mayhue, *Biblical Doctrine*, 911.

28. Chafer (1871–1952) was the founder and professor of Dallas Theological Seminary, and played a significant role in spreading dispensational theology and eschatology in the twentieth century beyond the English speaking world. Reflecting the judgment of the Great White Throne, revealed in Revelation 20:11–15, he falsely asserts that it is *only related to the judgment of unbelievers*: "This, the final judgment which consummates the judgment of the cross and the judgment of all people who are unredeemed, occurs at the close of the millennium. These people will be raised for that judgment and will be judged according to their works. These works are a matter of divine record in books which are opened at that judgment. The book of life is also in evidence, but probably with a view to demonstrating that no errors have been made and that those gathered before the great white throne have not the gift of God which is eternal life. The doom that awaits them is terrible beyond comprehension; but it is the last word of a holy God respecting sin and all unrighteousness. In view of the general tendency to confuse the judgment of the nations with that of the great white throne, the distinction between them should be observed. At the judgment of the nations three classes are present—'sheep,' 'goats,' and Christ's 'brethren,' while at the judgment of the great white throne there is but one class—the wicked dead. In the former the scene is on earth, while in the latter it is in space. In the former the issue is the treatment of the Jew, while in the latter it is the evil works of those being judged. In the former some enter the kingdom at its inception and some go to the lake of fire, in the latter all go to the lake of fire." Chafer, *Systematic Theology*, 4:411–12.

29. As an exponent of the historic premillennialism, Grudem insists that the time of final judgment will take place after the earthly millennial kingdom of Rev 20:1–6, the rebellion, and God's defeat as revealed in Rev 20:7–10: "The final judgment will occur after the millennium and the rebellion that occurs at the end of it. John pictures the millennial kingdom." Grudem, *Systematic Theology*, 1142.

reflecting their entire life on earth.[30] Meanwhile, "the book of life" will be open for the elect, and the covenantal basis for their final judgment will be the covenant of grace in the last Adam which was inaugurated in Genesis 3:15.[31] In juxtaposition, there will be *gradations of heavenly blessings* according to the good works in the process of progressive sanctification, although the salvation and inheritance of the eternal kingdom of God is purely God the Father's grant in Jesus Christ:[32]

30. Observing *the antithesis* between the blessings of heaven and curses of hell, Vos argues that there will be "a difference of degree" in the punishments of eternal hell: "In the punishments of hell there will be a *difference of degree*. That is clearly taught in Matthew 11:22; Luke 12:47–48; 'his portion,' Matt 24:51 (Luke 12:46). That does not allow for determining in detail. In Matthew 23:14 [cf. KJV] it is said of the scribes and Pharisees that they will receive more severe judgment." Vos, *Reformed Dogmatics*, 5:304.

31. Kline views God's final judgment in light of covenants. On the one hand, believers' vindication will be based upon "the grace of the new covenant in Christ, the second Adam." On the other hand, unbelievers' final judgment to hell will be founded upon "the primal covenant of works in Eden." In that sense, Kline *adequately applies the antithesis between the covenant of works and the covenant of grace* as the covenantal judicial ground of the final judgment: "Beyond the typological day of the Lord that would terminate the Old Covenant order as threatened in the curses of the Mosaic covenants, the Old Testament prophets foresaw an eschatological day of the Lord, a final judgment event at the conclusion of the coming new covenant age. For God's redeemed people it would prove to be a day of vindication. But for those who spurn the invitation to come under the grace of the new covenant in Christ, the second Adam, making instead the wretched choice to remain under the works principle in the first Adam, this final day of the Lord would bring the unmitigated doom threatened against man in the primal covenant of works in Eden." Kline, *God, Heaven and Har Magedon*, 188.

32. Vos properly recognizes that there will be gradations of the heavenly reward for believers, based upon their good works although their salvation is solely bestowed "on the basis of the imputed righteousness of Christ received by faith." Indeed, it motivates believers for evangelism, mission, and good works in their daily lives under the guidance of the Holy Spirit in Jesus Christ as we live in the Global Mission Age: "But works occur in yet another sense than as evidence of faith. Scripture also speaks of reward for believers ("their works follow them," Rev 14:13; Matt 5:12, 16; 6:1; Luke 6:23; Heb 10:34–38). This reward comes as compensation for the cross, as restitution for what was robbed, as recompense for love shown to the servants of the Lord, etc. There will be proportion in this reward (Matt 25:21, 23; Luke 6:38; 19:17, 19; 1 Cor 3:8). It is presented as a reaping that corresponds to what is sown (Gal 6:7–10). Salvation will be perfect for all, but nonetheless not entirely the same for all. This is certain: the difference will not possibly provide any occasion for unhappiness. Accordingly, for believers works are a *criterion* for the glory to be received. But this is *a reward out of grace* (Rom 11:35; 1 Cor 4:7; John 3:27). And the bestowing of salvation, as such, will take place solely on the imputed righteousness of Christ received by faith." Vos, *Reformed Dogmatics*, 5:293.

[11]Then I saw a great white throne and him who was seated on it. From his presence earth and sky fled away, and no place was found for them. [12]And I saw the dead, great and small, standing before the throne, and books were opened. Then another book was opened, which is the book of life. And the dead were judged by what was written in the books, according to what they had done. [13]And the sea gave up the dead who were in it, Death and Hades gave up the dead who were in them, and they were judged, each one of them, according to what they had done. [14]Then Death and Hades were thrown into the lake of fire. This is the second death, the lake of fire. [15]And if anyone's name was not found written in the book of life, he was thrown into the lake of fire. (Rev 20:11–15)[33]

Jesus Christ will sit on "a great white throne" as the final Judge. Likewise, after the final judgment of "a great white throne," the reprobate will be thrown "into the lake of fire" where they will be tormented with "the second death" forever, following the final destiny of Satan and demons.[34]

33. Interpreting Rev 20:11–15 in light of *the dispensational eschatology*, MacArthur and Mayhue falsely insist that "the great white throne judgment" will take place after the thousand years of "Jesus's kingdom reign" while "the sheep-goat judgment" will occur at the time of "Jesus's second coming" (Matt 25:31–32): "But a close examination reveals that these two judgments cannot be the same. First, the *timing* of the sheep-goat judgment occurs in close proximity to Jesus's second coming (see Matt 25:31–32). Jesus comes in glory with his angels and sits on his glorious throne (i.e., his Davidic throne), and then all the nations are gathered before him for judgment. So the sheep-goat judgment is closely connected to Jesus's second coming. On the other hand, the great white throne judgment occurs after the thousand-year reign of Jesus and his saints (Rev 20:4–7). Subsequent to the thousand years (Rev. 20:7), the great white throne judgment takes place (Rev 20:11–15). This point alone shows that these judgments are distinct. One judgment occurs at the beginning of Jesus's kingdom reign, while the other occurs after the millennium in the transition to the eternal state. Also, the resurrections, separated by a thousand years (see Rev 20:4–5) strongly suggest that these are distinct judgments." MacArthur and Mayhue, *Biblical Doctrine*, 869–70.

34. Kline views "the lake of fire" as the separate realm of the completed hell which will be consummated as the place of eternal curse against Satan, demons, and the reprobate when Jesus Christ returns on the day of the Lord: "The problem of corruption posed by Hades is actually one of cosmic proportions. It is not just a matter of freeing the earth of its cemetery status, but of eliminating Hades as the intermediate realm of the damned, fallen angels as well as fallen men. To deal with this God has prepared a separated place in the consummated order for the devil and his angels, a place to which reprobate men are also banished (Matt 25:41; Rev 20:15; 21:8). This realm, sealed off from the domain of the new heaven and earth, is symbolized by a lake of fire, the realm we call Hell. God has created Hell as a decontaminating, hermetically sealed

John's vision, "[14]Then Death and Hades were thrown into the lake of fire. This is the second death, the lake of fire. [15]And if anyone's name was not found written in the book of life, he was thrown into the lake of fire" (vv. 14–15), is the comprehensive and summary statement of God's final judgment in *the completed hell*.[35]

Once again, it is pertinent to know that the ultimate standard for the final judgment of believers will be the covenant of grace in the last Adam. On the other hand, the final reference point for unbelievers will be the covenant of works in the first Adam as pronounced by God in the holy garden of Eden in Genesis 2:15–17. This suggests that the proper distinction between the covenant of works and the covenant of grace is not only applicable and valid but will be decisively applied in the process of the final judgment when Jesus Christ returns.[36]

---

black hole against the time when he will consummate his holy kingdom. Into this lake of fire unclean Hades is cast (Rev 20:14). Hell thus serves as a cosmic catharsis.

At the same time, hell as the punitive (second) death of the reprobate satisfies the requirement for a forensic covering of martyr blood (cf. Num 35:33). The redemptive counterpart to this is the atoning sacrifice of the Cross, the shedding of Christ's blood as a covering for the bloodguiltiness of the elect." Kline, *God, Heaven and Har Madgedon*, 214.

35. Poythress properly views that " the book of life" includes "the roster of God's elect people" while "the lake of fire" is the picture of "hell" which will be completed at the day of the final judgment: "The book of life, the roster of God's elect people, symbolizes that he knows his own sheep (John 10:3, 27), keeps them all, and loses none of them (John 6:39; 10:28–29; cf. Rev 13:8). The lake of fire, or hell, demonstrates God's consummate justice and his utter frustration of all the devices of wickedness. The new heaven and the new earth will be free from all that has contaminated the world in the first order of things." Poythress, *Returning King*, 183.

36. Rejecting the proper distinction between law and gospel in hermeneutics and soteriology, Thomas Schreiner falls into the trap of monocovenantalism. So, he improperly argues that good works are *necessary* for justification and salvation. In doing so, he falsely insists that good works will be *necessary* for final salvation as well although he denies the application of *merit* into the arena of believers' good works: "To sum up, Paul teaches here that works play a role in the final judgment. They are necessary for final salvation. But how does that fit with Paul saying that justification cannot be obtained by works of law? Clearly, he doesn't think the necessary works *merit* salvation. What he does mean will be answered before this essay concludes. . . . Galatians knows nothing, then, of autonomous works or works produced by the virtue of the human being. Good works are energized and accomplished by the Holy Spirit, being rooted in the cross-work of Jesus Christ by which believers have been freed from the old creation and have been inducted into the new creation. Galatians makes it clear that these works are necessary for eternal life. . . . Paul clearly argues that good works are necessary for eternal life. Only those who sow to the Spirit will enjoy eternal life, and those who practice evil will not inherit the kingdom. James also teaches that

The Final Consummation of the Eternal
Kingdom of God and Kingdom of Satan

After the second coming of Jesus Christ, there will be the final redemptive judgment which will visibly separate the eternal kingdom of God and the kingdom of Satan. There will be no middle ground to stand for. All the resurrected believers, composed of the elect and holy angels, will inherit the eternal kingdom of God where Jesus Christ as King of kings and Lord of lords will rule the completed and glorified kingdom of God with the realization of the full presence of the Triune God.

The Triune God is not only the Creator par excellence but also the Consummator. The greatest artistic works and display ever will be revealed in the process of the Triune God's creative works and final touch for the Consummation. At the time of Noah, the Triune God used the mighty water as the means of redemptive judgment and recreation against the corrupt original world. However, in the process of final redemptive judgment and final recreation, the Triune God will use the mighty fire as the means of glorious artistic and architectural works. In that sense, we need to look at the new heaven and new earth, revealed in Revelation 21:1–4, in light of Consummation and final recreation. Mysteriously, the apostle John saw "a new heaven and a new earth" along with "the holy city, new Jerusalem, coming down out of *heaven* from God, prepared as a bride adorned for her husband" through "the revelation of Jesus Christ" (vv. 1–2):

> Then I saw a new heaven and a new earth, for the first heaven and the first earth had passed away, and the sea was no more. ²And I saw the holy city, new Jerusalem, coming down out of heaven from God, prepared as a bride adorned for her husband. ³And I heard a loud voice from the throne saying, "Behold, the dwelling place of God is with man. He will dwell with them, and they will be his people, and God himself will be with them as

justification is by works. No one will be justified if he or she fails to do good works. Such works are not autonomous but are the result of the new covenant works of the Holy Spirit. . . . Paul, like James, believes that works are necessary at the final judgment but the works are the fruit of the faith, the result of a faith that embraces and rests on Jesus Christ. I conclude, then, that the New Testament witness is consistent. Works are necessary for justification, but they are not the basis of justification or salvation since God requires perfection and all human beings sin. However, works constitute the necessary evidence or fruit of one's new life in Christ. We can even say that salvation and justification are through faith alone, but such faith is living and vital and always produces works." Schreiner, "Justification Apart From and By Good Works," 81–98.

their God. [4]He will wipe away every tear from their eyes, and death shall be no more, neither shall there be mourning nor crying nor pain anymore, for the former things have passed away." (Rev 21:1–4)

Jerusalem was the epicenter of the dwelling place of the covenant community of Israel on the present earth, with the inauguration of the Davidic covenant (2 Sam 7:1–17; 1 Chr 17:1–15). Furthermore, Jerusalem was the visible symbol and type of *heaven* where Jesus Christ as King of kings and Lord of lords currently rules and reigns the invisible and visible realms. In doing so, he receives the glorious praises from the justified believers on the earth and the glorified souls along with holy angels in *heaven*. The author of Hebrews codifies *heaven* as "the heavenly Jerusalem" under the inspiration of the Holy Spirit:

> [22]But you have come to Mount Zion and to the city of the living God, the heavenly Jerusalem, and to innumerable angels in festal gathering, [23]and to the assembly of the firstborn who are enrolled in heaven, and to God, the judge of all, and to the spirits of the righteous made perfect, [24]and to Jesus, the mediator of a new covenant, and to the sprinkled blood that speaks a better word than the blood of Abel. (Heb 12:22–24)

Under the old covenant, Jerusalem typified "the heavenly Jerusalem" which is a different expression of heaven or the kingdom of Heaven. Now, believers under the new covenant are spiritually united with Jesus Christ who is already seated "at the right hand of the throne of God" in "the heavenly Jerusalem." Later, John after the final fall of the earthly city of Jerusalem defines *the consummated heaven* as "the holy city, new Jerusalem" (v. 2) or "the holy city Jerusalem" (v. 10)

The present heaven and earth as a visible realm will be transformed as *the glorious realm* through the process of final recreation by God's mighty fire. The Holy Spirit will give the final touch as the Spirit of creation, recreation, and final recreation with the wondrous display of artistic beauty. After the Triune God completes the final recreation of "a new heaven and a new earth" by the means of the Mighty Fire, "a new heaven and a new earth" will be consummated as *the glorious realm* without the presence of any evil and corrupt beings.[37] Verse 1, "Then I

---

37. Interpreting the recreation of "a new heaven and a new earth" in light of the supernatural works of the Triune God, Horton notes that the new creation is, indeed, the harmonious works of the Father, the Son, and the Spirit: "Biblical eschatology has

saw a new heaven and a new earth, for the first heaven and the first earth had passed away, and the sea was no more," is the glorious pictorial vision that John saw after the final recreation process through God's mighty fire. The phrase "the first heaven and the first earth had passed away" provides a comprehensive idea that the present heaven and the present earth as the visible realm will not be annihilated but transformed into the glorious realm which will be the final visible inheritance for the glorified believers in Jesus Christ.[38]

Reflecting Revelation 21:1–4, Hoekema describes that after the completion of the new heaven and new earth, "holy city, new Jerusalem" will come down from *heaven* to the new earth. In that sense, the new earth and heaven will be united gloriously. And the glorified believers will live their everlasting life "in heaven" which will come down to the new earth:

> Verse 2 shows us the "holy city, new Jerusalem," standing for the entire glorified church of God, coming down out of heaven to earth. This church, now totally without spot or blemish, completely purified from sin, is now "prepared as a bride adorned for her husband," ready for the marriage of the Lamb (see Rev 19:7). From this verse we learn that the glorified church will not remain in a heaven far off in space, but will spend eternity on the new earth. From verse 3 we learn that the dwelling place of God will no longer be away from the earth but on the earth. Since where God dwells, there heaven is, we conclude that in the life to come heaven and earth will no longer be separated, as they

always run counter to the prevailing assumptions of paganism, Eastern and Western, affirming liberation of rather than from creation. Heaven is a real place, not just a state of mind (Luke 24:51; John 14:2–4; Acts 1:11; 7:55–56). Nevertheless, the biblical vision of a new heaven and a new earth is not the abolition of the old creation, but describes the new condition of the world that the Father has made and remade in his Son and by his Spirit." Horton, *Christian Faith*, 974.

38. In general, the Lutheran theologians have taught *the annihilation of the present heaven and earth* before the recreation of the new heaven and new earth. Critiquing them from a biblical theological perspective, Vos notes that "the substance of the presently existing world will be preserved but will be restored" as a glorified new heaven and earth: "Some propose an absolutely new world, so that in substance the old does not recur in the new and a new world comes in its place. The Lutheran dogmaticians until Gerhard were devoted to this view. But in general whenever they mention the new earth *pro forma*, they do not say much about it. The Reformed, for the most part, expressed support for the opposite view, namely that the substance of the presently existing world will be preserved but will be restored, purified in glory." Vos, *Reformed Dogmatics*, 5:308.

are now, but will be merged. Believers will therefore continue in heaven as they continue to live on the new earth. "He will dwell with them, and they shall be his people" are the familiar words of the central promise of the covenant of grace (cf. Gen 17:7; Exod 19:5–6; Jer 31:33; Ezek 34:30; 2 Cor 6:16; Heb 8:10; 1 Pet 2:9–10). The fact that this promise is repeated in John's vision of the new earth implies that only on that new earth will God finally grant his people the full riches which the covenant of grace includes. Here we receive the firstfruits; there we shall receive the full harvest."[39]

As the Triune God completes the final recreation of the new heaven and the new earth, he will unite *the glorious realms* together, namely "a new earth" and "the holy city, new Jerusalem." More specifically, the Triune God will unite "the holy city, new Jerusalem" with the glorified new earth as the eternal dwelling place of the glorified believers along with holy angels in the presence of the Triune God. Remarkably, John saw the glorious moment of union between the new earth and heaven, described as "the holy city, new Jerusalem." In verse 2, "And I saw the holy city, new Jerusalem, coming down out of heaven from God, prepared as a bride adorned for her husband," John describes the glorious picture of the final union of the glorious realms together.[40]

It is also the final ceremony of God the Father's grant to the victorious Son and the glorified believers while they celebrate the final consummation of the eternal kingdom of God. It will be a glorious celebration with the heavenly song and cantata which will be the song of the eternal kingdom of God. As the eternal kingdom of God is visibly consummated, the invisible and visible blessings of the covenant of grace will be fully realized.[41] Indeed, the clear message from the heavenly throne, "Behold,

---

39. Hoekema, *Bible and the Future*, 284–85.

40. Meanwhile, Hendriksen identifies "the holy city, new Jerusalem" as "the Church of the Lord Jesus Christ" which is a symbolical interpretation: "This Jerusalem is called 'new' in contradistinction to the earthly, Palestinian Jerusalem. It is called 'holy' because it is separate from sin and thoroughly consecrated to God. This new and holy Jerusalem is very clearly the Church of the Lord Jesus Christ, as is also plainly evident from the fact that it is here and elsewhere called the bride, the wife of the Lamb (Isa 54:5; Eph 5:32; etc.). Even in the Old Testament the Church is represented under the symbolism of a city (Isa 26:1; Ps 48; etc)." Hendriksen, *More Than Conquerors*, 218.

41. As Baugh properly indicates, Revelation 21:1–7 is not only the reflection of the full realization of believers' "covenant bond with God" but also "the consummation of the kingdom of God" along with all of its everlasting blessings: "As the Jeremiah quote also shows, the result of Christ's accomplishment for his people is the covenant bond

the dwelling place of God is with man. He will dwell with them, and they will be his people, and God himself will be with them as their God" (v. 3) is the prophecy that the spiritual and visible blessings of Immanuel and the covenant of grace will be fully realized in the New Jerusalem.[42]

The apostle John heard the glorious voice of Jesus Christ from the heavenly throne: "Behold, I am making all things new" (v. 5). This prophetic voice suggests that the Son of God is not only the Creator and Redeemer, but also the Consummator. As the final recreation of "a new heaven and a new earth," uniting with "the holy city, new Jerusalem" is complete, hell will be consummated in the kingdom of Satan as well:

> 5And he who was seated on the throne said, "Behold, I am making all things new." Also he said, "Write this down, for these

---

we discussed earlier as expressed in the covenant formula: 'I will be their God, and they shall be my people' (Heb 8:10; Jer 31:33). This mutual, covenant bond with God is true now, but its ultimate realization awaits the new creation as taught in a passage from Rev 21 we should read together with the one from Jeremiah and Hebrews just quoted. Here is the Revelation passage in full. . . . This is the consummation of the kingdom of God with all of its eternal benefits including its center of a fixed covenant bond with the triune God." Baugh, *Majesty on High*, 130–31.

42. Kline demonstrates that "the settling of the ark" on the mountains of Ararat after the flood judgment was "symbol of the consummate kingdom of the new heaven and earth." In addition, "Yahweh's kingdom" was established after "a holy war of annihilation" against the Canaanites in the promised land. Likewise, at the final judgment, the New Jerusalem as "the eternal holy city" will descend from heaven *after* God casts out all the evil beings to "the lake of fire." So, there will be *a logical order* from the final judgment of the eternal hell to the consummation of the eternal kingdom of God: "The Lord executes a thorough ethnic cleansing of the satanic genotype. The genocide is total; all fallen men and angels are eliminated from the world of the saints. This complete removal of Satan and his seed is a prerequisite for establishing the Glory-kingdom among men (logically so, even if chronologically they are simultaneous, complementary aspects of the final judgment event).

The typological judgment episodes exemplify this principle too. The ungodly of the wicked that then were erased en masse by the Deluge as a prelude to the settling of the ark, symbol of the consummate kingdom of the new heaven and earth, on the Ararat Har Magedon. The Canaanites must be obliterated by the Israelites in a holy war of annihilation to make way for setting up Yahweh's kingdom. . . . In keeping with this typological paradigm the coming of the antitypical kingdom of glory does not precede the elimination of the Satan-allied population of planet earth. It is only at the final judgment, when deceived men, small and great, all who receive the mark of the beast and worship his image, have been cast into the lake of fire, the second death, that the eternal holy city descends from heaven (Rev 20:15; 21:5–8; cf. 19:18). Stated in terms of the millennial issue, it is after 'the thousand years,' which lead up to the final judgment, that the kingdom comes in power and glory." Kline, *God, Heaven and Har Magedon*, 209–10.

words are trustworthy and true." **6**And he said to me, "It is done! I am the Alpha and the Omega, the beginning and the end. To the thirsty I will give from the spring of the water of life without payment. **7**The one who conquers will have this heritage, and I will be his God and he will be my son. **8**But as for the cowardly, the faithless, the detestable, as for murderers, the sexually immoral, sorcerers, idolaters, and all liars, their portion will be in the lake that burns with fire and sulfur, which is the second death." (Rev 21:5–8)

Verse 8 states, "But as for the cowardly, the faithless, the detestable, as for murderers, the sexually immoral, sorcerers, idolaters, and all liars, their portion will be in the lake that burns with fire and sulfur, which is the second death." This verse is the pictorial and vivid description of the dwellers in the completed hell, or the kingdom of Satan, which will be the absolutely separated wicked realm where Satan rules forever. Indeed, the dwellers in the completed hell will experience the eternal curse of "the second death" without ceasing. It is the prophetic voice from the heavenly throne that there will be the consummated separate realm which will be the realm of the eternal curse. In addition, it is an apologetical voice from *heaven* for those who reject the existence of hell. In other words, it is the divine confirmation of the existence of the final judgment in the completed hell against the unbelievers, Satan and demons.

Afterwards, John describes the detailed scenes of the New Jerusalem in Revelation 21:9—22:5 which he saw through the spectacular vision. In fact, the scene of Revelation 21:9–14 is a recapitulation of Revelation 21:1–4 where John saw the glorious union of the new earth and "the holy city, new Jerusalem." Once again, John saw "the Bride, the wife of the Lamb" who will be the glorified believers along with "the holy city Jerusalem coming down out of heaven from God" (vv. 9–10).[43] In short, it is *a prophecy of the glorious finale of the heavenly wedding* between the Bride and the Lamb in the New Jerusalem:

---

43. Baugh interprets Revelation 21:9 as the vision of "a marriage feast" which will take place between the Lamb and his bride when the Lord completes the creation of the eternal Kingdom of God: "Hence, for the people of God on that great day, the new covenant bond enjoyed with the Lord now by virtue of his blood of the covenant, will result in a marriage feast when the Lord consummates his new creational kingdom for his bride 'the wife of the Lamb' (Rev 21:9; cf. Rev 19:1–9; 21:1–2) whom he knows and loves now." Baugh, *Majesty on High*, 148.

⁹Then came one of the seven angels who had the seven bowls full of the seven last plagues and spoke to me, saying, "Come, I will show you the Bride, the wife of the Lamb." ¹⁰And he carried me away in the Spirit to a great, high mountain, and showed me the holy city Jerusalem coming down out of heaven from God, ¹¹having the glory of God, its radiance like a most rare jewel, like a jasper, clear as crystal. ¹²It had a great, high wall, with twelve gates, and at the gates twelve angels, and on the gates the names of the twelve tribes of the sons of Israel were inscribed— ¹³on the east three gates, on the north three gates, on the south three gates, and on the west three gates. ¹⁴And the wall of the city had twelve foundations, and on them were the twelve names of the twelve apostles of the Lamb. (Rev 21:9–14)

In the New Jerusalem, *the glory of God* will be fully consummated with the magnificent beauty, holiness, radiance, and righteousness. Indeed, John describes the glory of God which will beautifully fill New Jerusalem with spectacular radiance.

The Triune God is the beautiful God par excellence. Moreover, God is beauty itself. God's beauty and architectural majesty was visibly manifested and displayed in his original creation of the heavens and the earth (Gen 1:2—2:25). In that regard, God is the ultimate source of all artistic and architectural beauty and design. Moreover, God is the fountainhead and founder of aesthetics.[44] John saw the beauty of beauties from the architectural designs and structures in the New Jerusalem. Indeed, the aesthetic and architectural beauty will be culminated in the New Jerusalem with the fullness of the radiance of the glory of God:

¹⁵And the one who spoke with me had a measuring rod of gold to measure the city and its gates and walls. ¹⁶The city lies foursquare; its length the same as its width. And he measured the city with his rod, 12,000 stadia. Its length and width and height are equal. ¹⁷He also measured its wall, 144 cubits by human measurement, which is also an angel's measurement. ¹⁸The wall was built of jasper, while the city was pure gold, clear as glass. ¹⁹The foundations of the wall of the city were adorned with every kind of jewel. The first was jasper, the second sapphire, the third agate, the fourth emerald, ²⁰the fifth onyx, the sixth carnelian, the seventh chrysolite, the eighth beryl, the ninth

---

44. For a biblical theological discussion about the Beauty of the Triune God and its visible display and manifestation in the original creation of the heavens and earth, see Jeon, *Biblical Theology*, 8–10.

topaz, the tenth chrysoprase, the eleventh jacinth, the twelfth amethyst. [21]And the twelve gates were twelve pearls, each of the gates made of a single pearl, and the street of the city was pure gold, transparent as glass. (Rev 21:15–21)

Jerusalem, under the kingdom of Israel, was the epicenter of political and religious life of the covenant community of Israel. The temple in Jerusalem was the most sacred place of sacrifice and worship where the covenant community of Israel intimately encountered the living God under the guidance of the high priests. Moreover, the temple was the epicenter of the dwelling place of God where his glory was visibly manifested. However, John did not see the temple in the New Jerusalem because "its temple is the Lord God the Almighty and the Lamb" (v. 22):

> [22]And I saw no temple in the city, for its temple is the Lord God the Almighty and the Lamb. [23]And the city has no need of sun or moon to shine on it, for the glory of God gives it light, and its lamp is the Lamb. [24]By its light will the nations walk, and the kings of the earth will bring their glory into it, [25]and its gates will never be shut by day—and there will be no night there. [26]They will bring into it the glory and the honor of the nations. [27]But nothing unclean will ever enter it, nor anyone who does what is detestable or false, but only those who are written in the Lamb's book of life. (Rev 21:22–27)

In the glorious New Jerusalem, there will be no need for sunlight or moonlight because it will be *the consummated heaven*. There will be no more natural cycles of sunlight or moonlight in the new heaven and new earth. Remarkably, the fountainhead of the glory of God will be "the Lamb" because he will be the lamp of God's glory. It is so significant to note that after the Triune God recreates the new heaven and new earth, uniting with the New Jerusalem, Jesus Christ as the glorified Lamb will be the eternal source of the light of the glory of God, filling the New Jerusalem along with the new earth with beauty par excellence (v. 23). Because all evil will be eradicated in the new earth and New Jerusalem, the gates of the New Jerusalem will never be shut, and the dwellers of the New Jerusalem will have free access to both the New Jerusalem and new earth. John, under the inspiration of the Holy Spirit, describes how there will be no night or darkness in the glorified new earth and New Jerusalem while the citizens of the New Jerusalem will enjoy the abundant blessings of the new earth without barrier (vv. 24–26). Moreover, all the privileged dwellers of the New Jerusalem will be written in "the Lamb's book of life," which will finally reveal the precise numbers and names of the elect (v. 27).[45]

The garden of Eden before the fall was the earthly projection of *heaven* so that Adam and Eve were able to meditate on the abundant blessings of *heaven* as they dwelled the garden as priestly kings. There was the tree of life and the tree of the knowledge of good and evil in the midst of the garden of Eden. In addition, a river flowed out of the garden of Eden to water the garden, dividing into four rivers (Gen 2:4–25). The tree of life was a sacramental tree of the visible symbol of eternal life in heaven while the tree of knowledge of good and evil was a sacramental tree of the visible symbol of eternal death in hell (Gen 2:4–25). However, after the fall, God destroyed the original garden of Eden at the time of the Noahic flood judgment. As such, the original garden of Eden is not available or visible in the present earth (Gen 7:6–24). Remarkably, John saw the images of the original garden of Eden through a vision. To be sure, nevertheless, it was not an image of *the restoration* but the consummation of the holy garden of Eden. Furthermore, John saw "the river of the water of life," flowing from "the throne of God and of the Lamb." And "the tree of life" will be planted in the New Jerusalem as well (vv. 1–2). But, the tree of knowledge of good and evil will be unavailable because the New Jerusalem will be *the consummated heaven*, absent the presence of all evils:

> Then the angel showed me the river of the water of life, bright as crystal, flowing from the throne of God and of the Lamb ²through the middle of the street of the city; also, on either side of the river, the tree of life with its twelve kinds of fruit, yielding its fruit each month. The leaves of the tree were for the healing of the nations. ³No longer will there be anything accursed, but the throne of God and of the Lamb will be in it, and his servants

---

45. Calvin *organically* connects the biblical doctrines of election, adoption, and the book of life without any disjunction: "Accordingly, those whom God has adopted as his sons are said to have been chosen not in themselves but in Christ [Eph. 1:4]; for unless he could love them in him, he could not honor them with the inheritance of his Kingdom if they had not previously become partakers of him. But if we have been chosen in him, we shall not find assurance of our election in ourselves; and not even in God the Father, if we conceive him as severed from his Son. Christ, then, is the mirror wherein we must, and without self-deception may, contemplate our own election. For since it is into his body the Father has destined those to be engrafted whom he has willed from eternity to be his own, that he may hold as sons all whom he acknowledges to be among his members, we have a sufficiently clear and firm testimony that we have been inscribed in the book of life [cf. Rev 21:27] if we are in communion with Christ." Calvin, *Inst.* 3.24.5.

> will worship him. **4**They will see his face, and his name will be
> on their foreheads. (Rev 22:1–4)

The picture of the New Jerusalem that John saw is the glorious combination of the images of the original garden of Eden and Jerusalem under the Davidic Kingdom. In Jerusalem, there was the temple and the palace. In short, the temple was the visible symbol of the dwelling and ruling place of God the Father while the palace was the throne of the Davidic kings. The ultimate purpose of the earthly temple and palace in Jerusalem will be fulfilled in the New Jerusalem. This is what John saw. The throne of the Father and throne of the Son will be the central focus of the New Jerusalem. In that regard, John describes the scene, "**3**No longer will there be anything accursed, but the throne of God and of the Lamb will be in it, and his servants will worship him. **4**They will see his face, and his name will be on their foreheads" (vv. 3–4).[46] The glorified believers with heavenly angels will praise and worship the Triune God with the new song of the eternal kingdom of God. Verse 4 provides a glimpse into the glorious and intimate covenant relationship which was anticipated by the rich promises of the covenant of grace and will be fully realized in the New Jerusalem. Furthermore, the entire cosmos of the new heaven and new earth, united with the New Jerusalem will be the fully realized realm of the glorious temple of the Triune God.

Summary

In light of the new covenant, the fours Gospels are the historical process of God's covenant making with his elect, having his sworn oath to the covenant with sacrificing his only begotten Son once for all. However, from the perspective of the final fall of the kingdom of Israel in the promised land in A.D. 70 as Jesus' ministry, portrayed in the four Gospels is a covenant lawsuit history against the disobedient covenant community of Israel as the eschatological prophet. Furthermore, Jesus' covenant lawsuit against the disobedient Israel was carried and succeeded organically

46. Kline interprets "the throne of God and the Lamb" as "the closeness of the union of God and his Christ in their co-enthronement over creation." In that regard, the Father and the Son as the Lamb have been enthroned on the heavenly throne: "The Apocalypse softens the distinction of the two thrones. It describes the Lamb as in the midst of the throne (Rev 5:6; 7:17; cf. 3:21), which it even calls 'the throne of God and the Lamb' (Rev 22:1, 3). This reflects the closeness of the union of God and his Christ in their co-enthronement over creation." Kline, *Glory in Our Midst*, 224.

through the powerful ministry of the apostles and other sincere believers after the Pentecost. In that sense, the four Gospels and the book of Acts are the inerrant and infallible books of the new covenant which testify the historical process of the covenant lawsuit against a disobedient Israel who broke the Mosaic covenant of law. And then the kingdom of Israel faced the final judgment at A.D. 70 with the pouring out of God's wrath through the military power of the Roman Empire.

From the perspective of God's final judgment against the present world, the New Covenant Age is a covenant lawsuit history, based upon the covenant of works for those who remain in the first Adam and reject to believe in Jesus Christ who fulfilled the requirement of the broken covenant of works as the last Adam. In that regard, preaching the good news of the gospel in the New Covenant Age from Jerusalem to Judea, Samaria, and to the ends of the earth was not only the history of evangelism and mission but also the historical process of covenant lawsuit, based upon the covenant of works in the first Adam.

As we live in the global mission age, God intensifies the covenant lawsuit against the disobedient who reject the good news of the gospel in the global mission field. From the perspective of the second coming of Christ, the arrival of the global mission age due to the development of science and technology is the final stage of God's preparation for the day of the Lord which will be the day of the second coming of Christ and the final judgment. At the same time, great persecution, including martyrdom against sincere believers, will intensify in the global mission field. Yet, the great persecution against believers is also the visible process of God's covenant lawsuit against the persecutors.

After the end of the New Covenant Age, Jesus Christ will return *on the day of the Lord*. Christ's second coming will be glorious and visible because he will return as the final Judge and Consummator. In many ways, the day of the Lord will be the day of the final redemptive judgment. When Christ comes back, God will grant believers "the resurrection of life" which is the blessing of the covenant of grace in the last Adam. However, he will curse unbelievers with "the resurrection of judgment" because they are under the curse of the covenant of works in the first Adam (John 5:26–29). Meanwhile, the glorified believers with their bodily resurrection will meet Christ *in the air* while unbelievers with "the resurrection of judgment" will be *left on the present earth* (1 Thess 4:13–18). With the completion of visible separation between the elect and reprobate with their bodily resurrection, the preparation for the final holy war will be complete as well.

In the book of Revelation, the final holy war between the kingdom of God and the kingdom of Satan is revealed as the Armageddon Battle in Revelation 16:12–16. The same battle is recapitulated from different perspectives as the Battle of the Rider on a White Horse in Revelation 19:11–21 and as the Gog and Magog Battle in Revelation 20:7–10. In this final holy war, God will not use manmade weapons as he demonstrated when he waged the holy war against the corrupt world during the flood judgment and his holy war against the cities of Sodom and Gomorrah through the heavenly fire. Likewise, the Armageddon Battle as the final holy war will not be a military battle, using sophisticated destructive weapons although modernized weapons have been developed under the benefits of the covenant of common grace, inaugurated in Genesis 3:16–19. In short, the Armageddon Battle will be the final holy war between the kingdom of God and the kingdom of Satan as a means of the final redemptive judgment. In that regard, God will use the heavenly fire when he executes his final holy war against the kingdom of Satan, led by the victorious heavenly warrior Christ, using the mighty and transforming power of the heavenly fire (2 Pet 3:1–7).

At the end of the final holy war, the elect and reprobate will stand in the presence of "a great white throne" for the final judgment. The covenantal standard for the final judgment of the reprobate will be the covenant of works in the first Adam. Moreover, there will be gradations of hellish curses, reflecting unbelievers' lives on the earth as recorded in the "books." At the same time, the covenantal foundation for the final judgment of the elect will be the covenant of grace in the last Adam as inaugurated in Genesis 3:15. And the names of all the believers will be recorded in "the book of life," and there will be *gradations of heavenly blessings* according to the good works in the process of progressive sanctification in Christ (Rev 20:11–15).

Meanwhile, there will be *the final consummation* of the eternal kingdom of God after the final redemptive judgment. The visible appearance of the eternal kingdom of God will be manifested after the process of the recreation through heavenly fire. The present heaven and earth will not be annihilated but transformed as the glorious realm which will be identified as "a new heaven and a new earth." "A new earth" will be gloriously united with "the holy city, new Jerusalem, coming down out of heaven from God." In that sense, "the holy city, new Jerusalem" will be *the consummated heaven* united with the glorified new earth (Rev 21:1–4).

Conclusion

With the sudden outbreak of the coronavirus pandemic, we are experiencing a global pandemic that leads the global community into chaos, fear, and uncertainty of a future with the absence of a vaccine or other solution. This pandemic shatters the constant yearning and vision of the coming Utopian world driven by people with the development of modern science and technology and cultural advancement. It is a wakeup call for believers as God constantly stirs the global community through divergent disasters such as earthquakes, famine, hurricanes, tsunami, virus pandemics, and horrible wars which all are the signs of the last days under the New Covenant Age. However, God does not shelter believers from experiencing these disasters. Rather, people in the global community, including believers and unbelievers suffer and undergo these hardships. To be sure, God confirms that we live in the last days before the second coming of Jesus Christ who is the mediator and consummator of the new covenant.

Nevertheless, the present world will not end through catastrophic disasters, such as biological or nuclear wars, although many people anticipate the possibility. God will withhold and safeguard world history until the second coming of Jesus Christ no matter how tumultuous the state of the world may be. To do so, God will bestow and grant the abundant and rich blessings of the covenant of common grace without any discrimination and prejudice among believers and unbelievers in the global mission age (Gen 3:16–19; 8:20—9:17). The fact that we are living in the global mission age is an amazing and surprising reality that is possible because of the advancement of science and technology, a benefit of the covenant of common grace.

Many people who follow the lead of leading scientists believe that the world will end due to the catastrophic side effects of global warming, triggered by air and environmental pollution. God, however, will protect the environment of the present earth in his awesome providence, using the people's care and antipollution measures on behalf of the well-being of the environment of the earth until the second coming of Jesus Christ.

As we live in the global mission age, believers are members of the new covenant diaspora in Jesus Christ. The continual formation of different diaspora communities, including believers and unbelievers, is God's sovereign work under the powerful guidance of the Holy Spirit. The diaspora community was originally inaugurated when God expelled Adam and Eve from the holy garden of Eden after they committed the first sin, breaking the covenant of works by eating of the forbidden fruit of the knowledge of good and evil (Gen 3:21–24). Furthermore, in light of redemptive history, the new covenant diaspora was birthed when believers scattered from Jerusalem to Judea, Samaria, and other areas to the ends of the earth due to the great persecution of believers after the martyrdom of Stephen (Acts 8:1–8). In that sense, the new covenant church in the global community is the new covenant diaspora, scattered among all nations and tribes. God uses the members of the new covenant diaspora for evangelism and missions, sending forth faithful believers and missionaries to the global community.

In the twenty-first century, social media will become a powerful means to reach out to different ethnic and religious groups with the message of the good news of the gospel in Jesus Christ, especially for those of the communist regime like North Korea and radical Islamic fundamentalist regimes which don't allow religious freedom.

Stephen was the first martyr after the audible and visible inauguration of the New Covenant Age through the Pentecost event (Acts 7:54–60). Since then, countless believers have been persecuted and martyred in the new covenant church. As the gospel spread throughout the global community, the great persecution will intensify and numerous faithful believers will be persecuted and martyred on behalf of Jesus Christ and his kingdom. God, however, does not forget the sufferings that the new covenant community experiences. The omniscient God uses the persecution against the new covenant community as the covenant lawsuit against unbelievers and persecutors, based upon the covenant of works in the first Adam (Gen 2:15–17).

The Great Commission under the New Covenant Age was commanded and ordered by the risen Jesus Christ to his original disciples

(Matt 28:16–20). It will progressively and surely be accomplished by the sincere members of the new covenant community, reaching the global community under the invisible guidance and leadership of the Holy Spirit. In that process, the beauty and glory of the good news of the gospel will intrude on the hearts, minds, and souls of those who were oppressed by the destructive power of Satan.

In the end, on the day of the Lord, Jesus Christ as the final Judge and Consummator will come back in the air along with the host of heavenly and holy angels with the glorious sounds of the final trumpet. At the same time, believers as the bride with the glorious bodily resurrection will meet Jesus Christ the Bridegroom. However, the unbelievers with their bodily resurrection will be left on the earth. In doing so, the preparation of the final holy war by the mighty God will end.

There will be the final holy war between the kingdom of God and the kingdom of Satan. It will be the greatest holy war ever which will far surpass in scale a magnitude of the holy wars of the Noahic flood, Sodom and Gomorrah, and the conquest of Canaan, waged by the almighty God and warriors. It will be the universal holy war and God will finally terminate the benefits of the covenant of common grace which were bestowed to believers and unbelievers alike although he temporarily lifted over or removed during the Noahic flood judgment, redemptive judgment against Sodom and Gomorrah, and the conquest of Canaan. In the final holy war, Jesus Christ as the Son will lead with the heavenly fire while the holy angels and glorified believers will participate by the grace of God, cursing Satan, demons, and unbelievers into the lake of fire which will be the completed hell, the realm of the eternal kingdom of Satan.

As God completes his final redemptive judgment against the kingdom of Satan, God will consummate his kingdom at the eternal kingdom of God. God will use his heavenly fire to recreate the new heaven and the new earth, removing all evil out of the present heaven and earth. And then, the New Jerusalem, coming down from *heaven* will be united together with the new earth. In doing so, God's final recreation will be consummated. The Triune God will harmoniously and organically work together in the process of the final redemptive judgment and final recreation of the eternal kingdom of God.

The New Jerusalem on the new earth will be the epicenter of the glory of God, and the Son as the Bridegroom and believers as the bride will celebrate the feast of the heavenly wedding with the glorious cantata of the new song which will be the culmination of the heavenly music.

The promises and blessings of the covenant of grace in the last Adam will be visibly complete and consummated. The glorified believers along with the holy angels will enjoy the most intimate and spiritual relationship with the Triune God while they see in awe the beautiful and holy glory of Jesus Christ, enthroned in the New Jerusalem. Furthermore, the entire cosmos will be transformed into the glorious temple of the Triune God.

We as believers in the global mission age have to actively participate in evangelism and missions without ceasing no matter what difficult challenges we may face. God has called us in Jesus Christ to be "the salt of the earth" and "the light of the world" under the New Covenant Age which is the eschatological age before the second coming of Jesus Christ (Matt 5:13–16). Without a doubt, the eschatological mission as the Great Commission will be carried and accomplished through the sovereign guidance and work of the Holy Spirit.

As the book of Revelation reaches its conclusion, Jesus Christ boldly assured, "Surely, I am coming soon" (v. 20). And we as the new covenant community should shout together, yearning for the supernatural arrival of the eternal kingdom of God with a living faith, "Amen. Come, Lord Jesus!" (v. 20). Indeed, the new covenant canon is completed as follows:

> [16]"I, Jesus, have sent my angel to testify to you about these things for the churches. I am the root and the descendant of David, the bright morning star." [17]The Spirit and the Bride say, "Come." And let the one who hears say, "Come." And let the one who is thirsty come; let the one who desires take the water of life without price. [18]I warn everyone who hears the words of the prophecy of this book: if anyone adds to them, God will add to him the plagues described in this book, [19]and if anyone takes away from the words of the book of this prophecy, God will take away his share in the tree of life and in the holy city, which are described in this book. [20]He who testifies to these things says, "Surely I am coming soon." Amen. Come, Lord Jesus! [21]The grace of the Lord Jesus be with all. Amen. (Rev 22:16–21)

When Jesus Christ returns as the final Judge and Consummator, we will be surprised by the process of the grand scale of universal judgment and final recreation, separating the eternal kingdom of God and the kingdom of Satan. We will visibly realize the full benefits and blessings of the covenant of grace in the last Adam. Surely, the greatest gift of God for humans is the good news of the gospel in the present age. It should motivate all of us to actively participate in eschatological evangelism and mission, and the life of godliness and holiness as the members of the new covenant community who eagerly wait for the supernatural arrival of the age to come with the catastrophic disappearance of the present age.

Calvin and the Two Kingdoms

Calvin's Political Philosophy in Light of Contemporary Discussion

CALVIN'S CONCEPT OF "THE two kingdoms" has been very influential not only for the understanding of the relationship between church and state in the Reformed and evangelical traditions but also Western civilization as a whole since the Protestant Reformation in Europe.[1]

As we live in the global mission age due to the development of science and technology through the benefits of God's common grace, it is important to formulate and provide a biblical worldview not only for believers in the church but also for believers' lives in the present world so that they may glorify God through all facets of their lives, expanding God's kingdom throughout the world.

In this article, I will revisit Calvin's concept of "the two kingdoms" in light of contemporary discussion. In doing so, I will attempt to comprehensively and critically evaluate Calvin's view. Calvin understood and developed his concept of "the two kingdoms" in his own life through both religious and political contexts, which can be helpfully understood as a sixteenth-century form of European Christendom. Some scholars

---

1. For the comprehensive analysis on the concept of Calvin's two kingdoms and the divergent views in respect to the church and the state in European history, and its ethical implication in the Christian life, see Godfrey, "Kingdom and Kingdoms," 6–9; VanDrunen, "Calvin on the Church and Society," 10–13; VanDrunen, *Natural Law and the Two Kingdoms*, 67–118; VanDrunen, "Two Kingdoms Doctrine," 743–63; VanDrunen, "Two Kingdoms and the *Ordo Salutis*," 207–24; VanDrunen, "Two Kingdoms," 248–66; Spijker, "Kingdom of Christ according to Bucer and Calvin," 109–32.

suggest that Calvin made a clear distinction between church and state in his analysis of political philosophy, which was interpreted and explained by the concept of the two kingdoms. For example, VanDrunen argues that Calvin's political philosophy taught "clear distinctions between church and state": "In this article I discuss important aspects of Calvin's view of church and society and explain how, contrary to what we would expect from a theocratic tyrant, his theology taught clear distinctions between church and state and advocated significant yet distinct liberties in both realms. Calvin's legacy here has been profound and is still worth embracing today."[2]

However, it is my assessment that Calvin was unable to offer a clear distinction between church and state even though it was his goal to do so through his analysis of the concept of the two kingdoms. His concept of the two kingdoms left out a tension, and provided a hermeneutical, theological, and practical ground for his followers to pursue the idea of the Christian state or theocracy, which is the practical outcome of an amalgam of church and state.

---

2. VanDrunen, "Calvin on the Church and Society," 10. See also, VanDrunen, *Natural Law and the Two Kingdoms*, 68: "Contrary to those who find Calvin a precursor to popular contemporary Reformed views of culture and the kingdom of God, *Calvin clearly distinguished the two kingdoms* [emphasis added] and affirmed their continuing dual roles in this world (despite alleged tensions between his two kingdoms theology and the relation of church and state in Geneva). And certainly of significance for the present study, Calvin's views of natural law and the two kingdoms were dependent upon each other in significant respects." I am not critiquing VanDrunen's overall interpretation of Calvin's political philosophy. Rather, I insist that viewing Calvin's perspective as a clear distinction between church and state could mislead readers because Calvin opened a theological and practical door to the possibility of the Christian theocratic state as VanDrunen rightly notes. In that sense, my criticism of VanDrunen is not substantial but corrective and complimentary: "Calvin in the eyes of many, was the tyrant of Geneva who ruled both church and state with an iron hand and bequeathed a theocratic legacy that Western society has struggled to shake off. What are we make of this common conception of Calvin? This conception, in short, is partly true and partly false. Calvin was indeed not a mere theologian but one who thought extensively about how theological truth was to play out in real life. He was not merely a preacher but also the most prominent man in Geneva, who had significant (though certainly not unlimited) opportunities to implement his ideas in the affairs of both church and state. He did bequeath a legacy to subsequent history in both church and society. And his reputation as a theocratic tyrant is understandable in some respects, for he did advocate the state's enforcement of certain religious matters. On the whole, however, this reputation as a tyrant does serious injustice to his ecclesiastical and social views as well as to the character of his historical influence." VanDrunen, "Calvin on the Church and Society," 10.

I will argue that Calvin identified the Jewish theocracy under the Old Covenant as a type of the eternal heavenly kingdom, which is irreproducible in the present world but can only be consummated when the Parousia comes. However, his concept of the two kingdoms inconsistently allows for a Christian theocracy under the New Covenant because he advocated the concept of a Christian state or city as desirable in the present world where Christians are the dominant group in society.

In light of Calvin's understanding of the two kingdoms, Calvin's affirmation and support of Servetus' execution due to his denial of the doctrine of the Trinity in the city of Geneva was not an accidental one; it is the result of his political philosophy, carefully reflected upon and formulated by hermeneutical and theological principles. In that sense, I will argue that Calvin's idea of the two kingdoms should not be identified as a clear distinction between church and state. Rather, it is an inconsistent distinction between church and state that needs revision as we move into the global mission age.

Two Kingdoms

Medieval theology lost the correct theological and practical vision of the distinction between church and state. Medieval Christendom, without a proper separation between church and state, was a theological byproduct of an absence of the proper distinction between common grace and saving grace. Calvin, as a great Reformer, witnessed the unbiblical nature of medieval Christendom in his own religious and political contexts in sixteenth century Europe. As he adopted and developed his understanding of the two kingdoms, Calvin came to embrace the two kingdoms doctrine as pioneered by Luther. And he adopted and developed it further in light of the distinction between common grace and saving grace along with the recognition of natural law in the milieu of general revelation, which has been engraved by God on everyone's heart according to the principle of "the image of God" (*imago Dei*).[3]

---

3. I would argue that Augustine may be considered a forerunner of the idea of "the two kingdoms" although he did not use the terminology in his classical work of *The City of God* where he defined the two cities as "the city of God" and "the city of man." Cf. Augustine, *St. Augustine's City of God*, 1–511.

Reflecting the theological and practical problems of the medieval relationship between church and state, Luther coined the term, "two kingdoms" to explain the relationship between church and state. Calvin adopted the basic ideas and concepts

As such, Calvin carefully recognized the proper place of God's common grace and saving grace. He argued that God created human beings in his own image, so that human beings are distinguished from "brute beasts" as rational creatures due to "the general grace of God" (*generalem Dei gratiam*) although they are totally depraved due to the Fall. Interestingly, Calvin described God's common grace as two-fold with "the general grace of God" (*generalem Dei gratiam*) and "God's special grace" (*specialis Dei gratia*). Calvin argued that some people receive "God's special grace" as the benefit of God's common grace; God bestows it on selected political leaders or other gifted people as we have witnessed several examples within the covenant community of Israel in the Old Testament:

> We see among all mankind that reason is proper to our nature; it distinguishes us from brute beasts, just as they by possessing feeling differ from inanimate things. Now, because some are born fools or stupid, that defect does not obscure the general grace of God. Rather, we are warned by that spectacle that we ought to ascribe what is left in us to God's kindness. For if he had not spared us, our fall would have entailed the destruction of our whole nature. Some men excel in keenness; others are superior in judgment; still others have a readier wit to learn this or that art. In this variety God commends his grace to us, lest anyone should claim as his own what flowed from the sheer bounty of God. For why is one person more excellent than any other? Is

---

of the two kingdoms which Luther defined and explained in his treatise *On Secular Authority* in 1523. See Luther, *On Secular Authority*. For comprehensive and critical analysis of Luther's idea of the two kingdoms in the Reformation context, reflecting medieval Christendom, including Augustine in light of its historical reflection and criticism, see Bornkamm, *Luther's Doctrine of the Two Kingdoms*; Wright, *Martin Luther's Understanding of God's Two Kingdoms*. For favorable interpretations of Luther's 'two kingdoms,' see Ebeling, *Word and Faith*; Nygren, "Luther's Doctrine of the Two Kingdoms," 301–10. For the representative critique against Luther's thought on the two kingdoms, see Barth, *This Christian Cause*; Bonhoeffer, *Ethics*. Barth's critique of Luther's two kingdoms is consistent with his critical posture towards the contrast between law and gospel, which is a vital hermeneutical tool for formulating the doctrine of justification by faith alone, which was the Reformation consensus between Luther and Calvin. In addition, Barth's critique is his logical conclusion because he denies natural law in the milieu of general revelation, which is foundational for Luther's two kingdoms as well as Calvin's.

I have interacted with Calvin's doctrines of justification by faith in the milieu of the antithesis between law and gospel, union with Christ, double predestination, covenants, redemptive history, and sacramental theology in light of contemporary discussion. See Jeon, *Calvin and the Federal Vision*; Jeon, *Covenant Theology*, 11–29; Jeon, *Covenant Theology and Justification by Faith*, 3–26.

it not to display in common nature God's special grace, which, in passing many by, desires itself bound to none? Besides this, God inspires special activities, in accordance with each man's calling. Many examples of this occur in the Book of Judges, where it is said that "the Spirit of the Lord took possession" of those men whom he had called to rule the people [ch. 6:34]. In short, in every extraordinary event there is some particular impulsion. For this reason, Saul was followed by the brave men "whose hearts God had touched" [I Sam 10:26].[4]

Accepting the tradition, designating man as "a social animal" (*animal sociale*), Calvin insisted that God created man as "a social animal" so that he has a "natural instinct to foster and preserve society." As a result, we can witness "universal impressions of a certain civic fair dealing and order" (*civilis cuiusdam honestatis et ordinis universales impressiones*) within all human beings' minds. So, it is a universal phenomenon that all human organizations are regulated by laws, which reflect natural law. This law is implanted in all, "without teacher or lawgiver." Thus, Calvin summarizes the foundation of political organization as follows:

> Of the first class the following ought to be said: since man is by nature a social animal, he tends through natural instinct to foster and preserve society. Consequently, we observe that there exist in all men's minds universal impressions of a certain civic fair dealing and order. Hence no man is to be found who does not understand that every sort of human organization must be regulated by laws, and who does not comprehend the principles of those laws. Hence arises that unvarying consent of all nations and of individual mortals with regard to laws. For their seeds have, without teacher or lawgiver, been implanted in all men. . . . Yet the fact remains that some seed of political order has been implanted in all men. And this is ample proof that in the arrangement of this life no man is without the light of reason.[5]

---

4. Calvin, *Inst.* 2.2.17. The Latin phrases from Calvin's *Institutes* are cited from Calvini, *Institutio Christianae Religionis.*

It is important to note that Calvin viewed God's common grace in two categories such as "the general grace of God" and "God's special grace" as the editor of *Institutes* correctly recognizes: "Neither common grace nor the special grace here mentioned has any relation to the salvation of its possessor. Special grace is a special endowment of capacity, virtue, or heroism by which a man is fitted to serve the divine purpose in this world, while he himself may remain in the common state of human depravity." Calvin, *Inst.* 2.2.17, footnote 64.

5. Calvin, *Inst.* 2.2.13.

Interpreting Romans 2:14, the classical Pauline reference for the biblical validity of the affirmation of natural law, Calvin argued that Gentiles have "a law" although they do not have "a written law," which was given to the Jews in the Old Testament. Calvin added that Paul sets "nature in opposition to a written law," which signifies that the gentiles universally have had natural law as "the natural light of righteousness," which has functioned in the place of the moral law, written on two stone tablets for the Jews in the Old Testament:

> They have then a law, though they are without law: for though they have not a written law, they are yet by no means wholly destitute of the knowledge of what is right and just; as they could not otherwise distinguish between vice and virtue; the first of which they restrain by punishment, and the latter they commend, and manifest their approbation of it by honouring it with rewards. He sets nature in opposition to a written law, meaning that the Gentiles had the natural light of righteousness, which supplied the place of that law by which the Jews were instructed, so that they were a law to themselves.[6]

It is evident that Calvin had a clear theological consciousness of God's bestowal of grace in two different realms through "the divine Spirit" (*divini Spiritus*): one is the grace for "the common good of mankind" (*generis humani bonum*) which is in the realm of common grace and the other is in the application of personal salvation which is the sovereign work of "the Spirit of God" in the realm of saving grace. Interpreting Exodus 31:2–11 and 35:30–35, Calvin argued that "the Spirit of God" *communicates* to "the most excellent in human life" as demonstrated by the artistic gifts of Bezalel and Oholiab when building the Tabernacle. Meanwhile, "the Spirit of God dwells only in believers," bestowing "the Spirit of sanctification" (*Spiritu sanctificationis*) in the execution of saving grace as Paul states in Romans 8:9 and 1 Corinthians 3:16:

> Meanwhile, we ought not to forget those most excellent benefits of the divine Spirit, which he distributes to whomever he wills, for the common good of mankind. The understanding and knowledge of Bezalel and Oholiab, needed to construct the Tabernacle, had to be instilled in them by the Spirit of God [Exod 31:2–11; 35:30–35]. It is no wonder, then that the knowledge of all that is most excellent in human life is said to be communicated to us through the Spirit of God. Nor is there reason for

---

6. Calvin, *Romans*, 2:14, in *Calvin's Commentaries*.

anyone to ask, What have the impious, who are utterly estranged from God, to do with his Spirit? We ought to understand the statement that the Spirit of God dwells only in believers [Rom 8:9] as referring to the Spirit of sanctification through whom we are consecrated as temples to God [I Cor 3:16]. Nonetheless he fills, moves, and quickens all things by the power of the same Spirit, and does so according to the character that he bestowed upon each kind by the law of creation.[7]

Recognizing the benefits of God's common grace, Calvin emphasizes that believers ought to enjoy and share the benefits received by common grace such as "physics, dialectic, mathematics, and other like disciplines" although they were developed by non-Christians: "But if the Lord has willed that we be helped in physics, dialectic, mathematics, and other like disciplines, by the work and ministry of the ungodly, let us use this assistance. For if we neglect God's free gift freely offered in these arts, we ought to suffer just judgment for our sloths."[8]

As such, Calvin properly uses the concepts of natural law in the milieu of general revelation and the distinction between common grace and

7. Calvin, *Inst.* 2.2.16. Calvin had a clear theological consciousness of the distinction between common grace and saving grace. In that sense, saving grace as "special grace" (*gratia speciali*), according to Calvin, is bestowed to the elect alone: "If this be admitted, it will be indisputable that free will is not sufficient to enable man to do good works, unless he be helped by grace, indeed by special grace, which only the elect receive through regeneration. For I do not tarry over those fanatics who babble that grace is equally and indiscriminately distributed." Calvin, *Inst.* 2.2.6. For the classical affirmation of the distinction between common grace and saving grace in Calvin's theology, see Bavinck, "Calvin and Common Grace," 99–130; Kuiper, *Calvin on Common Grace*.

In general, Reformed theologians adopted the antithesis between common grace and saving grace after the pattern of Calvin, and developed and applied the doctrine of common grace to the areas of biblical worldview, Christian apologetics, biblical and systematic theology, etc. although there are variations of the understanding and implications of common grace. Here, I mention a few selective, yet influential and important works. See Bavinck, *Reformed Dogmatics*, 4 vols.; Kline, *God, Heaven and Har Magedon*; Kline, *Kingdom Prologue*; Kline, *Structure of Biblical Authority*; Kuyper, *Abraham Kuyper*; Kuyper, *De Gemeene Gratie*; Kuyper, *Lectures on Calvinism*; Murray, *Collected Writings of John Murray*, vol. 2; Van Til, *Common Grace and the Gospel*.

However, there are some who deny the validity of the doctrine of common grace in Calvin's theology and worldview. Representative theologians who reject the distinction between common grace and saving grace in Calvin's theology include Herman Hoeksema and Klass Schilder. Cf. Barber, "Common Grace"; Gritters, "Grace Uncommon"; Hoeksema, *God's Goodness Always Particular*; Hoeksema, *Reformed Dogmatics*, 2 vols.; Schilder, *Christ and Culture*.

8. Calvin, *Inst.* 2.2.16.

saving grace not only to present a biblical worldview but also the theological background of a distinction between church and state in terms of
the two kingdoms.[9]

Having used these theological sources and tools, Calvin developed
the concept of the two kingdoms to make a distinction between church
and state against the medieval ideal of the official state church. Calvin
viewed medieval European political philosophy as unbiblical, and then
developed the distinction between church and state in the milieu of the
two kingdoms. Certainly, Calvin viewed the idea of the official state
church as an amalgam of church and state. That is the reason why he carefully reflected upon the relationship between church and state in light of
the Bible. Calvin recognized that there is "a twofold government in man";
There are spiritual and political governments. The spiritual government
takes care of and concerns "the life of the soul" while the political government concerns "the present life":

> Therefore, in order that none of us may stumble on that stone,
> let us first consider that there is a twofold government in man:
> one aspect is spiritual, whereby the conscience is instructed in
> piety and in reverencing God; the second is political, whereby
> man is educated for the duties of humanity and citizenship that
> must be maintained among men. These are usually called "spiri-
> tual" and the "temporal" jurisdiction (not improper terms) by
> which is meant that the former sort of government pertains to
> the life of the soul, while the latter has to do with the concerns
> of the present life—not only with food and clothing but with
> laying down laws whereby a man may live his life among other
> men holily, honorably, and temperately.[10]

Calvin analyzed the church as an institution, which primarily takes
care of "the life of the soul" as "the spiritual kingdom" (*regnum spirituale*).
And he defines the role of the state, directly related to "the present life," as
"the political kingdom" (*regnum politicum*):

> The one we may call the spiritual kingdom, the other, the politi-
> cal kingdom. Now these two, as we divided them, must always
> be examined separately; and while one is being considered, we
> must call away and turn aside the mind from thinking about

9. Surprisingly, there is a general tendency for scholars who interpret Calvin's concept of the two kingdoms and political thought to relate it exclusively to natural law,
overlooking the importance of the distinction between common grace and saving grace.

10. Calvin, *Inst.* 3.19.15.

the other. There are in man, so to speak, two worlds, over which different kings and different laws have authority.[11]

Calvin carefully uses the distinction between church and state as an effective biblical concept to provide a succinct critique for those who oppose the idea of the two kingdoms. Calvin was aware of the unhealthy political philosophies, promoted by the Anabaptists, denying the authority of the state on the one hand, and the abuse of tyrannical power, promoted by the political philosophy of Machiavelli, represented by his monumental work, *Il Principe* on the other hand.[12] Calvin responded to the European political context of the sixteenth century, which was darkly overshadowed by medieval Christendom. Calvin argues that the Anabaptists endeavored to overturn the state, which is a "divinely established order," exclusively emphasizing Christ's spiritual kingdom while "the flatterers of princes" excessively praised their own political power," rejecting "the rule of God" in the arena of politics:

> For although this topic seems by nature alien to the spiritual doctrine of faith which I have undertaken to discuss, what follows will show that I am right in joining them, in fact, that necessity compels me to do so. This is especially true since, from one side, insane and barbarous men furiously strive to overturn this divinely established order; while, on the other side, the flatterers of princes, immoderately praising their power, do not hesitate to set them against the rule of God himself. Unless both these evils are checked, purity of faith will perish. Besides, it is of no slight importance to us to know how lovingly God has provided in this respect for mankind, that greater zeal for piety may flourish in us to attest our gratefulness.[13]

11. Calvin, *Inst.* 3.19.15.

12. The editor of *Institutes* rightly suggests that Calvin was aware of Machiavelli's political philosophy through the Latin translation of *Il Principe*. See *Inst.* 4.20.1, footnote 4: "These sentences (1559) evidently refer to the Anabaptists on the one hand, and on the other to Machiavelli, whose Italian *Il Principe* was only in 1553 translated into Latin. (OS V. 474.) Calvin may also have in mind the emperor-cult of antiquity." I would identify Machiavelli's political philosophy as a tyrannical political philosophy, which has been shown and practiced by different continents, especially in the twentieth century such as Hitler's German Nazism, Mussolini's Italian Facism, communistic regimes, military dictatorships, and others.

13. Calvin, *Inst.* 4.20.1. The ultimate kingship of Christ both in church and state in Calvin's idea of the two kingdoms is well summarized by Godfrey: "The language of two kingdoms (church and state) clearly did not mean for Calvin that one kingdom belonged to Christ and the other did not. It did not mean that one kingdom was for

Developing and adopting the idea of the two kingdoms, Calvin tried to balance the roles of church and state. During the Protestant Reformation, the Anabaptists denied the authority of the rulers of the state because they only recognized Christ's spiritual kingdom, denying Christ's indirect rule over the state through the ordination of earthly kings and magistrates.

The first Anabaptistic confession, *The Schleitheim Confession*, formulated in 1527, suggests that the political philosophy of the Anabaptists was based upon a radical dualism, which provided a pessimistic worldview and complete detachment from the activities of the political kingdom:

> IV. We have been united concerning the separation that shall take place from the evil and the wickedness which the devil has planted in the world, simply in this; that we have no fellowship with them, and do not run with them in the confusion of their abominations. So it is; since all who have not entered into the obedience of faith and have not united themselves with God so that they will to do His will, are a great abomination before God, therefore nothing else can or really will grow or spring forth from them than abominable things. Now there is nothing else in the world and all creation than good or evil, believing and unbelieving, darkness and light, the world and those who are [come] out of the world, God's temple and idols, Christ and Belial, and none will have part with the other.[14]

Christian living and the other was not. It did not mean that one kingdom glorified God and the other did not. Christ for Calvin was truly and fully king in both kingdoms, but ruled the two kingdoms differently." Godfrey, "Kingdom and Kingdoms," 7.

14. Yoder, *Schleitheim Confession*, IV. Hillerbrand, sympathetic to the Anabaptistic worldview and political philosophy, agrees with my interpretation that the Anabaptistic political philosophy was based upon a radical or sharp dualism as Farley briefly summarizes it: "As for the state, Hillerbrand notes that the Anabaptists have always recognized that it is ordained of God to punish evildoers and to protect the law-abiding. Hence 'the notion of rebellion or revolution must therefore have been utterly foreign to the Anabaptist mind.' With respect to the state substantial discrepancies appear between the Anabaptists and the Reformers only in the area of the limitations of government and religious liberty. Hillerbrand acknowledges, however, that 'Anabaptist thinking does not attempt a synthesis' of its rejection of office holding with its recognition of the state's divine institution. Hence, he admits that 'a basic paradox remains unanswered in Anabaptistic thinking'—the very paradox which Calvin probes.

Hillerbrand further explains that the Anabaptist view of the state is based on both a 'New Testament monism' and a sharp dualism between the kingdom of Christ and the 'world.' But then these are inseparable characteristics of the 'Anabaptist Vision.'" Calvin, *Treatises Against the Anabaptists and Against the Libertines*, 31–32. Cf. Hillerbrand, "Anabaptist View of the State," 83–110.

The Anabaptists also denied the Christian's right to be "a magistrate," who has the power and authority to use "the sword," arguing that Jesus rejected being the earthly King of Israel although his followers insisted:

> Third, is asked concerning the sword: whether the Christian should be a magistrate if he is chosen thereto. This is answered thus: Christ was to be made king, but He fled and did not discern the ordinance of His Father. Thus we should also do as He did and follow after Him, and we shall not walk in darkness. For He Himself says: "Whoever would come after me, let him deny himself and take up his cross and follow me." He Himself further forbids the violence of the sword when He says: "The princes of this world lord it over them etc., but among you it shall not be so."[15]

Observing the biblical nature of dualities such as "the flesh" as opposed to "the Spirit" and "worldly" as opposed to "Christians," the Anabaptists read these dualities from the perspective of a radical dualism. In doing so, they denied the Christian's dual citizenship in the spiritual kingdom which is ultimate, and his citizenship in the political kingdom which is temporary. And they concluded that "a Christian" should not be "a magistrate":

> Lastly one can see in the following points that it does not befit a Christian to be a magistrate: the rule of the government is according to the flesh, that of the Christians according to the Spirit. Their houses and dwelling remain in this world, that of the Christians is in heaven. Their citizenship is in this world, that of the Christians is in heaven. The weapons of their battle and warfare are carnal and only against the flesh, but the weapons of Christians are spiritual, against the fortification of the devil. The worldly are armed with steel and iron, but Christians are armed with the armor of God, with truth, righteousness, peace, faith, salvation, and with the Word of God.[16]

I briefly explored the Anabaptistic political philosophy that was founded upon a radical dualism which is a misrepresentation of dualities as presented in the Bible. In addition, this philosophy completely lacked the concept and implications of common grace, and the proper understanding and implications of natural revelation, which are foundational

---

15. Yoder, *Schleitheim Confession*, VI.
16. Yoder, *Schleitheim Confession*, VI.

not only for the biblical worldview but also for the idea of the two kingdoms, with which Calvin was dealing.

Calvin responded critically to the Anabaptistic rejection of the legitimacy of the use of sword by the state and the Christian participation
in political activities and the right to be the magistrate of a state. Alluding
to the principle of "the teaching of the gospel" in Luke 21:19 and Romans
12:21, Calvin argues that believers should be patient and conquer "evil
by doing good" in their personal lives. So, the believers' arms in their
personal lives are not "force and violence" but "prayer and gentleness in
order to pass their days." However, Calvin carefully notes that "the public
sword" was ordained by God to protect the citizens of a state as Paul
described in Romans 13:4. Moreover, "the Spirit of God Himself" warranted "the public sword," and "the magistrate" is "a minister of God" for
the benefit of citizens to restrain and prevent "the violence of the wicked."
In that sense, Calvin argues that the rejection of "the public sword" by the
Anabaptists is "a blasphemy against God Himself":

> Now it is true that the usage of the sword in particular must not
> be entrusted to just anyone for resisting evil. For the arms of
> Christians are prayer and gentleness in order to pass their days
> in patience and conquer evil by doing good, in accordance with
> the teaching of the gospel (Luke 21:19; Rom. 12:21). Thus the
> duty of each of us is to suffer patiently when someone offends us
> rather than to use force and violence.
>
> But to condemn the public sword which God ordained for
> our protection is a blasphemy against God Himself. The Spirit
> of God Himself proclaims through Saint Paul (Rom. 13:4) that
> the magistrate is a minister of God for our benefit and on our
> benefit, for the purpose of restraining and preventing the vio-
> lence of the wicked. And for that reason the sword is placed in
> his hands in order to punish crimes.[17]

Responding to the Anabaptists who argued that Christians cannot
become magistrates in the political kingdom, Calvin noted that the office of magistrate is a holy vocation that is "holy and lawful," ordained
and approved by God. In addition, Calvin responded to the Anabaptistic rejection of the believers' right to hold the position of magistrate
from the perspective of redemptive history. Calvin observed that the
Anabaptists correctly argued that "the civil government of the people
of Israel" was a type of "the spiritual kingdom of Jesus Christ," which

17. Calvin, *Treatises Against the Anabaptists and Against the Libertines*, 72.

lasted only until the first coming of Jesus. Agreeing with the Anabaptists about the typological nature of the kingdom of Israel in the Old Testament, Calvin deduced the important notion that the kingdom of Israel in the Old Testament was "a political government," and the principle itself should be applied to all nations:

> We worship the same God that the fathers of old did. We have the same law and rule that they had, showing us how to govern ourselves in order to walk rightly before God. It thus follows that a vocation that was considered holy and lawful then cannot be forbidden Christians today, for a vocation is the principal part of human life and the part that means the most to God. From which it follows that we should not deny ourselves the vocation of civil justice, nor drive it outside the Christian church. For our Lord has ordained it and approved it as good for the people of Israel. And He has appointed His most excellent servants to it and even His prophets.
>
> They will reply, possibly, that the civil government of the people of Israel was a figure of the spiritual kingdom of Jesus Christ and lasted only until His coming. I will admit to them that, in part, it was a figure, but I deny that it was nothing more than this, and not without reason. For in itself it was a political government, which is a requirement among all people.[18]

Critiquing the Anabaptistic understanding of the relationship between church and state, Calvin uses an analogy "between body and soul, between this present fleeting life and that future eternal life":

> First, before we enter into the matter itself, we must keep in mind that distinction which we previously laid down so that we do not (as commonly happens) unwisely mingle these two, which have a completely different nature. For certain men, when they hear that the gospel promises a freedom that acknowledges no king and no magistrate among men, but looks to Christ alone, think that they cannot benefit by their freedom so long as they see any power set up over them. They therefore think that nothing will be safe unless the whole world is reshaped to a new form, where there are neither courts, nor laws, nor magistrates, nor anything which in their opinion restricts their freedom. But whoever knows how to distinguish between body and soul, between this present fleeting life and that future eternal life, will

---

18. Calvin, *Treatises Against the Anabaptists and Against the Libertines*, 78.

without difficulty know that Christ's spiritual Kingdom and the civil jurisdiction are things completely distinct.[19]

Calvin was also critical of the Jewish political philosophy, which sought after Messiah's earthly and visible kingdom. This view, according to Calvin, is another example of the amalgam between the church as "Christ's spiritual kingdom" (*spirituale Christi regnum*) and the state as "the civil jurisdiction" (*civilem ordinationem*). Interpreting Pauline passages such as 1 Corinthians 7:21; Galatians 3:28; 5:1; and Colossians 3:11, Calvin argues that the distinction between church and state under the New Covenant is a biblical ideal:

> Since, then, it is a Jewish vanity to seek and enclose Christ's Kingdom within the elements of this world, let us rather ponder that what Scripture clearly teaches is a spiritual fruit, which we gather from Christ's grace; and let us remember to keep within its own limits all that freedom which is promised and offered to us in him. For why is it that the same apostle who bids us stand and not submit to the "yoke of bondage" [Gal. 5:1] elsewhere forbids slaves to be anxious about their state [I Cor. 7:21], unless it be that spiritual freedom can perfectly well exist along with civil bondage? These statements of his must also be taken in the same sense: In the Kingdom of God "there is neither Jew nor Greek, neither male nor female, neither slave nor free" [Gal. 3:28, Vg.; order changed]. And again, "there is not Jew nor Greek, uncircumcised and circumcised, barbarian Scythian, slave, freeman; but Christ is all in all" [Col. 3:11 p.]. By these statements he means that it makes no difference what your condition among men may be or under what nation's laws you live, since the Kingdom of Christ does not at all consist in these things.[20]

Reading through the historical accounts of the four Gospels and the book of Acts, Calvin notes that the Jews falsely expected a Messianic earthly kingdom for Israel. Jesus' disciples made similar mistakes "until after His resurrection" as Luke clearly witnesses the story in Acts 1:7. Thus, Jesus corrected the false expectation of the Messianic earthly kingdom that the Jews, including his disciples, anticipated. And he tried to correct it through his earthly ministry until his ascension:

19. Calvin, *Inst.* 4.20.1.
20. Calvin, *Inst.* 4.20.1.

Everyone knows the silly fantasy which the Jews had about the Messiah: that is, how they thought He would have a kingdom flourishing in this world, that they might live in this world in ease and comfort and triumph over others. So much so that even the apostles, until after His resurrection, held this notion in their heads, as Saint Luke points out in the first chapter of Acts (v.6). That is what motivated the people to want to make Jesus Christ king by force, in order that by this means they might be free of subjection to the Romans. Therefore it is no surprise that our Lord hid himself, since that wish derived from a wicked and perverse error and would have had a most pernicious consequence.[21]

Although Calvin tried to maintain a distinction between church and state, he was unable to do so because his theological vision allowed the civil authorities to have the right and duty to guard the doctrinal matters of the church, which should be the sole responsibility of the church under the New Covenant.

An Amalgam of Church and State

Calvin thought the concept of the Christian state or city was biblically warranted under the New Covenant, but he also thought the Jewish theocracy of the Old Testament Israel could not be reproduced. He considered the Jewish theocracy in the promised land as a type of eternal theocracy in heaven. Calvin, citing Cicero's *Laws*, viewed the law and the magistrate as essential components of the civil state:

Next to the magistracy in the civil state come the laws, stoutest sinews of the commonwealth, or, as Cicero, after Plato, calls them, the souls, without which the magistracy cannot stand, even as they themselves have no force apart from the magistracy. Accordingly, nothing truer could be said than that the law is a silent magistrate; the magistrate, a living law.[22]

Calvin recognized the formation and ruling of the Christian state or city where Christians are dominant. In doing so, Calvin called it "a Christian state" (*Christiana politia*) to separate it from medieval Christendom. Governing the Christian state, Calvin argues that laws may not apply and

21. Calvin, *Treatises Against the Anabaptists and Against the Libertines*, 86.
22. Calvin, *Inst.* 4.20.14.

directly imitate "the political system of Moses" (*Mose politicis*), but they reflect it because the ceremonial and judicial laws of the Jewish state are abrogated. Calvin insists that the "common laws of nations" (*communibus gentium legibus*), which are the diverse reflections of natural law, may be comprehensive enough to rule the Christian state:

> But because I have undertaken to say with what laws a Christian state ought to be governed, this is no reason why anyone should expect a long discourse concerning the best kind of laws. This would be endless and would not pertain to the present purpose and place. I shall in but a few words, and as in passing note what laws can piously be used before God, and be rightly administered among men.
>
> I would have preferred to pass over this matter in utter silence if I were not aware that here many dangerously go astray. For there are some who deny that a commonwealth is duly framed which neglects the political system of Moses, and is ruled by the common laws of nations. Let other men consider how perilous and seditious this notion is; it will be enough for me to have proved it false and foolish.[23]

Calvin accepted a theological tradition where "the whole law of God" (*universam Dei Legem*) is divided into "moral, ceremonial, and judicial laws" (*mores, ceremonias, iudicia*). In doing so, Calvin argues that the moral laws are perpetually binding while ceremonial and judicial laws are abrogated after the first coming of Jesus Christ. Calvin insisted that the moral law is essential for "true holiness of morals" because it is "an unchangeable rule of right living":

> We must bear in mind that common division of the whole law of God published by Moses into moral, ceremonial, and judicial laws. And we must consider each of these parts, that we may understand what there is in them that pertains to us, and what does not. In the meantime, let no one be concerned over the small point that ceremonial and judicial laws pertain also to morals. For the ancient writers who taught this division, although they were not ignorant that these two latter parts had some bearing upon morals, still, because these could be changed or abrogated while morals remained untouched, did not call them moral laws. They applied this name only to the first part,

---

23. Calvin, *Inst.* 4.20.14.

without which the true holiness of morals cannot stand, nor an unchangeable rule of right living.[24]

Calvin emphasizes the importance of "the moral law" (*lex moralis*) because it is perpetually binding as "the true and eternal rule of righteousness." God prescribed the moral law, transcending culture and time, to all human beings of "all nations and times." Calvin describes the perpetual nature of the moral law as follows:

> The moral law (to begin first with it) is contained under two heads, one of which simply commands us to worship God with pure faith and piety; the other, to embrace men with sincere affection. Accordingly, it is the true and eternal rule of righteousness, prescribed for men of all nations and times, who wish to conform their lives to God's will. For it is his eternal and unchangeable will that he himself indeed be worshiped by us all, and that we love one another.[25]

Reflecting upon Calvin's concepts about the Mosaic laws, their implications in the Jewish nation and the abrogation of judicial and ceremonial laws under the New Covenant, we are certain that Calvin believed that the Jewish theocracy is irreproducible because God allowed it only within the Jewish state in the Old Testament. Nevertheless, Calvin thought that the formation and government of the Christian state is desirable under the New Covenant where Christians are dominant. Desiring the Christian state, Calvin provided theological and practical grounds for its justification. Interpreting Romans 13:4 and 1 Timothy 2:2, Calvin provides the biblical rationale for the usefulness of "the laws, judgments, and magistrates" for "the common society of Christians" (*communem Christianorum societatem*), which is another expression of the Christian state or city:

> It now remains for us to examine what we had set in the last place: what usefulness the laws, judgments, and magistrates have for the common society of Christians. To this is also joined another question: how much deference private individuals ought to yield to their magistrates, and how far their obedience ought to go. To very many the office of magistrate seems superfluous among Christians, because they cannot piously call upon them for help, inasmuch as it is forbidden to them to take revenge,

24. Calvin, *Inst.* 4.20.14.
25. Calvin, *Inst.* 4.20.15.

to sue before a court, or to go to law. But Paul clearly testifies
to the contrary that the magistrate is minister of God for our
good [Rom. 13:4]. By this we understand that he has been so ordained of God, that, defended by his hand and support against
the wrongdoing and injustices of evil men, we may live a quiet
and serene life [Rom 13:4].[26]

Meanwhile, Calvin located both ceremonial and judicial laws in the
spectrum of redemptive history. He argued that "the ceremonial law"
(*ceremonialis*) served "the tutelage of the Jews" (*Iudaeorum paedagogia*)
so that it was abrogated when Jesus Christ came. Similarly, "the judicial
law" (*Iudicialis*) was given to the Jewish civil government in the Old Testament. Calvin had clarity of insight to connect the ceremonial law to "the
church of the Jews" (*Iudaeorum ecclesiam*), while he related the judicial
law to the "civil government" (*politiae*) of the Jews in the Old Testament.
In the end, Calvin properly concluded that both ceremonial and judicial
laws were abrogated while the moral law was perpetually binding:

> The ceremonial law was the tutelage of the Jews, with which it
> seemed good to the Lord to train this people, as it were, in their
> childhood, until the fullness of time should come [Gal 4:3–4; cf.
> ch. 3:23–24], in order that he might fully manifest his wisdom to
> the nations, and show the truth of those things which then were
> foreshadowed in figures. The judicial law, given to them for civil
> government, imparted certain formulas of equity and justice, by
> which they might live together blamelessly and peaceably. Those
> ceremonial practices indeed properly belonged to the doctrine
> of piety, inasmuch as they kept the church of the Jews in service
> and reverence to God, and yet could be distinguished from piety
> itself. In like manner, the form of their judicial laws, although
> it had no other intent than how best to preserve that very love
> which is enjoined by God's eternal law, had something distinct
> from that precept of love. Therefore, as ceremonial laws could
> be abrogated while piety remained safe and unharmed, so too,
> when these judicial laws were taken away, the perpetual duties
> and precepts of love could still remain.[27]

Calvin identifies the moral law as "a testimony of natural law"
(*naturalis legis testimonium*). God engraved and prescribed the moral
law on "the minds of men" throughout the history of human civilization.

26. Calvin, *Inst.* 4.20.17.
27. Calvin, *Inst.* 4.20.15.

So, Calvin suggests that equity, reflected by the moral law, should be "the goal and rule and limit of all laws." Calvin argues that the formation of laws should be flexible in different times and countries. And laws may be different from the Jewish judicial law in the Old Testament, which Calvin identifies as "the Jewish law" (*lege Iudaica*). Calvin specifies the judicial law in the Old Testament to govern "the Jewish state" (*politia Iudaeorum*) as "the Jewish law" because God does not demand it to be applied and obeyed outside of Old Testament Israel:

> It is a fact that the law of God which we call the moral law is noth-
> ing else than a testimony of natural law and of that conscience
> which God has engraved upon the minds of men. Consequently,
> the entire scheme of this equity of which we are now speaking
> has been prescribed in it. Hence, this equity alone must be the
> goal and rule and limit of all laws. Whatever laws shall be framed
> to that rule, directed to the goal, bound by that limit, there is no
> reason why we should disapprove of them, howsoever they may
> differ from the Jewish law, or among themselves.[28]

Calvin carefully observes that natural law and equity are the proper means to govern different nations under various circumstances. So, then we see that the judicial law which under the New Covenant is abrogated does not dishonor the Mosaic laws in the Old Testament, but rather prop-erly understands the implications of the appropriate context of redemp-tive history. God did not intend the judicial law to be "proclaimed among all nations and to be in force everywhere." Rather, he gave it uniquely to defend and keep "the Jewish nation" (*Iudaicam gentem*). Calvin carefully

---

28. Calvin, *Inst.* 4.20.16. There are numerous secondary writings which deal with Calvin and natural law in the Reformation context and its related issues in the milieu of medieval predecessors and other Reformers. I mention here a select few of the sec-ondary resources. For a comprehensive and critical discussion of Calvin's view of the natural law in relation to other Reformers, Aquinas, and other medieval theologians, its role in Calvin's thought, and its related topics, see Backus, "Calvin's Concept of Nat-ural and Roman Law," 7–26; Clark, "Calvin and the *Lex Naturalis*," 1–22; Helm, "Cal-vin and Natural Law," 5–22; Jue, "*Theologia Naturalis:* A Reformed Tradition," 168–89; Klempa, "John Calvin on Natural Law," 72–95; Lang, "Reformation and Natural Law," 56–98; McNeill, "Natural Law in the Teaching of the Reformers," 168–82; Pryor, "God's Bridle," 225–54; Schreiner, "Calvin's Use of Natural Law," 51–76; Schreiner, *Theater of His Glory*; VanDrunen, "Context of Natural Law," 503–25; VanDrunen, "Medieval Natural Law and the Reformation," 77–98; VanDrunen, "Natural Law, Custom, and Common Law," 699–717; VanDrunen, *Natural Law and the Two Kingdoms*, 21–118; Westburg, "Reformed Tradition and Natural Law," 103–17.

selects the words "the Jewish nation" to emphasize the unique application
of the judicial law to the nation of Israel in the Old Testament:

> For the statement of some, that the law of God given through
> Moses is dishonored when it is abrogated and new laws preferred
> to it, is utterly vain. For others are not preferred to it when they
> are more approved, not by a simple comparison, but with regard
> to the condition of times, place, and nation; or when that law is
> abrogated which was never enacted for us. For the Lord through
> the hand of Moses did not give that law to be proclaimed among
> all nations and to be in force everywhere; but when he had taken
> the Jewish nation into his safekeeping, defense, and protection,
> he also willed to be a lawgiver especially to it; and—as became a
> wise lawgiver—he had special concern for it in making its laws.[29]

Calvin argues that the governments of church and state are not antithetical, although he carefully maintained the distinction between church
and state. He was concerned with the Anabaptists who maintained a
complete detachment from the political matters of state. Indicating a
false interpretation of Colossians 2:20 by the Anabaptists and calling
them "certain fanatics" (*quidem fanatici*), Calvin strongly condemns the
Anabaptistic detachment to civil duties toward the state:

> Yet this distinction does not lead us to consider the whole na-
> ture of government a thing polluted, which has nothing to do
> with Christian men. That is what, indeed, certain fanatics who
> delight in unbridled license shout and boast: after we have died
> through Christ to the elements of this world [Col. 2:20], are
> transported to God's Kingdom, and sit among heavenly beings,

---

29. Calvin, *Inst.* 4.20.16. The close relationship between equity and natural law in
Calvin's ethics and political philosophy has been discussed by several scholars. See
Haas, *Concept of Equity in Calvin's Ethics*; Hancock, *Calvin and the Foundation of Mod-
ern Politics*, 86; Helm, *John Calvin's Ideas*, 363–67; VanDrunen, *Natural Law and the
Two Kingdoms*, 108–10.

I would argue that the Reformed theonomists' political vision of theonomic polity
is incompatible with Calvin. The Reformed theonomists, represented by Rushdoony,
Bahnsen, and their followers, insist that the judicial or civil law in the Old Testament
Israel should be applied in contemporary states under the New Covenant. In doing
so, they deny the abrogation of the Old Testament judicial law, which was a key principle in Calvin's understanding of the Mosaic laws and its application to his political
philosophy. See Bahnsen, *Theonomy in Christian Ethics*; Jordan, *Law of the Covenant*;
Rushdoony, *Institutes of Biblical Law*, 3 vols. For the critical evaluation of the Reformed theonomic ethics and political philosophy, see Barker and Godfrey, *Theonomy*;
Gordon, "Van Til and Theonomic Ethics," 271–78; Jeon, "Covenant Theology and Old
Testament Ethics," 3–33; VanDrunen, *Natural Law and the Two Kingdoms*, 408–11.

it is a thing unworthy of us and set far beneath our excellence to
be occupied with those vile and worldly cares which have to do
with business foreign to a Christian man[30]

Although Calvin makes the distinction between church and state
in light of the two kingdoms, his distinction is inconsistent because he
was not able to break away completely from the political philosophy of a
medieval Christendom. That evidence is clearly manifested through his
description of the appointed end of civil government:

> Yet civil government has its appointed end, so long as we live
> among men, to cherish and protect the outward worship of God,
> to defend sound doctrine of piety and the position of the church,
> to adjust our life to the society of men, to form our social behav-
> ior to civil righteousness, to reconcile us with one another, and
> to promote general peace and tranquility.[31]

I think Calvin's idea of the appointed end of civil government provides a hermeneutical and theological foundation to support the intrusion of government authorities in matters of doctrinal concern to the
church. And this foundation is evident in Calvin's support and affirmation of Servetus' execution for his heretical teachings in respect to the
doctrine of the Trinity.

Referring to Romans 13:1–4, Calvin argues that "the office of magistrate" is "an ordinance of God." He viewed the rulers of the state as
"ministers of God" (*ministros Dei*), for those who do "good unto praise";
for those who do "evil, avengers unto wrath." Mentioning the political
and religious leaders of Old Testament Israel, Calvin concludes that "civil
authority" (*civilis potestas*) is "a calling" (*vocatio*) in the presence of God:

> But Paul speaks much more clearly when he undertakes a just
> discussion of this matter. For he states both that power is an
> ordinance of God [Rom 13:2], and that there are no powers ex-
> cept those ordained by God [Rom 13:1]. Further, that princes
> are ministers of God, for those doing good unto praise; for those
> doing evil, avengers unto wrath [Rom 13:3–4]. To this may be
> added the examples of holy men, of whom some possessed
> kingdoms, as David, Josiah, and Hezekiah; others, lordships, as
> Joseph and Daniel; others, civil rule among a free people, as Mo-
> ses, Joshua, and the judges. The Lord has declared his approval

30. Calvin, *Inst.* 4.20.2.
31. Calvin, *Inst.* 4.20.2.

of their offices. Accordingly, no one ought to doubt that civil authority is a calling, not only holy and lawful before God, but also the most sacred and by far the most honorable of all callings in the whole life of mortal men.[32]

As such, Calvin argues that the magistrates and rulers of the state or city are ordained by God. And civil authority is a holy and lawful calling in the presence of God. However, Calvin's idea that the magistrates of the state have the right and duty to safeguard "sound doctrine of piety and the position of the church" opened a hermeneutical and theological door leading to Christian theocracy in the thinking of his followers. It also became the political ideal for the Puritans in the seventeenth century both in England and New England in America.

The prime example of Christian theocracy is found in the formulation and adaptation of this political philosophy by the Westminster divines. Like Calvin, the Westminster divines adopted Calvin's political philosophy that the government authorities of the state have the right and duty to interfere in the doctrinal and religious matters of the church, which should be dealt with solely by the church under the New Covenant. So, it is worthwhile to quote the political philosophy of the Westminster divines, which was amended later in 1789 when "the first American Assembly of 1789" amended it before its adoption:

> The civil magistrate may not assume to himself the administration of the Word and sacraments, or the power of the keys of the kingdom of heaven; *yet, he hath authority, and it is his duty, to take order that unity and peace be preserved in the church, that the truth of God be kept pure, and entire; that all blasphemies and heresies be suppressed; all corruptions and abuses in worship and discipline prevented or reformed; and all the ordinances of God duly settled, administered and observed. For the better effecting whereof, he hath power to call Synods, to be present at them, and to provide that whatsoever is transacted in them, be according to the minds of God* [emphasis added].[33]

32. Calvin, *Inst.* 4.20.4.

33. Westminster Confession of Faith, 23.3, in *Westminster Standards*. The American amendment in 1789 suggests that the newly adopted form of the Westminster Confession of Faith 23.3 avoids the concept of the Christian state, which was Calvin's political ideal as well as the Westminster divines who formulated the original Westminster Standards: "Civil magistrates may not assume to themselves the administration of the Word and sacraments; or the power of the kingdom of heaven; *or, in the least, interfere in the matter so faith. Yet, as nursing fathers, it is the duty of civil*

Calvin's idea of the role of the magistrate in the Christian state decisively contributed to the affirmation of Servetus' death sentence and execution in the city of Geneva although he maintained the distinction between church and state. In this sense, let us discuss Calvin's role in Servetus' death sentence and execution, which is a representative example of Calvin's political philosophy in his own life context.

Calvin and Servetus

Calvin was critical of the Anabaptists who were known as the Radical Reformers during the Protestant Reformation in Europe. Michael Servetus (1511–1553), one of the representative leaders of the Anabaptists, was one of the chief theological enemies of Calvin.[34]

Servetus was best known as an Anabaptist; he vehemently rejected the biblical doctrine of the Trinity. The culmination of Servetus' rejection of the doctrine of the Trinity was manifested in his publication of *Restitution of the Christian Religion* (*Christianismi restitutio*) in 1553, which suggests that he was attacking Calvin's theology, summarized in his *Institutes of the Christian Religion*. Calvin responded to Servetus' denial of the doctrine of Trinity in his *Institutes*. This historical evidence suggests that there was strong personal and theological animosity between Calvin and Servetus. Responding to Servetus' denial of the doctrine of Trinity,

---

magistrates to protect the Church of our common Lord, without giving the preference to any denomination of Christians above the rest, in such a manner that all ecclesiastical persons whatever shall enjoy the full, free, and unquestioned liberty of discharging every part of their sacred functions, without violence or danger. And, as Jesus Christ hath appointed a regular government and discipline in his Church, no law of any commonwealth should interfere with, let, or hinder, the due exercise thereof, among the voluntary members of any denomination of Christians, according to their own profession and belief. It is the duty of civil magistrates to protect the person and good name of all their people, in such an effectual manner as that no person be suffered, either upon pretense of religion or of infidelity, to offer any indignity, violence, abuse, or injury to any other person whatsoever: and to take order, that all religious and ecclesiastical assemblies be held without molestation or disturbance [emphasis added]."

34. For a comprehensive and critical sketch of Servetus' life and theology, his attitude towards Calvin, Calvin's affirmation of his execution in Geneva and evaluation from different perspectives, see Bainton, *Hunted Heretic*; Friedman, *Michael Servetus*; Godfrey, *John Calvin*, 132–34; Hillar, *Case of Michael Servetus (1511–1553)*; Hillar, *Michael Servetus*; Kayayan, "Case of Michael Servetus," 117–46; Kingdon, "Social Control and Political Control," 521–32; Parker, *John Calvin*, 146–54; Pettegree, "Michael Servetus and the Limits of Tolerance," 40–45.

Calvin pointed out that Servetus denied Christ as "the Son of God" due to the logic that he was "begotten of the Holy Spirit" in the virgin Mary's womb. Calvin rightly insisted that Servetus, denying "the distinction of the two natures" (*duplicis naturae distinctione*) in Christ, made a fatal theological mistake, mixing "some divine and some human elements." In the end, Calvin summarized that Servetus denied Christ as "both God and man." In this manner, Calvin writes as follows:

> But in our own age too, a no less deadly monster has emerged, Michael Servetus, who has supposed the Son of God to be a fig-ment compounded from God's essence, spirit, flesh, and three uncreated elements. First of all, he denies that Christ is the Son of God for any other reason than that he was begotten of the Holy Spirit in the virgin's womb. His subtlety takes this distinc-tion: having overturned the distinction of the two natures, he regards Christ to be a mixture of some divine and some human elements, but not to be reckoned both God and man. For his whole logic bears upon the point before Christ was revealed in the flesh there were only shadow figures in God; the truth or effect of these appeared only when the Word, who had been destined for this honor, truly began to be the Son of God.[35]

After publishing the controversial book, the Roman Catholic au-thorities in France arrested Servetus. However, he escaped, although he was condemned "*in absentia* for his heresy and would have been execut-ed" if he had been rearrested in France. For more than a thousand years, medieval Christendom in Europe practiced capital punishment, mostly burning at stake those who rejected and attacked the doctrine of the Trinity. Escaping France, Servetus entered the city of Geneva in August of 1553 and was arrested by the government authorities. In October, the trial

35. Calvin, *Inst.* 2.14.5. The culmination of the theological debate in respect to the doctrine of the Trinity between Calvin and Servetus is manifested when Calvin identi-fied Servetus as a "foul dog." I do not endorse Calvin's personal attitude in his theologi-cal debate against Servetus, although it is understandable when we reflect upon the religious and political contexts of the sixteenth century Protestant Reformation: "Sane readers will gather from this summary that the crafty evasions of this foul dog utterly extinguished the hope of salvation. For if flesh were divinity itself, it would cease to be the temple of divinity. Only he can be our redeemer who, begotten of the seed of Abraham and David, was truly made man according to the flesh. Servetus perversely bases his position on John's words: 'The Word was made flesh' [John 1:14]. For, as these words resist Nestorius' error, they also give no support to that impious fabrication whose author was Eutyches, inasmuch as the sole purpose of the Evangelist was to declare unity of person in the two natures." Calvin, *Inst.* 2.14.8

against Servetus took place in the city of Geneva. He was condemned for heresy and was executed due to his heretical teaching of the doctrine of the Trinity. In this trial, Calvin was the chief prosecutor. Godfrey briefly and comprehensively summarizes the process of Servetus' arrest, trial and execution in Geneva as follows:

> In October the trial finally took place. Members of the city council served as judges, and Calvin functioned as the chief prosecutor. Servetus was condemned and ordered to be executed by burning at the stake, the traditional medieval punishment for heresy. Calvin and the other ministers pled that the punishment should be changed to beheading, a much quicker and less painful form of execution. The city council refused. Justice moved swiftly in those days: he was tried on October 20, condemned on October 21, and executed on October 26.
>
> Calvin and the other ministers continued to appeal to Servetus to repent right up to the time of his execution, but Servetus adamantly maintained his heresy. His dying words were, "Jesus, son of the eternal God, have mercy on me." By those words Servetus maintained even in the flames that Jesus was not himself eternal God.[36]

Historically, Calvin, the chief prosecutor at Servetus' trial in the city of Geneva, affirmed and supported Servetus' capital punishment for his heretical teaching of the doctrine of the Trinity. It is my assessment that Calvin's affirmation of Servetus' death sentence and execution was not accidental but a result of his hermeneutical and theological reflection. Calvin thought that the government authorities of the Christian state had the right to prosecute and execute those who commit and teach heresy against the biblical religion, which was represented by Servetus in his own ecclesiastical and political contexts in the city of Geneva.[37] Calvin's affir-

36. Godfrey, *John Calvin*, 133–34.

37. For Calvin's political thought, its influence in the Reformation context and to the latter generations as well as the general principles and practices of the political system in Geneva, and Calvin's influence on them, and the relationship between church and state in the city of Geneva, see Ainsworth, *Relations between Church and State*; Hall, "Calvin on Human Government and the State," 411–40; Hall, *Legacy of John Calvin*, 20–26; Hancock, *Calvin and the Foundations of Modern Politics*, 62–81; Hopfl, *Christian Polity of John Calvin*; Kingdon, *Calvin and Calvinism*; Kingdon, "Calvin and the Government of Geneva," 49–67; McNeill, "Calvin and Civil Government," 260–74; McNeill, "John Calvin on Civil Government," 20–35; Monter, *Studies in Genevan Government*; Stevenson, "Calvin and Political Issues," 173–87. Calvin's influence in the shaping of political system in the city of Geneva is well summarized by Hall, *Legacy*

mation of Servetus' death sentence and execution is consistent with his political philosophy in light of his understanding of the two kingdoms.[38]

Although Calvin held the distinction between church and state, his distinction was inconsistent. He thought hermeneutically and theologically that the Christian state has a right to intrude in the doctrinal matters of the church and prosecute and even give a death sentence and execution due to heretical teachings.

---

of John Calvin, 24–25: "One of the procedural safeguards of the 1543 civic reform—a hallmark of the Calvinistic governing ethos—was that the various branches of local government (councils) could no longer act unilaterally; henceforth, at least two councils were required to approve measures before ratification. This early republican mechanism, which prevented consolidation of all governmental power into a single council, predated Montesquieu's separation of powers doctrine by two centuries—a Calvinistic contribution that is not always recognized. The driving rationale for this dispersed authority was a simple but scriptural idea: even the best of leaders could think blindly and selfishly, so they needed a format for mutual correction and accountability. This kind of thinking, already incorporated into Geneva's ecclesiastical sphere (embedded in the 1541 *Ecclesiastical Ordinances*) and essentially derived from biblical sources, anticipated many later instances of political federalism. The structure of Genevan Presbyterianism began to influence Genevan civil politics; in turn, that also furthered the separation of powers and provided protection from oligarchy. The result was a far more open and stable society than previously, and Calvin's orientation toward the practical is obvious in these areas."

38. As Parker properly indicates, Calvin's political philosophy in respect to the religious heresy and the attitude of the magistrate of the Christian state had been consistent from the publication of the first edition of *Institutes* in 1536 to the final edition of it in 1559: "Should the state punish heresy as a crime? Calvin's doctrine of civil government stands almost unaltered from the first edition of the *Institutio* to the last, and it is restated in the *Defensio orthodoxae fidei*, which he wrote on the Servetus affair at the request of the German cities. 'Is it lawful for Christian princes and judges to punish heretics?' The purpose of civil government is not only that 'men may breathe, eat, drink, and be warmed, although it certainly includes all these when it provides for human society. But it also exists so that idolatry, sacrilege of the name of God, blasphemies against his truth and other public offences against religion may not emerge and may not be disseminated. . . . Finally, that among Christians the public face of religion may exist and among men humanity.'

Thus it is the duty of the state to establish true religion and to maintain that religion once it is established. The state and its administration are in no way secular or unclean, a neutral or antagonistic realm to the church. On the contrary, the laws and those who administer them are ordained by God for the economy of the world. The rulers are ministers and servants of God and as such bear the authority not only of an earthly office but of the Lord by whom and for whom they execute their office. Granted that it is the duty of the state to establish and maintain true religion, what is a government to do if it sees true religion fundamentally attacked?" Parker, *John Calvin*, 152–53.

Conclusion

As we live in the global mission age, it is vital to have a sound biblical worldview as believers, missionaries, pastors, and theologians. I do not think it is biblical to promote and pursue the concept and ideal of the Christian state or theocracy under the New Covenant no matter what motivations people may have. In the history of redemption, God formed the Jewish theocracy under the Old Covenant as Calvin rightly perceived. However, the idea of the Jewish theocracy as a unique institution is not a biblical ideal to be reproduced under the New Covenant, even as the modified form of the Christian state or city. The Jewish theocracy under the Old Covenant was a type or shadow of the eternal heavenly theocracy, which will be consummated when Jesus Christ returns with his glory. That ideal should not be desired in the present world because believers' lives in the present world are, at best, a pilgrimage, yearning for the consummation of the ultimate heavenly theocratic kingdom, which was typified in the Jewish theocracy in the Old Testament.

Calvin was a great reformer, theologian, pastor, and political leader in the city of Geneva. His hermeneutical, theological, and practical contributions have been immense throughout the past five centuries, transcending linguistic, cultural, and political boundaries. However, his views on the two kingdoms require further reformation because the Bible teaches while heresy was punished as a capital offense in the Old Testament (for instance, by stoning to death) under the Jewish theocracy, during the New Covenant Age (the time between the first and second coming of Jesus Christ), heresy is to be punished by church authorities and does not involve any form of physical force. The famous dictum, "the Reformed church should be always reforming" (*Ecclesia reformata semper reformanda est*) may be the appropriate implication of Calvin's political philosophy, summed up in his adaptation and exposition of the two kingdoms.

Bibliography

Ainsworth, Arthur Davis. *The Relations between Church and State in the City and Canton of Geneva.* Atlanta, GA: Stein, 1965.

Alexander, T. Desmond, et al., eds. *New Dictionary of Biblical Theology.* Downers Grove, IL: InterVarsity, 2000.

Allis, Oswald T. *The Five Books of Moses.* Phillipsburg, NJ: P&R, 1949.

———. *Prophecy and the Church.* Phillipsburg, NJ: P&R, 1947.

Arnold, Bill T., and Bryan E. Beyer, eds. *Readings from the Ancient Near East.* Grand Rapids, MI: Baker Academic, 2002.

Augustine. *St. Augustine's City of God and Christian Doctrine.* In *A Select Library of the Nicene and Post-Nicene Fathers,* edited by Philip Schaff, 2:1–511. Grand Rapids, MI: Eerdmans, 1993.

Backus, Irena. "Calvin's Concept of Natural and Roman Law." *Calvin Theological Journal* 38 (2003) 7–26.

Bahnsen, Greg L. *Theonomy in Christian Ethics: Expanded Edition with Replies to Critics.* Phillipsburg, NJ: P&R, 1984.

Bainton, Roland H. *Hunted Heretic: The Life and Death of Michael Servetus (1511–1553).* Boston: Beacon, 1953.

Barber, John. "Common Grace: A Critical Assessment of Doctrine." https://web.archive.org/web/20160831150151/http://www.cornerstone-presbyterian.org/common_grace.pdf.

Barker, William S., and W. Robert Godfrey, eds. *Theonomy: A Reformed Critique.* Grand Rapids, MI: Academie Books, 1990.

Barth, Karl. *Church Dogmatics.* 5 vols. Edited by G. W, Bromiley and T. F. Torrance. Translated by G. W. Bromiley. Peabody, MA: Hendrickson, 2010.

———. "Gospel and Law." *Scottish Journal of Theology Occasional Papers* 8 (1959) 1–28.

———. *The Theology of Calvin.* Translated by Geoffrey W. Bromiley. Grand Rapids, MI: Eerdmans, 1995.

———. *This Christian Cause: A Letter to Great Britain from Switzerland.* Translated by E. L. H. Gordon and George Hill. New York: Macmillan, 1941.

Bartholomew, Craig G. "Covenant and Creation: Covenant Overload or Covenantal Deconstruction." *Calvin Theological Journal* 30 (1995) 11–33.

Bartsch, Hans Werner, ed. *Kerygma and Myth: A Theological Debate.* Translated by Reginald H. Fuller. New York: Harper & Row, 1961.

Bateman, Herbert W., IV, ed. *Three Central Issues in Contemporary Dispensationalism: A Comparison of Traditional and Progressive Views.* Grand Rapids, MI: Kregel, 1999.

Bauckham, Richard. *The Theology of the Book of Revelation.* Eugene, OR: Wipf & Stock, 2005.

Baugh, Steven M. *A First John Reader.* Phillipsburg, NJ: P&R, 1999.

———. *The Majesty on High: Introduction to the Kingdom of God in the New Testament.* N.p.: CreateSpace, 2017.

———. *A New Testament Greek Primer.* 3rd ed. Phillipsburg, NJ: P&R, 2012.

Bavinck, Herman. "Calvin and Common Grace." In *Calvin and the Reformation: Four Studies,* edited by William Park Armstrong, 99–130. Eugene, OR: Wipf & Stock, 2004.

———. *Reformed Dogmatics.* 4 vols. Edited by John Bolt. Translated by John Vriend. Grand Rapids, MI: Baker Academic, 2003–8.

Beale, G. K. *The Book of Revelation.* In *The International Greek Testament Commentary,* edited by I. Howard Marshal and Donald A. Hagner, 1–1157. Grand Rapids, MI: Eerdmans, 1999.

———. *Handbook on the New Testament Use of the Old Testament: Exegesis and Interpretation.* Grand Rapids, MI: Baker Academic, 2012.

———. *A New Testament Biblical Theology: The Unfolding of the Old Testament in the New.* Grand Rapids, MI: Baker Academic, 2011.

Beale, G. K., and Benjamin L. Gladd. *Hidden But Now Revealed: A Biblical Theology of Mystery.* Downers Grove, IL: IVP Academic, 2014.

Berkhof, Louis. *Introduction to Systematic Theology.* Grand Rapids, MI: Baker, 1988.

———. *Systematic Theology.* Grand Rapids, MI: Eerdmans, 1988.

Blaising, Craig A., and Darrell L. Bock, eds. *Dispensationalism, Israel and the Church: The Search for Definition.* Grand Rapids, MI: Zondervan, 1992.

———. "Premillennialism." In *Three Views on the Millennialism and Beyond,* edited by Darrell L. Bock, 157–227. Grand Rapids, MI: Zondervan, 1999.

———. *Progressive Dispensationalism.* Grand Rapids, MI: Baker, 2000.

Blomberg, Craig L., and Sung Wook Chung. *A Case for Historic Premillennialism: An Alternative "Left Behind" Eschatology.* Grand Rapids, MI: Baker, 2009.

Bock, Darrell L., ed. *Three Views on the Millennium and Beyond.* Grand Rapids, MI: Zondervan, 1999.

Bonhoeffer, Dietrich. *Ethics.* Edited by Eberhard Bethge. Translated by Neville Horton Smith. New York: Macmillan, 1955.

Bornkamm, Heinrich. *Luther's Doctrine of the Two Kingdoms in the Context of His Theology.* Translated by Karl H. Hertz. Philadelphia: Fortress, 1966.

Brenton, Sir Lancelot C. L. *Septuagint with Apocrypha: Greek and English.* Peabody, MA: Hendrickson, 2015.

Bright, John. *A History of Israel.* Philadelphia: Westminster, 1981.

Brown, Raymond E. *An Introduction to the New Testament.* New Haven: Yale University Press, 2010.

Bruce, F. F. *Paul: Apostle of the Heart Set Free.* Grand Rapids, MI: Eerdmans, 1984.

Brunner, Emil, and Karl Barth. *Natural Theology: Comprising "Nature and Grace" by Professor Emil Brunner and the Reply "No" by Dr. Karl Barth.* Translated by Peter Fraenkel. Eugene, OR: Wipf & Stock, 2002.

Bultmann, Rudolf. *History and Eschatology: The Presence of Eternity*. New York: Harper & Row, 1957.

———. *History of the Synoptic Tradition*. Translated by John Marsh. New York: Harper & Row, 1976.

———. *Jesus and the Word*. Translated by Louise P. Smith and Erminie H. Lantero. New York: Scribner's, 1958.

———. *New Testament & Mythology and Other Basic*. Edited and translated by Schubert M. Ogden. Philadelphia: Fortress, 1984.

———. *Theology of the New Testament*. Translated by Kendrick Grobel. New York: Scribner's, 1955.

Calvin, John. *Calvin's Commentaries*. 22 vols. Various translators. 1863. Reprint, Grand Rapids: Baker, 1996.

———. *Institutes of the Christian Religion in Two Volumes*. Edited by John T. McNeill. Translated by Ford Lewis Battles. The Library of Christian Classics 20–21. Philadelphia: Westminster, 1975.

———. *Treatises Against the Anabaptists and Against the Libertines*. Edited and translated by Benjamin Wirt Farley. Grand Rapids, MI: Baker, 1982.

Calvini, Ioannis [Calvin, John]. *Institutio Christianae Religionis* [*Institutes of the Christian Religion*]. 1559. Reprint, London: Berolnini, 1846.

Carlson, Richard F., and Tremper Longman III. *Science, Creation and the Bible: Reconciling Rival Theories of Origins*. Downers Grove, IL: IVP Academic, 2010.

Carson, D. A. "Evangelicals, Ecumenism, and the Church." In *Evangelical Affirmations*, edited by Kenneth S. Kantzer and Carl F. H. Henry, 347–85. Grand Rapids, MI: Zondervan, 1990.

Chafer, Lewis Sperry. "Dispensationalism." *Bibliotheca Sacra* 93 (1936) 390–449.

———. *Dispensationalism*. Dallas: Dallas Seminary Press, 1951.

———. *Systematic Theology*. 8 vols. Dallas: Dallas Seminary Press, 1948.

Charlesworth, James H., ed. *The Old Testament Pseudepigrapha*. Vol. 1, *Apocalyptic Literature & Testaments*. New York: Doubleday, 1983.

———, ed. *The Old Testament Pseudepigrapha*. Vol. 2, *Expansions of the "Old Testament" and Legends, Wisdom and Philosophical Literature, Prayers, Psalms and Odes, Fragments of Lost Judeo-Hellenistic Works*. New York: Doubleday, 1985.

Childs, Brevard S. *Biblical Theology of the Old and New Testaments: Theological Reflection on the Christian Bible*. Minneapolis, MN: Fortress, 1992.

———. *Old Testament Theology in a Canonical Context*. Philadelphia: Fortress, 1989.

Chilton, David. *The Days of Vengeance: An Exposition of the Book of Revelation*. Waterbury Center, VT: Dominion, 2006.

Cho, Ezra Jae Kyung. *The Rhetorical Approach to 1 Thessalonians In Light of Ancient Funeral Oration*. Eugene, OR: Wipf & Stock, 2020.

Clark, R. S. "Calvin and the *Lex Naturalis*." *Stulos Theological Journal* 6 (1998) 1–22.

Clouse, Robert G., ed. *The Meaning of the Millennium: Four Views*. Downers Grove, IL: InterVarsity, 1977.

Collins, C. John. "Adam and Eve as Historical People, and Why It Matters." *Perspectives on Science and Christian Faith* 62 (2010) 147–65.

———. *Did Adam and Eve Really Exist? Who They Were and Why You Should Care*. Wheaton, IL: Crossway, 2011.

———. *Genesis 1–4: A Linguistic, Literary, and Theological Commentary*. Phillipsburg, NJ: P&R, 2006.

Collins, John J. *Introduction to the Hebrew Bible*. Minneapolis, MN: Fortress, 2004.

Cross, Frank Moore. *From Epic to Canon: History and Literature in Ancient Israel*. Baltimore, MD: The Johns Hopkins University Press, 1998.

Darby, John Nelson. *Notes on the Book of the Revelation: To Assist Enquirers in Searching into That Book*. Middletown, DE: Forgotten Books, 2007.

———. *Synopsis of the Books of the Bible*. Middletown, DE: BiblioLife, 2015.

Darwin, Charles. *The Origin of Species: By Means of Natural Selection of the Preservation of Favoured Races in the Struggle for Life*. New York: Penguin, 2003.

Davis, D. Clair. "The Hermeneutics of Ernst Wilhelm Hengstenberg: Edifying Value as Exegetical Standard." ThD diss., Georg-August Universität, Göttingen, 1960.

Dennis, Lane T., ed. *ESV Study Bible: English Standard Version*. Wheaton, IL: Crossway, 2008.

Dennison, James T., Jr. "Merit or 'Entitlement' in Reformed Covenant Theology: A Review." *Kerux* 24 (2009) 3–152.

DeRouchie, Jason S., et al., eds. *For Our Good Always: Studies on the Message and Influence of Deuteronomy in Honor of Daniel I. Block*. Winona Lake, IN: Eisenbrauns, 2013.

Dillard, Raymond, and Tremper Longman III. *An Introduction to the Old Testament*. Grand Rapids, MI: Zondervan, 1994.

Dumbrell, William J. *Covenant and Creation: A Theology of Old Testament Covenants*. Eugene, OR: Wipf & Stock, 1984.

Dunn, James D. G. "The Incident at Antioch (Gal. 2:11–18)." *Journal for the Study of the New Testament* 18 (1983) 3–57.

———. *Jesus, Paul, and the Law: Studies in Mark and Galatians*. Louisville, KY: Westminster, 1990.

———. "The Justice of God: A Renewed Perspective on Justification by Faith." *Journal of Theological Studies* 43 (1992) 1–22.

———. *A New Perspective on Jesus: What the Quest for the Historical Jesus Missed*. Grand Rapids, MI: Baker Academic, 2006.

———. "The New Perspective on Paul." *Bulletin of the John Rylands University Library of Manchester* 65 (1983) 95–122.

———. *The New Perspective on Paul*. Grand Rapids, MI: Eerdmans, 2008.

———. *New Testament Theology: An Introduction*. Nashville: Abingdon, 2009.

———. "Works of the Law and the Curse of the Law (Galatians 3:10–14)." *New Testament Studies* 31 (1985) 523–42.

———. "Yet Once More—'The Works of the Law': A Response." *Journal for the Study of the New Testament* 46 (1992) 99–117.

Durham, John I. *Exodus*. Word Biblical Commentary 3. Waco, TX: Word, 1987.

Ebeling, Gerhard. *Word and Faith*. Translated by James W. Leith. Philadelphia: Fortress, 1963.

Edgar, William. *Created and Creating: A Biblical Theology of Culture*. Downers Grove, IL: IVP Academic, 2016.

Edwards, David L., and John Stott. *Evangelical Essentials: A Liberal-Evangelical Dialogue*. London: Hodder and Stoughton, 1988.

Edwards, Jonathan. *A History of the Work of Redemption: Containing the Outlines of a Body of Divinity*. Lexington: Hard, 2011.

———. *Sinners in the Hands of an Angry God*. Middletown, DE: CreateSpace, 2019.

Ehrman, Bart D. *The Bible: A Historical and Literary Introduction.* 2nd ed. Oxford: Oxford University Press, 2018.

———. *Heaven and Hell: A History of the Afterlife.* New York: Simon & Schuster, 2020.

Eichrodt, Walther. *Theology of the Old Testament.* Translated by J. A. Baker. The Old Testament Library 1. London: SCM, 1964.

———. *Theology of the Old Testament.* Translated by J. A. Baker. The Old Testament Library 2. Philadelphia: Westminster, 1967.

Elam, Andrew M., et al. *Merit and Moses: A Critique of the Klinean Doctrine of Republication.* Eugene, OR: Wipf & Stock, 2014.

Elliger, Karl, and Wilhelm Rudolph, eds. *Biblia Hebraica Stuttgartensia.* 5th ed. Stuttgart: Deutsche Bibelgesellschaft, 1997.

Enns, Peter. *The Bible Tells Me So: Why Defending Scripture Has Made Us Unable to Read It.* New York: HarperOne, 2014.

———. *The Evolution of Adam: What the Bible Does and Doesn't Say about Human Origins.* Grand Rapids, MI: Brazos, 2012.

———. *Inspiration and Incarnation: Evangelicals and Problem of the Old Testament.* Grand Rapids, MI: Baker Academic, 2005.

———. "Preliminary Observations on an Incarnational Model of Scripture: Its Validity and Usefulness." *Calvin Theological Journal* 42 (2007) 219–36.

Estelle, Bryan D., et al., eds. *The Law Is Not of Faith: Essays on Works and Grace in the Mosaic Covenant.* Phillipsburg, NJ: P&R, 2009.

Ferguson, Everett. *Backgrounds of Early Christianity.* 3rd ed. Grand Rapids, MI: Eerdmans, 2003.

Ferguson, Sinclair B. *The Holy Spirit: Contours of Christian Theology.* Downers Grove, IL: IVP Academic, 1997.

———. *The Whole Christ: Legalism, Antinomianism, and Gospel Assurance: Why the Marrow Controversy Still Matters.* Wheaton, IL: Crossway, 2016.

Ferry, Brenton C. "Cross—Examining Moses' Defense: An Answer to Ramsey's Critique of Kline and Karlberg." *Westminster Theological Journal* 67 (2005) 163–68.

———. "Works in the Mosaic Covenant: A Reformed Taxonomy." In *The Law Is Not of Faith*, edited by Bryan D. Estelle et al., 76–103. Phillipsburg, NJ: Presbyterian and Reformed, 2009.

Fesko, J. V. "Calvin and Witsius on the Mosaic Covenant." In *The Law Is Not of Faith*, edited by Bryan D. Estelle et al., 25–43. Phillipsburg, NJ: P&R, 2009.

———. "The Republication of the Covenant of Works." *The Confessional Presbyterian* 8 (2012) 197–212.

———. *The Theology of the Westminster Standards: Historical Context and Theological Insights.* Wheaton, IL: Crossway, 2014.

Frame, John M. *A History of Western Philosophy and Theology.* Phillipsburg, NJ: P&R, 2015.

———. *Systematic Theology: An Introduction to Christian Belief.* Phillipsburg, NJ: P&R, 2013.

Friedman, Jerome. *Michael Servetus: A Case Study in Total Heresy.* Geneva: Droz, 1978.

Fuller, Daniel P. *Gospel and Law: Contrast or Continuum? The Hermeneutics of Dispensationalism and Covenant Theology.* Grand Rapids, MI: Eerdmans, 1980.

———. "The Hermeneutics of Dispensationalism." ThD diss., Northern Baptist Theological *Seminary*, 1957.

———. "A Response on the Subjects of Works and Grace." *Presbyterion* 9 (1983) 72–79.

Funk, Robert W. *Honest to Jesus: Jesus for a New Millennium*. New York: HarperCollins, 1996.

Funk, Robert W., et al. *The Five Gospels: The Search for the Authentic Words of Jesus*. New York: HarperSanFrancisco, 1997.

Futato, Mark D. "Because It Had Rained: A Study of Genesis 2:5–7 with Implications for Gen. 2:4–25 and Gen. 1:1—2:3." *Westminster Theological Journal* 60 (1998) 1–21.

Gaffin, Richard B., Jr. "Biblical Theology and the Westminster Standards." In *The Practical Calvinists: An Introduction to the Presbyterian and Reformed Heritage: In Honor of D. Clair Davis' Thirty Years at Westminster Theological Seminary*, edited by Peter A. Lillback, 425–42. Great Britain: Christian Focus, 2002.

———. "Biblical Theology and the Westminster Standards." *Westminster Theological Journal* 65 (2003) 165–79.

———. *The Centrality of the Resurrection: A Study in Paul's Soteriology*. Grand Rapids, MI: Baker, 1978.

———. "The Holy Spirit." *Westminster Theological Journal* 43 (1980) 58–78.

———. *Perspectives on Pentecost: Studies in New Testament Teaching on the Gifts of the Holy Spirit*. Grand Rapids, MI: Baker, 1979.

———. *Resurrection and Redemption: A Study in Pauline Soteriology*. ThD diss., Westminster Theological Seminary, 1969.

———. *Resurrection and Redemption: A Study in Paul's Soteriology*. Phillipsburg, NJ: P&R, 1987.

———. "Review Essay: Paul the Theologian." *Westminster Theological Journal* 62 (2000) 121–41.

———. "Systematic Theology and Biblical Theology." In *The New Testament Student and Theology*, edited by John H. Skilton, 3:32–50. Philadelphia: P&R, 1976.

———. "The Vitality of Reformed Dogmatics." In *The Vitality of Reformed Theology: Proceedings of the International Theological Congress June 20–24th 1994, Noordwijkerhout, The Netherlands*, edited by J. M. Batteau et al., 16–50. Kampen: Uitgeverij Kok, 1994.

Gage, Warren A. *The Gospel of Genesis: Studies in Protology and Eschatology*. Winona Lake, IN: Carpenter, 1984.

Garlington, D. B. "The Obedience of Faith in the Letter to the Romans; Part I: The Meaning of *hupakoen pisteos* (Rom 1:5; 16:26)." *Westminster Theological Journal* 52 (1990) 201–24.

———. "The Obedience of Faith in the Letter to the Romans; Part II: The Obedience of Faith and Judgment by Works." *Westminster Theological Journal* 53 (1991) 47–72.

Garrett, Duane A. "Type, Typology." In *Evangelical Dictionary of Biblical Theology*, edited by Walter A. Elwell, 785–87. Grand Rapids, MI: Baker, 1996.

Gentry, Kenneth L., Jr. "Postmillennialism." In *Three Views on the Millennium and Beyond*, edited by Darrell L. Bock, 13–57. Grand Rapids, MI: Zondervan, 1999.

Gentry, Peter J., and Stephen J. Wellum. *Kingdom through Covenant: A Biblical Theological Understanding of the Covenants*. Wheaton, IL: Crossway, 2012.

Godfrey, W. Robert. *John Calvin: Pilgrim and Pastor*. Wheaton, IL: Crossway, 2009.

———. "Kingdom and Kingdoms." *Evangelium* 7 (2009) 6–9.

Golding, Peter. *Covenant Theology: The Key of Theology in Reformed Thought and Tradition*. Geanies House, Scotland: Christian Focus, 2004.

Goldsworthy, Graeme. *According to Plan: The Unfolding Revelation of God in the Bible.* Downers Grove, IL: InterVarsity, 1991.

———. *Christ-Centered Biblical Theology: Hermeneutical Foundations and Principles.* Downers Grove, IL: InterVarsity, 2012.

Gordon, T. David. "Van Til and Theonomic Ethics." In *Creator, Redeemer, Consummator: A Festschrift For Meredith G. Kline,* edited by Howard Griffith and John H. Muether, 271–78. Greenville, SC: Reformed Academic, 2000.

Greidanus, Sidney. *Preaching Christ from the Old Testament: A Contemporary Hermeneutical Method.* Grand Rapids, MI: Eerdmans, 1999.

Griffith, Howard, and John R. Muether, eds. *Creator, Redeemer, Consummator: A Festschirift For Meredith G. Kline.* Greenville, SC: Reformed Academic, 2000.

Gritters, Barry. "Grace Uncommon: A Protestant Reformed Look at the Doctrine of Common Grace." http://www.kalamazooprc.org/resources/pamphlets/Grace%20 Uncommon.pdf.

Grudem, Wayne. *Systematic Theology: An Introduction to Biblical Doctrine.* Grand Rapids, MI: Zondervan, 2000.

Gundry, Robert H. *A Survey of the New Testament.* 5th ed. Grand Rapids, MI: Zondervan, 2012.

Haas, Guenther H. *The Concept of Equity in Calvin's Ethics.* Waterloo: Wilfrid Laurier University Press, 1997.

Hagopian, David G., ed. *The Genesis Debate: Three Views on the Days of Creation.* Mission Viejo, CA: Crux, 2001.

Hahn, Scott W. *Kinship by Covenant: A Canonical Approach to the Fulfillment of God's Saving Promises.* New Haven, CT: Yale University Press, 2009.

Hall, David W. "Calvin on Human Government and the State." In *Theological Guide to Calvin's Institutes: Essays and Analysis,* edited by David W. Hall and Peter A. Lillback, 411–40. Phillipsburg, NJ: P&R, 2008.

———. *The Legacy of John Calvin: His Influence on the Modern World.* Phillipsburg, NJ: P&R, 2008.

Hancock, Ralph C. *Calvin and the Foundation of Modern Politics.* Ithaca, NY: Cornell University Press, 1989.

Harris, Stephen L. *Understanding the Bible.* Palo Alto, CA: Mayfield, 1985.

Harrison, Ronald K. *Introduction to the Old Testament.* Grand Rapids, MI: Eerdmans, 1988.

Hart, D. G. "Princeton and the Law: Enlightened and Reformed." In *The Law Is Not of Faith,* edited by Bryan D. Estelle et al., 44–75. Phillipsburg, NJ: P&R, 2009.

Hays, Richard B. *The Moral Vision of the New Testament: Community, Cross, New Creation: A Contemporary Introduction to New Testament Ethics.* New York: HarperCollins, 1996.

Hegel, G. W. F. *The Phenomenology of the Spirit.* Translated by A. V. Miller. Oxford: Oxford University Press, 1977.

———. *The Philosophy of History.* Translated by J. Sibree. Mineola, NY: Dover, 2004.

Hegg, Timothy J. *The Abrahamic Covenant and the Covenant of Grant in the Ancient Near East.* Northwest Baptist Seminary, 1980.

Heidel, Alexander. *The Babylonian Genesis: The Story of Creation.* Chicago: University of Chicago Press, 1963.

———. *The Gilgamesh Epic and Old Testament Parallels.* Chicago: University of Chicago Press, 1963.

Helm, Paul. "Calvin and Natural Law." *Scottish Bulletin of Evangelical Theology* 2 (1984) 5–22.

———. *John Calvin's Ideas*. Oxford: Oxford University Press, 2004.

Hendrikson, William. *More Than Conquerors: An Interpretation of the Book of Revelation*. Grand Rapids, MI: Baker, 1998.

Hillar, Marian. *The Case of Michael Servetus (1511–1553): The Turning Point in the Struggle for Freedom of Conscience*. Lewiston, NY: Edwin Mellen, 1997.

———. *Michael Servetus: Intellectual Giant, Humanist, and Martyr*. Lanham, MD: University Press of America, 2002.

Hillerbrand, Hans J. "The Anabaptist View of the State." *Mennonite Quarterly Review* 32 (1958) 83–110.

Hillers, Delbert R. *Covenant: The History of a Biblical Idea*. Baltimore, MD: The Johns Hopkins University Press, 1969.

Hodge, Charles. *1 & 2 Corinthians*. The Geneva Series of Commentaries. Carlisle, PA: The Banner of Truth Trust, 1978.

———. *The Epistle to the Romans: A Commentary on Romans*. Carlisle, PA: The Banner of Truth Trust, 1975.

———. *Systematic Theology*. 3 vols. 1871–73. Reprint, Grand Rapids, MI: Eerdmans, 1995.

Hoehner, Paul James. *The Covenant Theology of Jonathan Edwards*. Eugene, OR: Pickwick, 2021.

Hoekema, Anthony A. *The Bible and the Future*. Grand Rapids, MI: Eerdmans, 1994.

Hoeksema, Herman. *God's Goodness Always Particular*. Jenison, MI: Reformed Free Publishing Association, 1939.

———. *Reformed Dogmatics*. 2 vols. Jenison, MI: Reformed Free Publishing Association, 2005.

Höpfl, Harro. *The Christian Polity of John Calvin*. Cambridge: Cambridge University Press, 1982.

Horton, Michael. *The Christian Faith: A Systematic Theology for Pilgrims on the Way*. Grand Rapids, MI: Zondervan, 2011.

———. *Introducing Covenant Theology*. Grand Rapids, MI: Baker, 2006.

House, H. Wayne. "The Future of National Israel." *Bibliotheca Sacra* 166 (2009) 463–81.

Hughes, Philip E. *The True Image: The Origin and Destiny of Man in Christ*. Grand Rapids, MI: Eerdmans, 1989.

Irons, Lee. "Redefining Merit: An Examination of Medieval Presuppositions in Covenant Theology." In *Creator, Redeemer, Consummator: A Festschrift For Meredith G. Kline*, edited by Howard Griffith and John H. Muether, 253–68. Greenville, SC: Reformed Academic, 2000.

Jeon, Jeong Koo. "The Abrahamic Covenant and the Kingdom of God." *The Confessional Presbyterian* 7 (2011) 123–38, 249–50.

———. *Biblical Theology: Covenants and the Kingdom of God in Redemptive History*. Eugene, OR: Wipf & Stock, 2017.

———. *Calvin and the Federal Vision: Calvin's Covenant Theology in Light of Contemporary Discussion*. Eugene, OR: Wipf & Stock, 2009.

———. "Calvin and the Two Kingdoms: Calvin's Political Philosophy in Light of Contemporary Discussion." *Westminster Theological Journal* 72 (2010) 299–320.

———. "The Covenant of Creation and the Kingdom of God." *The Confessional Presbyterian* 9 (2013) 123–42.

———. *Covenant Theology and Justification by Faith: The Shepherd Controversy and Its Impacts.* Eugene, OR: Wipf & Stock, 2006.

———. "Covenant Theology and Old Testament Ethics: Meredith G. Kline's Intrusion Ethics." *Kerux* 16 (2002) 3–33.

———. *Covenant Theology: John Murray's and Meredith G. Kline's Response to the Historical Development of Federal Theology in Reformed Thought.* Lanham: University Press of America, 2004.

———. "The Noahic Covenants and Redemptive Judgment." *The Confessional Presbyterian* 15 (2019) 148–62, 220.

———. "The Noahic Covenants and the Kingdom of God." *Mid-America Journal of Theology* 22 (2013) 179–209.

———. Review of *Christ and Covenant Theology: Essays on Election, Republication, and the Covenants,* by Cornelis P. Venema. *Westminster Theological Journal* 80 (2018) 386–88.

———. Review of *Finding Favour in the Sight of God: A Theology of Wisdom Literature,* by Richard P. Belcher Jr. *Unio Cum Christo* 5 (2019) 222–25.

———. Review of *The Grace of Godliness: An Introduction to Doctrine and Piety in the Canons of Dordt,* by Matthew Barrett. *Unio Cum Christo* 4 (2018) 242–44.

———. Review of *Paul Against the Idols: A Contextual Reading of the Areopagus Speech,* by Flavian Pardigon. *Unio Cum Christo* 6 (2020) 237–40.

———. Review of *The Trinity and the Covenant of Redemption,* by John V. Fesko. *Unio Cum Christo* 3 (2017) 236–39.

Johnson, Dennis E. *Triumph of the Lamb: A Commentary on Revelation.* Phillipsburg, NJ: P&R, 2001.

Jones, G. H. "The Concept of Holy War." In *The World of the Old Testament,* edited by R. E. Clements, 299–322. Cambridge: Cambridge University Press, 1989.

———. "'Holy War' or 'Yahweh War'?" *Vetus Testamentum* 25 (1975) 642–58.

Jordan, James B. *The Law of the Covenant: An Exposition of Exodus 21–23.* Tyler, TX: Institute for Christian Economics, 1984.

Josephus, Flavius. *Josephus: The Complete Works.* Translated by William Whiston. Nashville, TN: Nelson, 1998.

Jue, Jeffrey K. "*Theologia Naturalis*: A Reformed Tradition." In *Revelation and Reason: New Essays in Reformed Apologetics,* edited by K. Scott Oliphint and Lane G. Tipton, 168–89. Phillipsburg, NJ: P&R. 2007.

Kaiser, Walter C., Jr. *The Promise-Plan of God: A Biblical Theology of the Old and New Testaments.* Grand Rapids, MI: Zondervan, 2008.

———. *Toward an Old Testament Theology.* Grand Rapids, MI: Zondervan, 1981.

Kang, Sa-Moon. *Divine War in the Old Testament and in the Ancient Near East.* New York: de Gruyter, 1989.

Karlberg, Mark W. *Covenant Theology in Reformed Perspective.* Eugene, OR: Wipf & Stock, 2000.

———. "Reformed Theology as the Theology of the Covenants: The Contributions of Meredith G. Kline to Reformed Systematics." In *Creator, Redeemer, Consummator: A Festschrift For Meredith G. Kline,* edited by Howard Griffith and John H. Muether, 235–52. Greenville, SC: Reformed Academic, 2000.

Kayayan, Eric. "The Case of Michael Servetus." *Mid-America Journal of Theology* 8 (1992) 117–46.

Kim, Seyoon. *Justification and God's Kingdom.* Tübingen: Mohr Siebeck, 2018.

———. *Justification and Sanctification: What Is Justification and Sanctification?* Seoul: Duranno, 2015.

———. *The Origin of Paul's Gospel.* 2nd ed. Tübingen: Mohr and Siebeck, 1984.

———. *Paul and the New Perspective: Second Thoughts on the Origin of Paul's Gospel.* Grand Rapids, MI: Eerdmans, 2002.

Kingdon, Robert M. *Calvin and Calvinism: Sources of Democracy.* Lexington, MA: Heath, 1970.

———. "Calvin and the Government of Geneva." In *Calvinus Ecclesiae Genevesis Custos*, edited by Wilhelm Neuser, 49–67. Frankfurt: Lang, 1984.

———. "Social Control and Political Control in Calvin's Geneva." In *Die Reformation in Deutschland und Europa: Interpretationen und Debatten*, edited by Hans R. Guggisberg, 521–32. Gütersloh: Gütersloloher Verlagshaus, 1993.

Klempa, William. "John Calvin on Natural Law." In *John Calvin and the Church: A Prism of Reform*, edited by Timothy George, 72–95. Louisville, KY: Westminster John Knox, 1990.

Kline, Meredith G. "Because It Had Not Rained." *Westminster Theological Journal* 20 (1958) 146–57.

———. *By Oath* Consigned: *A Reinterpretation of the Covenant Signs of Circumcision and Baptism.* Grand Rapids, MI: Eerdmans, 1968.

———. "Comments on an Old—New Error." Review of Greg L. Bahnsen's *Theonomy in Christian Ethics. Westminster Theological Journal* (1978–79) 173–89.

———. *Essential Writings of Meredith G. Kline.* Peabody, MA: Hendrickson, 2017.

———. *Genesis: A New Commentary.* Peabody, MA: Hendrickson, 2016.

———. *God, Heaven and Har Magedon: A Covenantal Tale of Cosmos and Telos.* Eugene, OR: Wipf & Stock, 2006.

———. "Gospel until the Law: Romans 5:13–14 and the Old Covenant." *Journal of the Evangelical Theological Society* 34 (1991) 433–46.

———. *Glory in Our Midst: A Biblical—Theological Reading of Zechariah's Night Visions.* Overland Park, KS: Two Age, 2001.

———. *Images of the Spirit.* Eugene, OR: Wipf & Stock, 1998.

———. "The Intrusion and the Decalogue." *Westminster Theological Journal* 16 (1953) 1–22.

———. *Kingdom Prologue: Genesis Foundations for a Covenantal Worldview.* Overland Park, KS: Two Age, 2000.

———. "Oracular Origin of State." In *Essential Writings of Meredith G. Kline.* Peabody, MA: Hendrickson, 2017.

———. *The Structure of Biblical Authority.* Eugene, OR: Wipf & Stock, 1997.

———. *Treaty of the Great King: The Covenant Structure of Deuteronomy: Studies and Commentary.* Eugene, OR: Wipf & Stock, 2012.

Köstenberger, Andreas J., and Richard D. Patterson. *Biblical Interpretation: Exploring the Hermeneutical Triad of History, Literature, and Theology.* Grand Rapids, MI: Kregel Academic, 2011.

Kugel, James L. *The Bible As It Was.* Cambridge, MA: Harvard University Press, 1997.

———. *The Great Poems of the Bible: A Reader's Companion with New Translations.* New York: Free Press, 1999.

———. *How to Read the Bible: A Guide to Scripture, Then and Now.* New York: Free Press, 2008.

———. *The Idea of Biblical Poetry.* New Haven: Yale University Press, 1981.

Kuiper, Herman. *Calvin on Common Grace.* Grand Rapids, MI: Smitter, 1928.

Kuyper, Abraham. *Abraham Kuyper: A Centennial Reader.* Edited by James D. Bratt. Grand Rapids, MI: Eerdmans, 1998.

———. *De Geemene Gratie.* Kampen: Kok, 1945.

———. *Lectures on Calvinism.* Grand Rapids, MI: Eerdmans, 1931.

Ladd, George Eldon. *The Blessed Hope: A Biblical Study of the Second Advent and the Rapture.* Grand Rapids, MI: Eerdmans, 1956.

———. *A Commentary on the Revelation of John.* Grand Rapids, MI: Eerdmans, 1972.

———. *Crucial Questions about the Kingdom of God.* Grand Rapids, MI: Eerdmans, 1952.

———. *The Gospel of the Kingdom: Scriptural Studies in the Kingdom of God.* Grand Rapids, MI: Eerdmans, 1959.

———. "Historic Premillennialism." In *The Meaning of the Millennium: Four Views,* edited by Robert G. Clouse, 17–40. Downers Grove, IL: InterVarsity, 1977.

———. *A Theology of the New Testament.* Grand Rapids, MI: Eerdmans, 1993.

Lang, August. "The Reformation and Natural Law." In *Calvin and the Reformation: Four Studies,* translated by J. Gresham Machen, 56–98. New York: Revell, 1909.

LaRondelle, Hans K. *Our Creator Redeemer: An Introduction to Biblical Covenant Theology.* Berrien Springs, MI: Andrews University Press, 2005.

Letham, Robert. "'Not a Covenant of Works in Disguise' (Herman Bavinck): The Place of the Mosaic Covenant in Redemptive History." *Mid-America Journal of Theology* 24 (2013) 143–77.

Lillback, Peter A. *The Binding of God: Calvin's Role in the Development of Covenant Theology.* MI: Baker, 2001.

Lillback, Peter A., ed. *The Practical Calvinist: An Introduction to the Presbyterian & Reformed Heritage In Honor of Dr. D. Clair Davis On the Occasion of His Seventieth Birthday And to Acknowledge His More Than Thirty years of Teaching At Westminster Theological Seminary in Philadelphia.* Fearn, Great Britain: Christian Focus, 2002.

———. *Seeing Christ in All of Scripture: Hermeneutics at Westminster Theological Seminary.* Philadelphia: Westminster Seminary Press, 2016.

Lillback, Peter A., and Richard B. Gaffin Jr., eds. *Thy Word Is Still Truth: Essential Writings on the Doctrine of Scripture from the Reformation to Today.* Phillipsburg, NJ: P&R, 2013.

Longman, Tremper, III. *The Story of God Bible Commentary: Genesis.* Grand Rapids, MI: Zondervan Academic, 2016.

Longman, Tremper, III, and Daniel G. Reid. *God Is a Warrior.* Grand Rapids, MI: Zondervan, 1995.

Longman, Tremper, III, and John H. Walton. *The Lost World of the Flood: Mythology, Theology, the Deluge Debate.* Downers Grove, IL: InterVarsity, 2018.

Longman, Tremper, III, and Raymond B. Dillard. *An Introduction to the Old Testament.* Grand Rapids, MI: Zondervan, 2006.

Lunn, Nicholas P. "Patterns in the Old Testament Metanarrative: Human Attempts to Fulfill Divine Promises." *Westminster Theological Journal* 72 (2010) 237–49.

Luther, Martin. *On Secular Authority.* In *Luther's Works,* edited by Walther I. Brandt. 45:81–129. Philadelphia: Fortress, 1962.

MacArthur, John. *The MacArthur Study Bible.* Wheaton, IL: Crossway, 2010.

MacArthur, John, and Richard Mayhue. *Biblical Doctrine: A Systematic Summary of Bible Truth*. Wheaton, IL: Crossway, 2017.

Machen, J. Gresham. *Christianity & Liberalism*. Grand Rapids, MI: Eerdmans, 2009.

———. *The New Testament: An Introduction to Its Literature and History*. Edited by W. John Cook. Carlisle, PA: The Banner of Truth Trust, 1997.

———. *The Origin of Paul's Religion*. Grand Rapids, MI: Eerdmans, 1976.

Marshall, I. Howard. *New Testament Theology*. Downers Grove, IL: InterVarsity, 2004.

Martin, Dale B. *New Testament History and Literature*. New Haven: Yale University Press, 2012.

Martinez, Florentino Garcia, ed. *The Dead Sea Scrolls Translated: The Qumran Texts in English*. Translated by Wilfred G. E. Watson. Grand Rapids, MI: Eerdmans, 1996.

Marx, Karl, and Frederick Engels. *The Communist Manifesto*. New York: International, 2016.

Mathison, Keith A. *Postmillennialism: An Eschatology of Hope*. Phillipsburg, NJ: P&R, 1999.

McCarthy, Dennis J. *Old Testament Covenant: A Survey of Current Opinions*. Richmond, VA: John Knox, 1972.

McComiskey, Thomas E. *The Covenant of Promise: A Theology of the Old Testament Covenants* Grand Rapids, MI: Baker, 1985.

McNeill, John T. "Calvin and Civil Government." In *Readings in Calvin's Theology*, edited by Donald McKim, 260–74. Grand Rapids, MI: Baker, 1984.

———. "John Calvin on Civil Government." In *Calvinism and the Political Order*, edited by George L. Hunt, 20–35. Philadelphia: Westminster, 1965.

———. "Natural Law in the Teaching of the Reformers." *Journal of Religion* 26 (1946) 168–82.

Meek, Charles S. *Christian Hope through Fulfilled Prophecy: An Exposition of Evangelical Preterism*. Spicewood, TX: Faith Facts, 2016.

Mendenhall, George E. "Ancient Oriental and Biblical Law." *The Biblical Archaeologist* 17 (1954) 26–46.

———. "Covenant Forms in Israelite Tradition." *The Biblical Archaeologist* 17 (1954) 50–76.

———. *Law and Covenant in Israel and the Ancient Near East*. Pittsburgh, PA: The Biblical Colloquium, 1955.

Meyer, Marvin, ed. *The Nag Hammadi Scriptures: The Revised and Updated Translation*. New York: HarperCollins, 2007.

Middleton, J. Richard. *A New Heaven and a New Earth: Reclaiming Biblical Eschatology*. Grand Rapids, MI: Baker Academic, 2014.

Millard, A. R. "A New Babylonian Genesis Story." *Tyndale Bulletin* 18 (1967) 3–18.

Monter, E. William. *Studies in Genevan Government, 1536–1605*. Geneva: Droz, 1964.

Morgan, Christopher W., and Robert A. Peterson, eds. *Hell under Fire: Modern Scholarship Reinvents Eternal Punishment*. Grand Rapids, MI: Zondervan, 2004.

Murray, John. *Collected Writings of John Murray*. 4 vols. The Banner of Truth Trust, 1976–83.

———. *The Covenant of Grace: A Biblico-Theological Study*. Phillipsburg, NJ: P&R, 1988.

———. *The Imputation of Adam's Sin*. Phillipsburg, NJ: P&R, 1959.

Niehaus, Jeffrey J. *Biblical Theology*. 3 vols. Woodster, OH: Weaber, 2017.

————. "Covenant and Narrative, God and Time." *Journal of the Evangelical Theological Society* 53 (2010) 535–59.

Nestle, Eberhard, and Kurt Aland, eds. *Novum Testamentum Graece*. 27th ed. Stuttgart: Deutsche Bibelgesellschaft, 1993.

Noth, Martin. *Exodus: A Commentary*. Translated by J. S. Bowden. In *The Old Testament Library*. Philadelphia: Westminster, 1962.

————. *The History of Israel*. Translated by P. R. Ackroyd. New York: Harper & Row, 1960.

————. *The Laws in the Pentateuch and Other Studies*. Translated by D. R. Ap-Thomas. London: SCM, 1984.

Nygren, Anders. "Luther's Doctrine of the Two Kingdoms." *The Ecumenical Review* 1 (1949) 301–10.

Olinger, Danny E., ed. *A Geerhardus Vos Anthology: Biblical and Theological Insights Alphabetically Arranged*. Phillipsburg, NJ: P&R, 2005.

Owen, John. *Biblical Theology: The History of Theology from Adam to Christ*. Translated by Stephen P. Westcott. Pittsburg, PA: Soli Deo Gloria, 2007.

Pardigon, Flavien. *Paul Against the Idols: A Contextual Reading of the Areopagus Speech*. Eugene, OR: Wipf & Stock, 2019.

Park, Hyung Ryong. *Dr. Hyung Ryong Park Systematic Theology*. Vol. 6, *Eschatology*. Seoul: Reformed, 2017.

Park, Yun Seon. *A Commentary on the Revelation of St. John*. Seoul: Yung Eum Sa, 1997.

Parker, T. H. L. *John Calvin: A Biography*. Louisville, KY: Westminster John Knox, 2006.

Peterson, Robert A. *Hell on Trial: The Case for Eternal Punishment*. Phillipsburg, NJ: P&R, 1995.

Pettegree, Andrew. "Michael Servetus and the Limits of Tolerance." *History Today* 40 (1990) 40–45.

Philo. *The Works of Philo: New Updated Edition*. Translated by C. D. Yonge. Peabody, MA: Hendrickson, 2011.

Pink, Arthur W. *The Divine Covenants*. Grand Rapids, MI: Baker, 1975.

Pinnock, Clark. "The Destruction of the Finally Impenitent." *Criswell Theological Review* 4 (1990) 243–59.

Poythress, Vern S. *God-Centered Biblical Interpretation*. Phillipsburg, NJ: P&R, 1999.

————. *The Returning King: A Guide to the Book of Revelation*. Phillipsburg, NJ: Presbyterian and Reformed, 2000.

————. *Theophany: A Biblical Theology of God's Appearing*. Wheaton, IL: Crossway, 2018.

————. *Understanding Dispensationalists*. Phillipsburg, NJ: P&R, 1993.

Pritchard, James B., ed. *The Ancient Near East: An Anthology of Texts & Pictures*. Princeton, NJ: Princeton University Press, 2011.

Pryor, C. Scott. "God's Bridle: John Calvin's Application of Natural Law." *Journal of Law and Religion* 22 (2006–7) 225–54.

Rad, Gerhard von. *Genesis: A Commentary*. In *The Old Testament Library*. Philadelphia: Westminster, 1972.

————. *Holy War in Ancient Israel*. Translated and edited by Marva J. Dawn. Grand Rapids, MI: Eerdmans, 1991.

————. *Old Testament Theology*. 2 vols. Translated by D. M. G. Stalker. New York: Harper & Row, 1962, 1965.

———. *Theologie Des Alten Testaments*. Band I and II. München: Chr. Kaiser Verlag, 1958, 1965.

Rahlfs, Alfred, and Robert Hanhart, eds. *Septuaginta*. Stuttgart: Deutsche Bibelgesellschaft, 2006.

Ramm, Barnard L. *The Christian View of Science and Scripture*. Grand Rapids, MI: Eerdmans, 1979.

Ramsey, D. Patrick. "In Defense of Moses: A Confessional Critique of Kline and Karlberg." *Westminster Theological Journal* 66 (2004) 373–400.

Reymond, Robert L. *A New Systematic Theology of the Christian Faith*. Nashville, TN: Nelson, 1998.

Ridderbos, Herman N. *The Coming of the Kingdom*. Translated by H. de Jongste. Edited by Raymond O. Zorn. Phillipsburg, NJ: P&R, 1962.

———. *Paul: An Outline of His Theology*. Translated by John Richard De Witt. Grand Rapids, MI: Eerdmans, 1990.

———. *Paul and Jesus*. Translated by David H. Freeman. Phillipsburg, NJ: P&R, 2002.

———. *When the Time Had Fully Come: Studies in New Testament Theology*. Grand Rapids, MI: Eerdmans, 1982.

Riddlebarger, Kim. *A Case for Amillennialism: Understanding the End Times*. Grand Rapids, MI: Baker, 2003.

Ritschl, Albrecht. *The Christian Doctrine of Justification and Reconciliation*. Edited by H. R. Mackintosh and A. B. Macaulay. New York: Scribner's, 1902.

———. *Three Essays*. Translated by Philip Hefner. Eugene, OR: Wipf & Stock, 2005.

Robertson, O. Palmer. *The Christ of the Covenants*. Phillipsburg, NJ: P&R, 1980.

———. *The Christ of the Prophets: Abridged Edition*. Phillipsburg, NJ: P&R, 2008.

———. "Genesis 15:6: New Covenant Expositions of an Old Covenant Text." *Westminster Theological Journal* 42 (1980) 259–89.

———. *The Israel of God: Yesterday, Today, and Tomorrow*. Phillipsburg, NJ: P&R, 2000.

Robinson, James M. *The Gospel of Jesus: A Historical Search for the Original Good News*. New York: HarperCollins, 2005.

———. *Jesus: According to the Earliest Witness*. Minneapolis, MN: Fortress, 2007.

Rushdoony, Rousas John. *The Institutes of Biblical Law*. 3 vols. Nutley, NJ: Craig, 1973.

Russell, James Stuart. *The Parousia: The New Testament Doctrine of Christ's Second Coming*. Bradford, PA: International Preterist Association, 2003.

Ryrie, Charles C. *Basic Theology: A Popular Systematic Guide to Understanding Biblical Truth*. Chicago: Moody, 1999.

———. *Dispensationalism*. Chicago: Moody, 2007.

———. *The Ryrie Study Bible: ESV*. Chicago: Moody, 2011.

Sanders, E. P. "The Covenant as a Soteriological Category and the Nature of Salvation in Palestinian and Hellenistic Judaism." In *Jews, Greeks and Christians: Religious Cultures in Late Antiquity*, edited by Robert Hamerton-Kelly and Robin Scroggs, 11–44. Leiden, 1976.

———. *Jesus and Judaism*. Philadelphia: Fortress, 1985.

———. *Jewish Law from Jesus to the Mishnah: Five Studies*. Philadelphia: Trinity, 1990.

———. *Paul*. Oxford: Oxford University Press, 1992.

———. *Paul and Palestinian Judaism*. Philadelphia: Fortress, 1977.

———. *Paul, the Law and the Jewish People*. Philadelphia: Fortress, 1983.

Saucy, Robert L. *The Case for Progressive Dispensationalism: The Interface between Dispensational & Non-dispensational Theology*. Grand Rapids, MI: Zondervan, 1993.

Schilder, Klass. *Christ and Culture*. Translated by G. van Rongen and W. Helder. Winnipeg: Premier, 1977. http://www.reformed.org/master/index.html?mainframe=/webfiles/cc/christ_and_culture.html.

Schreiner, Susan E. "Calvin's Use of Natural Law." In *A Preserving Grace: Protestants, Catholics, and Natural Law*, edited by Michael Cromartie, 51–76. Grand Rapids, MI: Eerdmans, 1977.

———. *The Theater of His Glory: Nature and the Natural Order in the Thought of John Calvin*. Durham: Labyrinth, 1992.

Schreiner, Thomas R. *Covenant and God's Purpose for the World*. Wheaton, IL: Crossway, 2017.

———. *Faith Alone: The Doctrine of Justification*. Grand Rapids, MI: Zondervan, 2015.

———. "Justification Apart From and By Good Works: At the Final Judgment Works Will Confirm Justification." In *Four Views on the Role of Works at the Final Judgment*, edited by Alan Stanley, 71–118. Grand Rapids, MI: Zondervan, 2013.

Schweitzer, Albert. *The Mystery of the Kingdom of God: The Secret of Jesus' Messiahship and Passion*. Translated by Walter Lowrie. New York: Dodd, Mead, 1914.

———. *The Quest of the Historical Jesus*. Translated by W. Montgomery. Mineola, NY: Dover, 2005.

Scofield, Cyrus I., ed. *The New Scofield Reference Bible: The Holy Bible Containing the Old and New Testaments*. Authorized King James Version. Edited by E. Schuyler English. New York: Oxford, 1967.

———, ed. *The Scofield Reference Bible: The Holy Bible Containing the Old and New Testaments*. Authorized Version. New and Improved ed. New York: Oxford, 1917.

Smick, Elmer B. "The Psalms as Response to God's Covenant Love: Theological Observations." In *Creator, Redeemer, Consummator: A Festschrift For Meredith G. Kline*, edited by Howard Griffith and John H. Muether, 77–86. Greenville, SC: Reformed Academic, 2000.

Sohn, Seock-Tae. *The Divine Election of Israel*. Grand Rapids, MI: Eerdmans, 1991.

———. *YHWH, the Husband of Israel: The Metaphor of Marriage between YHWH and Israel*. Eugene, OR: Wipf & Stock, 2002.

Song, Young Jae. *Theology and Piety in the Reformed Federal Thought of William Perkins and John Preston*. Lewiston, NY: Mellen, 1998.

Spijker, Willem van't. "The Kingdom of Christ according to Bucer and Calvin." In *Calvin and the State*, edited by Peter De Klerk, 109–32. Grand Rapids, MI: Calvin Studies Society, 1993.

Stek, John. "'Covenant' Overload in Reformed Theology." *Calvin Theological Seminary* 29 (1994) 12–41.

Stevenson, William R., Jr. "Calvin and Political Issues." In *The Cambridge Companion to John Calvin*, edited by Donald K. McKim, 173–87. Cambridge: Cambridge University Press, 2004.

Strimple, Robert B. "Amillennialism." In *Three Views on the Millennium and Beyond*, edited by Darrell L. Bock, 81–129. Grand Rapids, MI: Zondervan, 1999.

Turretin, Francis. *Institutes of Elenctic Theology*. 3 vols. Translated by George Musgrave Giger. Edited by James T. Dennison Jr. Phillipsburg, NJ: P&R, 1992–97.

VanDrunen, David. *A Biblical Case for Natural Law*. Studies in Christian Social Ethics and Economics 1. Grand Rapids, MI: Action Institute, 2006.

———. "Calvin on the Church and Society." *Evangelium* 6 (2008) 10–13.

———. "The Context of Natural Law: John Calvin's Doctrine of the Two Kingdoms." *Journal of Church and State* 46 (2004) 504–25.

———. *Living in God's Two Kingdoms: A Biblical Vision for Christianity and Culture.* Wheaton, IL: Crossway, 2010.

———. "Medieval Natural Law and the Reformation: A Comparison of Aquinas and Calvin." *American Catholic Philosophical Quarterly* 80 (2006) 77–98.

———. *Natural Law and the Two Kingdoms: A Study in the Development of Reformed Social Thought.* Grand Rapids, MI: Eerdmans, 2010.

———. "Natural Law, Custom, and Common Law in the Theology of Aquinas and Calvin." *University of British Columbia Law Review* 33 (2000) 699–717.

———. *Politics after Christendom: Political Theology in a Fractured World.* Grand Rapids, MI: Zondervan Academic, 2020.

———. "The Two Kingdoms: A Reassessment of the Transformationist Calvin." *Calvin Theological Journal* 40 (2005) 248–66.

———. "The Two Kingdoms and the *Ordo Salutis:* Life Beyond Judgment and the Question of a Dual Ethic." *Westminster Theological Journal* 70 (2008) 207–24.

———. "The Two Kingdoms Doctrine and the Relationship of Church and State in the Early Reformed Tradition." *Journal of Church and State* 49 (2007) 743–63.

Vangemeren, Willem. *The Progress of Redemption: The Story of Salvation from Creation to the New Jerusalem.* Grand Rapids, MI: Baker, 1995.

Van Til, Cornelius. *Common Grace and the Gospel.* Phillipsburg, NJ: P&R, 1972.

———. *Common Grace and the Gospel.* Phillipsburg, NJ: P&R, 1992.

———. *The Defense of the Faith.* Phillipsburg, NJ: P&R, 1967.

———. *In Defense of the Faith.* Vol. 3, *Christian Theistic Ethics.* Phillipsburg, NJ: P&R, 1980.

Venema, Cornelis P. "The Law of Moses: Not a Disguised Covenant of Works." *The Confessional Presbyterian* 8 (2012) 212–27.

———. "The Mosaic Covenant: A Republication of the Covenant of Works?" *Mid-America Journal of Theology* 21 (2010) 35–101.

Vos, Geerhardus. *Biblical Theology: Old and New Testaments.* Grand Rapids, MI: Eerdmans, 1988.

———. *The Eschatology of the Old Testament.* Edited by James T. Dennison Jr. Phillipsburg, NJ: P&R, 2001.

———. *Grace and Glory: Sermons Preached in the Chapel of Princeton Theological Seminary.* Carlisle, PA: The Banner of Truth Trust, 1994.

———. *The Pauline Eschatology.* Phillipsburg, NJ: P&R, 1994.

———. *Redemptive History and Biblical Interpretation: The Shorter Writings of Geerhardus Vos.* Edited by Richard B. Gaffin Jr. Phillipsburg, NJ: P&R, 1980.

———. *Reformed Dogmatics: A System of Christian Theology.* Translated and edited by Richard B. Gaffin Jr. Bellingham, WA: Lexam, 2020.

———. *Reformed Dogmatics.* Vol. 1, *Theology Proper.* Translated and edited by Richard B. Gaffin Jr. Bellingham, WA: Lexham, 2012–14.

———. *Reformed Dogmatics.* Vol. 2, *Anthropology.* Translated and edited by Richard B. Gaffin Jr. Bellingham, WA: Lexam, 2014.

———. *Reformed Dogmatics.* Vol. 5, *Ecclesiology, The Means of Grace, Eschatology.* Translated and edited by Richard B. Gaffin Jr. Bellingham, WA: Lexam, 2016.

———. *The Teaching of the Epistle to the Hebrews.* Edited by Johannes G. Vos. Phillipsburg, NJ: P&R, 1956.

————. *The Teaching of Jesus: Concerning the Kingdom of God and the Church.* Eugene, OR: Wipf & Stock, 1998.

Waltke, Bruce K. *An Old Testament Theology: An Exegetical, Canonical, and Thematic Approach.* Grand Rapids, MI: Zondervan, 2007.

Walton, John H. *The Lost World of Adam and Eve: Genesis 2–3 and the Human Origins Debate.* Downers Grove, IL: IVP Academic, 2015.

————. *Old Testament Theology for Christians: From Ancient Context to Enduring Belief.* Downers Grove, IL: IVP Academic, 2017.

Walton, John H., and J. Harvey Walton. *The Lost World of the Israelite Conquest: Covenant, Retribution, and the Fate of the Canaanites.* Downers Grove, IL: InterVarsity, 2017.

Weinfeld, Moshe. "The Covenant of Grant in the Old Testament and in the Ancient Near East." *Journal of the American Oriental Society* 90 (1970) 184–203.

Wellhausen, Julius. *Deuteronomy and the Deuteronomic School.* Oxford: Oxford University Press, 1972.

————. *Prolegomena to the History of Israel: With a Reprint of the Article Israel from the "Encyclopedia Britannica."* Translated by J. Sutherland Black and Allan Menzies. Edinburgh: A. & C. Black, 1885.

Wenham, Gordon J. *Genesis 1–15.* Word Biblical Commentary 1. Waco, TX: Word, 1987.

————. *Genesis 16–50.* Word Biblical Commentary 2. Waco, TX: Word, 1994.

Wenham, John. *Facing Hell: An Autobiography 1913–1995.* Paternoster: Send the Light, 1998.

Westburg, Daniel. "The Reformed Tradition and Natural Law." In *A Preserving Grace: Protestants, Catholics, and Natural Law,* edited by Michael Cromartie, 103–17. Grand Rapids, MI: Eerdmans, 1997.

Westerholm, Stephen. *Israel's Law and the Church's Faith: Paul and the Recent Interpreters.* Grand Rapids, MI: Eerdmans, 1988.

————. *Perspectives Old and New on Paul: The "Lutheran" Paul and His Critics.* Grand Rapids, MI: Eerdmans, 2004.

The Westminster Standards: An Original Fascimile. Original English Edition, 1648. Princeton, NJ: Old Paths, 1997.

Whitcomb, John C., Jr., and Henry M. Morris. *The Genesis Flood: The Biblical Record and Its Scientific Implications.* Grand Rapids, MI: Baker, 1979.

Williams, Michael D. *Far as the Curse Is Found: The Covenant Story of Redemption.* Phillipsburg, NJ: P&R, 2005.

Wright, N. Thomas. *The Climax of the Covenant: Christ and the Law in Pauline Theology.* Minneapolis, MN: Fortress, 1991.

————. "The Paul of History and the Apostle of Faith." *Tyndale Bulletin* 29 (1978) 61–88.

————. *Surprised by Hope: Rethinking Heaven, the Resurrection, and the Mission of the Church.* New York: HarperOne, 2008.

————. *What Saint Paul Really Said.* Grand Rapids, MI: Eerdmans, 1997.

Wright, N. Thomas, and Michael F. Bird. *The New Testament in Its World: An Introduction to the History, Literature, and Theology of the First Christians.* Grand Rapids, MI: Zondervan, 2019.

Wright, William J. *Martin Luther's Understanding of God's Two Kingdoms: A Response to the Challenge of Skepticism.* Grand Rapids, MI: Baker Academic, 2010.

Yoder, John Howard, ed. and trans. *The Schleitheim Confession*. Scottsdale, PA: Herald, 1977.

Young, Davis A. *The Biblical Flood: A Case Study of the Church's Response to Extrabiblical Evidence*. Grand Rapids, MI: Paternoster, 1995.

Young, Edward J. *Genesis 3: A Devotional and Expository Study*. Carlisle, PA: The Banner of Truth Trust, 1983.

———. *Studies in Genesis One*. Phillipsburg, NJ: P&R, 1964.

———. *The Study of Old Testament Theology*. London: Clark, 1958.

———. *Thy Word Is Truth: Some Thoughts on the Biblical Doctrine of Inspiration*. Carlisle, PA: The Banner of Truth Trust, 1991.